India

THE SOUTH

DAVID STOTT
VICTORIA McCULLOCH

CONTENTS

PLANNING YOUR TRIP	04
This is South India	04
Putting it all together	06
Mumbai–Hampi–Goa	08
Chennai–Madurai–Trivandrum	16
Kochi–Backwaters–Ooty–Bengaluru	24

MUMBAI → HAMPI → GOA → MUMBAI	33
Mumbai (Bombay)	35
Gateway of India and Colaba	37
Fort	38
Around the CST (VT)	40
Marine Drive to Malabar Hill	42
Central Mumbai	43
Bandra, Juhu Beach and Andheri	45
Elephanta Caves	46
Kanheri Caves	48
Ajanta and Ellora caves	51
Aurangabad	51
Daulatabad	54
Ajanta	55
Ellora	60
Hyderabad and around (below)	65
Hyderabad and Secunderabad	65
Golconda	72
Going further: Warangal and Nagarjunakonda	75
Northern Karnataka	79
Bidar	79
Gulbarga	82
Bijapur	83
Badami, Aihole and Pattadakal	86
Hampi and around	90
Goa (above)	96
South Goa	97
Going further: Gokarna	100
Central Goa	101
Margao and coastal Salcete	110
North Goa	114
Going further: Bhagwan Mahaveer and Goa's Hindu Heartland	124

CHENNAI → MADURAI → TRIVANDRUM			135
Chennai and around	137	Chettinad	174
Mahabalipuram (Mamallapuram)	149	Madurai and around	176
Puducherry and Auroville	156	Going further: Rameshvaram	182
Puducherry (Pondicherry)	156	Kodaikkanal to the coast	186
Auroville	159	Kodaikkanal	186
Going further: Gingee and		Around Kodaikkanal	188
Tiruvannamalai	161	Thekkady (Periyar National Park,	
Chola Heartland and Kaveri Delta	164	Kumily Town)	188
Chidambaram	164	Varkala (above)	191
Gangaikondacholapuram	167	Thiruvananthapuram (Trivandrum)	193
Kumbakonam	167	Kovalam and nearby resorts (below)	195
Thanjavur (Tanjore)	169	Going further: Kanyakumari	197
Tiruchirappalli (Trichy) and around	172		

KOCHI → BACKWATERS → OOTY → BENGALURU			201
Fort Kochi and Ernakulam	203	Coonoor	231
The Backwaters	210	Mettupalayam and the Nilgiri Ghat road	232
Alappuzha (Alleppey)	211	Mudumalai Wildlife Sanctuary	233
Kottayam and Kumarakom	212	Wayanad to the Western Plateau	235
Kollam (Quilon)	214	Wayanad	235
Kochi to Munnar	218	Mysore	237
Munnar	218	Around Mysore	240
Going further: River Nila and Palakkad	223	Western Plateau	243
Ooty and the Nilgiri hills	229	Going further: Coorg (Kodagu)	246
Udhagamandalam (Ooty)	229	Bengaluru (Bangalore)	250

PRACTICALITIES	257
Ins and outs	258
Best time to visit South India	258
Getting to South India	258
Transport in South India	260
Where to stay in South India	266
Food and drink in South India	268
Festivals in South India	270
Responsible travel	273
Essentials A-Z	274
Index	283
Credits	288

THIS IS
SOUTH INDIA

Tradition demands that we begin this book by telling you that India is an assault on your senses. It's both a lazy cliché and a cosmic understatement. India in places can feel like an all-out war on every value you've been taught to be right: a deluge of humanity whose one-and-a-quarter billion souls have no time for such bourgeois Western concepts as personal space and limits on the number of people permitted to ride a single motorcycle.

And then there's South India. While nobody will ever accuse India of living at a relaxed pace, the six states that collect like soft ice cream at the tip of India's cone stand out for a gentleness – a sense of life's needs being easily satisfied – that's nowhere to be found in the survivalist hardscrabble of the northern deserts and plains.

In the monsoon-softened far south, village folk weave their way from paddy field to temple under bounteous canopies of coconut, jackfruit and nutmeg. In the forests that blanket the spine of the Western Ghats you can hunt for hornbills and find your road blocked by herds of elephant. The Hindu heartland of Tamil Nadu is a focus for spiritual energy, where you can melt into a crowd of pilgrims pouring through the towering gateways of India's greatest temples, while the dusty Deccan Plateau is dotted with spectacular ruins that bear witness to the ancient artistry of craftsmen of every religious stripe.

Yet for all its archaeological and natural treasures, South India's greatest riches are in its people: an intelligent, poetic, incurably curious folk who'll welcome you into their lives, whether lavish or humble, with a startling generosity that expects no repayment. Even amid the quickening modernity of megacities such as Mumbai and Bengaluru, the ageless Indian impulse to seek, understand and merge with the divine remains unvanquished.

And the Indian soul knows many ways to heaven. You might find yours in a rosy sunset over the Arabian Sea with Goa's warm waves lapping at your toes, in a lazy afternoon watching life ooze by from the shady deck of a Backwaters houseboat, or tiptoeing through the cloistered silence of an exquisitely carved Hampi temple. Or it might come from less obvious sources: the heady waft of freshly crushed cardamom on a spice plantation in the Malabar hinterland, or the gauzy light of 'cow dust hour' as you drift through rural Tamil Nadu on an afternoon train.

Many travellers hesitate on the brink of India. Travel here can still present real challenges – to your patience, your compassion, your sense of hygiene – but the voice that tells you India is too overwhelming is like the voice telling you not to jump into a cold pool on a hot summer's day. Throw yourself in, and once the air returns to your lungs you'll find every sinew of your being revived, wide awake and renewed.

Before you jump, a friendly warning. There's a good reason people leave India until last. One visit sparks a yearning to return, which grows into an obsession, and finally an addiction. After India, nowhere else will be quite the same. And if you give a small part of yourself up to its thundering current of life, neither will you.

David Stott

Victoria McCulloch

Chinese fishing nets, Kochi

FIRST STEPS
PUTTING IT ALL TOGETHER

The area covered in this book could swallow France and Germany whole, and throw the Netherlands in as a snack.

South India is a vast and hugely varied slice of the globe, and there's no way you'll 'do' all of it in the space of a typical holiday. The area covered in this book could swallow France and Germany whole, and throw the Netherlands in as a snack. In sharp contrast to those countries, travel in India is neither predictable nor quick; what looks on the map like a short journey can easily consume a day or more.

The secret to eating this particular elephant is to take small bites and chew thoroughly. Choose one area to focus on, take your time, and accept that you'll return in the future to take care of the rest.

South India has an exceptional number of international airports, allowing great flexibility when planning your trip. If you're prepared to fly via the Gulf or Southeast Asia, many airlines sell open-jaw fares that make it easy to enter through one gateway and leave from another at little or no extra cost. This book makes the most of that flexibility: only one of the three itineraries featured here is a circular journey.

If you've only got a short holiday and want plenty of time to relax, you might fly into Mumbai, sample a few of Goa's beaches and take a brief detour inland to Hampi – though many people land in Goa and never breach its borders.

→ DOING IT ALL

Mumbai → Aurangabad → Ajanta → Ellora → Hyderabad → Bijapur → Badami → Hampi → Goa → Chennai → Mahabalipuram → Puducherry → Thanjavur → Chettinad → Madurai → Kanyakumari → Thiruvananthapuram → Varkala → Backwaters → Kochi → Munnar → Ooty → Wayanad → Nagarhole → Mysore → Hassan → Bengaluru

If temples and spiritual quests are more your thing, Chennai is the logical starting point for trips in the far southeast, where the delta country of the Kaveri River provides a lush backdrop to hundreds of ornate temples, all humming with life and a palpable sense of the sacred.

If you're interested in exploring the beaches and backwaters of Kerala, it's most logical to fly into Thiruvananthapuram or Kochi, while either Kochi or Bengaluru serve as convenient gateways to the lush mountain forests and wildlife parks of the Western Ghats.

India's excellent domestic air network makes it easy to cover the ground between cities quickly and, though expensive in comparison to getting around by land, fares are still very affordable. It's therefore quite straightforward to combine a tour of the south with some highlights of North India – for details of which, see the companion guide to North India.

The itineraries we've created for this book are designed to show you some of the best of South India, at a pace that packs in the sights without forcing you to run yourself ragged. These Dream Trips cover a selection of the very best the south has to offer, both on and off the beaten track – the finest landscapes, the most bewitching ruins, the cleanest beaches and the most atmospheric temples. Let the itineraries inspire and inform you, not restrict you. Use them as a starting point, and a springboard to further exploration.

1 Painters at work, Hyderabad **2** Kerala's Backwaters

DREAM TRIP 1
MUMBAI → HAMPI → GOA → MUMBAI

Best time to visit South India's tourist season runs from October to March, and as long as you come somewhere within that window you'll have a good time. The interior gets unbearably hot from April onwards, while the summer-monsoon months from May to September see Goa's beaches virtually deserted, and not in a good way – you'll be hard pressed to get a room or a meal outside the main cities. Christmas and New Year are crowded and expensive on the beaches, making the ideal times for this trip October and February to March, when most things are open and prices are moderate.

Our first itinerary takes you on a circular journey through South India's richly varied landscapes, from arid boulder-strewn plains to lush coastal forests, and on a whirlwind journey back in time through layers of Hindu, Muslim and European colonial history. You'll need a minimum of three weeks to do it in full, though if you only have a fortnight you could pick off many of the historical highlights and still have time for some beachside relaxation.

Begin at the deep end in Mumbai (page 35), India's frenetic capital of business and pop culture, whose anarchic street life is immortalized in a million movie scenes. If you're a connoisseur of urban life and you don't mind the odd mind-numbing traffic jam, you could easily spend your entire holiday here, wandering through markets, exploring the Victorian Gothic monuments of SoBo, clubhopping with the Bollywood glitterati and exploring the slums where sweltering workers in tin-shack factories convert Mumbai's muck into brass.

From Mumbai you jump on a train or plane to Aurangabad (page 51). A busy provincial city rich in historical sights, this is an interesting base from which to explore the mesmerizing hand-carved cave temples of Ajanta (page 55) and Ellora (page 60). You'll need at least two days to see the caves properly.

An overnight journey across the Deccan Plateau, Hyderabad (page 65) is a city undergoing a transformation. The palaces and mosques of the Nizams still stand in quiet decrepitude, while the new city expands out in a mushroom cloud of IT parks, film studios and

1 Auto-rickshaws, Mumbai 2 Ibrahim Rauza, Bijapur 3 Kailasanatha Temple, Ellora

shopping malls. A couple of days here are enough for most people, and allow time to explore nearby sights such as Golconda Fort.

The journey back west leads through Bidar (page 79) and Gulbarga (page 82) – little-visited towns with striking medieval monuments left behind by the Muslim Deccan dynasties – before rejoining the beaten track at the walled city of Bijapur (page 83). If you're short on time, you can slice off a few days (at the cost of a tough day's travel) by cutting southward directly from Aurangabad to Bijapur.

South of Bijapur lie South India's most evocative ruins. You can easily spend a day or two trotting between the villages of Badami (page 86), Pattadakal (page 88) and Aihole (page 89), where the foundations of Hindu temple architecture were developed and subsequently spread throughout the country.

The palaces and mosques of the Nizams still stand in quiet decrepitude, while the new city expands out in a mushroom cloud of IT parks, film studios and shopping malls.

DREAM TRIP 1
MUMBAI → HAMPI → GOA → MUMBAI

Further south are the unmissable ruins of Hampi (page 90) – once the capital of an empire that covered most of South India, now a series of temples and palaces open to the sky, bejewelled with exquisite carvings and surrounded by spectacular boulder-strewn hills. A three-day stay here is enough to cover all the widely dispersed ruins, though you could easily spend far longer soaking up the atmosphere.

The road to Goa (page 96) is a well-worn stretch of the South Indian backpacker trail. Whether you travel by car, juddering overnight bus, or on the sinuous railway track that winds down the face of Dudhsagar Falls (page 129), the journey through the lush forests of the Western Ghats takes you to a very different India, with a culture, cuisine and standards of acceptable dress utterly unrelated to the rest of the country.

Many people choose a beach and settle in for a few weeks, but finding the right beach for you takes a little exploration. The far south, centred around idyllic Palolem (page 98), is where you'll find secluded palm-fringed coves, some still relatively undeveloped. Central Goa has long unbroken stretches of sand and small resorts favoured by Indian families, while inland the slowly decaying remains of Portuguese colonial society melt into the forest around Old Goa (page 105). Northern Goa, while not quite the hippy stronghold of old, still retains elements of its tie-dyed past, with some

1 Dudhsagar Falls, Goa **2** Anjuna market, Goa **3** Boulder-strewn ruins, Hampi **4** Palolem beach, Goa **5** Cricket on Gokarna beach

of India's most popular yoga retreats hidden in the paddy fields around Anjuna (page 117) and Arambol (page 119).

Idyllic Palolem is where you'll find secluded palm-fringed coves, some still relatively undeveloped.

You can, of course, reverse this itinerary, taking the Konkan Railway from Mumbai south to Goa and giving yourself a softer entry point to India. However, the beaches provide a tantalizing rest at the end of a substantial trip through the 'real India'. This approach also insures you against the risk that Goa's all-round chilled lifestyle proves so beguiling that you never go any further.

→ GOING FURTHER

From Hyderabad, visit **Warangal Fort** and the Buddhist remnants of **Nagarjunakonda**. Head south of Goa to check out the beaches of **Gokarna**, and inland for the forests and birding of **Bhagwan Mahaveer Wildlife Sanctuary**. → page 75, page 100, page 124

→ ROUTE PLANNER

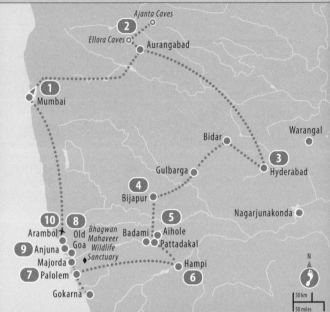

1 Char Minar, Hyderabad **2** Virupaksha Temple, Hampi

→ WISH LIST

1 India's biggest city, Mumbai shocks you with its sheer current of life. Wander the workaday lanes of Fort, take a ride on the world's busiest railway, and strut your stuff alongside movie royalty as a Bollywood extra. **2** The Hindu, Buddhist and Jain cave temples hewn into volcanic rock at Ellora and Ajanta rank among India's most astonishing works of art. **3** A tech capital to rival Bengaluru, Hyderabad still retains stone-carved bazaars, giant medieval forts and crumbling palaces that offer poignant glimpses into its glorious past. **4** Minarets and mausoleums dominate the skyline of Bijapur, with the hulking dome of the Gol Gumbaz in centre stage. **5** Go back to the drawing board of Hindu architecture in Aihole, where craftsmen created temple styles that have been exported to every corner of India. **6** The one-time capital of the Vijayanagar Empire, Hampi's ruins are a heady brew of superb sculpture and magnificently surreal boulder-strewn landscapes. **7** The curving bay of Palolem is Goa's perfect postcard beach, with other quieter bays nearby. **8** Wander the lanes of Old Goa, where the cathedrals and grand mansions left behind by the Portuguese gently crumble into the jungle. **9** Sharpen your elbows and dive into the consumerist melee of north Goa's biggest social event: the legendary Wednesday flea market in Anjuna. **10** Book in for a body and mind experience at one of the first-class yoga retreats that dot the paddy fields around Arambol.

Panoramic view of Old Goa

Best time to visit If you're at all rain-shy, plan your trip for the cool and dry time – generally from December to March. Tamil Nadu gets two monsoons – the famous Southwest Monsoon that sweeps up the coast of Kerala in June, and the oft-forgotten Southeast Monsoon which drenches the east coast in October. Either one can cause havoc on the mountain roads in the Western Ghats. As elsewhere in South India, crippling heat hits the plains of Tamil Nadu in April and May.

The first part of this itinerary takes you through the sandalwood-scented heart of Tamil Nadu, home to some of the liveliest and most colourful Hindu temples in India, then takes a diversion through the cool Palani Hills – and one of South India's most intriguing wildlife parks – before finishing with a beach break on the Kerala coast.

You start in Chennai (page 137), a vast and crowded city by any measure, and one that doesn't readily reveal its charms to short-term visitors. It's worth allowing a day to explore the ancient Brahmin enclave of Mylapore, where bustling sari shops and dingy pure-vegetarian Brahmin cafés service the crowds who descend upon the hugely atmospheric Kapaleeswarar Temple.

Less than an hour south of the city, the fascinating beachside backpacker town of Mahabalipuram (page 149) makes for a touristy but enjoyable first stop. A centre of excellence in stone sculpture since at least the seventh century, you'll need a full day here to see the best of the carvings and the World Heritage Shore Temple, though the beach and a ready supply of chilled-out rooftop cafés might well seduce you into staying longer.

An interesting diversion inland leads through boulder-strewn countryside to Tiruvannamalai (page 161). Meanwhile, the main route continues south to the former French colony of Puducherry (page 156). Inland is the fascinating experimental community of

1 Meenakshi Temple, Madurai 2 Matrimandir, Auroville 3 Brihadisvara Temple, Thanjavur 4 Karaikkudi mansion, Chettinad

Auroville (page 159), a showpiece of modern sacred architecture and co-operative low-impact living that deserves more than the cursory glance that most visitors give it.

The temple trail begins in earnest at Chidambaram (page 164), where non-Hindus get a unique chance to enter the inner sanctum for a glimpse of the idol of Nataraja – Shiva as creator, preserver and destroyer of the universe. From here it's a day's drive to Thanjavur (page 169), home of the superb World Heritage Brihadisvara Temple. Thanjavur makes a good base to visit nearby temple towns including Gangaikondacholapuram (page 167), Kumbakonam (page 167) and Srirangam (page 173).

Continuing south, Chettinad (page 174) offers a break from temple fatigue. The Chettiar traders made immense fortunes in the Burmese

Thronged with pilgrims night and day, the arcades of the Meenakshi Temple are a haven for frantic activity both spiritual and commercial.

teak trade, and their conspicuously ornamented mansions line the quiet country lanes of villages around Karaikudi. Several of the finest have opened as luxury hotels, while others welcome visitors during the day. A couple of days here will give you time to poke through the lifestyles of the formerly rich, and see workshops where craftsmen carve temple statues and make hand-dyed tiles.

The temple trail has one more cosmic treat in store: the absorbing Meenakshi Temple of Madurai (page 176). Thronged with pilgrims night and day, its shaded arcades are a haven for frantic activity both spiritual and commercial, and the nightly ritual in which the idol of Sundareswar is transported, in a cloud of incense smoke and drum rumble, to the bed chamber he shares with Meenakshi, is one of Tamil Nadu's unmissable rituals. Spend a couple of nights here to absorb the medieval atmosphere

The standard tourist route continues south from Madurai to Kanyakumari. We take a more roundabout route, leaving behind the hot plains and heading into the Palani Hills where Kodaikkanal (page 186) awaits with promises of crisp air, waterfalls, long walks through pine-scented woods, and a refreshing absence of parping horns.

A day's drive away, Thekkady (page 188) is the base for exploring Periyar National Park (page 188), which offers the rare opportunity to hike in country populated with elephant, tigers and sloth bear, guided by former poachers.

A few days by the beach in Varkala (page 191) make for an ideal decompression after some demanding travel, and the salty blend

1 Sloth bear cub, Periyar National Park **2** Inside the Meenakshi Temple, Madurai **3** Kerala beach **4** Vivekananda Memorial, Kanyakumari

of fishing village, Hindu pilgrimage centre and tourist bazaar make this a more textured seaside spot than most. Strong ocean currents make a stay here more about the atmosphere than spending time in the water.

It's a short hop from here to Thiruvananthapuram (page 193), Kerala's capital and a genial transport hub with a handful of interesting museums and temples. A one-night stopover is plenty, but if you've got time and energy it's definitely worth a diversion to Kanyakumari (page 197), where three seas meet at the southernmost tip of India.

With more time you could combine this itinerary with Dream Trip 3 to create a genuine highlights package of India's far south; or you could add in a couple of days on the Backwaters between Thekkady and Varkala. Alternatively, you could convert the trip into a 'best of Tamil Nadu' by diverting north after Kodaikkanal towards Ooty and the Nilgiri Mountain Railway (see Dream Trip 3).

A few days by the beach in Varkala make for an ideal decompression after some demanding travel, and the salty blend of fishing village, Hindu pilgrimage centre and tourist bazaar make this a more textured seaside spot than most.

→ GOING FURTHER

Explore sacred hills, cavernous temples and fort-topped boulder hills in **Tiruvannamalai** and **Gingee**; take a holy dip in the temple at **Rameswaram**; and watch sunset and moon-rise over the sea at **Kanyakumari**. → page 161, → page 182, → page 197

Meenakshi Temple, Madurai

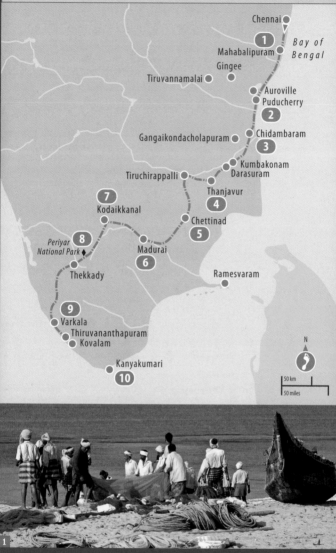

1 The journey south begins in the fascinating beachside hamlet of Mahabalipuram, famed for its stone carving and World Heritage temples. **2** The colonial core of Puducherry (Pondicherry) offers a brief respite from India, with decent French food, a nascent café scene, and art galleries hidden away in shady courtyards. **3** Chidambaram marks the beginning of the temple trail, and it's worth staying a night to experience the atmospheric Nataraja Temple as the lanterns come alight. **4** The drive south is littered with superb examples of Tamil temple architecture, none more exalted than Thanjavur's vast and ornate Brihadisvara Temple. **5** Poke your nose into the gently decaying mansions of Chettinad for an insight into the lifestyles and tastes of Tamil Nadu's one-time trading elites. **6** Madurai is home to one of India's greatest spiritual sites, the mind-boggling Meenakshi Temple. **7** The winding mountain road to Kodaikkanal whisks you away from the sweltering plains to a land of cool pine woods, pedal boats, horse rides and log fires. **8** Across the Kerala border, the forests of Periyar National Park offer a rare opportunity to track wild elephants on foot and by raft in the company of reformed poachers. **9** A piquant mix of fishing village, pilgrimage centre and backpacker beach ghetto, Varkala is one of the far south's best chill-out spots. **10** At the southern tip of India, Kanyakumari offers the chance to witness a unique celestial spectacle as the sunset and moonrise occur simultaneously over two different seas.

1 Fishermen, Varkala **2** Arjuna's Penance bas-relief, Mahabalipuram

DREAM TRIP 3
KOCHI → BACKWATERS → OOTY → BENGALURU

Best time to visit The standard advice of October to March applies again here, though nights can get very chilly in the hills in winter. If you can stand the occasional blast of heat, mid-May would be a surprisingly good time to do this itinerary in reverse. The hill towns will be at their busiest, but the dry late summer is the best time for a shot at a tiger sighting, and Kerala's festival season will be in full swing. Time it right and you might be here to see the monsoon make landfall – a magical moment of crashing thunder and spontaneous dancing in the street.

Our third itinerary takes you from the languid lily-strewn lagoons of Kerala's backwaters to the frantic tech hub of Bengaluru (formerly Bangalore), via the tea towns of Munnar and Ooty, the lush cloud forests and tiger reserves of Nagarhole National Park, and the charming regional hub of Mysore, surrounded by ancient temples and riverside fortresses. This route covers some of the most heavily travelled parts of South India, but there are some fascinating options here for stepping off the beaten track.

Kochi (page 203) serves as an intriguing and easy-going entry point to the charms of coastal Kerala. Most visitors see little of the bustling downtown district of Ernakulam, preferring to ensconce themselves in the raintree-shaded haven of Fort Cochin. The old garrison town is a wonderful place to wander for a day, exploring the warren of quiet streets that bear the stamp of Portuguese, Dutch, Jewish and British colonists, stopping in for a proper espresso in an art gallery, and watching the sun set over the elegant Chinese nets that now catch more tourists than fish.

The Backwaters (page 210) stretch south from Kochi in a glistening web of broad palm-fringed canals. Budget for at least one night aboard a *kettuvallom* (the romantically palm-thatched houseboats that ply the waterways) and one or two nights on land, exploring by bike or canoe from one of the stunning small hotels that dot the shore of Lake Vembanad.

Budget for at least one night aboard a kettuvallom, the romantically palm-thatched houseboats that ply the waterways.

From the Backwaters you begin the journey north. The main road parallels the coast, heading north through Thrissur (page 223), famous for its riotous July Pooram festival, before turning inland towards Palakkad (page 225). This part of Kerala is a renowned hotbed of both traditional Keralite culture and Ayurvedic healing, and if you're looking to spend a few days rebooting your body there are several excellent retreats hidden away in the wonderfully tranquil hinterland of the Malabar coast.

A more scenic alternative is to head inland from the Backwaters up the winding mountain road to Munnar (page 218). Surrounded by tea estates with wilder country close at hand, Munnar is a wonderful place to walk in cooler climes, and explore the subalpine landscapes of Eravikulam National Park (page 222).

The coast and mountain roads meet across the Tamil Nadu border at Mettupalayam (page 232), an obligatory overnight stop if you

1 Ancient Chinese fishing methods, Kochi 2 Houseboat tour, Kerala's Backwaters 3 Pooram festival, Thrissur 4 Tea plantations, Munnar

DREAM TRIP 3
KOCHI → BACKWATERS → OOTY → BENGALURU

want to catch the dawn departure of the Nilgiri Mountain Railway (page 232). A veritable icon of Indian rail travel, steam trains have been chugging up the narrow-gauge track to Ooty (page 229) since 1899. While Ooty itself has lost some of its shine, you can hop off at Coonoor (page 231) for an enjoyable overnight stop among the eucalypts and tea plantations. Ooty also makes a convenient jumping-off point for exploring Mudumalai National Park (page 233) and Bandipur National Park (page 233), home to huge herds of elephant which are frequently seen jaywalking across the highways.

Back across the Kerala border lies Wayanad (page 235), a magical hill station that keeps a lower profile than Ooty and is infinitely more appealing for that. Hidden away among the rolling tea plantations and spice farms, lie patches of montane shola rainforest, Neolithic caves and beautiful waterfalls. One of the lesser-known gems of Kerala, it's worth spending at least two days here.

North of Wayanad, Nagarhole National Park (page 236) offers some of the best tiger and elephant sightings in South India. Though rooms in the park come at a hefty premium, it's worth allowing two or three full days with two safaris a day if you want a shot at glimpsing the king of the Indian jungle.

Mysore (page 237), a charmingly anarchic little city centred on the domed and gilded Mysore Palace, serves as an excellent base from

1 Nilgiri Mountain Railway **2** Tea garden, Tamil Nadu **3** Elephant in Nagarhole National Park **4** Mysore Palace **5** Gommateshwara statue, Sravanabelagola **6** Fruit vendors, Bengaluru

Mysore, a charmingly anarchic little city centred on the domed and gilded Mysore Palace, serves as an excellent base from which to explore the hills, bird sanctuaries and ancient temples in the surrounding countryside.

which to explore the hills, bird sanctuaries and ancient temples in the surrounding countryside. An interesting day's drive north takes you via Tipu Sultan's island fortress at Srirangapatnam (page 240), and the monolithic naked statue of Jain sage Bahubali at Sravanabelagola (page 243), to Hassan, a bustling regional centre from where you can explore the superbly carved Hoysala temples of Belur (page 244) and Halebid (page 245).

The last stop on this route is Bengaluru (page 250), a watchword for India's economic reinvention as a tech and innovation hub. There are enough sights here to keep you occupied for a couple of days, and plenty of glitzy malls and buzzing markets if you need to fill a space in your suitcase.

This route would work equally well in reverse, trading a fast-paced start in Bengaluru for a relaxing finish on the Backwaters. With more time you could turn west from Hassan, skipping Bengaluru, and head north up the little-travelled coast of Karnataka towards Gokarna and eventually Goa; alternatively, with a long day's drive from Hassan you can reach Hampi and connect with Dream Trip 1.

→ ROUTE PLANNER

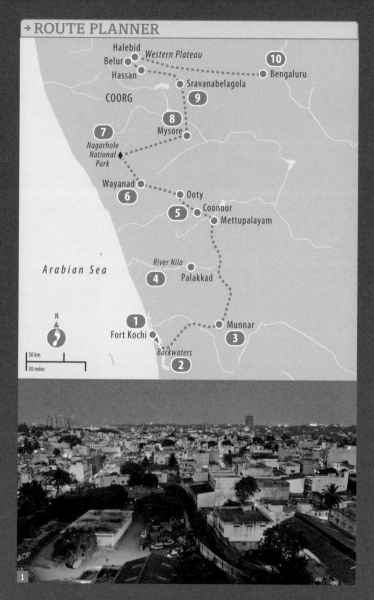

Halebid
Belur
Hassan
Western Plateau

10 Bengaluru

COORG

9 Sravanabelagola

7
Nagarhole National Park ◆

8 Mysore

Wayanad **6**

Ooty **5**

Coonoor

Mettupalayam

Arabian Sea

River Nila

4 Palakkad

N

50 km
50 miles

1 Fort Kochi

Munnar **3**

2 *Backwaters*

1

1 Bengaluru **2** Houseboat in Kerala's Backwaters

1 The atmospheric old town of Fort Kochi makes for a soft landing in India. Explore the spice warehouses and synagogues of Jew Town and watch sunset over the old Chinese fishing nets that nowadays catch more tourists than fish. 2 Hire a converted rice barge and spend a day or two cruising Kerala's languid lily-choked Backwaters. 3 Tiptoe through the tea bushes in Munnar, and take a jeep ride to Kolukkumalai Estate to watch the sun rise over the blue ridges and misty valleys. 4 Check in for a proper Ayurvedic cleansing at an ancient *illam* on the banks of the River Nila, a hotbed of traditional Keralite culture. 5 Asia's steepest train ride, the rack-and-pinion Nilgiri Mountain Railway is a trip back to the days of the Raj. 6 Wake up in a treehouse amid the cloud forests of Wayanad, surrounded by spice and coffee plantations, and explore the Neolithic carvings of Edakkal Caves. 7 Search for tigers, elephants and giant squirrels in the forests of Nagarhole National Park. 8 Wander through the fabulously kitsch palace of Mysore, and visit the fort from which Tipu Sultan terrorized the British in the 18th century. 9 Climb the granite monolith of Sravanabelagola, where the 17-m-high statue of Gommateshwara has stood naked and serene for a thousand years. 10 Take the pulse of 21st-century India amid the malls, boutiques and gridlocked streets of Bengaluru, then retreat to one of the city's genteel parks.

2

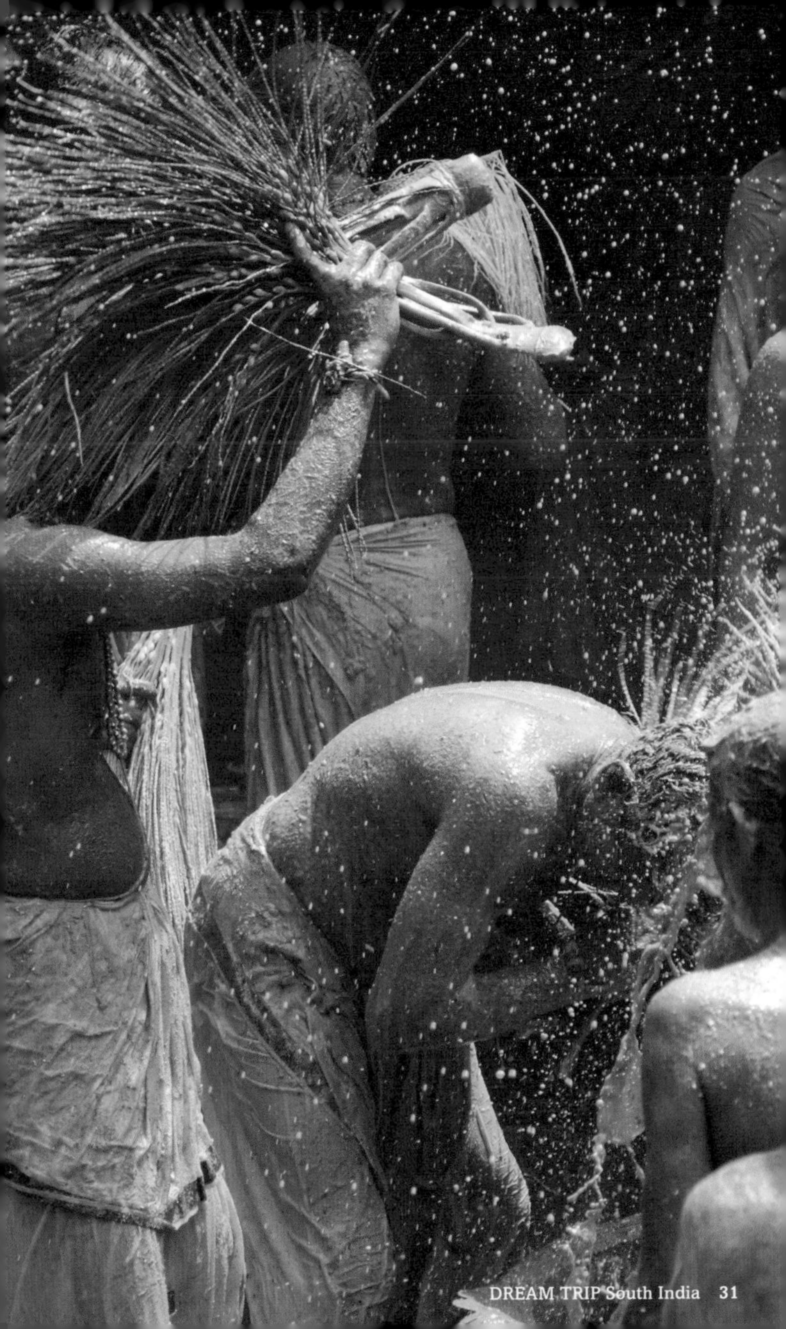

DREAM TRIP 1
Mumbai→Hampi→Goa→Mumbai 21 days

Mumbai 3 nights, page 35

Aurangabad (Ajanta Caves and Ellora Caves) 2 nights, page 51
Flight/train from Mumbai (1 hr/7 hrs).

Hyderabad 2 nights, page 65
Overnight train from Aurangabad (10 hrs)

Bidar 1 night, page 79
Train/taxi from Hyderabad (3½ hrs/2½ hrs)

Gulbarga en route, page 82

Bijapur 2 nights, page 83
Taxi from Bidar via Gulbarga (5-8 hrs)

Badami, Aihole and Pattadakal
1 night, page 86
Train/taxi from Bijapur (3 hrs/2 hrs)

Hampi 3 nights, page 90
Taxi from Badami (5 hrs); or bus from Badami to Hospet (5 hrs) then bus/auto-rickshaw to Hampi (30 mins); or train Badami to Gadag, Gadag to Hospet, then auto-rickshaw or bus to Hampi (5 hrs)

South Goa 2 nights, page 97
Train from Hospet to Madgaon (7½ hrs) then bus or taxi to Palolem (2 hrs)

Central Goa 2 nights, page 101
Taxi from Palolem to Majorda Beach (2 hrs)

North Goa 3 nights, page 114
Taxi from Majorda to Arambol/Anjuna (3 hrs)

Mumbai stopover, page 35
Flight/train from Goa (1 hr/8+ hrs)
for international flight home

GOING FURTHER

Warangal page 75
Train from Hyderabad (3½ hrs)

Nagarjunakonda page 76
Bus from Hyderabad (4 hrs) or
guided day trip from Hyderabad

Gokarna page 100
Train from Madgaon to Gokarna Rd
then taxi to Gokarna (2½ hrs)

Bhagwan Mahaveer and Goa's Hindu heartland page 124
For Bhagwan Mahaveer, bus to Molem then taxi to Bhagwan Mahaveer. For spice farms and Wildernest, bus/taxi/scooter to Ponda, then taxi/scooter to spice farms. Guided tours from Panjim or the coastal resorts are also a strong option

DREAM TRIP 1
Mumbai→Hampi→Goa→Mumbai

From the multisensory urban assault of downtown Mumbai, through silent sunsets over boulder-strewn ruins, to the mellow surf and colonial relics of Goa, this exhilarating circuit peels back layer upon layer of South Indian history.

Your immersion begins in the concrete jungle of Mumbai – a city that, despite its immense size and its 21 million souls striving for survival, makes for an utterly absorbing and surprisingly hassle-free introduction to India.

From Mumbai you head east across the Western Ghats into the Deccan Plateau. Here are the astonishing rock-carved temples of Ellora and Ajanta, and further east, the great fort of Golconda – now incongruously crowded by the suburbs of Hyderabad, whose gleaming IT parks sprawl outwards from the fascinating old city of the Nizams.

The route now turns west into the red plains of Karnataka, passing a sequence of dusty medieval Muslim towns en route to Bijapur, a beguiling citadel of mosques and mausoleums. South of Bijapur lie Pattadakal and Aihole, where Chalukyan architects spent six centuries forging the blueprints for Hindu temple designs that spread to every corner of India. These serve as a fine appetizer for the surreal wonder that is Hampi – the ghostly remains of South India's greatest ancient city, spread across a fantastical landscape of tumbled orange boulders.

From here the route once again turns west, crossing the mountains and descending to the lush coastal plains of Goa. For some a pallid pastiche of the 'real India', for others a blessed escape from it, Goa is a palm-shaded world unto itself, and somewhere along its surprisingly varied coastline you'll almost certainly find a beach that provides the right kind of recharge before your journey onwards.

MUMBAI (BOMBAY)

Maximum City, the City of Dreams, India's economic capital and melting pot. You can throw epithets and superlatives at Mumbai until the cows come home, but it refuses to be understood on a merely intellectual level. Like London and New York, it's a restless human tapestry of cultures, religions, races, ways of surviving and thriving, and one that evokes palpable emotion; whether you love it or hate it, you can't stay unaffected.

From the cluster of fishing villages first linked together by the British East India Company in 1668, Mumbai has swelled to sprawl across seven islands, which now groan under the needs of 19 million stomachs, souls and egos. Its problems – creaking infrastructure, endemic corruption coupled with bureaucratic incompetence, and an ever-expanding population of whom more than two thirds live in slums – are only matched by the enormous drive that makes it the centre of business, fashion and film-making in modern India, and both a magnet and icon for the country's dreams, and nightmares.

The taxi ride from the airport shows you both sides of the city: slum dwellers selling balloons under billboards of fair-skinned models dripping in gold and reclining on the roof of a Mercedes; the septic stench as you cross Mahim Creek, where bikers park on the soaring bridge to shoot the breeze amid fumes that could drop an elephant; the feeling of diesel permeating your bloodstream and the manically reverberating mantra of Horn OK Please as you ooze through traffic past Worli's glitzy shopping malls and the fairytale island mosque of Haji Ali. And finally the magic moment as you swing out on to Chowpatty Beach and the city throws off her cloak of chaos to reveal a neon-painted skyscape that makes you feel like you've arrived at the centre of all things.

Gothic clocktowers and glass skyscrapers, mill chimneys and minarets, vibrant temples and tarpaulin-roofed shacks mingle below the smog. Stitching them together are streets aswarm with panel-beaten double-decker buses, yellow and black taxis, long wooden carts stacked with hessian-stitched parcels being towed by teams of grimacing Bihari migrant workers, and white-hatted dabbawalas weaving their way through the chaos carrying stacks of metal tins – the guardians of a hundred thousand office lunches.

Hundreds of fresh migrants arrive in the city daily, and whether they come by plane, sweeping in over the crescent bays and the smog-wrapped slums bound for South Mumbai, where real estate is more expensive than Manhattan, or by packed train carriage through the endless sprawl of apartment blocks to eke out a space among the poorest of the poor in Dharavi, Mumbai, somehow, finds a way to absorb them all.

→ ARRIVING IN MUMBAI

GETTING THERE

Chhatrapati Shivaji International Airport is 30 km from Nariman Point, the business heart of the city. The domestic terminals at Santa Cruz are 5 km closer. Prepaid taxis to the city centre are good value and take 40-90 minutes; buses are cheaper but significantly slower. If you arrive at night without a hotel booking it is best to stay at one of the hotels near the airports. If you're travelling light (and feeling brave), local trains head into the city from Vile Parle (International) and Santa Cruz (Domestic) stations, but these are daunting at any time (passengers leap off while the train is still moving and will 'help' you if you're in their way) and become impossibly crowded during the morning and evening rush hours.

MOVING ON

As one of India's most important transport hubs, Mumbai is well connected by air, bus and rail to the rest of the country. After three nights here, you can either take a one-hour flight to **Aurangabad** (see page 51) or jump on a train from CST station, a short taxi ride from the main sights and hotel districts of South Mumbai. The most useful of the three daily trains is the Tapovan Express, which departs at 0610 and reaches Aurangabad around 1330; this is a popular route and you'll need to book tickets well in advance to avoid a cramped and uncomfortable journey. CST station has a special counter for overseas visitors, where you can sometimes get tickets on otherwise full trains under the Foreign Tourist Quota. You'll need your passport and an ATM receipt or money exchange receipt.

GETTING AROUND

The sights are spread out and you need transport. Taxis are metered and good value. Older taxis carry a rate card to convert the meter reading to the correct fare. You can download the rate card in advance from www.hindustantimes.com/farelist, and various fare conversion apps are available for smartphones. There are frequent buses on major routes, and the two suburban railway lines are useful out of peak hours, but get horrendously crowded. Auto-rickshaws are only allowed in the suburbs north of Mahim Creek.

TOURIST INFORMATION

Government of India ① *123 M Karve Rd, opposite Churchgate, T022-2207 4333, Mon-Sat 0830-1730 (closed 2nd Sat of month from 1230); counters open 24 hrs at both airports; Taj Mahal Hotel, Mon-Sat 0830-1530 (closed 2nd Sat from 1230).* **Maharashtra Tourist Development Corporation (MTDC)** ① *CDO Hutments, Madam Cama Rd, T022-2204 4040, www.maharashtratourism.gov.in; Koh-i-Noor Rd, near Pritam Hotel, Dadar T022-2414 3200; Gateway of India, T022-2284 1877.* Information and booking counters at international and domestic terminals and online.

→BACKGROUND

Hinduism made its mark on Mumbai long before the Portuguese and British transformed it into one of India's great cities. The caves on the island of Elephanta were excavated under the Kalachuris (AD 500-600). Yet, only 350 years ago, the area occupied by this great metropolis comprised seven islands inhabited by Koli fishermen. The British acquired these marshy and malarial islands as part of the marriage dowry paid by the Portuguese when Catherine of Braganza married Charles II in 1661. Four years later, they took possession of the remaining islands and neighbouring mainland area and in 1668 the East India Company leased the whole area from the crown for £10 a year, which was paid for nearly 50 years. The East India Company shifted its headquarters to Mumbai in 1672.

Isolated by the sharp face of the Western Ghats and the constantly hostile Marathas, Mumbai's early fortunes rested on the shipbuilding yards established by progressive Parsis. It thrived entirely on overseas trade and, in the cosmopolitan city this created, Parsis, Sephardic Jews and the British shared common interests and responded to the same incentives.

After a devastating fire on 17 February 1803, a new town with wider streets was built. Then, with the abolition of the Company's trade monopoly, the doors to rapid expansion were flung open and Mumbai flourished. Trade with England boomed, and under the governorship of Sir Bartle Frere (1862-1869) the city acquired a number of extravagant

Indo-Gothic landmarks, most notably the station formerly known as the Victoria Terminus. The opening of the Suez Canal in 1870 gave Mumbai greater proximity to European markets and a decisive advantage over its eastern rival Kolkata. It has since become the headquarters for many national and international companies, and was a natural choice as home to India's stock exchange (BSE). With the sponsorship of the Tata family, Mumbai has also become the primary home of India's nuclear research programme, with its first plutonium extraction plant at Trombay in 1961 and the establishment of the Tata Institute for Fundamental Research, the most prestigious science research institute in the country.

Mumbai is still growing fast, and heavy demand for building space means property value is some of the highest on earth. As in Manhattan, buildings are going upward: residential skyscrapers have mushroomed in the upscale enclaves around Malabar Hill. Meanwhile, the old mill complexes of Lower Parel have been rapidly revived as shopping and luxury apartment complexes. An even more ambitious attempt to ease pressure on the isthmus is the newly minted city of Navi Mumbai, 90 minutes east of the city, which has malls, apartments and industrial parks, but little of the glamour that makes Mumbai such a magnet.

The latest project is the controversial redevelopment of Dharavi, a huge chunk of prime real estate that's currently occupied by Asia's biggest slum – home to one third of Mumbai's population, in desperately squalid makeshift hovels originally designed to house migrant mill workers. In addition, an uncounted number live precariously in unauthorized, hastily rigged and frequently demolished corrugated-iron or bamboo-and-tarpaulin shacks beside railways and roads, while yet more sleep in doorways and on sheets across the pavement.

In recent decades, the pressure of supporting so many people has begun to tell on Mumbai. Communal riots between Hindus and Muslims have flared up several times since the destruction by militant Hindus of the Babri Masjid in 1992, and the disastrous 2005 monsoon, which dumped almost a metre of rainfall on the city overnight and left trains stranded with water up to their windows, laid bare the governmental neglect which had allowed drainage and other infrastructure to lag behind the needs of the populace.

The unprecedented attacks of 26 November 2008, when Lashkar-e-Taiba terrorists held staff and foreign guests hostage in the Taj Mahal and Oberoi hotels, have been widely read as a strike against the symbols of India's overseas business ambitions. They further served to illustrate that money cannot buy protection from the harsh realities of Indian life. Yet the citizens did not vent their anger on each other, but at the government that had failed to deal effectively with the attacks. Within weeks the front of the Taj had been scrubbed clean and tourists were packing out the Leopold Café, while CST station emerged from the bullets a cleaner, calmer, less chaotic place. Somehow, whether through economic imperative or a shared mentality of forward thinking, the city always finds a way to bounce back.

→ GATEWAY OF INDIA AND COLABA

The Indo-Saracenic-style Gateway of India (1927), designed by George Wittet to commemorate the visit of George V and Queen Mary in 1911, is modelled in honey-coloured basalt on 16th-century Gujarati work. The great gateway is an archway with halls on each side capable of seating 600 at important receptions. The arch was the point from which the last British regiment left on 28 February 1948, signalling the end of the empire. The whole area has a huge buzz at weekends. Scores of boats depart from here for **Elephanta Island**, creating a sea-swell which young boys delight in diving into. Hawkers, beggars and the general throng of people all add to the atmosphere. A short distance behind the Gateway is an impressive **statue of Shivaji**.

The original red-domed **Taj Mahal Hotel** was almost completely gutted by fire in the aftermath of the 26/11 terrorist attacks, which saw guests and staff of the hotel taken hostage and several killed, but the glorious Old Wing has since been fully restored to its original opulence. Even if you're not staying it's worth braving the airport-style security checks to wander through the palatial corridors, or stop for afternoon tea. Unfortunately, drug addicts, drunks and prostitutes frequent the area behind the hotel, but you can also find couples and young families taking in the sea air around the Gateway at night.

South of the Gateway of India is the crowded southern section of Shahid (literally 'martyr') Bhagat Singh Marg, or Colaba Causeway, a brilliantly bawdy bazar and the epicentre of Mumbai's tourist scene; you can buy everything from high-end jeans to cheaply made *kurtas* and knock-off leather wallets at the street stalls, and the colourful cast of characters includes Bollywood casting agents, would-be novelists plotting a successor to *Shantaram* in the **Leopold Café** (another bearer of bullet scars from 26/11), and any number of furtive hash sellers. The Afghan Memorial **Church of St John the Baptist** (1847-1858) is at the northern edge of Colaba itself. Early English in style, with a 58-m spire, it was built to commemorate the soldiers who died in the First Afghan War. Fishermen still unload their catch early in the morning at **Sassoon Dock**, the first wet dock in India; photography prohibited. Beyond the church near the tip of the Colaba promontory lie the **Observatory** and **Old European cemetery** in the naval colony (permission needed to enter). Frequent buses ply this route.

→ FORT

The area stretching north from Colaba to CST (Victoria Terminus) is named after Fort St George, built by the British East India Company in the 1670s and torn down by Governor Bartle Frere in the 1860s. Anchored by the superb Chhatrapati Shivaji Museum to the south and the grassy parkland of Oval Maidan to the west, this area blossomed after 1862, when Sir Bartle Frere became governor (1862-1867). Under his enthusiastic guidance Mumbai became a great civic centre and an extravaganza of Victorian Gothic architecture, modified by Indo-Saracenic influences. This area is worth exploring at night, when many of the old buildings are floodlit.

Chhatrapati Shivaji (Prince of Wales) Museum ⓘ *Oct-Feb Tue-Sun 1015-1800, last tickets 1645; foreigners Rs 300 (includes audio guide), Indians Rs 15, camera Rs 15 (no flash or tripods), students Rs 10, children Rs 5, avoid Tue as it is busy with school visits*, is housed in an impressive building designed by George Wittet to commemorate the visit of the Prince of Wales to India in 1905. The dome of glazed tiles has a very Persian and Central Asian flavour. The archaeological section has three main groups: Brahminical; Buddhist and Jain; Prehistoric and Foreign. The art section includes an excellent collection of Indian miniatures and well displayed *tankhas* along with a section on armour that is worth seeing. There are also works by Gainsborough, Poussin and Titian as well as Indian silver, jade and tapestries. The Natural History section is based on the collection of the Bombay Natural History Society, founded in 1833. Good guidebooks, cards and reproductions on sale. **Jehangir Art Gallery** ⓘ *within the museum complex, T022-2284 3989*, holds short-term exhibitions of contemporary art. The **Samovar** café is good for a snack and a chilled beer in a pleasant, if cramped, garden-side setting. Temporary members may use the library and attend lectures.

The **National Gallery of Modern Art** ① *Sir Cowasji Jehangir Hall, opposite the museum, T022-2285 2457, foreigners Rs 150, Indians Rs 10,* is a three-tiered gallery converted from an old public hall which gives a good introduction to India's contemporary art scene.

St Andrew's Kirk (1819) ① *just behind the museum, daily 1000-1700,* is a simple neoclassical church. At the south end of Mahatma Gandhi (MG) Road is the renaissance-style **Institute of Science** (1911) designed by George Wittet. The Institute, which includes a scientific library, a public hall and examination halls, was built with gifts from the Parsi and Jewish communities.

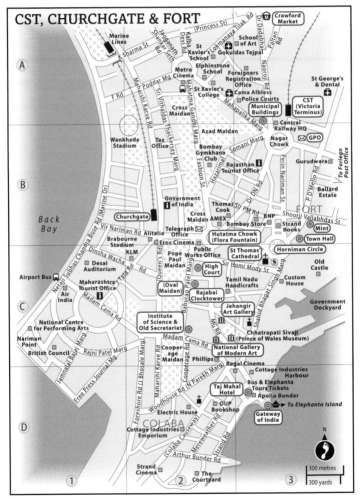

CST, CHURCHGATE & FORT

The **Oval Maidan** has been restored to a pleasant public garden and acts as the lungs and public cricket pitch of the southern business district. On the east side of the **Pope Paul Maidan** is the Venetian Gothic-style **old Secretariat** (1874), with a façade of arcaded verandas and porticos that are faced in buff-coloured porbander stone from Gujarat. Decorated with red and blue basalt, the carvings are in white *hemnagar* stone. The **University Convocation Hall** (1874) to its north was designed by Sir George Gilbert Scott in a 15th-century French decorated style. Scott also designed the adjacent **University Library** and the **Rajabai clock tower** (1870s) next door, based on Giotto's campanile in Florence. The sculpted figures in niches on the exterior walls of the tower were designed to represent the castes of India. Originally the clock could chime 12 tunes including *Rule Britannia*. The **High Court** (1871-1879), in early English Gothic style, has a 57-m-high central tower flanked by lower octagonal towers topped by the figures of Justice and Mercy. The Venetian Gothic **Public Works Office** (1869-1872) is to its north. Opposite, and with its main façade to Vir Nariman Road, is the gorgeously wrought former **General Post Office** (1869-1872). Now called the Telegraph Office, it stands next to the original Telegraph Office adding romanesque to the extraordinary mixture of European architectural styles.

From here you can walk east and delve into the dense back lanes of the Fort district, crossing the five-way junction of **Hutatma Chowk** ('Martyrs' Corner', in the centre of which stands the architecturally forgettable but useful landmark of the Flora Fountain (1869). This is an interesting area to explore although there are no particular sights

Vir Nariman Road cuts through to the elegant tree-shaded oval of **Horniman Circle**, laid out in 1860 and renamed in 1947 after Benjamin Horniman, editor of the pro-independence *Bombay Chronicle* – one of the few English names remaining on the Mumbai map. The park in the middle is used for dance and music performances during the **Kala Ghoda Arts Festival**, held in January. On the west edge are the Venetian Gothic **Elphinstone Buildings** (1870) in brown sandstone, while to the south is the **Cathedral Church of St Thomas** (1718), which contains a number of monuments amounting to a heroic 'Who's Who of India'.

South of Horniman Circle on Shahid Bhagat Singh Marg, the **Custom House** is one of the oldest buildings in the city, believed to incorporate a Portuguese barrack block from 1665. Over the entrance is the crest of the East India Company. Remnants of the old Portuguese fort's walls can be seen and many Malabar teak 'East Indiamen' ships were built here. Walk north from here and you'll reach the **Town Hall** (1820-1823), widely admired and much photographed as one of the best neoclassical buildings in India. The Corinthian interior houses the **Assembly Rooms** and the **Bombay Asiatic Society**. Immediately north again is the **Mint** (1824-1829) ① *visit by prior permission from the Mint Master, T022-2270 3184, www.mumbaimint.org*, built on the Fort rubbish dump, with Ionic columns and a water tank in front of it. The nearby **Ballard Estate** is also worth a poke around while you're in the area, with some good hotels and restaurants, as well as Hamilton Studios, the swanky offices of *Vogue* magazine, and the Mumbai Port Authority.

→ AROUND THE CST (VT)

Chhatrapati Shivaji Terminus (1878-1887), formerly Victoria Terminus and still known to many elder taxi drivers as 'VT', is far and away the most remarkable example of Victorian Gothic architecture in India. Opened during Queen Victoria's Golden Jubilee year (1887), over three million commuters now swarm through the station daily, though the bustling chaos of old has been reined in somewhat since November 2008's terror attacks, when at least 50 people were shot dead here. Several scenes from *Slumdog Millionaire* were filmed on the suburban platforms at the west end of the station.

The station was built at a time when fierce debate was taking place among British architects working in India as to the most appropriate style to develop to meet the demands of the late 19th-century boom. One view held that the British should restrict themselves to models derived from the best in Western tradition. Others argued that architects should draw on Indian models, trying to bring out the best of Indian tradition and encourage its development. By and large, the former were dominant, but the introduction of Gothic elements allowed a blending of Western traditions with Indian (largely Islamic) motifs, which became known as the Indo-Saracenic style. The station that resulted, designed by FW Stevens, is its crowning glory: a huge, symmetrical, gargoyle-studded frontage capped by a large central dome and a 4-m-high statue of Progress, with arcaded booking halls, stained glass and glazed tiles inspired by St Pancras. The giant caterpillar-like walkway with perspex awnings looks truly incongruous against the huge Gothic structure.

There are many more Victorian buildings in the area around CST, particularly along Mahapalika Marg (Cruickshank Road), which runs northwest of the station past the grand **Municipal Buildings** (also by Stevens, 1893), and Lokmanya Tilak Marg (Camac Road), which joins Mahapalika Marg at the Metro Cinema traffic circle – a landmark known to every Mumbai cabbie.

Immediately to the north of CST lies **Crawford Market** (1865-1871), now renamed **Mahatma Jyotiba Phule Market** after a Maharashtran social reformer, designed by Emerson in 12th-century French Gothic style, with paving stones imported from Caithness and fountains carved by Lockwood Kipling. The market is divided into bustling sections for fruit, vegetables, fish, mutton and poultry, with a large central hall and clock tower.

Running northwest of Crawford Market towards Mumbai Central Railway Station is **Falkland Road**, the centre of Mumbai's red-light district. Prostitutes stand behind barred windows, giving the area its other name, 'The Cages' – many of the girls are sold or abducted from various parts of India and Nepal. AIDS is very widespread, and a lot of NGOs are at work in the area educating the women about prevention.

North of Crawford Market is **Masjid Station**, the heart of the Muslim quarter, where agate minarets mingle with the pollution-streaked upper storeys of 1960s residential towers. The atmosphere here is totally different from the crumbling colonial architectural glory of the Colaba and Fort area: balconies on faded apartment blocks are bedecked with fairy lights, laundry dries on the window grilles, and at sunset the ramshackle roads hum with taxis, boys wielding wooden carts through traffic and Muslim women at a stroll. One of the city's most interesting markets, the **Chor Bazar** (Thieves' Market) ① *Sat to Thu 1100-1900*, spreads through the streets between the station and Falkland Road. The bazar is a great place to poke around in with tonnes of dealers in old watches, film posters, Belgian- or Indian-made temple lamps, enamel tiles and door knobs. The area around Mutton Street is popular with film prop-buyers and foreign and domestic bric-a-brac hunters.

When the hustle of the city becomes too much, do as the Mumbaikars do and head for the water. The 3-km sweep of **Marine Drive** (known as the 'Queen's Necklace' for the lines of streetlights that run its length) skirts alongside the grey waters of the Arabian Sea from Nariman Point in the south to exclusive Malabar Hill in the north. This is where you'll see Mumbai at its most egalitarian: servants and *babus* alike take the air on the esplanades in the evening. For an interesting half-day trip, start downtown at Churchgate Station and follow the curving course of the Queen's Necklace to the Walkeshwar Temple out on the end of Malabar Hill; start at lunchtime and you can be strolling back down Marine Drive, ice cream in hand, among the atmospheric sunset crush of power-walking executives and festive families.

Churchgate Station (1894-1896), on Vir Nariman Road at the north end of the Oval Maidan, was the second great railway building designed by FW Stevens. With its domes and gables, Churchgate has an air of Byzantine simplicity that contrasts with CST's full-tilt Gothic overload, but the rush hour spectacle is no less striking: Sebastião Salgado's famous photograph of commuters pouring out of suburban trains was taken here.

A block to the west is Netaji Subhash Road, better known as **Marine Drive**, which bends northwest past Wankhede cricket stadium, several luxury hotels and the run-down Taraporewala Aquarium. At the north end in the crook of Malabar Hill is **Chowpatty Beach**, a long stretch of grey-white sand that looks attractive from a distance, but is polluted. Swimming here is not recommended but there is a lot of interesting beach activity in the evening. Chowpatty was the scene of a number of important 'Quit India' rallies during the Independence Movement. During important festivals, like **Ganesh Chaturthi** and **Dussehra**, it is thronged with jubilant Hindu devotees.

Mahatma Gandhi Museum (Mani Bhavan) ① *west of Grant Rd station at 19 Laburnum Rd, www.gandhi-manibhavan.org, 0930-1800, Rs 10, allow 1 hr*, is north of Chowpatty on the road to Nana Chowk. This private house, where Mahatma Gandhi used to stay on visits to Mumbai, is now a memorial museum and research library with 20,000 volumes. There is a diorama depicting important scenes from Gandhi's life, but the display of photos and letters on the first floor is more interesting, and includes letters Gandhi wrote to Hitler in 1939 asking him not to go to war, and those to Roosevelt, Einstein and Tolstoy.

At the end of Chowpatty, Marine Drive becomes Walkeshwar Road and bends southwest to pass the **Jain Temple** (1904), built of marble and dedicated to the first Jain Tirthankar. Much of the colourful decoration depicts the lives of the Tirthankars. Visitors can watch various rituals being performed. Jains play a prominent part in Mumbai's banking and commerce and are one of the city's wealthiest communities. Beyond, on the tip of Malabar Point, is **Raj Bhavan**, now home to the Governor of Maharashtra.

Behind the Jain Temple, Gangadhar Kher Rd (Ridge Road) runs up Malabar Hill to the **Hanging Gardens** (**Pherozeshah Mehta Gardens**) so named since they are located on top of a series of tanks that supply water to Mumbai. The gardens are well kept with lots of topiary animals and offer an opportunity to hang out with Mumbai's elite, whose penthouse apartments peer down on the park from all sides; there are good views over the city and Marine Drive from the **Kamala Nehru Park** across the road. It's worth a visit after 1700 when it's a bit cooler, but it's reputed to be unsafe after nightfall. Immediately to the north are the Parsi **Towers of Silence**, set in secluded gardens donated by Parsi industrialist Sir Jamshetji Jeejeebhoy. This very private place is not accessible to tourists but it can be glimpsed from the road. Parsis believe that the elements of water, fire and earth must not be polluted by the dead, so they lay their 'vestments of flesh and bone' out on the top of the towers to be picked clean by vultures. The depletion in the number of vultures is a cause for concern, and more and more agiarys now opt for solar panels to speed up the process of decay.

At the end of the headland behind Raj Bhavan stands the **Walkeshwar Temple** ('Lord of Sand'), built about AD 1000 and one of the oldest buildings in Mumbai. In legend this was a resting point for Lord Rama on his journey from Ayodhya to Lanka to free Sita from the demon king Ravana. One day Rama's brother failed to return from Varanasi at the usual time with a *lingam* that he fetched daily for Rama's worship. Rama then made a *lingam* from the beach sand to worship Siva. You'd also do well to visit **Banganga**, a freshwater tank that's part of an 12th-century temple complex. Legend has it that when Rama got thirsty Lakshman raised his bow and shot a *baan* (arrow) into the ground, bringing forth fresh water from the Ganga in this ocean locked island. The site is being renovated and is regularly used as a venue for concerts, festivals and pilgrimages alike.

→ CENTRAL MUMBAI

Other than to catch a train from Mumbai Central Station, relatively few visitors venture into the area north of Marine Drive, yet it contains some fascinating only-in-Mumbai sights which, with judicious use of taxis and the odd suburban train, can easily be combined into a day trip with the coastal sights described above.

On the coast, 1 km north of the Ghandi Museum on Bhulabhai Desai (Warden Road), are the **Mahalakshmi temples**, the oldest in Mumbai, dedicated to three goddesses whose images were found in the sea. Lakshmi, goddess of wealth, is the unofficial presiding deity of the city, and the temple is host to frenzied activity – pressing a coin into the wall of the main shrine is supposed to be a sign of riches to come. Just to the north, **Haji Ali's Mosque** sits on an islet 500 m offshore. The mosque, built in 1431, contains the tomb of Muslim saint Haji Ali, who drowned here while on pilgrimage to Mecca, and as a last request demanded that he be buried neither on land nor at sea. A long causeway, usable only at low tide, links the mosque and tomb to the land, and is lined by Muslim supplicants. The money changers are willing to exchange one-rupee coins into smaller coins, enabling pilgrims to make several individual gifts to beggars rather than one larger one, thereby reputedly increasing the merit of the gift.

From Haji Ali's Tomb go east along Keshavrao Khade Road, passing the **Mahalakshmi Race Course** ⓘ *racing season Nov-Apr, www.rwitc.com*, to SG Maharaj Chowk (**Jacob's Circle**), and turn north to Mahalakshmi Bridge, reachable by local trains from Churchgate. From the bridge there is a view across the astonishing Municipal **dhobi ghats**, where Mumbai's dirty laundry is soaked, smacked in concrete tubs and aired in public by the *dhobis* (washerfolk); vistas unfold in blocks of primary colours, though you may have to fend off junior touts to enjoy them in peace. A short distance further north are the disused Victorian cotton mills of **Lower Parel**. Closed in 1980 after an all-out strike, some remain standing in a state of picturesque ruin (local residents may offer to show you round for Rs 50-100) while others, notably the Phoenix, Mathuradas and Bombay Dyeing mill compounds, have been converted into slick new malls, nightclubs and studio spaces popular with publishers and advertising agencies.

Southeast of Mahalakshmi station in Byculla are the **Veermata Jijibai Bhonsle Udyan** gardens, formerly Victoria Gardens. The attractive 20-ha (48-acre) park is home to

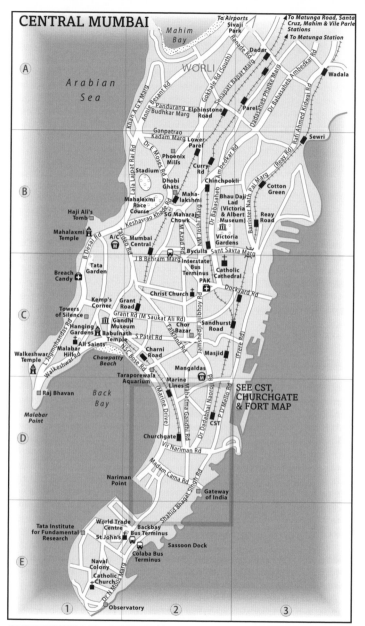

ON THE ROAD
Dabbawallahs

If you go inside Churchgate station at mid-morning or after lunch, you will see the *dabbawallahs*, members of the Bombay Union of Tiffin Box Carriers. Each morning, the 2500 *dabbawallahs* call on suburban housewives who pack freshly cooked lunch into small circular stainless steel containers – *dabbas*. Three or four are stacked one on the other and held together by a clip with a handle. Typically the *dabbawallah* will collect 30-40 tiffin boxes, range them out on a long pole and cycle to the nearest station. Here he will hand them over to a fellow *dabbawallah* who will transport them into the city for delivery.

Over 100,000 lunches of maybe *sabze* (vegetable curry), chappattis, dahl and pickle make their way daily across town to the breadwinner. The service, which costs a few rupees a day, is a good example of the fine division of labour in India, reliable and efficient, for the *dabbawallahs* pride themselves on never losing a lunch. He makes sure that the carefully prepared *pukka* (proper) food has not in any way been defiled.

Mumbai's **zoo** ⓘ *Thu-Tue 0900-1800, Rs 5*, be warned though, the signboards are missing and while the birds are gorgeous – they have birds of paradise, white peacocks and pink pelicans among others – there's no indication of what you're looking at. The gardens share space with the newly renovated **Bhau Daji Lad Museum** (**Victoria and Albert Museum**) ⓘ *www.bdl museum.org, Thu-Tue, 1000-1730, foreigners Rs 100, Indians Rs 10, children half price*. Inspired by the V&A in London and financed by public subscription, it was built in 1872 in a palladian style and is the second oldest museum in India. The collection covers the history of Mumbai and contains prints, maps and models that show how the seven disjointed islands came to form Mumbai.

→ BANDRA, JUHU BEACH AND ANDHERI

If you really want to get under the skin of the city, a jaunt into the far-flung northern suburbs is essential. Close to the airports and relatively relaxed compared to living in the city centre, Bandra and Juhu are popular with Mumbai's upper crust, and most Bollywood A-listers have at least one of their homes here. **Bandra** is a lively suburb, full of the young and wealthy, with some exciting places to eat and some of the coolest bars, coffee shops, gyms and lounges in the city. Linking Road is home to a long open-air shoe bazar where you can find cheap, colourful sandals and knock-offs of every brand of clothing. Bandra's two seaside promenades, one at Bandra Bandstand by the Taj Lands End Hotel and one at Carter Road, the next bay northwards, feature sea-facing coffee shops with spectacular sunset views.

Juhu Beach, 20 km north of the centre, used to be an attractive and relaxed seaside area, but one sniff of the toxic water oozing out of Mahim Creek is enough to dissuade anyone from dipping so much as a toe in the ocean. Hordes of people still visit every day to walk on the beach, eat *bhel puri* and other spicy street food that delicate stomachs had best avoid, while kids buy balloons and take rides on horse-driven chariots. Beyond the beach Juhu is primarily a residential area, full of luxurious apartments, elegant old bungalows (Bollywood megastar Amitabh Bachchan has a place here) and day spas.

Andheri, spreading north of the airports, is the biggest suburb in Mumbai: it covers 50 sq km, is home to between 1.5 million and four million people depending on who's counting, and has sprung up from villages and mangrove swamps in a mere 30 years. There are few sights of note, but as a city within a city, with its own social subdivisions (mega-trendy residential enclaves and malls to the west, business parks and down-at-heel slums to the east, and even a suburban monorail system in construction), Andheri may well come to represent Mumbai's second city centre. If you want to explore, the areas to know about are Lokhandwala, New Link Road and Seven Bungalows/Versova; all are in Andheri West.

→ ELEPHANTA CAVES

Ten kilometres east of the Gateway of India, the heavily forested **Elephanta Island**, barely visible in the haze from Mumbai, rises out of the bay like a giant whale. The setting is symbolically significant; the sea is the ocean of life, a world of change (Samsara) in which is set an island of spiritual and physical refuge. The 'caves', excavated over 1000 years ago in the volcanic lava high up the slope of the hill, saw Hindu craftsmen express their view of spiritual truths in massive carvings of extraordinary grace. Sadly a large proportion have been severely damaged, but enough remains to illustrate something of their skill.

BACKGROUND
The vast majority of India's 1200 **cave sites** were created as temples and monasteries between the third century BC and the 10th century AD. Jain, Buddhist and Hindu caves often stand side by side. The temple cave on Elephanta Island, dedicated to Siva, was probably excavated during the eighth century by the Rashtrakuta Dynasty which ruled the Deccan AD 757-973, though the caves may have had earlier Buddhist origins. An earlier name for the island was Garhapuri ('city of forts') but the Portuguese renamed it after the colossal sculpted elephants when they captured Mumbai from the Sultan of Gujarat in 1535, and stationed a battalion there. They reportedly used the main pillared cave as a shooting gallery causing some of the damage you see. Muslim and British rulers were not blameless either.

ARRIVING IN ELEPHANTA CAVES
Boats to Elephanta Island leave every few minutes from 0900, from the jetty in front of the Gateway of India. The crossing takes about an hour. From the landing place, a 300-m unshaded path along the quayside and then about 110 rough steps lead to the caves at a height of 75 m. The walk along the quay can be avoided when the small train functions (Rs 10 return). The climb can be trying for some, especially if it is hot, though *doolies* (chairs carried by porters) are available for Rs 300 return, Rs 200 one-way. At the start of the climb there are stalls selling refreshments, knick-knacks and curios (including models of the Eiffel Tower), but if you're carrying food watch out for aggressive monkeys. **Maharashtra Tourism** normally organizes a festival of classical music and dance on the island in the third week of February. Early morning is the best time for light and also for avoiding large groups with guides which arrive from 1000. The caves tend to be quite dark so carry a powerful torch.

THE SITE
ⓘ *Tue-Sun, sunrise to sunset; foreigners Rs 250, Indians Rs 10, plus Rs 5 passenger tax. Weekends are very busy.*
Entrance Originally there were three entrances and 28 pillars at the site. The entrances on the east and west have subsidiary shrines which may have been excavated and used for different ceremonies. The main entrance is now from the north. At dawn, the rising

sun casts its rays on the approach to the *garbagriha* (main shrine), housed in a square structure at the west end of the main hall. On your right is a carving of Siva as Nataraj. On the left he appears as Lakulisa in a much damaged carving. Seated on a lotus, the Buddha-like figure is a symbol of the unconscious mind and enlightenment, found also in Orissan temples where Lakulisa played a prominent role in attempting to attract Buddhists back into Hinduism. From the steps at the entrance you can see the *yoni-lingam*, the symbol of the creative power of the deity.

Main Hall The ribbed columns in the main hall, 5- to 6-m high and in a cruciform layout, are topped by a capital. At the corner of each pillar is a dwarf signifying *gana* (the earth spirit), and sometimes the figure of Ganesh (Ganapati). To the right, the main **Linga Shrine** has four entrances, each corresponding to a cardinal point guarded by a *dvarpala*. The sanctum is bare, drawing attention to the *yonilingam* which the devotee must walk around clockwise.

Wall panels To the north of the main shrine is **Bhairava killing the demon Andhakasura**. This extraordinarily vivid carving shows Siva at his most fearsome, with a necklace of skulls, crushing the power of Andhaka, the Chief of Darkness. It was held that if he was wounded each drop of his blood would create a new demon. So Siva impaled him with his sword and collected his blood with a cup, which he then offered to his wife Shakti. In winter this panel is best seen in the early afternoon.

Opposite, on the south side of the main shrine is the damaged panel of **Kalyan Sundari**, in which Siva stands with Parvati on his right, just before their wedding (normally a Hindu wife stands on her husband's left). She looks down shyly, but her body is drawn to him. Behind Parvati is her father Himalaya and to his left Chandramas, the moon god carrying a gift – *soma*, the food of the gods. On Siva's left is Vishnu and below him Brahma.

At the extreme west end of the temple are **Nataraja** (left) and **Yogisvara Siva** (right). The former shows a beautiful figure of Ganesh above and Parvati on his left. All the other gods watch him. Above his right shoulder is the four-headed God of Creation, Brahma. Below Brahma is the elephant-headed Ganesh.

On the south wall, opposite the entrance are three panels. **Gangadhara** is on the west. The holy River Ganga (Bhagirathi) flowed only in heaven but was brought to earth by her father King Bhagiratha (kneeling at Siva's right foot). Here, Ganga is shown in the centre, flanked by her two tributaries, Yamuna and Saraswati. These three rivers are believed to meet at Allahabad.

To the left of these is the centre piece of the whole temple, the remarkable **Mahesvara**, the Lord of the Universe. Here Siva is five-headed, for the usual triple-headed figure has one face looking into the rock and another on top of his head. Nearly 6 m high, he unites all the functions of creation, preservation and destruction. Some see the head on the left (your right) as representing Vishnu, the Creator, while others suggest that it shows a more feminine aspect of Siva. To his right is Rudra or Bhairava, with snakes in his hair, a skull to represent ageing from which only Siva is free, and he has a look of anger. The central face is Siva as his true self, Siva Swarupa, balancing out creation and destruction. In this mode he is passive and serene, radiating peace and wisdom like the Buddha. His right hand is held up in a calming gesture and in his left hand is a lotus bud.

The panel to the left has the **Ardhanarisvara**. This depicts Siva as the embodiment of male and female, representing wholeness and the harmony of opposites. The female half is relaxed and gentle, the mirror in the hand symbolizing the woman reflecting the man. Siva has his 'vehicle', Nandi on the right.

To the east, opposite the *garbha-griha*, was probably the original entrance. On the south is Siva and Parvati **Playing chaupar on Mount Kailash**. Siva is the faceless figure. Parvati has lost and is sulking but her playful husband persuades her to return to the game. They are surrounded by Nandi, Siva's bull, celestial figures and an ascetic with his begging bowl.

On the north is **Ravana Shaking Mount Kailash** on which Siva is seated. Siva is calm and unperturbed by Ravana's show of brute strength and reassures the frightened Parvati. He pins down Ravana with his toe, who fails to move the mountain and begs Siva's forgiveness which is granted.

→ KANHERI CAVES

Sanjay Gandhi National Park, north of the city at Goregaon, is worth a visit in itself for its dense deciduous and semi-evergreen forest providing a beautiful habitat for several varieties of deer, antelope, butterflies, birds and the occasional leopard. However, the main reason for visiting is for the **Kanheri Caves** situated in the heart of the park.

Some 42 km north of Mumbai, the caves (also known as Mahakali Caves) are on a low hill midway between Borivli and Thane. The hills used to form the central part of Salsette Island, but the surrounding land has long since been extensively built on. Further up the ravine from the caves there are some fine views across the Bassein Fort and out to sea. Still shaded by trees, the entrance is from the south. There are 109 Buddhist caves, dating from the end of the second to the ninth century AD with flights of steps joining them. The most significant is the **Chaitya Cave** (cave 3) circa sixth century. The last Hinayana chaitya hall to be excavated is entered through a forecourt and veranda. The pillared entrance has well carved illustrations of the donors, and the cave itself comprises a 28 m x 13 m colonnaded hall of 34 pillars. At one end these encircle the 5-m-high *dagoba*. Some of the pillars have carvings of elephants and trees. Fifty metres up the ravine is **Darbar of the Maharajah Cave** (Cave 10). This was a *dharamshala* (resthouse) and has two stone benches running down the sides and some cells leading off the left and back walls. Above Cave 10 is **Cave 35** which was a *vihara* (monastery), which has reliefs of a Buddha seated on a lotus and of a disciple spreading his cloak for him to walk on. All the caves have an elaborate drainage and water storage system, fresh rainwater being led into underground storage tanks.

Above the cave complex is **Ashok Van**, a sacred grove of ancient trees, streams and springs. From there, a three-hour trek leads to 'View Point', the highest in Mumbai. There are breathtaking views. Photography is prohibited from the radar station on top of the hill; there are excellent opportunities just below it.

The park is also home to hyena and panther, though rarely seen, while three lakes have ducks, herons and crocodiles. Nature trails lead from Film City (reached by bus from Goregaon station). A lion safari leaves from **Hotel Sanjay** near Borivli station.

MUMBAI LISTINGS

WHERE TO STAY

$$$$ Ascot, 38 Garden Rd, Colaba, T022-6638 5566, www.ascothotel.com. The tan-wood rooms, shoehorned into a graceful 1930s building, veer dangerously close to IKEA anonymity, but they're generously proportioned and new, with safe deposit boxes, work desks and granite shower stalls. Great views from the upper floors. Breakfast included.

$$$$ Leela, near International Terminal, T022-6000 2233, www.theleela.com. One of the best of the airport hotels, with 460 modern rooms, excellent restaurants, pricey but excellent bar (residents only after 2300), all-night coffee shop, happening nightclub.

$$$$ The Oberoi, Nariman Pt, T022-6632 5757, www.oberoimumbai.com. Newly renovated and reopened, with beautiful sea-view rooms, glass-walled bathrooms, and 3 top-class restaurants.

$$$$ Taj Mahal, Apollo Bunder, T022-6665 3366, www.tajhotels.com. The grand dame of Mumbai lodging, over a century old. The glorious old wing has been fully restored and updated after the 26/11/08 attacks, joining the 306 rooms in the **Taj Mahal Intercontinental** tower. Several top-class restaurants and bars, plus fitness centre, superb pool and even a yacht on call.

$$$ Godwin, 41 Garden Rd, Colaba, T022-2287 2050, hotelgodwin@mail.com. 48 large, clean, renovated, a/c rooms with superb views from upper floors, mostly helpful management and a good rooftop restaurant – full of wealthy Mumbaikars on Fri and Sat night.

$$$ Juhu Residency, 148B Juhu Tara Rd, Juhu Beach, T022-6783 4949, www.juhuresidency.com. Across the road from Juhu Beach, with just 28 attractive refurbished rooms, free Wi-Fi, friendly efficient staff and 2 excellent restaurants. A decent deal by Mumbai standards.

$$$ YWCA International Centre, 18 Madame Cama Rd, Colaba, T022-2202 0598, www.ywcaic.info. For both sexes, 34 clean and pleasant rooms with bath, and breakfast and buffet dinner included in the price. A reliable and sociable budget option, though the deposit required to hold your booking is a slight hassle.

$$-$ Traveller's Inn, 26 Adi Murzban Path, Ballard Estate, Fort, T022-2264 4685, www.hoteltravellersinn.co.in. A relatively new addition to Mumbai's backpacker repertoire, with simple, clean rooms, a 3-bed dormitory, internet and Wi-Fi, and friendly staff.

RESTAURANTS

$$$ Indigo, 4 Mandlik Rd, behind **Taj Hotel**, T022-6636 8999. Excellent Mediterranean in smart restaurant, good atmosphere and wine list, additional seating on rooftop.

$$$ Khyber, 145 MG Rd, Kala Ghoda, T022-4039 6666. North Indian. For an enjoyable evening in beautiful surroundings, outstanding food, especially lobster and *reshmi* chicken kebabs, try *paya* soup (goats' trotters).

$$$ Ling's Pavilion, 19/21 KC College Hostel Building, off Colaba Causeway

(behind **Taj** and Regal Cinema), T022-2285 0023. Stylish decor, good atmosphere and delightful service, colourful menu, seafood specials, generous helpings. Recommended.

$$$ Olive, Union Park, Pali Hill, Bandra, T022-2605 8228. 'Progressive Mediterranean' food, served in an upscale environment to a cast of Bollywood celebs. Packed on Thu, when there's live music, and for brunch on Sun. Also has a branch at Mahalaxmi racecourse, T022-4085 9595.

$$$ Pali Village Cafe, Ambedkar Rd, Bandra (W), T022-2605 0401. Super-trendy new restaurant done out in shabby-chic industrial style, cascading across different rooms and levels. Good desserts and tapas-style starters, though the wine list and general vibe outweigh the quality of food and service.

$$$ Trishna, Sai Baba Marg, next to Commerce House, T022-2270 3213. Good coastal cuisine, seafood, excellent butter garlic crab. Recommended.

$$ Britannia, Wakefield House, Sprott Rd, opposite New Custom House, Ballard Estate, T022-22615264. Mon-Sat 1200-1600. Incredible Parsi/Iranian fare with a delicious berry *pullav* made from specially imported Bol berries (cranberries from Iran). Try the *dhansak* and the egg curry. Recommended.

$$ Café Churchill, 103-8, East West Court Building, opposite Cusrow Baug, Colaba Causeway, T022-2284 4689. Open1000-2330. A tiny little café with 7 tables crammed with people basking in a/c, towered over by a cake counter and a Winston Churchill portrait. Great breakfasts, club sandwiches, seafood, fish and chips, lasagne and Irish stew.

$$ Leopold's, Colaba, T022-2282 8185. An institution among Colaba backpackers and Mumbai shoppers. The food, predominantly Western with a limited choice of Indian

vegetarian, is average and pricey (similar cafés nearby are far better value) but Leo's gained cachet from its cameo role in the novel *Shantaram*, and was the first target of the terror attacks in Nov 2008.

$ Bade Miyan, Tullock Rd behind Ling's Pavilion. Streetside Kebab corner, but very clean. Try *baida roti*, *shammi* and *boti* kebabs. The potato *kathi* rolls are excellent veg options.

$ Kailash Parbat, 1st Pasta La, Colaba. Excellent snacks and *chats*, in an old-style eatery also serving Punjabi *thalis*. The milky-sweet *pedas* from the counter are a Mumbai institution.

$ Kamat Samarambh, opposite Electric House, Colaba Causeway. Very good and authentic South Indian food, *thalis* and snacks. Try the moist, fluffy *uttapam* and *upma*. Clean drinking water.

$ Swati Snacks, Tardeo Rd, opposite Bhatia Hospital, T022-6580 8405. Gujarati and Parsi snacks along with street foods made in a hygienic fashion: try *khichdi, sev puri, pav bhaji, dahi puri* here. Be prepared for a 20- to 40-min wait, but it's worth it.

$ Tea Centre, 78 Vir Nariman Rd, near Churchgate. A little old-fashioned and colonial, but dozens of refreshing tea options, and a menu of heavy Indian food. Good value and a/c.

WHAT TO DO

Be the Local, T(0)9930-027370, www.be thelocaltoursandtravels.com. Fascinating walking tours of Dharavi, which take you through some of the cottage industries – from traditional Gujarati pottery to plastic – which sustain Mumbai from within Asia's largest slum. Owned and run by local students, the tours are neither voyeuristic nor intrusive, and photography is prohibited. Rs 400 per person includes transport from Colaba; private tours Rs 3500 for up to 5 people.

MTDC, Madam Cama Rd, opposite LIC Building, T022-2202 6713. City tour Tue-Sun 0900-1300 and 1400-1800, Rs 100. Evening open-top bus tour of Colaba, Marine Drive

and Fort, runs Sat and Sun at 1900 and 2015; Rs 150 (lower deck Rs 50). Elephanta tours from Gateway of India. Boat, 0900-1415, Rs 130 return; reserve at Apollo Bunder, T022-2284 1877.

Mumbai Magic, T(0)98677-07414, www. mumbaimagic.com. A vast range of tours covering every inch of the city from Colaba to Bandra and beyond. Highlights include South Indian cuisine tours of Matunga, a walk through the Chor Bazaar, and the Mumbai Local tour which hops you around the city by taxi, local train and bus. Personalized itineraries available. Professional and highly recommended.

AJANTA AND ELLORA CAVES

The splendid carved volcanic caves (Hindu, Jain and Buddhist) at Ellora and Ajanta, dating from the sixth and second centuries AD respectively, are among India's finest sights, including monasteries, meditation chambers, cloisters, chapels and colonnaded halls gouged from rock, graced with friezes and shrines. The triumphant Kailasanatha Temple is the star of Ellora. Ajanta's exquisite craftsmanship – Buddha's story etched into a sheer cliff face – was nearly lost to the world, lying hidden under dense jungle from the seventh to the 19th century. Aurangabad, Mughal ruler Aurangzeb's military headquarters during his Deccan campaign, is a spacious town to base yourself en route to the caves.

→ AURANGABAD

A pleasantly spacious town, Aurangabad is the most common starting point for visiting the superb caves at Ellora and Ajanta. The gates are all that remain of the old city walls. There is a university, medical and engineering colleges and an airport to complement the town's industrial and commercial activities.

ARRIVING IN AURANGABAD
Getting there and around Chikalthana airport is 10 km east of the town with taxis (Rs 250, a/c Rs 350) or hotel transport into the town centre. The railway station is on the southern edge of town, within walking distance of most hotels and the Central Bus Stand just under 2 km north on Dr Ambedkar Road. The city is easy to navigate. There are plenty of autos to see the sights, most of which are too scattered to see on foot.

Moving on Ajanta Caves (see page 55) are a 2½-hour drive or bus ride north of Aurangabad. Some buses go direct to the caves, others require a change at Fardapur. A car and driver will cost around Rs 2000 for the return trip. **Ellora** (see page 60) is a 45-minute drive from Aurangabad. Buses drop you right at the entrance to the caves, or take an auto-rickshaw for around Rs 400-500; a taxi for the day will cost Rs 1000-1500 – worthwhile if you want to visit other sights on the way back from Ellora. Good tours are available from Aurangabad to both Ajanta and Ellora (around Rs 200/Rs150 per person) – allow a day for each as trying to combine the two in one day is too rushed. Four daily trains leave Aurangabad for **Hyderabad** (see page 65); most useful is the Ajanta Express, which leaves late in the evening and reaches Secunderabad station around 0900.

Tourist information India Tourism ① *Krishna Vilas, Station Rd, T0240-236 4999, Mon-Fri 0830-1830, Sat 0830-1330; airport counter open at flight times.* MTDC ① *TRC Bldg, Station Rd, T0240-234 3169; also at railway station, 0430-0830, 1100-1600, Tue-Sun 0900-1600.*

BACKGROUND
Originally known as Khadke, the town was founded in 1610 by Malik Ambar, an Abyssinian slave who became the *wazir* (prime minister) to the King of Ahmadnagar. It was later changed to Aurangabad in honour of the last great Mughal, Aurangzeb. His wife is buried in the Bibi ka Maqbara and he is buried in a simple grave at Rauza. It acted as the centre of operations for his Deccan campaign which occupied him for the second half of his 49-year reign.

PLACES IN AURANGABAD

The British **cantonment** area is in the southwest quadrant, along the Kham River and can be seen on the way to Ellora. The old Holy Trinity church is in very poor condition. To the northwest is the **Begampura** district in which there is the attractive Pan Chakki water mill and the Bibi ka Maqbara, both worth visiting.

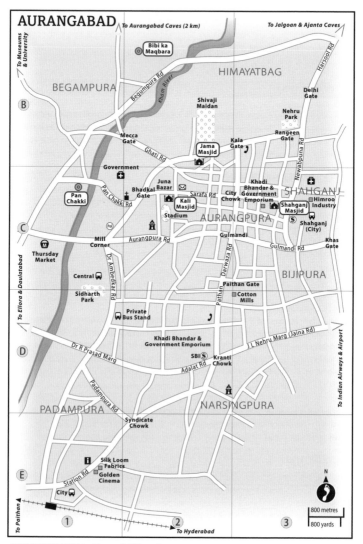

Aurangzeb built the 4.5-m-high crenellated city walls in 1682 as defence against the Marathas. **Killa Arrak** (1692), his citadel, lay between the Delhi and Mecca Gates. Little remains, though when it was Aurangzeb's capital over 50 maharajahs and princes attended the court. With Aurangzeb gone, the city's significance faded. At the centre in a grove of trees lies the **Jama Masjid**, a low building with minarets and a broad band carved with Koranic inscriptions running the length of the façade.

Other interesting monuments include: **Kali Masjid** (1600), a six-pillared stone mosque built by Malik Ambar; **Shahganj Masjid** (circa 1720) in the market square with shops on three sides; **Chauk Masjid** (1665), built by Shayista Khan, Aurangzeb's uncle, with five domes; and **Lal Masjid** (1655) in red-painted basalt. The **City Chowk** is worth visiting.

Bibi ka Maqbara ① *sunrise to 2000, foreigners Rs 100, Indians Rs 5, floodlit at night*, beyond the Mecca Gate, is the mausoleum of Aurangzeb's wife, Rabia Daurani (1678). The classic lines of a garden tomb give it an impressive setting. However, it is less impressive close up. Modelled on the Taj Mahal, which was completed 25 years earlier, it is about half its size. Far less money was spent (one three hundredth by some estimates) and the comparative poverty of the finish is immediately obvious. It uses marble on the bottom 2 m of the mausoleum and four of the *jali* screens, but plaster elsewhere. The proportions are cramped and the minarets are too heavy in relation to the main mausoleum. Despite its failings it is one of the finest buildings of its period. The brass door carries an inscription which says Ata Ullah was the chief architect and Haibat Rai the maker of the door. On the tomb itself, in place of a marble slab, there is bare earth covered with a decorated cloth, a sign of humility. Light enters through a precisely angled shaft, allowing the early morning sun's rays to light the tomb for three minutes. The second tomb in the corner is said to be that of Rabia Daurani's nurse.

On the same side of the river is the **Pan Chakki** (1696) ① *sunrise to 2000, Rs 5, refreshments*, which has a white marble shrine to Baba Shah Muzaffar, the devout Aurangzeb's spiritual adviser. The pre-Mughal 17th-century water mill for turning large grinding stones was powered by water channelled from a spring some distance away and released through a dam.

AURANGABAD CAVES
① *3 km north of Aurangabad, sunrise to sunset, foreigners Rs 100, Indians Rs 5.*
The Aurangabad Caves are very interesting though not a substitute for Ajanta and Ellora. Overlooking the town they fall into two groups of five each, about 1.5 km apart. They date from the Vakataka (fourth and fifth centuries AD) and Kalachuri dynasties (sixth to eighth centuries), though the older Hinayana Cave 4 is believed to be at least first century, if not earlier. Waiting charges for auto-rickshaws can be high – bargain. Or, if it is cool and you are fit, you can walk back to the edge of town and get an auto-rickshaw back.

The **Western Group** are all *viharas* except for the earlier Cave 4 which is a *chaitya*. Cave 1 (incomplete) has finely carved pillars with ornamentation around doorways and walls and figures on brackets. Cave 2 has a shrine and columned hallways, a large Buddha and intricately carved panels. The larger Cave 3 has a plain exterior but superb carvings on 12 pillars of the hallway; the sanctuary has panels illustrating *jataka* stories and a fine large Buddha figure on his throne with attendant devotees illustrating contemporary dress and style. Cave 4, the *chaitya* has a rib-vaulted ceiling with a *stupa* containing relics and a Buddha figure outside. Cave 5 is damaged and retains little of its original carvings.

The hillside around Deogiri was made steeper to make scaling the fort extremely difficult. The three concentric walls had strong gates, surrounded by a deep moat and the path climbed through the gates then up the steep slope towards the citadel. Today a new path has been cut to avoid the obstacles that were designed to prevent attackers from gaining entry. There is an L-shaped keep, a long, tortuous tunnel which could be sealed by an iron cover at the top after firing with hot coals, and a chamber which could be filled with noxious fumes. At one point the tunnel divides and meets, to fool attackers to kill each other in the dark. The only genuine access was narrowed so that an invader would have to crawl through the last few metres, making it possible for defenders to kill them on sight. The bodies were disposed of by chutes down into the crocodile infested moat 75 m below. A guide will take you through. Take a torch and allow two hours to get the most out of the extraordinary site.

The **Eastern Group** has more sculptures of women and Bodhisattvas. Cave 6 has a large Buddha supporting Ganesh, indicating a later period when Hinduism was gaining in importance over Buddhism. Note the paintings on the ceiling of the balcony. Cave 7 is regarded as the most interesting of both groups. Columned shrines at each end of the veranda house images of Hariti (right) and six goddesses, including Padmini (left). The central shrine has an ambulatory passage around it and a large preaching Buddha at the back. The wall carvings depict deliverance and numerous female dancers and musicians. The importance of Tara and of Tantric Buddhism is evident here. There is little to see in the unfinished Cave 9; the carvings of pre-Nirvana figures suggest Buddhism was waning. The incomplete Cave 10 illustrates the first stages of cave excavation.

→ DAULATABAD

Some 13 km from Aurangabad is the fort of Deogiri on a volcanic lava rock towering 250 m above the surrounding countryside. The fort dates from the Yadava period of the 11th-14th centuries although the first fort had probably been built in the ninth century. Before that it had been a Buddhist monastery. It is an extraordinary site, particularly attractive in the late afternoon when the crowds have gone. If you are lucky you may get the resident guide who takes visitors through the dark tunnels with a flaming torch.

DEOGIRI FORT
ⓘ *Sunrise to sunset, Rs100 foreigners, Rs 5 Indians, allow 3 hrs.*
From Ala-ud-din Khalji's capture of Deogiri in 1296 until Independence in 1947, by which time it was under the control of the Nizam of Hyderabad, the fort remained in Muslim hands. Muhammad bin Tughluq determined to extend his power south, seized Daulatabad, deciding to make it his capital and populate it with the residents from Delhi. Thousands died as a result of his misconceived experiment. The outermost of the three main ring walls and the bastion gates were probably built by the Muslims. For snacks there are numerous dhabas opposite the entrance.

The Persian style **Chand Minar** (1435) stands at the bottom of the fort, towering as a celebration of victory like the Qutb Minar in Delhi. Its original covering of Persian blue tiles must have made it even more striking. Opposite is the **Jama Masjid** (1318), with 106 pillars taken from a Hindu temple, and a large tank. The 31 m high victory tower built by Ala-ud-din Bahmani to celebrate his capture of the fort has at its base 24 chambers and a small mosque. The path passes bastions, studded gates, a drawbridge and the **Chini Mahal** where Abdul Hasan Tana Shah, the last King of Golconda, was imprisoned in 1687 for 13 years. The 6.6-m-long Kila Shikan (Fort Breaker) iron cannon is on the bastion nearby. At the end of the tunnel (see box, opposite) inside the citadel is a flight of steps leading up to the **Baradari** (Pavilion), said to be the palace of the Yadavi Queen and later Shah Jahan. The **citadel** is reached by climbing 100 more steps and passing through two more gateways. At the top is another cannon with a ram's head on the butt; the Persian inscription around the muzzle reads 'Creator of Storms'.

→ AJANTA

The exquisite carved Buddhist caves of Ajanta lay hidden under dense jungle for 12 centuries before a British hunting party stumbled across them in 1819. One of India's greatest surviving works of craftsmanship, the caves were cut from the volcanic lavas of the Deccan Trap from about 200 BC to AD 650, and lie hidden in a steep crescent-shaped hillside in a forested ravine of the Sahyadri.

ARRIVING IN AJANTA
Getting there The bus or taxi drive from Aurangabad (106 km) takes 2½ to three hours. Shilod (Silod) is a popular halting place and has a number of restaurants. About 10 km from Ajanta, the road descends from the plateau offering dramatic views of the Waghora Valley, where the caves are located.

Getting around There's a small settlement with a restaurant, curio market and aggressive salesmen at the approach to the caves. The entrance is a short uphill walk along a stepped concrete path. *Dhoolis* are available for hire if you wish to be carried. You can approach the caves from the river bed in the bottom of the valley, where the bus stops; the View Point, is worth getting to. You have to buy your ticket from the kiosk first, and if there is water in the stream you have to wade through, but it is much shadier than the path cut out of the cliff.

BACKGROUND
In 1819, a party of British army officers from Madras noticed the top of the façade of Cave 10 while tiger hunting. They investigated and discovered some caves, describing seeing 'figures with curled wigs'. Others made exploratory trips to the fascinating caves. In 1843, James Fergusson, horrified by the ravages of the elements, requested that the East India Company do something to preserve and protect the deteriorating caves.

In 1844 **Captain Robert Gill**, an artist, was sent to copy the paintings on the cave walls. He spent 27 years living in a small encampment outside, sending each new batch of paintings to Bombay and London. After nearly 20 years his work was almost complete and displayed in the Crystal Palace in London. In December 1866 all but a few of the paintings were destroyed in a fire. Gill soldiered on for another five years before giving up, and died from illness soon afterwards. He is buried in the small European cemetery at **Bhusawal**, 60 km to the north, 27 km from Jalgaon.

THE SITE

① Tue-Sun 0900-1730, foreigners US$10, Indians Rs 10. No flash photography. Some caves have electric lights for illuminating the paintings; hawkers sell cheap postcards and slides (Rs 100). In the Mahayana caves with paintings there is a restriction on the number of visitors allowed in at any one time. Computer kiosks are planned, designed to show a 'virtual' history of the caves.

Hiuen-Tsang, recorded in the seventh century (although he did not visit it), a description of the "monastery in a deep defile ... large temple with a huge stone image of the Buddha with a tier of seven canopies".

The terrain in which the caves were excavated was a sheer cliff facing a deeply incised river meander. At the height of Ajanta's importance the caves are thought to have housed about 200 monks and numerous craftsmen and labourers. The masterpieces retell the life story of the Buddha and reveal the life and culture of the people of the times, royal court settings, family life, street scenes and superb studies of animals and birds. The *Jatakas* relate the Buddha's previous births – showing the progress of the soul.

Originally the entrance to the caves was along the river bed and most had a flight of stairs leading up to them. The first to be excavated was Cave 10, followed by the first Hinayana caves (in which the Buddha is not depicted in human form), on either side. Later Mahayana caves were discovered, completing the spectrum of Buddhist development in India.

There is a round trip walk, up the side of the valley where all the caves are located then down to the river to cross to the other side. An attractive low level walk through forest brings you back to the roadhead. **Caves 1, 2, 10, 16** and **17** have lights. **11, 19** and **26** are also particularly worth visiting.

Mahayana group Cave 1 (late fifth century) is one of the finest *viharas* (monasteries), remarkable for the number and quality of its murals. A veranda with cells and porches either side has three entrances leading into a pillared hall. Above the veranda are friezes depicting the sick man, old man, corpse and saint encountered by the Buddha, who is shown above the left porch. The hall has 20 ornamented pillars, a feature of the late period caves. Five small monks' cells lead off three sides, and in the centre of the back wall is a large shrine of the Buddha supported by Indra, the rain god. At the entrance are the river goddesses Yamuna and Ganga and two snake-hooded guardians at the base.

The **murals** are among the finest at Ajanta. In the four corners are panels representing groups of foreigners. The Mahajanaka jataka (where the Buddha took the form of an able and just ruler) covers much of the left-hand wall including Renunciation, and the scenes where he is enticed by beautiful dancing girls.

On either side of the entrance to the antechamber of the shrine room are two of the best known murals at Ajanta. On the left is the **Bodhisattva Padmapani** (here holding a blue lotus), in a pose of spiritual detachment, whilst on the right is the **Bodhisattva Avalokitesvara**. Together compassion and knowledge, the basis of Mahayana Buddhism, complement one another. Their size dwarfs the attendants to enhance the godlike stature of the bodhisattva. The Buddha inside the shrine is seated in the teaching position, flanked by the two carved bodhisattvas. Under the throne appears the **Wheel of Life**, with deer representing Sarnath where he preached his first sermon.

One of the sculptural tricks that a guide will display is that when the statue is lit from the left side (as you face it), the facial expression is solemn, suggesting contemplation. Yet

ON THE ROAD
The challenge of preservation

Preservation of the murals poses enormous challenges. Repeated attempts to reproduce and to restore them have faced major problems. After all but five of Robert Gill's paintings were destroyed by fire, the Bombay School of Arts sent out a team to copy the wall paintings under the guidance of the principal John Griffiths in the 1870s. The copies were stored in the Victoria and Albert Museum in London but this also had a fire in 1885, when 87 were destroyed.

In 1918 a team from Kyoto University Oriental Arts Faculty arrived at Ajanta to copy the sculptures. This they did by pressing wet rice paper against the surface to make casts which were then shipped back to Japan. In the early 1920s they were all destroyed by an earthquake.

In 1920 the Ajanta paintings were cleaned by the former Hyderabad Government under whose jurisdiction the caves lay. Two Italian restorers were commissioned and they set about fixing the peeling paintings to the walls of the caves. They first injected casein between the paintings and the plastered wall, then applied shellac as a fixative. The Griffiths team from Bombay had also applied a coat of varnish to bring out the colours of the paintings.

However, these varnishes darkened over the years, rendering the murals less visible. They also cracked, aiding the peeling process and the accumulation of moisture between the wall and the outer membrane. The Archaeological Survey of India is now responsible for all restoration at the site.

from the other side, there is a smile of joy, while from below it suggests tranquillity and peace. Note the paintings on the ceiling, particularly the elephant scattering the lotus as it rushes out of the pond, and the charging bull. Also look for the 'black princess' and the row of the dancer with musicians. On the way out is a pillar that has four deer sculpted skilfully, sharing the same head.

Cave 2 (sixth century) is also a *vihara* hall, 14.6 sq m with 12 pillars, with five cells on each side of the left and right hand walls and two chapels on each side of the ante-chamber and shrine room. The veranda in front has a side chapel at each end. The doorway is richly carved. On the left hand wall is the mural depicting **The Birth of The Buddha**. Next to this is the **'Thousand' Buddhas**, which illustrates the miracle when the Buddha multiplied himself to confuse a heretic. On the right are dancing girls before the king, shown with striking three-dimensional effect.

The cave is remarkable for its painted ceiling, giving the effect of the draped cloth canopy of a tent. The *mandala* (circular diagram of the cosmos) is supported by demon-like figures. The Greek key designs on the border are possibly influenced by Gandharan art, first to third centuries AD. The ceiling decorations portray a number of figures of Persian appearance apparent from the style of beard and whiskers and their clothing.

The *Yaksha* (nature spirits) Shrine in the left chapel is associated with fertility and wealth. The main shrine is that of Buddha in the teaching position, again flanked by the two bodhisattvas, both holding the royal fly whisk. The **Hariti** Shrine on the right is to the ogress who liked eating children! The panel on your left as you leave the hall is a *jataka* telling the story of the Bodhisattva's life as the Pandit Vidhura.

Caves 3-7 are late fifth century. **Cave 3** has no veranda and **Cave 4** is the largest *vihara* at Ajanta, planned on an ambitious scale and not completed. The hall is 27 sq m and supported on 28 pillars. Along the walls are cells whilst at the rear is a large shrine. **Cave 5** is unfinished.

Hinayana group A Hinayana group comes next (**Caves 6-10** and **12**, **13** and **15**) dating from the second century BC. **Cave 6** is on two levels with only seven of the 16 octagonal pillars standing. A shrine contains a seated Buddha. **Cave 7** has no hall. The veranda has two porches each supported by heavy octagonal Elephanta-type columns. These lead to four cells. These and the antechamber are profusely carved. The shrine is that of Buddha, his hand raised in blessing. **Cave 8** (first century BC) is a small vihara. **Cave 9** (circa 100 BC), a *chaitya*, is 14 m long, 14 columns run the length of each side and 11 continue round the *stupa*. The vaulted roof was once wooden ribbed and leads back from a huge arched *chaitya sun* window which throws light on the *stupa* at the rear. Two phases of wall painting have been identified. The earlier ones dating from the construction of the cave can be seen at the far left side and consist of a procession to a *stupa* as well as a thin band above the left colonnade. Above this are later Buddha figures from the Mahayana period when the figures of the Buddha on either side of the entrance were painted.

Cave 10 (circa 150 BC) is much larger. Like the previous cave the roof was once fitted with wooden ribs which subsequently collapsed. The long hall with an apse housing the *stupa* was one of the first excavated and also the first rediscovered by army officers. An inscription above the façade, now destroyed, dated the excavation to the second century BC through a generous donation by the king. The *dagoba* or *stupa* resembles that of Cave 9 and is a double-storey drum. There are also paintings dating from the Hinayana and Mahayana periods. The early ones depict figures in costumes resembling those seen at Sanchi. Traces of later paintings survive on the pillars and aisle ceilings and later Buddha figures are often superimposed on earlier works. The main subjects of the Hinayana paintings are *jataka* stories. On the rear wall are the King (in a ceremonial headdress) and Queen approaching the Sacred Bodhi Tree, one of the earliest Ajanta paintings.

Cave 11 (originally second century BC, with sixth century alterations), has a veranda and roof painted with birds and flowers, a hall supported by four heavy pillars and a stone bench running along the right side. There are five cells and a shrine of a seated Buddha. **Cave 12** (with glauconite rock wall) and **Cave 13** (second century BC) are small *viharas*. **Cave 14** (fifth century AD) was planned on a grand scale but not completed and can be missed along with **Cave 15** (fifth century) which is a long hall with a Buddha carved out of the rock.

Later Mahayana period The remaining caves all belong to the Later Mahayana period and date from the fifth century. **Cave 16**, with kneeling elephants at the entrance and the Cobra King, has a 20 m long and 3.5 m deep veranda that carries six plain octagonal pillars. There is a good view of the ravine from here. The magnificent columned hall inside has six cells on each side and a beamed ceiling. The Teaching Buddha is seated on a lion throne. On the left the 'Dying Princess' portrays Nanda's new bride being told that he has been ordained a monk and renounced the world. Her misery is shared by all and everything around her. On the right wall are the remains of a picture of Prince Siddhartha, later the Buddha, using a bow.

Cave 17 (late fifth century) is similar to No 16 in layout and has the greatest number of murals. On the left of the veranda is a painted Wheel of Life. Over the entrance door is a

ON THE ROAD
Tempera techniques in cave painting

To prepare the rock for painting it was chiselled to leave a rough surface. Two layers of mud-plaster containing fibrous material (grain-husk, vegetable fibres and rock grit) was applied, the first coarse, the second fine. Metal mirrors must have been used by the artists, to reflect sunlight into the dark caves. It is thought that the tempera technique was used. On a dry surface, a red cinnabar outline defined the picture, filled in, possibly initially with grey and then numerous colour pigments usually mixed with glue; the completed painting was burnished to give a lustrous finish. The pigments were mainly taken from the land around, the principal ones being red and yellow ochre, white from lime and kaoline, green from glauconite, black from lamp-black and blue from imported lapis lazuli. The shellac used in restoration after 1819 was found to be cracking. Since 1951 this has been removed by the Archaeological Survey of India, with UNESCO's help. PVA is now used.

row of seven Past Buddhas and the eighth, the Maitreya or Future Buddha, above a row of amorous Yaksha couples. Sculpted deities are carved on either side.

Murals show scenes from 17 *jatakas*: the worship of the Buddha, the Buddha preaching; Hansa *jataka*, with paintings of geese; Vessantara *jataka*, where the greedy Brahmin is portrayed, grinning; the miraculous 'Subjugation of the rogue elephant', sent to kill the Buddha; and the ogress who turns into a beautiful maiden by day! There are also panels showing royal processions, warriors, an assembled congregation from which you can get an accurate and detailed picture of the times. **Cave 18** (late fifth century) has little of merit and can be missed.

Cave 19 (late fifth century) is a Mahayana *chaitya* hall and was painted throughout. The façade is considered to be one of the most elegant in terms of execution and elaborate ornamentation, and has the arched *chaitya* window set into it. The interior is in the layout seen before, two rows of richly decorated columns leading up to and around the back of the standing Buddha, which here is in front of the slender *stupa*. This tall shrine has a triple stone umbrella above it. Note the seated Nagaraja with attendants.

Cave 20 is comparatively small and has imitation beams carved into the ceiling.

Later caves The final few caves belong to the seventh century and are a separate and distinct group at the farthest end of the horseshoe near the waterfall. Only one, **Cave 26**, need be visited. **Cave 21** (early seventh century) has a fallen veranda with flanking chapels. **Cave 24** was intended to be the largest *vihara* but was not completed.

Cave 26 is a large *chaitya* hall. A partly damaged columned façade stretches across the front with the customary side chambers at each end. The 3-m-high window is flanked by sculptured Buddha reliefs. Inside, 26 pillars run in an elongated semi circle around the cylindrical *stupa* which is decorated with Buddhas. The walls are decorated with sculpture, including the temptations by Mara's daughters, but the most striking being a 9-m reclining image of the Parinirvana Buddha, about to enter Nirvana, his death mourned by his followers.

The walk back along the promenade connecting the shrines is pleasant enough but the return via the river, waterfall and forest walkway is delightful. Steps lead down from Cave 16 (with the carved elephants). The hilltop opposite the caves offers a fine view of the horseshoe-shaped gorge.

The Hindu, Jain and Buddhist caves carved in the volcanic rocks at Ellora are among the finest in India, centred on the Kailashnatha cave – vast and very much still a living temple, carved from the roof down in an astonishing feat of craftsmanship and architectural imagination. Lying near an important ancient trade route between Ujjain in Madhya Pradesh and the west coast, the caves are thought to be the work of priests and pilgrims who used the route.

ARRIVING IN ELLORA

Ellora, 26 km from Aurangabad, takes about 45 minutes. Tour buses usually arrive at the car park, directly in front of the Kailashnatha temple itself. Arrive early and see the Kailashnatha first to avoid the very large crowds. Take lunch and drinks as decent options are limited. Also wear a hat and comfy shoes and take a strong torch.

THE SITE

ⓘ *Wed-Mon 0900-1730, Kailashnatha entry Rs 250 foreigners (other caves remain free), Rs 10 Indians. Cameras may be used outside, flash photography and tripods are not allowed inside. Guides available (some European languages and Japanese spoken). 'Light passes' for groups wishing to see darker caves illuminated are available (best to join a group if on your own). Painted caves open at 1000, others at 0900 – light is better in the afternoon. For the elderly and infirm, dhoolies (chairs carried by men) are available.*

Like the caves at Ajanta, Ellora's caves were also abandoned and forgotten. Twelve of the 34 caves are Buddhist (created from circa AD 600-800), 17 Hindu (AD 600-900) and five Jain (AD 800-1100). Most have courtyards in front. They face west and are best seen in the afternoon. To see the caves in chronological order, start at the east end and visit the Buddhist *viharas* first. In this way the magnificent Hindu Kailashnatha temple is seen towards the end.

Buddhist Caves (Nos 1-12) These belong to the **Vajrayana** sect of the Mahayana (Greater Vehicle) School. The caves include *viharas* (monasteries) and *chaityas* (chapels) where the monks worshipped. It has been suggested that the stone-cut structures were ideally suited to the climate which experienced monsoons, and rapidly became the preferred medium over more flimsy and less durable wood.

Cave 1 A simple *vihara*.

Cave 2 Adjoining is reached by a flight of steps. At the door of the cave are *dwarapala* (guardians) flanked by windows. The interior (14.5 sq m) comprises a hall supported by 12 pillars, some decorated with the pot and foliage motif. In the centre of the back wall is a 3-m-high seated Buddha and two standing Buddhas while along each of the side walls are five Buddhas accompanied by Bodhisattvas and *apsaras* (celestial nymphs).

Cave 3 Similar to Cave 2, having a square central chamber with a Buddha image, this time seated on a lotus. Around the walls are 12 meditation cells.

Cave 4 Two-storeyed and contains a Buddha sitting under the Bo (pipal) tree.

Cave 5 The **Maharwada**, is the largest of the single-storeyed caves in this group (17.6 m by 36 m). Two rows of 10 columns each run the length of the cave, as do two raised platforms which were probably tables, suggesting that this cave was a dining hall. There are attractive carvings on the first pillar on the left. The Buddha at the back is guarded on the left by Padmapani, a symbol of purity. On the right is Vajrapani holding a thunderbolt, the symbol of esoteric knowledge and the popular deity of the sect responsible for creating the caves. The Buddha is seated, not cross-legged on the floor as is usual, but on a chair or stool. He demonstrates some of the 32 distinctive marks: three folds in the neck, long ear lobes and the third eye. The *mudra* here signifies the Buddha's first sermon at the Deer Park, and is a teaching pose.

The next four caves can be bypassed as they contain nothing new.

Cave 10 Viswakarma, or 'Carpenter's Cave', is the only *chaitya* (chapel) cave in the group. It used to be a monastery. This is on the ground floor and above are what are presumed to have been the monks' living quarters. In front is a large courtyard approached by a flight of steps. The galleries around it have square-based pillars at the foot of which was a lion facing outwards. At the back of these galleries are two elaborately carved chapels. The exterior decoration gives the impression that instead of stone, wood was the building material, hence 'Viswakarma'. The façade has a trefoil window with *apsara* groups for ornamentation. The main hall is large (26 m by 13 m, 10 m high). The curved fluted 'beams' suggest to some the upturned hull of a ship. The chamber has 28 columns, each with a vase and foliage capital, dividing it up into a nave and aisles. The aisle runs round the decorated *stupa* (*dagoba*) with a colossal 4.5-m 'Preaching Buddha' carved in front of it. The upper gallery, reached by an internal flight of steps, was supposed to have subsidiary shrines at either end but the left hand one was not finished. Decorating the walls are loving couples, indicating how much Buddhism had changed from its early ascetic days. You can get a view of the friezes above the pillars which show Naga queens, symbolic precursors of the monsoon, and dwarfs as entertainers, dancing and playing musical instruments. Sunlight pouring through the circular window at the entrance to the cave gives the cave a truly ethereal quality.

Cave 11 (Do Thal – two-storeyed) was found to have a third storey in 1876 when the basement was discovered. The lowest level is a veranda with a shrine and two cells at the back of it. The middle level has eight front pillars and five rear cells of which only the central three are completed and decorated. The upper level has a porch opening into a long colonnaded hall with a Buddha shrine at the rear. Images of Durga and Ganesh suggest that the cave was later used by Hindus. Cave 11 and 12 illustrate the use of the upper levels of these caves as a residence for monks and pilgrim hostels.

Cave 12 (Tin Thal – three-storeyed) has cells for sleeping (note the stone benches) on the lower floors but it is the figures of the Buddha which are of particular interest. The rows of seven Buddhas are symbolic of the belief that he appears on earth every 5000 years and has already visited it seven times.

Hindu Caves (Nos 13-29) These caves lie in the centre of the group and are the most numerous. **Cave 13** is a plain room while **Cave 14** (**Ravana ki khai**, seventh century), is single storeyed and the last of the collection from the early period. River goddesses and guardians stand at the doorway while inside is a broken image of Durga and figurative panels on the walls of the principle deities, Vishnu, Siva, Lakshmi and Parvati. **Cave 15** (**Das Avatara**, mid-eighth century), reached by a flight of steps, has a large courtyard and is two storeyed.

Kailasanatha Temple (mid-eighth century onwards) This is the most magnificent of all the rock-cut structures at Ellora, and is completely open to the elements. It is the only building that was begun from the top. Carved out of 85,000 cu m of rock, the design and execution of the full temple plan is an extraordinary triumph of imagination and craftsmanship. Excavating three deep trenches into the rock, carving started from the top of the cliff and worked down to the base. Enormous blocks were left intact from which the porch, the free standing pillars and other shrines were subsequently carved. The main shrine was carved on what became the upper storey, as the lower floor was cut out below. It is attributed to the Rashtrakuta king Dantidurga (AD 725-755) and must have taken years to complete. **Mount Kailasa** (6700 m), the home of Siva, is a real mountain on the Tibetan plateau beyond the Himalaya. Its distinctive pyramidal shape, its isolation from other mountains, and the appearance to the discerning eye of a swastika etched by snow and ice on its rock face, imbued the mountain with great religious significance to Hindus and Buddhists alike. Kailasa was seen as the centre of the universe, and Siva is Lord of Kailasa, Kailasanatha. To imitate the real snow-covered peaks, the *sikharas* here were once covered with white plaster.

Entrance The temple is 50 m long and 33 m wide and the tower rises 29 m above the level of the court. At the entrance gate, the threshold between the profane and sacred worlds, the goddesses **Ganga** and **Yamuna** form the door jambs. Just inside are two seated sages: **Vyasa**, the legendary author of the *Mahabharata*, and **Valmiki** to whom the *Ramayana* has been ascribed. In the porch four columns carry the North Indian vase and foliage motif, a symbol of fertility and well-being. On each side of the doorway there are images of **Kubera**, the god of wealth, with other symbols of well-being such as the conch shell and the lotus. Two more figures complete the welcoming party. They are **Ganesh** (left), the elephant headed son of Siva, bringer of good fortune, and **Durga** (right), Siva's wife who fought the demons.

In the antechamber opposite is **Lakshmi**, the goddess of wealth. In the courtyard, to your right and left are free-standing elephants. On the left round the corner is a panel depicting **Kama**, the god of desire, carrying his bow and five arrows, one for each of the senses. On the far wall to your left of the entrance, behind the pillars, is the shrine of the **Three River Goddesses** – Ganga (centre), Yamuna (left) and Sarasvati (right). Symbolically they stand for purity, devotion and wisdom respectively. This is a good place to photograph the central shrine. The two carved monolithic pillars are probably stylized flagstaffs indicating royal patronage – a practice that Asoka popularized in the third century BC.

There are two distinct levels taking the worshipper from the courtyard by two staircases flanking the central hall, to the lower level with its processional path and then rising even higher to the upper level of the *mandapa*.

Central Assembly Hall Around the central shrine is a colonnaded hall gouged from the rock, which in places overhangs menacingly. Inside this cloister is a series of panels portraying Siva and Vishnu myths. The whole can be viewed as a sort of instructional picture gallery, a purpose it served for worshippers from ancient times who could not read.

The south facing wall has *Ramayana* stories – **Ravana** offering his heads; Siva and Parvati with Nandi the bull and the lingam (creative power); Siva playing the vina; Siva and Parvati playing dice in a spirit of harmony; the marriage of Siva and Parvati; the origin of the lingam, the symbol of Siva and creative (male) energy; Siva dancing and Siva tricking Parvati. The panel on the south of the mandapa of Ravana shaking Mount Kailasa, attempting to carry it off, disturbing Parvati and her attendants, one of whom is seen frightened and fleeing, and Siva restoring order with the movement of his toe.

Along the north-facing wall are stories from the *Mahabharata* above and Krishna legends below. The panels include **Krishna** stealing buttermilk; Vishnu as **Narasimha**, half man, half lion; Vishnu reclining on **Ananda** the serpent inbetween incarnations; Vishnu the **Preserver**. Finally there is **Annapurna**, Goddess of Plenty.

The inner porch contains two panels, Siva as **Lord of Knowledge** and Siva as **Bhairava** killing the Elephant Demon.

Main Shrine Steps lead to the upper floor which contains a *mandapa* (central hall, 17 m by 16 m) of 16 stout pillars arranged in groups of four, with aisles that correspond to the cardinal points leading to an open central area. At the far end is the *garbhagriha* (shrine) with **Ganga** and **Yamuna** as door guardians. Inside is the *yoni lingam*, symbol of Siva's creative power. Running around the back is a passageway with five small shrine rooms off it, each with a replica of the main temple. The Nataraja painting on the *mandapa* ceiling. There are remnants of paintings on the porch ceilings (particularly to the west) where you will see *apsaras*, dwarfs and animals. The temple rises in a pyramid, heavier and more squat looking than later towers in the north. The shape suggests enormous strength. As you leave, the path to the left leads up and around the temple, giving an interesting bird's-eye view of the magnificent complex.

Cave 21 (**Ramesvara**, late sixth century) has a court with a stone Nandi bull in the middle and side shrines. A *linga* sanctuary leads off the veranda. This cave is celebrated for its fine sculptures of amorous couples and the gods. **Cave 29** (**Dhumar Lena**, late sixth century) is very similar to Elephanta (see page 46) in concept. Access is from three sides, there is a spacious hall with a separate small sanctuary with a *lingam* at the end. Wall panels depict Siva legends especially as Destroyer.

Jain Caves (Nos 30-34) These caves are an anticlimax after the Hindu ones, but they have an aura of peace and simplicity. **Cave 30** (**Chhota Kailasa**, early ninth century) was intended as a smaller scale replica of the Kailasanatha Temple but never completed. The columned shrine has 22 *tirthankaras* with *Mahavira* in the sanctuary. **Cave 32** (**Indra Sabha**, early ninth century) is the finest of the Jain series and is dedicated to Mahavir. A simple gateway leads into an open court in the middle of which stands the shrine. The walls have carvings of elephants, lions and *tirthankaras*. The lower of the two is incomplete but the upper has carvings of Ambika and also Mahavir flanked by guardians of earlier *tirthankaras*. The ceiling is richly carved with a massive lotus at the centre and you can see signs of painted figures among clouds.

AJANTA AND ELLORA CAVES LISTINGS

WHERE TO STAY

Aurangabad

$$$$ Residency (Taj), Ajanta Rd, 8 km from railway station, 9 km from the airport, T0240-661 3737, www.tajhotels.com. 40 large rooms, quiet swimming, excellent service, imposing building in lovely gardens, on outskirts, beautiful gardens, difficult for the less able (no lift, some rooms on 1st floor, reception and restaurant on ground floor).

$$$$-$$$ The Meadows, Gat 135-136, Mitmita village, Ellora Rd, T0240-267 7412, www.themeadowsresort.com. A pleasant change from Aurangabad's corporate offerings, with 40 comfortable cottages set among 26 ha (11 acres) of bird-filled gardens. Quiet and relaxing.

$$ Khemi's Inn, 11 Town Centre, CIDCO (4 km from town, 1st left after **Ambassador Ajanta**, then first right), T0240-248 4868, khemis@ vsnl.com. 10 spotless a/c rooms with hot bath, good home cooking, quiet, pleasant garden, has the feel of an English B&B, very hospitable.

$ Printravel, Dr Ambedkar Rd, T0240-232 9707. Old-fashioned but large clean rooms with bath, good **Patang** restaurant, very well run. Recommended.

Ajanta

$$ Holiday Resort (MTDC), Fardapur, 5 km from Ajanta caves, T02438-244230. 12 basic rooms with bath (mosquito net vital, not provided), 16 a/c rooms in gardens are better value, dorm (mattress only), restaurant.

Ellora

$$-$ Kailas, near the bus stand, T02437-244543, www.hotelkailas.com. 25 decent rooms in group of 'cottages', best a/c face the caves, dorm in annexe, restaurant, very pleasant garden, good service.

RESTAURANTS

Aurangabad

$$ Angeethi, next to **Jet Airways**, Jalna Rd, T0240-244 1988. Excellent Marathi specialities, book ahead.

$ Bhoj, Ambedkar Marg (above **Manas Hotel**) near Central Bus Stand. Excellent Gujarati and Rajasthani *thalis*. Arrive at 1845 to listen to *puja* in the kitchen with chanting and cymbals.

WHAT TO DO

Classic Travels, TRC Building, Station Rd, T0240-233 7788, and at **Ambassador Ajanta**. Helpful and efficient; car hire, ticketing, hotels, Ajanta/Ellora and city tour, Rs 300/250 pp.

MTDC see page 51. Good sightseeing tours to Ajanta, Ellora and the City. Ajanta tour highly recommended, but Ellora and City tour visits too many places in too little time. Tours start from **MTDC Holiday Resort**, Station Rd, T0240-233 1513, and pickup from major hotels and the **Central Bus Stand**: Ellora and City Wed-Mon 0930-1800, Rs 200; Ajanta Tue-Sun 0830-1730, Rs 200; book at Window 1 (behind book stall) at bus stand; check times.

HYDERABAD AND AROUND

Hyderabad, one of the poster boys for India's biotech and software boom, has emerged as a great place to soak up the atmosphere of the New India. It's also a city that heaves with history: splendid markets, mosques, architecture and museums and pearl bazars. On the outskirts of the city are film-set theme parks, the grand medieval fortress of Golconda, and a collection of 17th-century tombs of old rulers lying in gardens of frilly bougainvillea. A day's drive to the southeast lies Nagarjunakonda, where the relocated ruins of one of India's richest Buddhist civilizations rise from the middle of an artificial lake.

→ HYDERABAD AND SECUNDERABAD

The Twin Cities of Hyderabad and Secunderabad, founded by the rulers of two separate Muslim dynasties, have long since bled into one conglomerate metropolis. The southern half, **Hyderabad**, holds the dusty and congested Old City; here you will find the beautiful but faded palaces of Islamic architecture, while the atmospheric lanes around the Char Minar throb with a contemporary Muslim mania. **Secunderabad**, which served as a prominent British army base prior to independence and remains the biggest military cantonment in the country, is separated from Hyderabad by the Hussain Sagar lake.

N Chandrababu Naidu, Andhra's chief minister from the late 1990s until 2004, had development dreams as lofty as the legendarily eccentric Nizam. The result is a city with town planning unequalled in India, including huge theme resorts where you can stand at minus temperatures (a tribute to the famous heat of Andhra), and Hitech City (brilliantly named 'Cyberabad'; a rival to Silicon Valley and home to Microsoft's first overseas base). The success of these high-tech and biotech industries has spawned a new elite to keep the old pearl peddlers in business since trade from the jewel-draped Nizams dried up.

ARRIVING IN HYDERABAD
Getting there Trains from Aurangabad arrive at Secunderabad station, one of three main stations in Hyderabad's vast urban sprawl. There are a few hotels clustered within a 10-minute walk of the station, including some good high-end options, but the best choices are in Banjara Hills, a 30-minute ride by auto-rickshaw, while budget hotels congregate around Deccan Nampally station, 20 minutes away. To save hassle getting to your hotel, take a prepaid auto-rickshaw from the booth outside the station entrance.

Moving on The next section of this journey, from Hyderabad to **Bijapur** (see page 83), is best done with a car and driver, as the distances are long and public transport is sketchy. A two-day trip with an overnight stop in **Bidar** (see page 79) should cost Rs 10,000-15,000, depending on the size of car. You can, however, reach Bidar by bus from the enormous Imlibun bus terminal, or by one of four daily trains; the least delay-prone of these is the Bidar **Intercity Express**, which leaves Deccan Nampally at 1845 every day except Sunday (3½ hours).

Getting around Autos or taxis are the best means of getting about the city north of the Musi and in Secunderabad, but in the congested old quarter you are best off walking, though there are cycle-rickshaws.

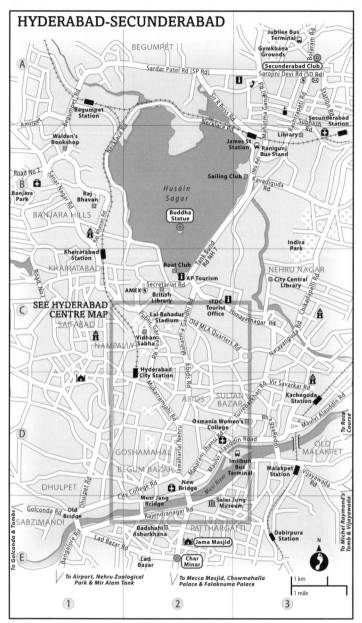

HYDERABAD-SECUNDERABAD

BEGUMPET

Jubilee Bus Terminal

Gymkhana Grounds

Secunderabad Club

Sardar Patel Rd (SP Rd)

Sarojini Devi Rd (SD Rd)

Begumpet Station

Sir R Ross Rd

Necklace Rd

Mahatma Gandhi Rd

Rashtrapati Rd

Secunderabad Station

Amirpet

Walden's Bookshop

James St Station

Library

Ranigunj Bus Stand

Road No 1

Husain Sagar

Sailing Club

Kavadiguda Rd

Banjara Park

Raj Bhavan

BANJARA HILLS

Buddha Statue

Indira Park

NEHRU NAGAR

Khairatabad Station

KHAIRATABAD

Boat Club

AP Tourism

Tank Bund Rd NH 7

City Central Library

SEE HYDERABAD CENTRE MAP

AMEX

Secretariat Rd

British Library

ITDC Tourist Office

Himayatnagar Rd

SAIFABAD

Lal Bahadur Stadium

Old MLA Quarters Rd

NAMPALLY

Vidhan Sabha

Public Garden Rd

Mahatma Gandhi Rd

Naravanguda Rd

Vir Savarkar Rd

Kacheguda Station

Hyderabad City Station

Abids Rd

Mukarramjahi Rd

ABIDS

SULTAN BAZAR

Turrebazkhan Rd

Maulvi Alauddin Rd

To Race Course

Osmania Women's College

GOSHAMAHAL

Jawaharlal Nehru

Maulvi Alauddin Road

Imlibun Bus Terminal

OLD MALAKPET

BEGUM BAZAR

Malakpet Station

Vijayawada Rd

DHULPET

City College Rd

New Bridge

Musi River

Salar Jung Museum

Dabirpura Station

To Golconda & Tombs

Golconda Rd

Old Bridge

Musi Jang Bridge

Rajendranagar Rd

PATTHARGATTI

To Michel Raymond's Tomb & Vijayawada

SABZIMANDI

Bangalore Rd

Lad Bazar Rd

Badshahi Ashurkhana

Jama Masjid

N

Lad Bazar

Char Minar

1 km

1 mile

To Airport, Nehru Zoological Park & Mir Alam Tank

To Mecca Masjid, Chowmahalla Palace & Falaknuma Palace

① ② ③

Tourist information Government of Andhra Pradesh ① *Yatri Nivas, SP Rd, Secunderabad, T040-6457 7598, www.aptdc.gov.in; Tank Bund Rd, near Secretariat, T040-6558 1555.* **Andhra Pradesh Tourism Development Corporation (APTDC)** ① *Tourism House, Himayatnagar, T040-2326 2151.* **India Tourism** ① *Netaji Bhavan, Himayatnagar, T040-2326 1360,* runs an excellent walking tour of the old city.

OLD CITY AND CHAR MINAR

To celebrate the founding of Hyderabad, Sultan Mohammed Quli Qutb Shah built the lofty archway of **Char Minar** ① *0900-1730, Rs 5,* at the entrance to his palace complex. Capped with four soaring minarets (*char minar* means 'four towers') and holding the city's original mosque on its roof, it has been the showpiece of the city since construction was finished in 1612. Today it stands at the centre of a busy crossroads, surrounded by the Old City's sprawling bazar of pearl, perfume and jewellery shops. The monument is lit up every evening from 1900-2100.

Immediately to the southwest is the vast **Mecca Masjid**, so named because of the red clay bricks from Mecca embedded in its impressive outer walls. The second largest mosque in India and among the seven biggest in the world, construction of the building began in 1614 under the sixth Sultan Abdulla Qutb Shah and was completed by Aurangzeb when he annexed Golconda in 1692. Comprising huge slabs of black granite quarried nearby, the mosque was designed to hold 10,000 people at prayer times. The tombs of the Asaf Jahi rulers, the Nizams of Hyderabad, are in an enclosure with a roof, to the left of the courtyard.

Towards the river is the **Jama Masjid**, the second mosque built in the old city at the end of the 16th century, beyond which on Sadar Patel Road are the four arches of **Charkaman**. The eastern Black Arch was for the drums, the western arch led to the palaces, the northern was the Fish Arch, and the southern arch was for the Char Minar.

Lad Bazar area The heart of the Muslim part of the city, the area around the Mecca Masjid and the Char Minar is a fascinating hive of bazars, made up of beautiful wooden buildings with stone carvings and pink elephant gates, packed with people. You arrive at the **chowk** which has a mosque and a Victorian clock tower.

Southeast of the Lad Bazar is the enormous complex of palaces which were built by the different Nizams, including the grand **Chowmahalla Palace** ① *1000-1700, closed holidays, Rs 150; T040-2452 2032,* a facsimile of the Shah's Palace in Tehran. Nizam Salabhat Jung began the splendid palace complex in 1750, but it was only completed more than a century later by Nizam Afzar-ud-Dawla Bahadur. Refreshed and sparkling after a thorough restoration undertaken at the behest of Princess Esra, the eighth Nizam's wife, the four ('chow') stuccoed and domed palaces ('mahal') of the complex's name – the Afzal Mahal, Mahtab Mahal, Tahniyat Mahal and Aftab Mahal – now play host to a museum packed with artefacts from the Nizam's reign, while the central Khilawat Mubarak (Durbar Hall) has been brought back to its original glory, complete with 19 Belgian crystal chandeliers and a platform of pure marble on which the *Takht-e-Nishan* (royal seat) was placed.

SALAR JUNG MUSEUM AND THE BANKS OF THE MUSI

The modern **Salar Jung Museum** ① *Salar Jung Marg, T040-2452 3211, Sat-Thu 1030-1700, closed public holidays, allow 1½ hrs, Rs 150, cameras and bags must be left at counter, recorded guides at ticket office,* houses the collection of Sir Yusuf Ali Salar Jung III, the *wazir* (prime minister) to the Nizam between 1899-1949. The fact that it is one of only three national museums in India is a telling indication of the extant of the riches he amassed. Originally housed on the edge of the city in one of the palaces, it was rehoused in this purpose-built museum in 1968. Exhibits are described in English, Urdu, Hindi and Telugu. The collection includes Indian textiles, bronzes, paintings and fine ivory art pieces, armoury, Far Eastern porcelain and entertaining curiosities. The Indian miniatures are stunning.

The **High Court**, built on the new roads laid out along the Musi's embankments after the great flood, is a splendid Mughal-style building in the old Qutb Shahi gardens **Amin Bagh**, near Afzal Ganj Bridge. This was Vincent Esch's most striking work. It was built in 1916 from local pink granite, with red sandstone carved panels and columns, a large archway and domes. These days it is painted pink. A further change is the enclosure of the verandas. The detail is Mughal, but some argue that the structure and internal form are Western.

Next door to the High Court is Esch's **City College** (1917-1920), originally the City High School for boys. Built largely of undressed granite, there are some distinctive Indian decorative features including some marble *jalis*. Esch deliberately incorporated Gothic features, calling his style Perpendicular Mogul Saracenic.

In the opposite direction along the riverbank from the Salar Jung Museum is one of the oldest *imambaras* in the country, the **Badshahi Ashurkhana** (house of mourning), built in the Qutb Shahi style in the late 16th century. It has excellent tile mosaics and wooden columns in the outer chamber, both later additions.

Over the river is the **Osmania Women's College**, the former British residency built by James Achilles Kirkpatrick – the central character of William Dalrymple's history, *White Mughals* – in 1803. This imposing colonial structure, whose grounds run down to the river bank, was the first symbol of British presence in the city. It was deliberately built to the same proportions as the Char Minar in order to be the only equal to its minarets on the city skyline. After decades of decline, the World Monuments Fund is carrying out structural conservation as well as fundraising for further restoration, while it continues to function as an educational institute for 4000 girl students (whose modesty visitors are urged to respect). The ornate palace Kirkpatrick built for his Muslim bride was razed in 1861 as a symbol of his perceived immorality. Dalrymple's book was launched from the stately, ochre-painted stately building's Durbar Hall. This is a room of giant chandeliers, French windows, mirrors shipped in from Brighton palaces, tatty fans and glorious floral tracings on its ceiling. The Palladian-villa style central complex, the entrance porch with Corinthian columns, the Durbar Hall, oval offices, billiard rooms and bedrooms were initially independent of the flanking wings, separated by drawbridges, whose pulleys are still in place. Outlying buildings hold printing presses dating from the 1900s. Turn out of the King's Gate then left down a pathway towards the pigeon rookery to see the model of the Residency that Kirkpatrick had made so his Hyderabadi princess Khairunnissa could see the main house without breaking her *purda*.

HYDERABAD CENTRE: NEW CITY

The **Osmania General Hospital** (1918-1921) is the third of Vincent Esch's impressive buildings in Hyderabad. It stands across the river, opposite the High Court. The 200-m-long building was one of the largest and best equipped hospitals in the world when it opened. To its east, also on the river, is the imposing **Asafia State Central Library** (1929-1934) with its priceless collection of Arabic, Persian and Urdu books and manuscripts.

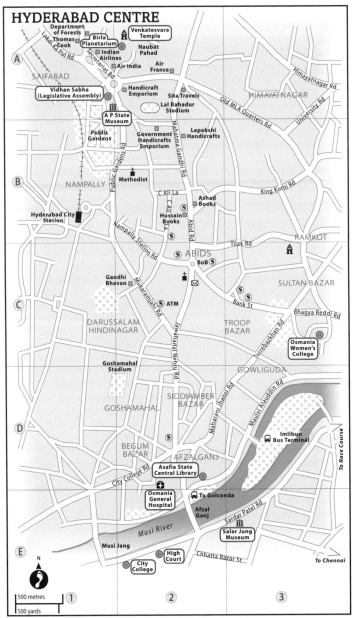

HYDERABAD CENTRE

Department of Forests

Thomas Cook

Birla Planetarium

Venkatesvara Temple

Lakdi Ka Pul Rd

Secretariat Rd

Indian Airlines

Air India

Naubat Pahad

Air France

Himayatnagar Rd

SAIFABAD

Vidhan Sabha (Legislative Assembly)

Handicraft Emporium

Sita Travels

HIMAYATNAGAR

University Rd

A P State Museum

Lal Bahadur Stadium

Old MLA Quarters Rd

Public Gardens

Government Handicrafts Emporium

Lepakshi Handicrafts

Public Gardens Rd

Mahatma Gandhi Rd

Methodist

NAMPALLY

King Kothi Rd

C Ali La

Ashad Books

Abid Rd

Hyderabad City Station

Nampally Station Rd

Hussain Books

CALI

RAMKOT

Tilak Rd

ABIDS

SULTAN BAZAR

BoB

Gandhi Bhavan

Mukarramjahi Rd

ATM

Bank St

DARUSSALAM HINDINAGAR

TROOP BAZAR

Bhagya Reddi Rd

Jawaharlal Nehru Rd

Osmania Women's College

GOWLIGUDA

Goshamahal Stadium

Turrebazkhan Rd

GOSHAMAHAL

SIDDIAMBER BAZAR

Maharani Jhansi Rd

Maulvi Alauddin Rd

To Race Course

BEGUM BAZAR

AFZALGANJ

Imlibun Bus Terminal

City College Rd

Asafia State Central Library

Osmania General Hospital

To Golconda

Afzal Ganj

Sardar Patel Rd

To Chennai

Musi River

Salar Jung Museum

Musi Jang

High Court

Chhatta Bazar St

500 metres
500 yards

N

City College

The **Public Gardens** ⓘ *closed public holidays,* in Nampally, north of Hyderabad Station, contain some important buildings including the Archaeological Museum and Art Galleries and the State Legislative Assembly (Vidhan Sabha).

Andhra Pradesh State Museum ⓘ *near the Lal Bahadur Shastri Stadium, 10 mins by car from Banjara Hills area, 1030-1700, closed public holidays, nominal entrance fee, photography Rs 10, guidebook Rs 15*, is a small museum with a crowd-drawing 4000-year-old Egyptian mummy. Behind the museum in Ajanta Pavilion are life-size copies of frescoes from the Ajanta Caves while the Nizam's collection of rare artefacts is housed in the Jubilee Hall.

The **City Railway Station** (1914) was intended by Esch to be pure Mughal in style but built entirely of the most modern material then available: pre-cast, reinforced concrete. It has a wide range of distinctively Indian features including the *chhattris* of royalty, wide *chajjas* (eaves) and onion domes.

Naubat Pahad (Kala Pahad or Neeladri) are two hills situated north of the Public Gardens. The Qutb Shahis are believed to have had their proclamations read from the hill tops accompanied by drums. In 1940 pavilions were built and a hanging garden was laid out on top of one; it's now occupied by the **Birla Planetarium** ⓘ *Fri-Wed at 1130, 1600 and 1800, Rs 20*, and **Science Centre** ⓘ *1030-2000, Rs 20.*

The nearby **Venkatesvara Temple** (Birla Mandir) ⓘ *reached by a stall-lined path opposite Thomas Cook on Secretariat Rd, 0700-1200, 1400-2100, photography of inner sanctum prohibited*, is a modern, stunning white marble temple with an intricately carved ceiling which overlooks Husain Sagar. It was built by the Birlas, the Marwari business family who were responsible for building important new Hindu temples in several major cities, including Laxmi Narayan Temple in New Delhi. Completed in 1976, the images of the deities are South Indian, although the building itself drew craftsmen from the north as well, among them some who claimed to have ancestors who built the Taj Mahal.

The massive State Legislative Assembly building, **Vidhan Sabha**, originally the Town Hall, was built by the Public Works Department (PWD) in 1922. Although Esch had nothing to do with its design, he reportedly admired it for its lightness and coolness, which the building maintained even on the hottest day. **Jubilee Hall** (1936), behind the Vidhan Sabha, is another remarkable PWD building, with clear simple lines.

The deep **Husain Sagar Lake** ⓘ *boat trips organized by APTDC leave from Lumbini Park, near the APTDC office on Secretariat Rd, T040-2345 3315,* was created in the mid-16th century by building the *bund* that links Hyderabad and Secunderabad, and was named to mark the gratitude of Ibrahim Quli Qutb Shah to Hussain Shah Wali, who helped him recover from an illness. The *bund* is a favourite evening promenade for the city dwellers. At the far end of the lake is the **Nizamia Observatory**. The 17.5-m-high, 350-tonne granite **statue of Buddha** was erected in the lake after years of successive disasters and finally inaugurated by the Dalai Lama in 1993. The tank, fed by streams originating from the Musi River, supplies drinking water to Hyderabad. Although it supports a rich birdlife and is used for fish culturing it also receives huge amounts of industrial effluent, agricultural waste and town sewage.

OUTSIDE THE CITY CENTRE

Originally a rich nobleman's house, **Falaknuma Palace** was built in 1873 in a mixture of classical and Mughal styles. Bought by the Nizam in 1897, it has a superb interior (particularly the state reception room) with marble, chandeliers and paintings. The palace houses Eastern and European treasures, including a collection of jade, crystal and precious stones and a superb library. Currently operating as one of India's most luxurious hotels – a high bar to jump – it's particularly atmospheric in the evening, when the lights of Hyderabad twinkle at your feet.

Osmania University ① *T040-2709 6048*, built by the Nizam in 1939, is just outside the city towards the east. Inaugurated in 1917 in temporary buildings, its sprawling campus with its black granite Arts College combines Moorish and Hindu Kakatiya architectural styles. There is a botanical garden and the State Archives.

The **tomb of Michel Raymond** is off the Vijayawada Road, about 3 km from the Oliphant Bridge. The Frenchman joined the second Nizam's army in 1786 as a common soldier and rose to command 15,000 troops. His popularity with the people earned him the combined Muslim-Hindu name Moosa Ram, and even today they remember him by holding a commemorative **Urs fair** at his grey granite tomb, which is 7 m high and bears the initials JR.

Mir Alam Tank, to the southwest of the old city, is a large artificial lake. It was built by French engineers under instructions of the grandfather of Salar Jung III and is a popular picnic spot. It is now part of the **Nehru Zoological Park** ① *Apr-Jun 0800-1730, Jul-Mar 0830-1700, closed Mon, Rs 20 (extra charges for nocturnal house, safari ride, etc), camera Rs 20, video Rs 100, bus 7Z from Secunderabad Station and Public Garden Rd,* which occupies a remarkable 153-ha (380-acre) site studded with huge boulders. The hilly grounds offer a welcome relief from the bustle of the city, and birdwatching here provides a good introduction to Indian avifauna, but this is also one of India's best zoos (the animals are kept in natural surroundings) and well worth a visit. There's also a lion safari park and a nocturnal house. The **Natural History Museum**, **Ancient Life Museum** and **Prehistoric Animals Park** are here as well.

West of the city centre lies **Hitec City**, a major technology township set up by former Chief Minister Chandrababu Naidu to promote the IT industry in Andhra Pradesh. In a distinctly more low-tech vein, nearby Madhapur is home to **Shilparamam** ① *1100-2300*, a crafts village spread over 12 ha, where you can interact with artisans and craftsman from all over the country.

Ramoji Film City ① *25 km southeast of Hyderabad on the Vijayawada road, T08415-246555, www.ramojifilmcity.com, 0900-1800, Rs 700 (children under 12 Rs 600) includes guided tour and various shows, take bus 204, 205, 206 or 207 from Hyderabad (Women's College stop, Koti), or 290 from Secunderabad's Uppal bus stop,* is a sherbet-dipped shrine to the many uses of plaster of Paris. Bus tours take visitors around the 'city', and though they're conducted mainly in Hindi, you'll still gather that everywhere from Mumbai's Chor Bazar to Mysore's Brindavan Gardens have been re-created since media baron Ramoji Rao founded his film lot in 1991. Over 3000 films have been shot here since then. It's oddly compelling to see an audience sit in rapt thrall to a show of aspiring film dancers gyrating in spandex hot pants, while their male opposite numbers inexplicably morris dance; this is only for the committed Indian film buff. It doesn't have the diversionary value of Universal Studios, but there is a theme park, **Fundustan**, for kids. AP Tourism runs daily bus tours from Hyderabad.

Golconda, one of the most accessible of great medieval fortresses in India, was the capital of the Qutb Shahi kings who ruled over the area from 1507 to 1687. Nizam-ul-Mulk repossessed it in 1724 and restored it to its former glory for a time. Modern-day restorations are being carried out by the Archaeological Survey of India.

ARRIVING IN GOLCONDA

Golconda is 11 km west of Hyderabad, Buses 119 or 142M from Nampally or 66G from Char Minar take one hour to the fort. Buses 123 and 142S go direct from Char Minar to the Qutb Shahi Tombs, Rs 10. Autos take 30 minutes, Rs 150. Cycling in the early morning is a good option as it's an easy journey. Both the fort and the tombs are popular sites and get crowded and very noisy after 1000; if you arrive early it's worth asking to be allowed in.

THE FORT

ⓘ T040-2351 2401, 0900-1930, Rs 100, Indians Rs 10. Official guides wait at the entrance (Rs 250), unofficial ones greet you under the Fateh Darwaza. Allow 2-3 hrs. There is an excellent 1-hr son et lumière show in English (Mar-Oct 1800, Nov-Feb 1900; Rs 50/100); tickets go on

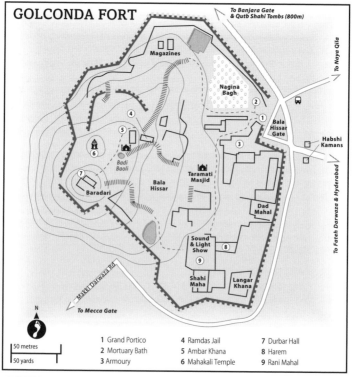

GOLCONDA FORT

To Banjara Gate & Qutb Shahi Tombs (800m)

To Naya Qila

Magazines

Nagina Bagh

Bala Hissar Gate

Habshi Kamans

Badi Baoli

Taramati Masjid

Bala Hissar

Dad Mahal

Baradari

To Fateh Darwaza & Hyderabad

Sound & Light Show

Shahi Maha

Langar Khana

Makki Darwaza Rd

To Mecca Gate

N

50 metres
50 yards

1 Grand Portico
2 Mortuary Bath
3 Armoury
4 Ramdas Jail
5 Ambar Khana
6 Mahakali Temple
7 Durbar Hall
8 Harem
9 Rani Mahal

sale at Golconda 1 hr before the start, Rs 25. Some people buy buy their sound and light ticket as soon as the office opens and take a quick tour (45 minutes) of the fort before sunset in time for the show.

Originally built of mud in the 12th century by the Hindu Kakatiyas, the fort was reinforced by masonry by the Bahmanis who occupied it from 1363. The massive fort, built on a granite hill, was surrounded by three walls. One encircled the town, another the hill on which the citadel stood and the last joined huge boulders on the high ridge with parts of masonry wall. The citadel's 5-km double wall had 87 bastions with cannons and eight huge gates with outer and inner doors and guardrooms between. Some of the guns of the Qutb Shahis are still there with fortifications at various levels on the way up. Another of India's supposed underground tunnels is believed by some to run for about 8 km from a corner of the summit to Gosha Mahal. The fort had an ingenious system of laminated clay pipes and huge Persian Wheels to carry water to cool the palace chambers up to the height of 61 m where there were hanging gardens. The famous diamond vault once held the *Koh-i-noor* and *Hope* diamonds. The fort fell to Emperor Aurangzeb after two attempts, an eight-month siege and the help of a Qutb general-turned-traitor. English traveller Walter Hamilton described it as being almost deserted in 1820: "the dungeons being used by the Nizam of Hyderabad as a prison for his worst enemies, among whom were several of his sons and two of his wives".

The Fateh Darwaza or Victory Gate at the **Grand Portico (1)** entrance, made of teak, with a Hindu deity engraved, is studded with iron spikes as a defence against war elephants. The superb acoustics enabled a drum beat, bugle call or even a clap under the canopy of this gate to be heard by someone at the very top of the palace; it is put to the test by the visiting crowds today. A couple of glass cases display a map and some excavated finds.

Beyond the gate the **Mortuary Bath (2)** on the right has beautiful arches and a crypt-like ceiling; you see the remains of the three-storey **armoury (3)** and the women's palaces on the left. About halfway up is a large water tank or well and to the north is what was once the most densely populated part of the city. Nearby, the domed storehouse turned into the **Ramdas Jail (4)** and has steps inside that lead up to a platform where there are relief sculptures of deities on the wall, dominated by Hanuman. The **Ambar Khana (5)** (granary) has a Persian inscription on black basalt stating that it was built between 1626 and 1672. The steps turn around an enormous boulder with a bastion and lead to the top passing the Hindu **Mahakali Temple (6)** on the way. The breezy **Durbar Hall (7)** is on the summit. It is well worth climbing the stairs to the roof here for good views. The path down is clearly signposted to take you on a circular route through the **harem (8)** and **Rani Mahal (9)** with its royal baths, back to the main gate. AP Tourism conducts regular bus tours from Hyderabad.

QUTB SHAHI TOMBS
① Sat-Thu 0930-1830, Rs 100, Indians Rs 10, camera Rs 10, car Rs 20, bicycle Rs 5. Allow 2 hrs, or half a day for a leisurely exploration. Inexpensive guidebook available.

About 800 m north-northwest of Golconda fort on a low plateau (a road leaves the fort through the Banjara Gate) are the Qutb Shahi Tombs. Each tomb of black granite or greenstone with plaster decoration is built on a square or octagonal base with a large onion dome and arches with fine sculptures, inscriptions and remains of glazed decoration. The larger tombs have their own mosque attached which usually comprises an eastward opening hall with a *mihrab* to the west. The sides have inscriptions in beautiful Naksh script, and remnants of the glazed tiles that used to cover them can still be seen in places. The tombs of the rulers were built under their own supervision but fell into disrepair and the gardens ran wild until the end of the 19th century when Sir Salar Jang restored them and replanted the gardens. It is now managed and kept in an excellent state of repair by the Archaeological Survey of India. The gardens are being further improved.

The road north from Golconda fort passes the tomb of **Abdullah Qutb Shah** (1626-1672) as it approaches the entrance to the tombs, which is at the east gate of the compound. On the left side of the road just outside the compound is the tomb of **Abul Hasan Tana Qutb Shahi** (ruled 1672-1687). He was the last of the kings to be buried here as the final king in the line of the Qutb Shahi Dynasty, Abul Hasan, died in the fort at Daulatabad in 1704. To the right of the entrance are the tomb of Princess **Hayat Baksh Begum** (died 1677), the daughter of Ibrahim Qutb Shah, and a smaller mosque, while about 100 m directly ahead is the granite tomb of **Muhammad Qutb Shah** (ruled 1612-1626). Tucked away due north of this tomb is that of **Pemamati**, one of the mistresses of Muhammad Qutb Shah, dating from 1663. The path turns south and west around the tomb of Muhammad Qutb Shah. About 100 m to the south is a tank which is still open. The **Badshahi Hammam**, the oldest structure in the compound, is the bath where the body of the king was washed before burial. You can still see the channels for the water and the special platforms for washing the body. The Badshahi kings were Shi'a Muslims, and the 12 small baths in the Hammam stand symbolically for the two *imams* revered by the Shi'a community. Next door, a small **Archaeological Museum** ① *1000-1300, 1400-1630,* has interesting items in glass cases.

To the south of the hammam is a series of major tombs. The most striking lies due south, the 54-m-high mausoleum of **Muhammad Quli Qutb Shah** (ruled 1581-1612), the poet king founder of Baghnagar (Hyderabad). It is appropriate that the man responsible for creating a number of beautiful buildings in Hyderabad should be commemorated by such a remarkable tomb. The underground excavations here have been turned into a Summer House. You can walk right through the tomb and on to the tomb of the fourth king of the dynasty, **Ibrahim Qutb Shah** (ruled 1550-1580), another 100 m to the south. At the west edge of the compound is the octagonal tomb of **Kulsum Begum** (died 1608), granddaughter of Mohammad Quli Qutb Shah. To its east is the tomb of **Jamshid Quli Qutb Shah** (ruled 1543-1550), who was responsible for the murder of his 90-year-old father and founder of the dynasty, **Sultan Quli Qutb Shah** (ruled 1518-1543). This has the appearance of a two-storey building though it is in fact a single-storey structure with no inscription. There are some other small tombs here.

GOING FURTHER
Warangal and Nagarjunakonda

→ WARANGAL

The capital of the Kakatiya Empire in the 12th and 13th centuries, Warangal's name is derived from the Orugallu (one stone) Hill, a massive boulder with ancient religious significance that stands where the modern town is situated.

ARRIVING IN WARANGAL

Warangal is 156 km northeast of Hyderabad, and is served by frequent trains (two to three hours) and buses (three to four hours). The railway and bus stations are next to each other south of the centre. Auto-rickshaws are the best way to get around the town. **Warangal Tourist Office** ① *1st floor, Talwar Hyndai Show Room, Chaitanyapuri, opposite REC Petrol Pump, Kazipet, T0870-244 6606.*

BACKGROUND

The city was probably laid out during the reigns of King Ganapatideva (1199-1262) and his daughter Rudrammadevi (until 1294). Warangal was captured by armies from Delhi in 1323, enforcing the payment of tribute. Control of Warangal fluctuated between Hindus and Muslims but between the 14th and 15th centuries it remained in Bahmani hands. Thereafter it repeatedly changed hands, and some argue that although the military fortifications were repeatedly strengthened, the religious buildings were largely destroyed, including the great Siva temple in the middle of the city. Marco Polo was highly impressed by Warangal's riches, and it is still famous for the remains of its temples, its lakes and wildlife, and for its three circuits of fortifications.

PLACES IN WARANGAL

At the centre of the **'fort'** ① *0600-1800, Rs 100, Indians Rs 5,* is a circular area about 1.2 km in diameter. Most of it is now farmland with houses along the road. Near the centre are the ruins of the original Siva temple. Remains include the large beautifully carved stone entrance gateways, replicas of which adorn many of the government offices, hotels and even private residences in the city. The gateways lead to the almost square enclosure, aligned along the cardinal directions and beyond are overturned slabs, smashed columns, brackets and ceiling panels.

Nearby Siva temples are still in use, and to the west is the **Khush Mahal**, a massive royal hall used by the Muslim Shitab Khan in the early 16th century for state functions. It may well have been built on the site of earlier palaces, near its geometric centre, while some structures in the central area may have been granaries.

From the centre, four routes radiate along the cardinal directions, passing through gateways in the three successive rings of fortification. The innermost ring is made of massive granite blocks, and is up to 6 m high with bastions regularly spaced along the wall. The middle wall is of unfaced packed earth, now eroded, while the outermost circuit, up to 5 m high, is also of earth. The four main roads pass through massive gateways in the inner wall, and there are also incomplete gateways in the second ring of fortifications. Some of the original roads that crossed the city have disappeared.

Some suggest that the plan of Warangal conforms to early Hindu principles of town planning. **'Swastika towns'**, especially suited to royalty, followed the pattern of concentric circles and swastika of the *yantras* and *mandalas*. They were a miniature representation of the universe, the power of god and king recognized symbolically, and in reality, at the centre.

The Chalukya-style '1000-pillar' **Siva Rudresvar temple** ① *0500-1200, 1600-2000*, on the slopes of the Hanamakonda Hill, 4 km to the north, has beautiful carvings. It is a low, compact temple, built on several stepped platforms with subsidiary shrines to Vishnu and Surya, rock-cut elephants, a large superbly carved *Nandi* in the courtyard and an ancient well where villagers have drawn water for 800 years.

If you want to spend a night in Warangal, **$$ Suprabha** (Nakkalagutta, Hanamkonda, T0870-257 3888) is a new hotel near the railway station, with 52 clean airy rooms (a/c and non a/c), excellent service, internet and breakfast included.

→ AROUND WARANGAL

PAKHAL, ETHURNAGARAM AND LAKHNAVARAM

① *Warangal Bus Station to Narsampet. Regular bus service from Narsampet to Pakhal Lake or take a taxi.*

The great artificial lakes 40 km northeast of Warangal – from the south, Pakhal, Lakhnavaram, Ramappa and Ghanpur – were created as part of the Kakatiya rulers' water management and irrigation schemes in the 12th and 13th centuries and are still in use. The lakes are fringed with an emerging marsh vegetation and surrounded by extensive grasslands, tropical deciduous forests and evergreens.

This is the richest area for wildlife in the state, with tiger, panther, hyena, wild dogs, wild boars, gaur, foxes, spotted deer, jackals, sloth bears and pythons. There are also otters and alligators and a variety of waterbirds and fish in the lakes.

PALAMPET

Palampet lies close to the Ramappa Lake. The **Ramappa Temple**, dedicated to Siva as Rudreswara, was built in 1234 and is one of the finest medieval Deccan temples. The black basalt sculpture is excellent (even richer than that at the 1000-pillar temple) with famous Mandakini figures of female dancers which appear on brackets at the four entrances. The base of the temple has the typical bands of sculpture, the lowest of elephants, the second, a lotus scroll, the third which is the most interesting depicting figures opening a window on the life of the times and finally another floral scroll. There are more fine sculptures inside, some displaying a subtle sense of humour in common with some of the figures outside, and paintings of scenes from the epics on the ceiling. Note that no bottled water is available.

→ NAGARJUNAKONDA

Some 150 km southeast of Hyderabad is one of India's richest Buddhist sites, now almost entirely under the lake created by the Nagarjunasagar Dam, completed in 1960. The remains of a highly cultured Buddhist civilization had remained almost undisturbed for 1600 years until their discovery by AR Saraswati in March 1926. The reconstructed buildings are on a comparatively small scale, in a peaceful setting on top of the hilltop fort, now an island planted with low trees.

ARRIVING IN NAGARJUNAKONDA

Buses from Hyderabad arrive at Vijayapuri, which is 7 km from the boat jetty for Nagarjuna-konda. Boats leave for the island roughly every hour from 0930; prepare for a chaotic scrum to get on board. The last ferry leaves the island at 1600. Enquiries T08642-243457. Other ferries are reserved for **APTDC** tours, which can be organized locally or from Hyderabad. **AP State Tourist Office** ① *Project House, Hill Colony, T08680-277364/276540.* A guide is available through this office; others can be arranged from the **APTDC** in Hyderabad.

BACKGROUND

Rising from the middle of the artificial lake is the Nagarjuna Hill which was once nearly 200 m above the floor of the secluded valley in the northern ranges of the Nallamalais (black hills) which surround the lake on three sides. On the fourth side was the great river Krishna, superimposed on the hills as it flows towards the Bay of Bengal.

Early archaeological work showed the remnants of Buddhist monasteries, many limestone sculptures and other remains. The survey carried out a full excavation of the sites before they were covered by the rising waters of the lake. More than 100 distinct sites ranging from the prehistoric early Stone Age period to the late medieval were discovered. Some of the most important remains have been moved and reconstructed on the hilltop fort. These include nine monuments, rebuilt in their original form, and 14 large replicas of the ruins.

The Ikshvakus made Nagarjunakonda the centre of extraordinary artistic activity from the third century AD. In the mid-fourth century AD the Pallavas pushed north from Tamil Nadu and eclipsed the Ikshvaku Kingdom, reducing Nagarjunakonda to a deserted village. However, during the Chalukya period a Saiva centre was built at Yellaswaram, on the other bank of the Krishna. In the 15th and 16th centuries the hill became a fortress in the contest for supremacy between the Vijayanagar, Bahmani and Gajapati kings. After the fall of the Vijayanagar Empire both the hill and the valley below lost all importance.

PLACES IN NAGARJUNAKONDA

The Ikshvaku's capital was a planned city on the right bank of the Krishna – **Vijayapuri** (city of victory). The citadel had rampart walls on three sides with the river on the fourth. The buildings inside including houses, barracks, baths and wells were probably destroyed by a great fire. The nine **temples** show the earliest developments of Brahmanical temple architecture in South India. The Vishnu temple (AD 278) had two beautifully carved pillars which were recovered from its site. Five temples were dedicated to Siva or Karttikeya. The river bank was dotted with Brahmanical shrines.

Nagarjunakonda excavations also revealed some of India's finest early sculptures and memorial pillars. Over 20 pillars were raised in the memory not just of rulers and nobles but also of artisans and religious leaders. The sculptures represent the final phase of artistic development begun at Amaravati in the second century BC.

The **hill fort** (early 14th-century) has remnants of the Vijayanagar culture though the present layout of the fort probably dates from as recently as 1565. The main entrance was from the northeast, near where the ferry now lands on the island. In places the walls are still over 6 m high, with regular bastions and six gateways. There are two temples in the east, where the museum now stands.

The **museum** ① *Sat-Thu 0900-1600,* has a collection of coins and ornaments, but most importantly sculptures (including a 3-m-high standing Buddha). There are also prehistoric and protohistoric remains and several panels and friezes depicting Buddhist scenes.

The best accommodation option in Nagarjunakonda is **$$ Vijay Vihar** (APTDC, Nagarjuna Sagar, T08680-277362), whose fantastic views make up for the poorly maintained lake-facing rooms and suites (all a/c, though frequent power cuts are the norm).

HYDERABAD AND AROUND LISTINGS

WHERE TO STAY

Hyderabad

$$$$ Taj Falaknuma, Engine Bowli, Falaknuma, T040-6629 8585, www.taj hotels.com. The most opulent palace ever built by the Hyderabadi Nizams has been restored to its original condition and now plays host to one of India's most extraordinary hotels. The pick of the 60 rooms are the Historical and Royal suites, fitted out with Edwardian antiques and Italian marble floors, with sweeping views over the city or carefully tended lawns. Public areas are similarly exquisite, with cavernous ballrooms and dining tables that stretch for miles, and the overall feeling is akin to being a private guest in a stately home. Even if you don't stay it's worth splashing out on a meal here; book ahead and dress up.

$$$ Minerva Grand Banjara, Road No 11, Banjara Hills, T040-6612 7373, www.minervagrand.com. A boutique hotel with 44 designer rooms and suites in the upmarket Banjara Hills, close to the main commercial, retail and entertainment centres. Breakfast included.

$$-$ Taj Mahal, 4-1-999 Abid Rd, T040-2475 8250, www.hoteltajmahalindia.com. 20 good-sized simple a/c rooms in 1940s building. Busy South Indian vegetarian restaurant, meals, laundry, good value, friendly and the most characterful of the budget options. Recommended.

Secunderabad

$$$ Green Park, Begumpet, T040-6651 5151, www.hotelgreenpark.com. A sedate and large Indian business and family hotel with 146 rooms. Rooms come with bath, a/c and TV. Free Wi-Fi.

RESTAURANTS

Hyderabad

To foodies, the city is synonymous with one dish: the Hyderabadi biryani. Succulent mounds of rice, piled high with meat and spices and served with emergency bowls of yoghurt to counter the blistering heat, emerge from the kitchens of grubby and basic cafés along Pathergatti Rd, in the old city near the Char Minar. **Hotel Shaadab** is one of the most famous purveyors. While you're here, sample another Hyderabad insitution – a cup of extra-sweet and extra-milky Irani *chai*.

$$$ The Water Front, Eat St, Necklace Rd, T040-2330 8899. Lunch and dinner. When Hyderabadi's need to impress, they go to this open-air restaurant right on Hussain Sagar Lake. The food is coastal Indian and

Asian, the bill hefty, the atmosphere stylish and romantic.

$$$-$$ Firdaus, Taj Krishna hotel, Road No 1, Banjara Hills, T040-6666 2323. Excellent Mughlai cuisine and one of the only places in the city where you can get the special Hyderabadi treat, *haleem*. Meaning 'patience', this meat, wholewheat and gram dish is slow-cooked and is traditionally made to break the Ramadan fast.

$$-$ Paradise Food Court, 38 Sarojini Devi Rd/MG Rd. T040-6631 3721. Open 1100-2400. The best biryani in Secunderabad and such an institution that the surrounding area is now named 'Paradise'. You can get parcels from downstairs, eat standing up at the fast-food section, or go upmarket at **Persis Gold**.

NORTHERN KARNATAKA

Down the centuries, the red soil plains of northeast Karnataka have been host to a profusion of Deccani rulers. Bidar, Gulbarga and Bijapur are rich in Islamic relics, with crumbling archways leading into empty zenanas and plots of silent domed tombs – all the more atmospheric for their lack of visitors. The cluster of temples in the villages of Aihole, Pattadakal and Badami, built in the sixth century, bear witness to a moment of unique architectural inspiration in which the Chalukyans created the prototypes for the distinctive northern and southern styles of Hindu temple design. Finally, most famous of all, comes Hampi, site of the capital of the Vijayanagar Hindu empire that rose to conquer the entire south in the 14th century. An extraordinary collection of tumbledown temples, elephant stables and pleasure baths somehow moulded into a breathtakingly surreal landscape of jumbled orange boulders, this is one of India's most compelling destinations, its silence and mystery a potent siren song to settle into one of the laid-back guesthouses along the Tungabhadra River and stay for weeks.

→ BIDAR

The scruffy bungalow town that is modern-day Bidar spreads out in a thin layer of buildings both within and outside of the imposing rust-red walls of the 15th-century fort that once played capital to two Deccan-ruling Muslim dynasties. Little now remains of the succession of immaculately made palaces that must once have glowed incandescent with bright blue, green and yellow designs – just the occasional tile tucked into a high corner of the laterite brick structures that now stand in their place.

Yet the old fort still commands grand vistas across the empty cultivated lands of North Karnataka, and although the buildings are new, there's still something of a medieval undercurrent to life here. Islam still grows sturdily, and the outskirts are littered with long white prayer walls to mop up the overspill from packed mosques during Id.

ARRIVING IN BIDAR

Getting there Buses arrive at the main bus stand on the northwestern edge of Bidar, a five-minute ride by auto-rickshaw from the town centre and railway station.

Moving on It's a long drive from Bidar to **Bijapur** (see page 83), and an ordeal by bus, so it's worth hiring a car and breaking the journey in **Gulbarga** (see page 82). Travel agents charge Rs 5000-6000 for a one-way trip.

BACKGROUND

The walled fort town, once the capital of the **Bahmanis** and the **Barid Shahis**, remained an important centre until it fell to Aurangzeb in 1656. The Bahmani Empire fragmented into four kingdoms, and the ninth Bahmani ruler, **Ahmad Shah I**, shifted his capital from Gulbarga to Bidar in 1424, rebuilding the old Hindu fort to withstand cannon attacks, and enriching the town with beautiful palaces and gardens. With the decline of the Bahmanis, the Barid Shahi Dynasty founded here ruled from 1487 until Bidar was annexed to Bijapur in 1619.

PLACES IN BIDAR

The intermingling of Hindu and Islamic architectural styles in the town has been ascribed to the use of Hindu craftsmen, skilled in temple carving in stone (particularly hornblende), who would have been employed by the succeeding Muslim rulers. They transferred their skill to Muslim monuments, no longer carving human figures, forbidden by Islam, but using the same technique to decorate with geometric patterns, arabesques and calligraphy, wall friezes, niches and borders. The pillars, often of wood, were intricately carved and then painted and burnished with gold to harmonize with the encaustic tiles.

The **Inner Fort** built by Muhammad Shah out of the red laterite and dark trapstone was later embellished by Ali Barid. The steep hill to the north and east provided natural defence. It was protected to the south and west by a triple moat (now filled in). A series of gates and a drawbridge over the moat to the south formed the main entrance from

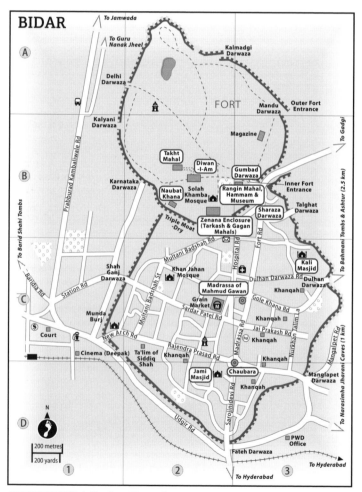

the town. The second gate, the **Sharaza Darwaza** (1503) has tigers carved in bas-relief on either side (Shia symbols of Ali as protector), the tile decorations on the walls and the *Nakkar Khana* (Drum gallery) above. Beyond this is a large fortified area which brings you to the third gate, the huge **Gumbad Darwaza**, probably built by Ahmad Shah Wali in the 1420s, which shows Persian influence. Note the decorated *gumbad* (dome).

You will see the triple moat to the right and after passing through the gateway, to your left are steps leading to the **Rangin Mahal** (Coloured Palace) where Muhammad Shah moved to, after finding the nearby Shah Burj a safe refuge in 1487 when the Abyssinians attacked. This small palace (an indication of the Bahmanis' declining years) was built by him, elaborately decorated with coloured tiles, later enhanced by Ali Barid with mother-of-pearl inlay on polished black granite walls as well as intricate wood carvings. If locked, ask at the museum (see below) for a key.

The old banyan tree and the **Shahi Matbak** (once a palace, but served as the Royal Kitchens) are to the west, with the **Shahi Hammam** (Royal Baths) next to it, which now houses a small **museum** ① *0800-1700*. Exhibits include Hindu religious sculptures, Stone Age implements and cannon balls filled with bits of iron.

The **Lal Bagh**, where remains of water channels and a fountain witness to its former glory, and the *zenana*, are opposite the hammam. The **Sola Khamba** (16 columns) or **Zanani Mosque** is to the west (1423). The adjacent **Tarkash Mahal** (possibly refurbished by the Barid Shahis for the harem), to the south of Lal Bagh, is in ruins but still retains some tilework. From behind the mosque you can get to the **Gagan Mahal** (Heavenly Palace) that once carried fine decorations and is believed to have allowed the women to watch animal fights in the moat below from the back of the double hall. There's a good view from the roof. The **Diwan-i-Am** (Hall of Public Audience) is to the northwest of the *Zenana* which once held the *Takht-i-Firoza* (turquoise throne). To the north stands the **Takht Mahal** with royal apartments, audience hall and swimming baths. The steep staircase will take you down to underground chambers.

South of the Royal Apartments is the well that supplied water to the fort palaces through clay pipes. Of the so-called **Hazar** ('thousand') **Kothri** ① *cycling is a good way of exploring the site, free,* you can only see a few underground rooms and passages which enabled a quick escape to the moat when necessary. Further south, the **Naubat Khana** probably housed the fort commander and the musicians. The road west from the Royal Apartments leads to the encircling Fort Wall (about 10 km) with bastions carrying vast cannons, the one to the northwest being the most impressive. You can see the ammunition magazine inside the **Mandu Darwaza** to the east before returning to the main fort entrance.

As you walk south from the fort you can see the ruins of the **Madrassa of Mahmud Gawan** (1472). It is a fine example of his native Persian architecture and still bears signs of the once-brilliant green, white and yellow tiles which covered the whole façade with swirls of floral patterns and bold calligraphy.

The **Chaubara** is a 23-m circular watchtower at the crossroads, south of the town centre (good views from the top). South of this is the **Jami Masjid** (1430) which bears the Barid Shahis' typical chain and pendant motif. The **Kali Masjid** (1694), south of the Talghat Darwaza, is made of black trapstone. It has fine plaster decorations on the vaulted ceiling. There are also a number of **khanqahs** (monasteries).

The road east from the Dulhan Darwaza, opposite the General Hospital, leads to the eight **Bahmani tombs** ① *Ashtur, 0800-1700, free, carry your own torch*. These are best seen in the morning when the light is better for viewing the interiors.

The square tombs, with arched arcades all round, have bulbous domes. The exteriors have stone carvings and superb coloured tile decoration showing strong Persian influence, while the interiors have coloured paintings with gilding. The tomb of **Ahmad Shah I**, the ninth Bahmani ruler, is impressive with a dome rising to nearly 35 m, and has a particularly fine interior with coloured decorations and calligraphy in the Persian style, highlighted with white borders. To the east and south are minor tombs of his wife and son. The tomb of **Alauddin Shah II** (1458) is possibly the finest. Similar in size to his father's, this has lost its fine painting inside but enough remains of the outer tilework to give an impression of its original magnificence.

On the way back is the **Chaukhandi of Hazrat Khalil-Ullah** which is approached by a flight of steps. Most of the tilework has disappeared but you can see the fine carvings at the entrance and on the granite pillars.

The **Barid Shahi tombs**, each of which once stood in its own garden, are on the Nanded Road to the west of the old town. That of **Ali Barid** is the most impressive, with the dome rising to over 25 m, with granite carvings, decorative plasterwork and calligraphy and floral patterns on the coloured tiles, which sadly can no longer be seen on the exterior. Here, abandoning the customary *mihrab* on the west wall, Ali Barid chose to have his tomb left open to the elements. It includes a prayer hall, music rooms, a combined tomb for his concubines and a pool fed by an aqueduct.

→ GULBARGA

The dry and undulating plains from Bidar to Bijapur are broken by rocky outcrops providing superb sites for commanding fortresses, such as the one that sits in ruins overlooking Gulbarga. From 1347 to 1525 Gulbarga served as the first capital of the Bahmanis, but it is also widely known among South Indian Muslims as the home of Saiyid Muhammad Gesu Daraz Chisti (1320-1422) who was instrumental in spreading pious Islamic faith in the Deccan. The annual **Urs festival** in his memory can attract up to 100,000 people.

PLACES IN GULBARGA

The town's sights and hotels are quite spread out so it is worth hiring an auto for half a day. The most striking remains in the town are the fort, with its citadel and mosque, the Jami Masjid, and the great tombs in its eastern quarter – massive, fortress-like buildings with their distinctive domes over 30 m high.

The **fort** is just 1 km west of the centre of the present town. Originally built by Ala-ud-din Bahmani in the 14th century, most of the outer structures and many of the buildings are in ruins. The outer door of the west gate and the *bala hissar* (citadel), a massive structure, however, remain almost intact although the whole place is very overgrown. A flight of ruined steps leads up to the entrance in the north wall; beware of dogs. It's easy to see why the Bahamis were so keen to upgrade their fortress. The fat fort walls at Gulbarga – romantically named as the 'bouquet of lovers' – may sit proud above the more modern artificial lake, and the *bala hissar* itself stands high with its plump rotund columns, but the whole is all too pregnable and modest. And there's no commanding hilltop to provide the impenetrability that the plateaux around Bidar bequeathed the dynasty's subsequent rulers.

All that remains of the palace structures are solitary walls stamped with arches, but the **Jami Masjid**, with its incongruous, uncanny likeness to the mosque at Córdoba in southern Spain, is both active and well maintained (similarities with the mosque at Córdoba have contributed to the legend that it was designed by a North African architect from the Moorish court). Beautiful geometrical angles of archways form as you walk under the 75 small roof domes zagging between the four corner domes. The whole area of 3500 sq m is covered by a dome over the *mihrab*, four corner domes and 75 minor domes, making it unique among Indian mosques. It was built by Firoz Shah Bahmani (1397-1432).

The **tombs** of the Bahmani sultans are in two groups. One lies 600 m to the west of the fort, the other on the east of the town. The latter have no remaining exterior decoration though the interiors show some evidence of ornamentation. The Dargah of the Chisti saint, **Hazrat Gesu Nawaz** – also known as Khwaja Bande Nawaz – who came to Gulbarga in 1413 during the reign of Firoz Shah Tughlaq, is open to visitors. The two-storey tomb with a highly decorated painted dome had a mother-of-pearl canopy added over the grave. Note that women are not allowed to enter the tombs. The **Dargah library**, which has 10,000 books in Urdu, Persian and Arabic, is open to visitors.

The most striking of all the tombs near **Haft Gumbaz**, the eastern group, is that of **Taj-ud-Din Firuz** (1422). Unlike the other tombs it is highly ornate, with geometrical patterns developed in the masonry.

→ BIJAPUR

Mohammed Adil Shah was not a man to be ignored; the tomb he built from the first day of his rule in anticipation of his own death hovers with dark magnificence over Bijapur and is so large it can be seen from over 20 km away. His brooding macabre legacy threw down the gauntlet to his immediate successor, Ali Adil Shah II, who took over from Mohammed in 1656, began his own tomb, which would surely have been double in size and architectural wonder had he not died too soon, 26 years into his reign, with only archways complete.

With its mausoleums, palaces and some of the finest mosques in the Deccan, Bijapur has the air of a northern Muslim city and retains real character. The chowk between the bus station and MG Road is quite atmospheric in the evening.

ARRIVING IN BIJAPUR
Getting there The road from Gulbarga enters Bijapur from the east, becoming MG Road which cuts across the middle of the walled city. Most of the hotels and main sights are on or within a couple of blocks of MG Road. Long-distance buses pull into the colourful new bus stand just south of MG Rd towards the east end of the citadel.

Moving on Six trains a day go from Bijapur to **Badami** (see page 86; 2½ to three hours). If your time is short it's worth hiring a taxi and visiting **Pattadakal** (see page 88) and **Aihole** (see page 89) on the way to Badami – travel agents quote around Rs 3000-4500 for a one-way trip.

Getting around It is easy to walk or cycle round the town. There are also autos and *tongas*; negotiate for the 'eight-sight tour price' (around Rs 250).

Tourist information There's a **tourist office** ⓘ *opposite the stadium, T08352-250359, Mon-Sat 1030-1330 and 1415-1730*, but it's not very useful.

BACKGROUND

The Chalukyas who ruled over Bijapur were overthrown in the late 12th century. In the early years of the 14th century the Delhi Sultans took it for a time until the Bahmanis, with their capital in Gulbarga, ruled through a governor in Bijapur who declared Independence in 1489 and founded the Adil Shahi Dynasty. Of Turkish origin, they held power until 1686.

The 55-ton canon was employed against Vijayanagar. Ali Adil Shah I, whose war it was, was somewhat chastened at the destruction his marauding Muslim armies had wreaked on the Hindu empire at Hampi. By way of atonement, and in a show of the inordinate riches that had fallen into his lap by supplanting Vijayanagar, he did his communal civic duty and built the exquisite Jama Masjid. It was his nephew Mohammed, he of the giant Gol Gumbaz, who later commissioned the Quaranic calligraphy that so sumptuously gilds the western wall.

PLACES IN BIJAPUR

Hulking in the background wherever you look in Bijapur, the **Gol Gumbaz** ⓘ*0630-1730, foreigners Rs 100, Indians Rs 5, video camera Rs 25, some choose to just view it from the gate*, is the vast whitewashed tomb of Mohammad Adil Shah, buried here with his wife, daughter and favourite court dancer, underneath the world's second largest dome (unsupported by pillars) – and one of its least attractive. Its extraordinary **whispering gallery** carries a

message across 38 m which is repeated 11 times. However, noisy crowds make hearing a whisper quite impossible; it's quietest in the early morning. Numerous narrow steps in one of the corner towers lead to the 3-m-wide gallery. The plaster here was made out of eggs, cow dung, grass and jaggery. There is an excellent view of the city from the base of the dome. The **Nakkar Khana**, or gatehouse, is now a museum ① *1000-1700, Rs 2*, housing an excellent collection of Chinese porcelain, parchments, paintings, armoury, miniatures, stone sculpture and old Bijapur carpets.

To the south is the **Jama Masjid**, one of the finest in the Deccan, with a large shallow, onion-shaped dome and arcaded court. Built by Ali Adil Shah I (ruled 1557-1579) during Bijapur's rise to power it displays a classic restraint. The Emperor Aurangzeb added a grand entrance to the mosque and also had a square painted for each of the 2250 worshippers that it can accommodate. West of here is the **Mehtar Mahal** (1620), whose delicate minarets and carved stone trellises were supposedly built for the palace sweepers.

Bijapur's **Citadel**, encircled by its own wall, now has few of its grand buildings intact. One is the Durbar Hall, **Gagan Mahal** (Sky Palace), open to the north so that the citizens outside were not excluded. It had royal residential quarters on either side with screened balconies for the women to remain unseen while they watched the court below. Another worth visiting is the **Jal Manzil**, or the water pavilion, a cool sanctuary. Just to the east is the **Asar Mahal** (circa 1646), once used as a court house with teak pillars and interesting frescoes in the upper floor.

The **Bara Kaman** was possibly a 17th-century construction by Adil Shah III. Planned as a huge 12-storey building with the shadow of the uppermost storey designed to fall onto the tomb of the Gol Gumbaz, construction was ended after two storeys with the death of the ruler. An impressive series of arches on a raised platform is all that remains.

The western gateway to the walled city, **Sherza Burj** (Lion Gate), has the enormous 55-tonne, 4.3-m-long, 1.5-m-diameter cannon *Malik-i-Maidan* (Ruler of the Plains). Cast in the mid-16th century in Ahmadnagar, it was brought back as a prize of war pulled by "400 bullocks, 10 elephants and hundreds of soldiers". The muzzle, a lion's head with open jaws, has an elephant being crushed to death inside, and the gun's roar was said to be so loud that the gunner used to dive into the tank off the platform to avoid being deafened. Inside the city wall nearby is **Upli Burj**, a 24-m-high watchtower with long guns and water tanks.

West of the city centre is the **Ibrahim Rauza** ① *0600-1800, Rs 100, Indians Rs 5, video camera Rs 25, visit early morning to avoid crowds,* the palatial 17th-century tomb and mosque built by Ibrahim Adil Shah. Raised during the dynasty's most prosperous period (after the sacking of Vijayanagar) when the arts and culture flourished, the corners of both buildings are decorated with slender minarets and decorative panels carved with lotus, wheel and cross patterns as well as bold Arabic calligraphy, bearing witness to the tolerance of the Adil Shahi Dynasty towards other religions. Near the Rauza is a huge tank, the **Taj Bauri**, built by Ibrahim II in memory of his wife. The approach is through a giant gateway flanked by two octagonal towers.

Although Bijapur became an important Muslim regional capital, its surrounding region has several villages which, nearly 1500 years ago, were centres of Chalukyan power and the heart of new traditions in Indian temple building. At a major Indian crossroads, the temples at Aihole represent the first finely worked experiments in what were to become distinct North and South Indian temple styles.

ARRIVING IN BADAMI, AIHOLE AND PATTADAKAL

Getting there Trains from Bijapur to Gadag stop at Badami, which makes a useful hub for visiting other sights. Badami is the most useful transport hub for visiting the temples. The railway station is 5 km north of the village; shared and private auto-rickshaws take you into the centre.

Moving on Buses chug through the countryside from Badami to **Hospet** (see page 94), a slow but quite pleasant trip with lots of stops. Six trains a day leave for Gadag (two hours), from where you can connect to buses or trains to Hospet (a further 1½ hours). A taxi direct to **Hampi** (see page 90) should cost around Rs 3000-4000.

Getting around If you're travelling by bus it's best to visit Badami first, then Pattadakal and Aihole, but since it takes half a day to see Badami, visiting the sites by bus doesn't allow time for Mahakuta. If you want to see all the sights comfortably in a day it is well worth hiring a car.

Tourist information Tourist office ① *next to Mayura Chalukya, Badami, T08357-220414.*

BADAMI

Badami occupies a dramatic site squeezed in a gorge between two high red sandstone hills. Once called Vatapi, after a demon, Badami was the Chalukyan capital from AD 543-757. The ancient city has several Hindu and Jain temples and a Buddhist cave and remains peaceful and charming. The transcendent beauty of the Hindu cave temples in their spectacular setting warrants a visit. The village with its busy bazar and a large lake has whitewashed houses clustered together along narrow winding lanes up the hillside. There are also scattered remains of 18 stone inscriptions (dating from the sixth to the 16th century). The sites are best visited early in the morning. They are very popular with monkeys, which can be aggressive, especially if they see food. End the day by watching the sun set from the eastern end of the tank. The area is well worth exploring by bicycle.

The **South Fort** ① *foreigners Rs 100, Indians Rs 5,* is famous for its cave temples, four of which were cut out of the hillside in the second half of the sixth century. There are 40 steps to **Cave 1**, the oldest. There are several sculpted figures, including Harihara, Siva and Parvati, and Siva as Nataraja with 18 arms seen in 81 dancing poses. **Cave 2**, a little higher than Cave 1, is guarded by *dvarapalas* (door keepers). Reliefs of Varaha and Vamana decorate the porch. **Cave 3**, higher still, is dedicated to Vishnu. According to a Kannada inscription (unique in Badami) it was excavated in AD 578. It has numerous sculptures including Narasimha (man-lion), Hari-Hara (Siva-Vishnu), a huge seated Vishnu and interesting friezes. Frescoes executed in the tempera technique are similar to that used in the Ajanta paintings, and so are the carved ceilings and brackets. **Cave 4**, probably about

100 years later than the three earlier caves, is the only Jain cave. It has a statue of the seated Parsvanatha with two *dvarapalas* at the entrance. The fort itself above the caves is closed to the public.

The **Buddhist Temple** is in the natural cave close to the ancient artificial Bhutanatha Lake (Agasthya Lake), where the mossy green water is considered to cure illnesses. The Yellamma Temple has a female deity, while one of the two Shaivite temples is to Bhutanatha (God of souls); in this form, Siva appears angry in the dark inner sanctuary.

The seventh-century **Mallegitti Sivalaya Temple**, which is one of the finest examples of the early Southern style, has a small porch, a *mandapa* (hall) and a narrower *vimana* (shrine), which Harle points out is typical of all early Western Chalukya temples. The slim pilasters on the outer walls are reminders of the period when wooden pillars were essential features of the construction. Statues of Vishnu and Siva decorate the outer walls, while animal friezes appear along the plinth and above the eaves. These are marked by a moulding with a series of ornamental small solid pavilions.

Jambulinga Temple is an early temple in the centre of the town near the rickshaw stand. Dating from AD 699 as attested by an inscription and now almost hidden by houses, the visible brick tower is a late addition from the Vijayanagar period. Its three chapels, dedicated to Brahma, Vishnu and Siva, contain some fine carving, although the deities are missing and according to Harle the ceiling decoration already shows signs of deteriorating style. The carvings here, especially that of the Nagaraja in the outside porch, have helped to accurately date the Lad Khan Temple in Aihole (see page 89). Opposite the Jambulinga temple is the 10th-century Virupaksha Temple.

The mainly seventh-century **North Fort temples** ① *Rs 2, carry water*, provide an insight into Badami's history. Steep steps, almost 1 m high, take you to 'gun point' at the top of the fort which has remains of large granaries, a treasury and a watchtower. The **Upper Sivalaya Temple**, though damaged, still has some friezes and sculptures depicting Krishna legends. The North Fort was taken in a day by Colonel Munro in 1918, when he broke in through the east side.

An ancient **dolmen** site can be reached by an easy hike through interesting countryside; allow 3½ hours. A local English-speaking guide, Dilawar Badesha, at Tipu Nagar, charges about Rs 2.

The Archaeological Survey's **Medieval Sculpture Gallery** ① *Sat-Thu 1000-1700, free*, north of the tank, has fine specimens from Badami, Aihole and Pattadakal and a model of the natural bridge at Sidilinapadi, 5 km away.

MAHAKUTA

Once reached by early pilgrims over rocky hills from Badami, 5 km away, Mahakuta is a beautiful complex of Chalukyan temples dating from the late seventh century and worth a detour. The superstructures reflect influences from both North and South India and one has an Orissan *deul*.

The restored temple complex of two dozen shrines dedicated to Siva is built around a large spring-fed tank within an enclosure wall. The old gateway to the southeast has fasting figures of Bhairava and Chamunda. On entering the complex, you pass the *Nandi* in front of the older **Mahakutesvara Temple** which has fine scrollwork and figures from the epics carved on the base. Larger Siva figures appear in wall niches, including an *Ardhanarisvara*. The temple is significant in tracing the development of the super-structure which began to externally identify the position of the shrine in Dravidian temples. Here the tower is dome-like and octagonal, the tiers supported by tiny 'shrines'. The **Mallikarjuna Temple** on the other side of the tank is similar in structure with fine carvings at the entrance and on the ceiling of the columned *mandapa* inside, depicting Hindu deities and *mithuna* couples. The enclosure has many smaller shrines, some carrying fine wall carvings. Also worth visiting is the **Naganatha Temple**, 2 km away.

PATTADAKAL

On the banks of the Malaprabha River, Pattadakal, a World Heritage Site, was the second capital of the Chalukyan kings between the seventh and eighth centuries and the city where the kings were crowned. Ptolemy referred to it as 'Petrigal' in the first century AD. Two of their queens imported sculptors from Kanchipuram. Most of the **temples** ① *sunrise to sunset, foreigners Rs 250, Indians Rs 10*, cluster at the foot of a hill, built out of the pink-tinged gold sandstone, and display a succession of styles of the southern Dravida temple architecture of the Pallavas (even miniature scaled-down models) as well as the North Indian Nagara style, vividly illustrating the region's position at the crossroads of North and South Indian traditions. With one exception the temples are dedicated to Siva. Most of the site is included in the archaeological park. Megalithic monuments dating from the third to fourth centuries BC have also been found in the area.

Immediately inside the entrance are the small eighth-century **Jambulinga** and **Kadasiddheshvara Temples**. Now partly ruined, the curved towers survive and the shrine of the Jambulinga Temple houses a figure of the dancing Siva next to Parvati. The gateways are guarded by *dvarapalas*.

Just to the east is the eighth-century **Galaganatha Temple**, again partly damaged, though its curved tower characteristic of North Indian temples is well preserved, including its *amalaka* on top. A relief of Siva killing the demon Andhaka is on the south wall in one of three original porches.

The **Sangameshvara Temple** dating from the reign of Vijayaditya (AD 696-733) is the earliest temple. Although it was never completed it has all the hallmarks of a purely Dravidian style. Beautifully proportioned, the mouldings on the basement and pilasters divide the wall. The main shrine, into which barely any light is allowed to pass, has a corridor for circumambulation and a *lingam* inside. Above the sanctuary is a superbly proportioned tower of several storeys.

To the southwest is the late-eighth century North Indian-style **Kashi Vishveshvara Temple**, readily distinguishable by the *Nandi* in front of the porch. The interior of the pillared hall is richly sculpted, particularly with scenes of Krishna.

The largest temples, the **Virupaksha** (AD 740-744) with its three-storey *vimana* and the **Mallikarjuna** (745), typify the Dravida style, and were built in celebration of the victory of the Chalukyan king Vikramaditya II over the Pallavas at Kanchipuram by his wife, Queen Trailokyamahadevi. The king's death probably accounted for the fact that the Mallikarjuna temple was unfinished, and you can only mark out some of the sculptures. However, the king's victory over the Pallavas enabled him to express his admiration for Pallava architecture by bringing back to Pattadakal one of the chief Pallava architects. The Virupaksha, a Shaivite temple, has a sanctuary surrounded by passageways and houses a black polished stone Siva *lingam*. A further Shaivite symbol is the huge 2.6-m-high chlorite stone *Nandi* at the entrance, contrasting with the pinkish sandstone surrounding it. The three-storey tower rises strikingly above the shrine, the outside walls of which, particularly those on the south side, are richly carved. Many show different forms of Vishnu and Siva, including some particularly striking panels which show Siva appearing out of a *lingam*. Note also the beautifully carved columns inside. They are very delicate, depicting episodes from the *Ramayana*, *Mahabharata* and the *Puranas*, as well as giving an insight into the social life of the Chalukyas. Note the ingenuity of the sculptor in making an elephant appear as a buffalo when viewed from a different side.

In the ninth century the Rashtrakutas arrived and built a Jain temple with its two stone elephants a short distance from the centre. The carvings on the temples, particularly on the **Papanatha** near the village which has interesting sculpture on the ceiling and pillars, synthesizes North and South Indian architectural styles.

AIHOLE

ⓘ *The main temples are now enclosed in a park, open sunrise to sunset, foreigners Rs 100, Indians Rs 5, flash photography prohibited.*

Aihole was the first Chalukyan capital, but the site was developed over a period of more than 600 years from the sixth century AD and includes important Rashtrakuta and late Chalukyan temples, some dedicated to Jain divinities. It is regarded as the birthplace of Indian temple architectural styles and the site of the first built temples, as distinct from those carved out of solid rock. Most of the temples were dedicated to Vishnu, though a number were subsequently converted into Shaivite shrines.

There are about 140 temples – half within the fort walls – illustrating a range of developing styles from Hoysala, Dravida, Jain, Buddhist, Nagara and Rekhanagara. There is little else. All the roads entering Aihole pass numerous temple ruins, but the road into the village from Pattadakal and Bagalkot passes the most important group of temples which would be the normal starting point for a visit. Some prefer to wander around the dozens of deserted (free) temples around town instead of joining the crowds in the park.

Durgigudi Temple is named not after the Goddess Durga but because it is close to the *durga* (fort). Dating from the late seventh century, it has an early *gopuram* structure and semi-circular apse which imitates early Buddhist *chaitya* halls. It has numerous superb sculptures, a series contained in niches around the ambulatory: walking clockwise they represent Siva and Nandi, Narasimha, Vishnu with Garuda, Varaha, Durga and Harihara.

According to recent research **Lad Khan Temple** has been dated from around AD 700, not from AD 450 as suggested by the first Archaeological Survey of India reports in 1907. This is indicated by the similarity of some of its sculptures to those of the Jambulinga Temple at Badami, which has been dated precisely at AD 699. Originally an assembly hall and *kalyana mandapa* (marriage hall), it was named after Lad Khan, a pious Muslim who stayed in the temple at the end of the 19th century. A stone ladder through the roof leads to a shrine with damaged images of Surya, Vishnu and Siva carved on its walls. It bears a striking resemblance to the megalithic caves that were still being excavated in this part of the Deccan at the beginning of the period. The roof gives an excellent view of the village.

Gaudar Gudi Temple, near the Lad Khan temple, is a small, rectangular Hindu temple, probably dating from the seventh century. It has a rectangular columned *mandapa*, surrounded on three sides by a corridor for circumambulation. Its roof of stone slabs is an excellent example of North Indian architecture. Beyond the Gaudar Gudi Temple is a small temple decorated with a frieze of pots, followed by a deep well. There are others in various states of repair. To see the most important of the remaining temples you leave the main park. Excavations are in progress, and the boundaries of the park may sometimes be fenced. Turning right out of the main park, the Bagalkot road leads to the **Chikki Temple**. Similar in plan to the Gaudar Gudi, this temple has particularly fine carved pillars. The beams which support the platform are also well worth seeing.

Ravan Phadi Cave Temple is reached from the main park entrance on the left, about 300 m from the village. The cave itself (formerly known as the Brahman) is artificial, and the sixth-century temple has a variety of carvings of Siva both outside and inside. One is in the *Ardhanarisvara* form (half Siva, half Parvati), another depicts Parvati and Ganesh dancing. There is a huge lotus carved in the centre of the hall platform; and two small eighth-century temples at the entrance, the one to the northwest dedicated to Vishnu and that to the south, badly weathered, may have been based on an older Dravidian-style temple.

The **Buddhist Temple** is a plain two-storey Buddhist temple on a hill beyond the end of the village on the way to the Meguti Temple. It has a serene smiling Buddha with the Bodhi Tree emerging from his head, on the ceiling of the upper floor. Further uphill is the **Jain temple**, a plain structure lacking the decorations on the plinth, columns and *gopuram* of many Hindu temples. It has a statue of Mahavira in the shrine within. Climb up through the roof for a good view of Aihole.

The **Meguti Temple** (AD 634) is reached from the Buddhist Temple down a path leading to a terrace. A left-hand route takes you to the foot of some stairs leading to the top of a hill which overlooks the town. This is the site of what is almost certainly the oldest building in Aihole and one of the oldest dated temples in India. Its 634 date is indicated by an inscription by the court poet to the king Ravikirtti. A Dravidian-style temple, it is richly decorated on the outside, and although it has elements which suggest Shaivite origins, it has an extremely impressive seated Jain figure, possibly Neminath, in the sanctuary which comprises a hall of 16 pillars.

The **Kunti Group** is a group of four Hindu temples (dating from seventh to ninth centuries). To find them you have to return down to the village. The oldest is in the southeast. The external columns of its *mandapa* are decorated with *mithuna*, or erotic couples. The temple to the northwest has beautifully carved ceiling panels of Siva and Parvati, Vishnu and Brahma. The other two date from the Rashtrakuta period.

Beyond these temples is the **Hucchappayya Math**, seventh century, which has sculptures of amorous couples and their servants, while the beams inside are beautifully decorated. There is a tourist resthouse close to the temples should you wish to stay.

→ HAMPI AND AROUND

Climb any boulder-toppled mountain around the ruins of the Vijayanagar Empire and you can see the dizzying scale of the Hindu conquerors' glory; Hampi was the capital of a kingdom that covered the whole of southern India. Little of the kingdom's riches remain; now the mud huts of gypsies squat under the boulders where noblemen once stood, and the double decker shopfronts of the bazar where diamonds were once traded by the kilo is now geared solely towards profiting from Western tourists and domestic pilgrims. Away from the hubbub and hassle of the bazar, Hampi possesses a romantic, hypnotic desolation. You'll need at least a full day to get a flavour of the place, but for many visitors the chilled-out vibe has a magnetic attraction, and some end up staying for weeks.

ARRIVING IN HAMPI

Getting there Buses and trains arrive in **Hospet** (see page 94), from where it's a 30-minute bus or auto-rickshaw ride to Hampi Bazar.

Moving on By far the best way to reach **Goa** (see page 96) is by train. The **Hampi Express** leaves Hospet four mornings a week, arriving in **Madgaon** (see page 111) early in the afternoon; book tickets in advance. Travel agents in Hospet and Hampi sell tickets for overnight sleeper buses, but this is a punishing trip on potholed roads.

Tourist information Tourist office ⓘ *on the approach to Virupaksha Temple, T08394-241339, 0800-1230, 1500-1830.* A four-hour guided tour of the site (without going into the few temples that charge admission) costs around Rs 400.

BACKGROUND

Hampi was founded on the banks of the Tungabhadra River in 1336 by two brothers, Harihara and Bukka, and rose to become the seat of the mighty Vijayanagar Empire and a major centre of Hindu rule and civilization for 200 years. The city, which held a monopoly on the trade of spices and cotton, was enormously wealthy – some say greater than Rome – and the now-sorry bazar was packed with diamonds and pearls, the crumbled palaces plated with gold. Although it was well fortified and defended by a large army, the city fell to a coalition of northern Muslim rulers, the Deccan Sultans, at Talikota in 1565. The invading armies didn't crave the city for themselves, and instead sacked it, smiting symbolic blows to Hindu deities and taking huge chunks out of many of the remaining white granite carvings. Today, the craggy 26-sq-km site holds the ghost of a capital complete with aqueducts, elephant stables and baths as big as palaces. The dry arable land is slowly being peeled back by archaeologists to expose more and more of the kingdom's ruins.

The site for the capital was chosen for strategic reasons, but the craftsmen adopted an ingenious style to blend in their architectural masterpieces with the barren and rocky landscape. Most of the site is early 16th century, built during the 20-year reign of Krishna Deva Raya (1509-1529) with the citadel standing on the bank of the river. Today Hampi has a population of 3000 across its 62 sq km. Once that figure was closer to 1.5 million.

SACRED CENTRE

The road from the west comes over Hemakuta Hill, overlooking the sacred centre of Vijayanagar (the 'Town of Victory'), with the Virupaksha Temple and the Tungabhadra River to its north. On the hill are two large monolithic Ganesh sculptures and some small temples. The road runs down to the village and the once world-famous market place. You can now only see the wide pathway running east from the towering **Virupaksha** (*Pampapati*) **Temple** with its nine-storey *gopuram*, to where the bazar once hummed with activity. The temple is still in use; note the interesting paintings on the *mandapam* ceiling.

RIVERSIDE

You can walk along the river bank (1500 m) to the famous Vitthala Temple. The path is easy and passes several interesting ruins including small 'cave' temples – worthwhile with a guide. Alternatively, a road skirts the Royal Enclosure to the south and goes all the way to the Vitthala Temple. On the way back (especially if it's at sunset) it's worth stopping to see

Raghunatha Temple, on a hilltop, with its Dravidian style, quiet atmosphere and excellent view of the countryside from the rocks above.

After passing **Achyuta Bazar**, which leads to the Tiruvengalanatha Temple 400 m to the south, the riverside path goes near **Sugriva's Cave**, where it is said that Sita's jewels, dropped as she was abducted by the demon Ravana, were hidden by Sugriva. There are good views of the ancient ruined bridge to the east, and nearby the path continues past the only early period Vaishnavite shrine, the 14th-century **Narasimha Temple**. The **King's Balance** is at the end of the path as it approaches the Vitthala Temple. It is said

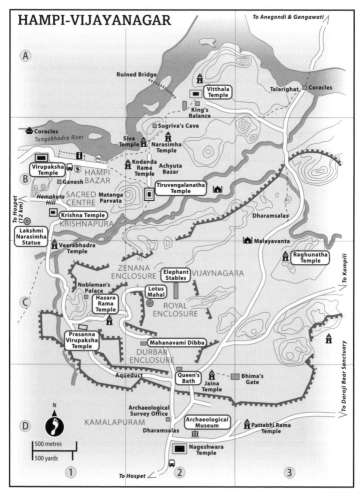

that the rulers were weighed against gold, jewels and food, which were then distributed to Brahmins.

Vitthala Temple ① *0830-1700, US$5/Rs 250, allows entry to Lotus Mahal on the same day*, a World Heritage Monument, is dedicated to Vishnu. It stands in a rectangular courtyard enclosed within high walls. Probably built in the mid-15th century, it is one of the oldest and most intricately carved temples, with its *gopurams* and *mandapas*. The *Dolotsava mandapa* has 56 superbly sculpted slender pillars which can be struck to produce different musical notes. It has elephants on the balustrades and horses at the entrance. The other two ceremonial *mandapas*, though less finely carved, nonetheless depict some interesting scenes, such as Krishna hiding in a tree from the *gopis* and a woman using a serpent twisted around a stick to churn a pot of buttermilk. In the courtyard is a superb chariot carved out of granite, the wheels raised off the ground so that they could be revolved!

KRISHNAPURA

On the road between the Virupaksha Bazar and the Citadel you pass Krishnapura, Hampi's earliest Vaishnava township with a Chariot Street 50 m wide and 600 m long, which is now a cultivated field. **Krishna temple** has a very impressive gateway to the east. Just southwest of the Krishna temple is the colossal monolithic **statue of Lakshmi Narasimha** in the form of a four-armed man-lion with fearsome bulging eyes sheltered under a seven-headed serpent, Ananta. It is over 6 m high but sadly damaged.

The road south, from the Sacred Centre towards the Royal Enclosure, passes the excavated **Prasanna Virupaksha** (misleadingly named 'underground') **Temple** and interesting watchtowers.

ROYAL ENCLOSURE

At the heart of the metropolis is the small **Hazara Rama Temple**, the Vaishanava 'chapel royal'. The outer enclosure wall to the north has five rows of carved friezes while the outer walls of the *mandapa* has three. The episodes from the epic *Ramayana* are told in great detail, starting with the bottom row of the north end of the west *mandapa* wall. The two-storey **Lotus Mahal** ① *0600-1800, US$5/Rs250, allows entry to Vitthala Temple on the same day*, is in the **Zenana** or ladies' quarter, screened off by its high walls. The watchtower is in ruins but you can see the domed **stables** for 10 elephants with a pavilion in the centre and the guardhouse. Each stable had a wooden beamed ceiling from which chains were attached to the elephants' backs and necks. In the **Durbar Enclosure** is the specially built decorated platform of the **Mahanavami Dibba**, from which the royal family watched the pageants and tournaments during the nine nights of *navaratri* festivities. The 8-m-high square platform originally had a covering of bricks, timber and metal but what remains still shows superb carvings of hunting and battle scenes, as well as dancers and musicians.

The exceptional skill of water engineering is displayed in the excavated system of aqueducts, tanks, sluices and canals, which could function today. The attractive **Pushkarini** is the 22-sq-m stepped tank at the centre of the enclosure. The road towards Kamalapuram passes the **Queen's Bath**, in the open air, surrounded by a narrow moat, where scented water filled the bath from lotus-shaped fountains. It measures about 15 m by 2 m and has interesting stucco work around it.

DAROJI BEAR SANCTUARY

① 15 km from Hampi Bazar, daily 0600-1800.

The relatively new Daroji sanctuary protects 55 sq km of boulder-strewn scrubland, which is home to around 120 sloth bears. The bears have become accustomed to regular treats of honey, courtesy of the park rangers, and a handful of them come regularly to a particular rock to feed. A watchtower placed high above the spot makes this perhaps the best place in India to observe the species in the wild. The sanctuary also has leopard, wolf, jackal, Eurasian horned owl, and good populations of the beautiful painted sandgrouse.

HOSPET

The transport hub for Hampi, Hospet is famous for its sugar cane; the town exports sugar across India, villagers boil the milk to make *jaggery* and a frothing freshly wrung cup costs you just Rs 4. Other industries include iron ore, biscuit making and the brewing of Royal Standard rum. The main bazar, with its characterful old houses, is interesting to walk around. **Tungabhadra Dam** *① 6 km west, Rs 5, local bus takes 15 mins,* is 49 m high and offers panoramic views. One of the largest masonry dams in the country, it was completed in 1953 to provide electricity for irrigation in the surrounding districts.

Muharram, the Muslim festival that marks the death of Mohammed's grandson Imam Hussein, is celebrated with a violent vigour both here and in the surrounding villages and with equal enthusiasm by both the area's significant Muslim population and Hindus. Ten days of fasting is broken with fierce drum pounding, drink and frequent arguments, sometimes accompanied by physical violence. Each village clusters around icons of Hussein, whose decapitation is represented by a golden crown on top of a face covered with long strings of jasmine flowers held aloft on wooden sticks. Come evening, fires are lit. When the embers are dying villagers race through the ashes, a custom that may predate Islam's arrival. The beginnings or ends of livestock migrations to seasonal feeding grounds are marked with huge bonfires. Cattle are driven through the fires to protect them from disease. Some archaeologists suggest that Neolithic ash mounds around Hospet were the result of similar celebrations over 5000 years ago.

NORTHERN KARNATAKA LISTINGS

WHERE TO STAY

Bidar
$ Mayura Barid Shahi (KSTDC), opposite New Bus Stand, T08482-228142. Small but well-kept rooms, and some larger suites, with a good restaurant downstairs. A good deal for the price.

Bijapur
$$ Hotel Pearl, opposite Gol Gumbaz, Station Rd, T08352-256002, www.hotel pearlbijapur.com. 32 rooms (17 a/c) in a modern, 3-storey, scrupulously clean, modest, mint pastel-coloured hotel set round a central courtyard with vegetarian basement restaurant (booze and non-vegetarian food through room service). Telephones, cable TV in all rooms, laundry and parking.

$ Hotel Navaratna International, Station Rd, T08352-222771. The grand colonnaded drive belies the modest price tag of the 34 rooms here (12 a/c). Communal areas scream with huge modernist paintings and rooms are done up with colour-coded care. TV, phone and smaller rooms have sit-outs. Very popular non-vegetarian courtyard restaurant, bar and pure vegetarian restaurant. They also have rooms and baths for drivers – a giant leap in the humane direction for an Indian hotel.

Badami
$$ Heritage Resort, Station Rd, T08357-220250, www.theheritage.co.in. Smart and spacious rooms in handsome stone cottages, each with its own sit-out opening on to a green lawn. There's a vegetarian restaurant, and the staff can arrange transport and guides.

Hampi
As of mid-2013, bulldozers have moved into the modern village of Hampi Bazaar and knocked down many buildings, including popular guesthouses and restaurants. It's possible that by the time you get there the only rooms will be across the river in the relaxed backpacker ghetto of Virupapur Gaddi – though these too may come under threat. Hotels around Hampi tend to be basic. if you crave comforts, Hospet has more options but less atmosphere.

$$ Mayura Bhuvaneswari, 2 km from site, Kamalapuram, T08394-241574. Government-run place that feels by turns weird and worn out; the budget rooms are overpriced, grimy and falling apart, while the newer suites have bizarre ultraviolet tube lights that lend the feel of sleeping in an abandoned nightclub. Decent food and chilled beer, but service is stretched.

$ Mowgli Guest House, 1.5 km from ferry in Virupapur Gaddi, T08533-287033, www.mowglihampi.com. A wide selection of rooms, from basic cells with shared bath to cute circular huts and lovely bright a/c rooms on the 2nd floor with expansive views over stunningly green paddy fields terracing down to the river. Hot water a few hours a day, international restaurant and pool table. Mellow without being too mellow. Boats across the river run from 0900-1700, making sunrise or sunset in the ruins a tough undertaking.

Hospet
$$$$-$$$ Malligi, 6/143 Jambunatha Rd, T08394-228101, www.malligihotels.com. 188 a/c rooms and large suites, restaurant and bar by pool (non-residents pay Rs 25 per hr), health club, exchange, travel (good Hampi tour), creakingly slow internet and overpriced STD/ISD service, but generally pleasant. 2-tier pricing in place: Indians pay Rs2-3000 less.

GOA

Goa, like San Francisco, Kathmandu and Spain, became a mecca for alternative living in the 1960s. Nowadays, it doesn't take much searching to find Costa Brava beer bellies and big-screen soccer intruding among the California tie-dye and palm-hung prayer flags, but if you don't need your sand Mr Whippy-white this tiny tranche of land remains, in pockets, unmatched. In most places you'll find little more than drowsy one-storey guesthouses strung along the beach, and away from the St George crosses and Kashmiri carpet shops the heartbeats of Goa's multilayered culture still pump good and strong: fishermen's boats rest on the sand beside sun loungers, Portuguese fados drift on the air in colonial villages, and the feral trance crew still hold their own at Anjuna's thrumming Saturday night market.

The relics of Goa's colonial past, though no match for the giant landmarks of broader India, are still rococo and baroque gems, half swallowed up by nature. Lush jungles twist their way around ruined forts, and huge banyans shelter centuries-old church spires and lavish basilicas.

There is humble everyday beauty to be had elsewhere too. At dawn in the villages, blue mists lie low and hazy across paddy fields and curl at the crumbling fronts of 18th-century Portuguese manors in pink, umber and blue. Exotic birds dive about sprawling raintrees and ravens caw as delivery boys push bicycles stacked with freshly baked breads. At sunset, the amber hues blaze against the mottled green Arabian Sea, fire embers smoke at the feet of chickens and pigs, bullock carts dredge through muddy fields of paddy and boys in board shorts swing their cricket bats in the straw stubble. Then at velvet twilight Goa's fisherfolk steal out of quiet harbours in brightly coloured trawlers, whose torches twinkle like a thread of fairy lights along the night horizon as they fill their nets with silvery pomfret and snapper. These gentle-paced and easy-living people also enjoy a shared flair for food, wine and song.

→ ARRIVING IN GOA

GETTING THERE

The train from Hospet stops in Margao (Madgaon), where a prepaid taxi booth lists fixed prices to destinations throughout Goa.

If you reverse this itinerary and come south from Mumbai, you can be in Goa in just over an hour on one of the many direct flights to Dabolim airport. There's a prepaid taxi stand here too: state your destination at the booth, pay the fare and obtain a receipt that will give the registration number of your taxi. A phalanx of drivers will sweep forth to commandeer your luggage and hustle you into the right cab.

MOVING ON

As a scenic last hurrah, return to **Mumbai** (see page 35) via the Konkan railway, a beautiful 12-hour journey up the coastal plain. You can board in Madgaon, or from the northern beaches jump on at Thivim or Pernem. There are plenty of direct flights from Dabolim airport to Mumbai's domestic terminal, or, if you're continuing your journey in India, direct flights also go to Chennai, Bengaluru and New Delhi. Finally, as we went to print news was emerging that the steamer service between Panjim and Mumbai is due to be reinstated by the end of 2013. Check online for details.

CABO DE RAMA, PALOLEM AND THE FAR SOUTH

Palolem's sheer prettiness has made it popular and perhaps less pretty than it once was, prompting some travellers to drift south to the tranquil beaches of neighbouring Colomb, Patnem and Galgibaga (beautiful Rajbag is ring-fenced by a five-star resort). Patnem, hemmed in by crags and river at either end, has mopped up most of Palolem's overspill, though it doesn't have the same rash of coconut trees that made Palolem so shadily alluring. To the north, Agonda is fast growing as a rival to Palolem's crown, yet for now retains its charm as a pretty fishing village strung out along a windswept casuarina-backed bay. There are more dramatic waves here than the calm waters of Palolem and Patnem. Further north again, the dramatic ruined fort at Cabo de Rama yields some of Goa's most dramatic views from its ramparts and has empty coves tucked about at its shores.

Getting there The nearest major transport junction for all these beaches is Canacona, also known as Chaudi, on the NH17 between Panjim and Karwar in Karnataka. Buses from here shuttle fairly continuously down to Palolem, and less frequently to Agonda, while there's a less frequent service from the beaches direct to Margao (37 km) which takes about an hour. Canacona station on the Konkan railway is only 2 km from Palolem. Canacona's main square has the bus and auto-rickshaw stands; rickshaws cost Rs 50-150 to any of these bays.

Moving on To return to **Margao** (see page 110), jump on one of the few daily buses from Palolem, or return to Canacona and jump on any northbound bus.

Getting around Once you're installed, the distances between beaches are small, and wandering between them becomes a leisure pursuit in itself. However, it can be worth hiring a scooter or motorbike to go further afield. The drive to Cabo de Rama, although riddled with hairpin bends, is particularly lovely, and going under your own steam means you can hunt out tucked away beaches nearby and stop over at the fishing dock at the estuary north of Agonda. Buses run along this route between the bays roughly hourly.

Cabo de Rama (Cape Rama) Legend has it that the hero of the Hindu epic *Ramayana* lived in this desolate spot with his wife Sita during their exile from Ayodhya, and the fort predated the arrival of the Portuguese who seized it from its Hindu rulers in 1763. Its western edge, with its sheer drop to the Arabian Sea, gives you a stunning vista onto a secluded stretch of South Goa's coastline.

The main entrance to the **fort** seems far from impregnable, but the outer ramparts are excellently preserved with several cannons still scattered along their length. The gatehouse is only 20 m or so above the sea, and is also the source of the fort's water supply. A huge tank was excavated to a depth of about 10 m, which even today contains water right through the dry season. If a local herdsman is about ask him to direct you to the two springs, one of which gives out water through two spouts at different temperatures.

Agonda Snake through forests and bright paddy south from Cabo De Rama towards Palolem to uncover artless Agonda, a windswept village backed by mountains of forestry full of acrobatic black-faced monkeys. Local political agitators thwarted plans for a five-star hotel and so have, temporarily at least, arrested the speed of their home's development as a tourist destination. However year on year, more restaurants and coco-huts open up along the length of the beach. There's no house music, little throttling of Enfield engines and you need to be happy to make your own entertainment to stay here for any serious length of time. Less photogenic than Palolem, Agonda Bay has pine-like casuarina trees lining the beach instead of coconuts and palms. The swimming is safe but the sea is livelier than in neighbouring Palolem. The northern end of the beach, close to the school and bus stop, has a small block of shops including the brilliantly chaotic and original **Fatima stores and restaurant** (Fatima Rodrigues, not one to be a jack of all trades, has limited her menu to just spaghetti and *thali*) and **St Annes bookstore**, a video library.

Palolem For a short spell, when the police cracked down most severely on parties up north, Palolem looked like it might act as the Anjuna overflow. Today, **Neptune's Point** has permission to hold parties every Saturday, but so far, Palolem's villagers are resisting the move to make the beach a mini-party destination and authorities are even stumping up the cash to pay for litter pickers. The demographic here is chiefly late 20s and 30-something couples, travellers and students. The large church and high school of **St Tereza of Jesus** (1962) are on the northern edge of town.

Beaches further south Over the rocky outcrops to the south you come to the sandy cove of **Colomb**. Wholly uncommercial, its trees are pocked with long-stayers' little picket fences and stabs at growing banana plants, their earthy homesteads cheek by jowl with fishermen's huts. The locals are currently holding firm against a controversial development planned by a Russian group, and for now the only sounds here are the rattle of coconut fronds and bird song. Although just a bay away, you could almost be on a different planet to Palolem.

At the end of the track through Colomb, a collection of huts marks the start of the fine sweep of **Patnem Beach**. The 500 villagers here have both put a limit on the number of shacks and stopped outsiders from trading, and as a result the beach has conserved much of its unhurried charm. The deep sandbanks cushion volleyball players' falls and winds whip through kite flyers' sails: but fishing boats far outnumber sun loungers. A hit with old rockers, Israelis and long-stayers, there is no nightlife, no parties and, no coincidence, a healthy relationship between villagers and tourism. Hindu temples in Patnem have music most Fridays and Saturdays, with tabla, cymbals and harmonica.

Further south, wade across a stream (possible before the monsoon) to reach the dune- and casuarina-fringed **Rajbag Beach**, its southern waters a-bob with fishing boats. Although it's virtually unvisited and has perfect swimming, the luxury five-star that opened here in 2004 provoked a storm of protest; allegations against the hotel have included the limited access to the sea, the failure to meet local employment quotas, and the rebuilding of the ancient Shree Vita Rukmayee Temple, which villagers argue was tantamount to the hotel 'swallowing our God'. The isolated **Kindlebaga Beach** is east of Rajbag, 2 km from Canacona.

Galgibaga Nip across the Talpona River by the ferry to reach a short strip of land jutting out to sea, where well-built houses lie among lucrative casuarina plantations. Like Morjim,

Galgibaga Beach is a favourite stopover for Olive Ridley **turtles**, which travel vast distances to lay their eggs here each November. Shacks are mushrooming, to environmentalists' concern.

Partagali and Cotigao Wildlife Sanctuary Some 7 km south of Canacona, a left turn off the NH17 leads through a massive concrete gateway to the **Shri Sausthan Gokarn Partagali Jeevotam Math**, a centre for culture and learning on the banks of the river Kushavati. The *math* (religious establishment) was set up in AD 1475 at Margao when the followers, originally Saivites, were converted and became a Vaishnav sect. During the period of Portuguese Christianization (1560-1568), the foundation was moved south to Bhatkal (in northern Karnataka). The sixth Swami returned the *math* to Partagali, and built its Rama, Lakshman, Sita and Hunuman temple. An ancient *Vatavriksha* (banyan tree) 65 m by 75 m, which represents this Vaishnav spiritual movement, is a sacred meditation site known as *Bramhasthan*. The tree and its *Ishwarlinga* (the *lingam* of the Lord, ie Siva) have drawn pilgrims for more than a millennium. The temple, which also has a typical tall Garuda pillar, celebrates its festival in March/April.

Just beyond the *math*, another road heads inland to **Cotigao Wildlife Sanctuary** ⓘ *www. goaforest.com/wildlife mgmt/body_cotigao.htm, year-round 0730-1730 (but may not be worthwhile during the monsoon), Rs 5, 2-wheelers Rs 10, cars Rs 50, camera Rs 25, video Rs 100*, one of the most densely forested areas of the state. The 86-sq-km sanctuary is hilly to the south and east and has the Talpona River flowing through it. There is a nature interpretation centre with a small reference library and map of the park roads at the entrance. The vegetation is mostly moist deciduous with some semi-evergreen and evergreen forest cover. You may be very lucky and spot gazelles, panther, sloth bear, porcupine and hyena, and several reptiles, but only really expect wild boar, the odd deer and gaur and many monkeys. Bird-spotting is more rewarding; rare birds include rufous woodpecker, Malabar crested lark and white-eyed eagle. You need your own vehicle to reach the treetop watchtowers and waterholes that are signposted, 3 km and 7 km off the main metalled road on a variable rough track. There are no guides available, but the forest paths are easy to follow – just make sure you have drinking water and petrol. The chances of seeing much wildlife, apart from monkeys, are slim, since by the opening time of 0730 animal activity has already died down to its daytime minimum.

The first tower by a waterhole is known as **Machan Vhutpal**, 400 m off the road, with great views of the forest canopy. The second tower is sturdier and the best place to spend a night (permission required).

Most visitors come for a day trip, but if you are keen on walking in the forest this is a great place to spend a day or two. You can either stay near the sanctuary office or spend a night in a watchtower deep in the forest. A short way beyond the sanctuary entrance the metalled road passes through a small hamlet where there is a kiosk for the villagers living within the reserve, which sells the usual array of basic provisions. If you are planning to spend a few days in the park it is best to bring your own fresh provisions and then let the staff prepare meals. Rudimentary facilities like snake proof campsites, with canvas tents available from the forest office. You'll also need written permission to stay in the forest rest house or watchtower from the **Deputy Conservator Of Forests** ⓘ *3rd floor, Junta House, Panaji*, as far in advance of a visit as possible.

The cheapest way to visit the park is to get a group together from Palolem. If you leave the beach just before 0700 you will be at the park gates when they open. Motorbikes are also allowed in the sanctuary.

GOING FURTHER
Gokarna

Shaivite pilgrims have long been drawn to Gokarna by its temples and the prospect of a holy dip in the Arabian Sea, but it's the latter half of the equation that lures backpackers. The long, broad expanses of beach stretching along the coast, of which the graceful double curve of Om Beach is the most famous, provide an appealing alternative hideaway to Goa, and the busy little town centre plays host to some fascinating cultural inversions: pilgrims wade in the surf in full *salwar kameez* while hippy castaways in bikinis sashay past the temple. Whilst the unspoiled beaches south of town remain the preserve of bodysurfers, *djembe* players and frisbee throwers, travellers spending time in the village would do well to respect local sensitivities.

Gokarna's name, meaning 'cow's ear', possibly comes from the legend in which Siva emerged from the ear of a cow – but also perhaps from the ear-shaped confluence of the two rivers here. Ganesh is believed to have tricked Ravana into putting down the famous Atmalinga on the spot now sanctified in the **Mahabalesvara Temple**. As Ravana was unable to lift the lingam up again, it is called *Mahabala* ('the strong one'). The **Tambraparni Teertha** stream is considered a particularly sacred spot for casting the ashes of the dead.

Most travellers head for the beaches to the south, reached by a rugged but easy to follow track over the headlands. **Kudle Beach** is an appealing crescent of sand hemmed in by low cliffs, occasionally good for low-key bodysurfing, while the fabled beauty of **Om Beach** attracts hordes of day trippers at weekends; both are backed by a wall of small hotels and coconut shacks. Both Om and Kudle beaches can get extremely busy in season, when the combination of too many people, a shortage of fresh water and poor hygiene can result in dirty beaches.

Beyond Om lie **Half Moon Beach** and **Paradise Beach**, popular with long-stayers, most easily reached by motorboat from Gokarna.

Trains on the Konkan railway from Goa stop at Gokarna Road, a 20-minute auto-rickshaw or taxi ride from the village. You can ask the driver to drop you on the hilltop above Om or Kudle beaches for an extra few rupees.

WHERE TO STAY

$$$$ SwaSwara, Om Beach, 15 mins from town, T08386-257132, www.swaswara.com. An elite retreat with "yoga for the soul" on a 12-ha complex on the curve of gorgeous Om Beach. Classes taught by Indian swamis are: ashtanga, hasya, kundalini, yoga nidra (psychic sleep) and meditation. From the hilltop the thatched Konkan stone villas look like an Ewok village, with private gardens and a pool; beds are strewn with flowers in the day and philosophical quotes in the evening. But despite its size and expense the resort has virtually no visual impact on the beach, and fishermen can still shelter under the mangroves out front. Also offered are Ayurveda, archery, kayaking, trekking, butterfly and birdwatching, and jungle walks.
$ Nirvana Café, Om Beach, T08386-329851. A pleasant complex under coconut trees, with a choice of basic huts and solid concrete-and-tile cottages.
$ Shanti Nivas, Gayatri Rd, behind Nimmu's, T08386-256983. Set in a coconut grove just inland from the south end of Gokarna Beach. Choose from clean simple rooms in the main house, apartments in the annexe, or a couple of solid hexagonal huts with mosquito nets and mattresses.

The prosperous midriff of Goa is where the Portuguese were most deeply entrenched. Hidden away in the interior lie the beautiful fossilized remnants of centuries-old mansion estates built by the Goan elite, their sprawling drawing rooms paved with marble and stuffed with chandeliers and antiques. Closer to the beach, lush coconut thickets blend with stretches of iridescent paddy field, punctuated at intervals by the piercingly bright white spears of church steeples.

PANJIM (PANAJI) AND OLD GOA

Sleepy, dusty Panjim was adopted as the Portuguese capital when the European empire was already on the wane, and the colonizers left little in the way of lofty architecture. A tiny city with a Riviera-style promenade along the Mandovi, it's also splendidly uncommercial: the biggest business seems to be in the sale of *kaju* (cashews), gentlemen-shaves in the *barbieris* and *feni*-quaffing in the booths of pokey bars – and city folk still insist on sloping off for a siesta at lunch. The 18th- and 19th-century bungalows clustered in the neighbouring quarters of San Thome and Fontainhas stand as the victims of elegant architectural neglect. Further upriver, a thick swathe of jungle – wide fanning raintrees, the twists of banyan branches and coconut palms – has drawn a heavy, dusty blanket over the relics of the doomed Portuguese capital of Old Goa, a ghost town of splendid rococo and baroque ecclesiastical edifices.

Getting there Panjim is the transport hub of central Goa, with frequent buses running up the highway from Margao. The closest railway station is at Karmali, 10 km east. From the bus station it's a short walk or auto-rickshaw ride across Ourem Creek into the centre.

Moving on Frequent buses head north to **Mapusa** (see page 116), with connections to the beaches of north Goa.

Getting around Panjim is laid out on a grid and the main roads run parallel with the seafront. The area is very easy to negotiate on foot, but autos are readily available. Motorcycle rickshaws are cheaper but slightly more risky. Local buses run along the waterfront from the City Bus Stand past the market and on to Miramar.

Tourist information Goa Tourism Development Corporation (GTDC) ① *east bank of the Ourem Creek, beside the bus stand at Patto, T0832-243 8750, www.goa-tourism.com, Mon-Sat 0900-1130, 1330-1700, Sun 0930-1400.* Also has an information counter at Dabolim airport, and runs a moderately helpful information line, T0832-241 2121. **India Tourism** ① *Church Sq, T0832-222 3412, www.incredibleindia.com.*

Panaji is the official spelling of the capital city, replacing the older Portuguese spelling Panjim. It is still most commonly referred to as Panjim, so we have followed usage.

Background The Portuguese first settled Panjim as a suburb of Old Goa, the original Indian capital of the sea-faring *conquistadores*, but its position on the left bank of the Mandovi River had already attracted Bijapur's Muslim king Yusuf Adil Shah in 1500, shortly before the Europeans arrived. He built and fortified what the Portuguese later renamed the Idalcao Palace, now the oldest and most impressive of downtown Panjim's official buildings. The palace's service to the sultan was short-lived: Alfonso de Albuquerque seized it, and Old Goa upstream – which the Islamic rulers had been using as both a trading port and their main starting point for pilgrimages to Mecca – in March 1510. Albuquerque, like his Muslim predecessors, built his headquarters in Old Goa, and proceeded to station a garrison at Panjim and made it the customs clearing point for all traffic entering the Mandovi.

The town remained little more than a military outpost and a staging post for incoming and outgoing viceroys on their way to Old Goa. The first Portuguese buildings, after the construction of a church on the site of the present Church of Our Lady of Immaculate Conception in 1541, were noblemen's houses built on the flat land bordering the sea. Panjim had to wait over two centuries – when the Portuguese Viceroy decided to move from Old Goa in 1759 – for settlement to begin in earnest. It then took the best part of a century for enough numbers to relocate from Old Goa to make Panjim the biggest settlement in the colony and to warrant its status as official capital in 1833.

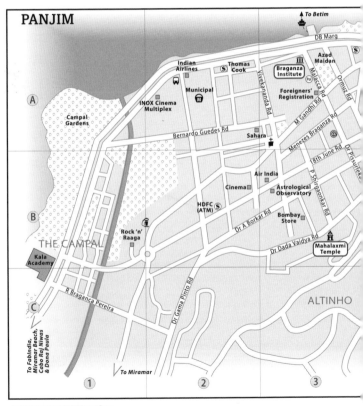

The waterfront The leafy boulevard of Devanand Bandodkar (DB) Marg runs along the Mandovi from near the New Patto Bridge in the east to the Campal to the southwest. When Panjim's transport and communication system depended on boats, this was its busiest highway and it still holds the city's main administrative buildings and its colourful market.

Walking from the east, you first hit **Idalcao Palace** ⓘ *behind the main boat terminal, DB Marg*. Once the castle of the Adil Shahs, the palace was seized by the Portuguese when they first toppled the Muslim kings in 1510 and was rebuilt in 1615 to serve as the Europeans' Viceregal Palace. It was the official residence to Viceroys from 1759 right up until 1918 when the governor-general (the viceroy's 20th-century title) decided to move to the Cabo headland to the southwest – today's Cabo Raj Niwas – leaving the old palace to become government offices. After Independence it became Goa's secretariat building (the seat of the then Union Territory's parliament) until that in turn shifted across the river to Porvorim. It now houses the bureaucracy of the state passport office. Next to it is a striking dark statue of the **Abbé Faria** (1756-1819) looming over the prone figure of a woman. José Custodio de Faria, who went on to become a celebrated worldwide authority

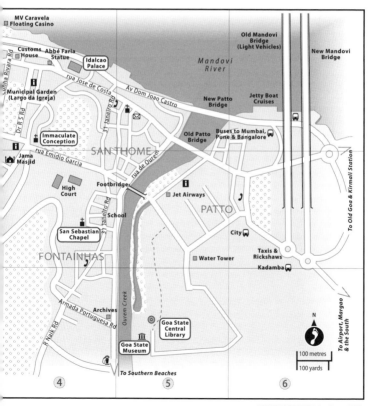

on hypnotism, was born into a Colvale Brahmin family in Candolim. The character in Dumas' Count of Monte Cristo may have been based on this Abbé.

Further west, on Malacca Road, almost opposite the wharf, are the central library and public rooms of the **Braganza Institute** ① *Mon-Fri 0930-1300, 1400-1745*. It was established as the Instituto Vasco da Gama in 1871 (the anniversary of the date that the Portuguese explorer da Gama sailed round the Cape of Good Hope), to stimulate an interest in culture, science and the arts. It was renamed for Luis Menezes de Braganza (1878-1938), an outstanding figure of social and political reform in early 20th-century Goa. The blue tile frieze in the entrance, hand painted by Jorge Colaco in 1935, is a mythical representation of the Portuguese colonization of Goa. An art gallery upstairs has paintings by European artists of the late 19th and early 20th centuries and Goan artists of the 20th century.

City centre The giant whitewashed 16th-century **Church of the Immaculate Conception** ① *Church Sq, Emidio Gracia Rd, Mon-Sat 0900-1230, 1530-1730, Sun 1100-1230, 1530-1700, free, English Mass Mon-Fri 0800, Sun 0830*, looms pristine and large up a broad sweep of steps off the main square, Largo Da Igreja, blue and white flags fluttering at its fringes. Its dimensions were unwarranted for the population of what was at the time of its construction in 1541, in Panjim, little more than a marshy fishing village; its tall, Portuguese baroque twin towers were instead built both to act as a landmark for and to tend to the spiritual needs of arriving Portuguese sailors, for whom the customs post just below the hill at Panjim marked their first step on Indian soil. The church was enlarged in 1600 to reflect its status as parish church of the capital and in 1619 was rebuilt to its present design. Inside is an ornate jewel in Goan Catholicism's trademark blue, white and gold, wood carved into gilt corkscrews, heavy chandeliers and chintz. The classic baroque main altar *reredos* (screens) are sandwiched between altars to Jesus the Crucified and to Our Lady of the Rosary, in turn flanked by marble statues of St Peter and St Paul. The panels in the Chapel of St Francis, in the south transept, came from the chapel in the Idalcao Palace in 1918. Parishioners bought the statue of Our Lady of Fatima her crown of gold and diamonds in 1950 (candlelight procession every 13 October). The church's feast day is on 8 December.

The Hindu **Mahalaxmi Temple** ① *Dr Dada Vaidya Rd, free*, (originally 1818, but rebuilt and enlarged in 1983) is now hidden behind a newer building. It was the first Hindu place of worship to be allowed in the Old Conquests after the close of the Inquisition. The **Boca de Vaca** ('Cow's Mouth') spring, is nearby.

There are some great themed walks with **Cholta Cholta** (www.choltacholta.com) around Panjim. *Cholta cholta* means 'whilst walking' in Konkani and their popular tours offer real insight into the city and its history. Many of the walks focus on the areas of San Thome and Fontainhas and its beautiful architecture.

San Thome and Fontainhas On Panjim's eastern promontory, at the foot of the Altinho and on the left bank of the Ourem Creek, sit first the San Thome and then, further south, Fontainhas districts filled with modest 18th- and 19th-century houses. The cumulative prettiness of the well-preserved buildings' colour-washed walls, trimmed with white borders, sloping tiled roofs and decorative wrought-iron balconies make it an ideal area to explore on foot. You can reach the area via any of the narrow lanes that riddle San Thome or take the footbridge across the Ourem Creek from the New Bus Stand and tourist office that feeds you straight into the heart of the district. A narrow road that runs east past the Church of the Immaculate Conception and main town square also ends up here. But probably the best way in is over the Altinho from the Mahalaxmi Temple: this route gives great views over the estuary from the steep eastern flank of the hill, a vantage point that was once used for defensive purposes. A footpath drops down between the Altinho's 19th- and 20th-century buildings just south of San Sebastian Chapel to leave you slap bang in middle of Fontainhas.

The chief landmark here is the small **San Sebastian Chapel** ① *St Sebastian Rd, open only during Mass held in Konkani Mon-Tue, Thu-Sat 0715-0800, Wed 1800-1900, Sun 0645-0730, English Mass Sun 0830-0930, free,* (built 1818, rebuilt 1888) which houses the large wooden crucifix that until 1812 stood in the Palace of the Inquisition in Old Goa where the eyes of Christ watched over the proceedings of the tribunal. Before being moved here, it was in Idalcao Palace's chapel in Panjim for 100 years.

The **Goa State Museum** ① *Patto, 0930-1730, free, head south of Kadamba Bus Stand, across the Ourem Creek footbridge, right across the waste ground and past the State Bank staff training building,* is an impressive building that contains a disappointingly small collection of religious art and antiquities. Most interesting are the original Provedoria lottery machines built in Lisbon that are on the first-floor landing. A few old photos show how the machines were used. Next to the museum, the new building housing Goa's **central library** has a collection that dates from 1832, including rare religious texts.

OLD GOA AND AROUND

The white spires of Old Goa's glorious ecclesiastical buildings burst into the Indian sky from the depths of overgrown jungle that has sprawled where admirals and administrators of the Portuguese Empire once tended the oriental interests of their 16th-century King Manuel. The canopies of a hundred raintrees cast their shade across the desolate streets, adding to the romantic melancholy beauty of the deserted capital. Tourists and pilgrims continue to flock to the remains of St Francis Xavier in the giddying baroque Basilica of Bom Jesus, where hawkers thrust spindly votive candles into their hands and compete to slake thirsts with fresh coconut, lime or sugarcane juice.

Getting there Old Goa lies on the south bank of the Mandovi on the crest of a low hill 8 km from Panjim. The frequent bus service takes 15-20 minutes. Buses drop you off opposite the Basilica of Bom Jesus; pick up the return bus near the police station. Karmali station on the Konkan Railway, just east of the centre, has taxis for transfers.

Getting around The major monuments are within easy walking distance of the bus stop. All monuments are open daily year-round 0830-1730.

Background Old Goa is to Christians the spiritual heart of the territory. It owes its origin as a Portuguese capital to Afonso de Albuquerque and some of its early ecclesiastical development to St Francis Xavier who was here, albeit for only five months, in the mid-16th century. Before the Portuguese arrived it was the second capital of the Muslim Bijapur Kingdom. Today, all the mosques and fortifications of that period have disappeared and only a fragment of the Sultan's palace walls remain.

Under the Portuguese, Old Goa was grand enough to be dubbed the 'Rome of the East', but it was a flourishing port with an enviable trade even before the Portuguese arrived. The bustling walled city was peopled by merchants of many nationalities who came to buy and sell horses from Arabia and Hormuz, to trade silk, muslin, calico, rice, spices and areca nuts from the interior and other ports along the west coast. It was a centre of shipbuilding and boasted fine residences and public buildings.

After the arrival of the Portuguese, Old Goa swelled still further in size and significance. In the west lay barracks, mint, foundry and arsenal, hospital and prison. The banks of the Mandovi held the shipyards of Ribeira des Gales and next door lay the administrative and commercial centre. Streets and areas of the city were set aside for different activities and merchandise, each with its own character. The most important, Rua Direita ou dos Leiloes (Straight Street), was lined with jewellers, bankers and artisans. It was also the venue for auctions of precious goods, held every morning except Sunday. To the east was the market and the old fortress of Adil Shah, while the true centre of the town was filled with magnificent churches built by the Franciscans, themselves joined by waves of successive religious orders: first the Dominicans in 1548, the Augustinians from 1572, the Carmelites from 1612 and finally the Theatines from 1655. By the mid-17th century, the city, plagued by cholera and malaria and crippled economically, was abandoned for Panjim.

Basilica of Bom Jesus The Renaissance façade of Goa's most famous church, the Basilica of Bom (the Good) Jesus, a UNESCO World Heritage Site, reflects the architectural transition to baroque then taking place in Europe. Apart from the elaborate gilded altars, wooden pulpit and the candy-twist Bernini columns, the interior is very simple.

The church has held the treasured remains of **St Francis Xavier**, a former pupil of soldier-turned-saint Ignatius Loyola, the founder of the Order of Jesuits since the 17th century. Francis's canonization was in 1622.

The tomb, which lies to the right of the main chancel (1698), was the gift of one of the last of the Medicis, Cosimo III, Grand Duke of Tuscany, and took the Florentine sculptor

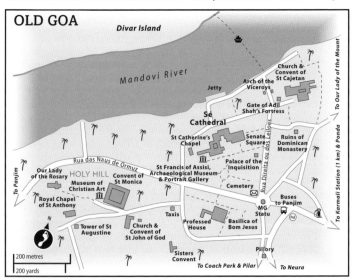

Giovanni Batista Foggini 10 years to complete. It is made of three tiers of marble and jasper; the upper tier holds scenes from the saint's life. The casket is silver and has three locks, the keys being held by the Governor, the Archbishop and the Convent Administrator. You can look down on to the tomb from a small window in the art gallery next to the church.

After his canonization, St Francis's body was shown on each anniversary of his death until 1707, when it was restricted to a few special private expositions. In 1752, the cadaver was again paraded to quash rumours that the Jesuits had removed it. The exhibition now happens every 10 to 12 years (the last exposition was in 2005), when the relics are taken to the Sé Cathedral. Feast Day is 3 December.

Sé Cathedral Across the square sits the Sé Cathedral, dedicated to St Catherine on whose day (25 November) Goa was recaptured by Albuquerque. Certainly the largest church in Old Goa, it could even be the biggest in Asia and was built on the ruins of a mosque by the Dominicans between 1562 and 1623. The building is Tuscan outside and Corinthian inside, with a barrel-vaulted ceiling and east-facing main façade. One of the characteristic twin towers collapsed in 1776 when it was struck by lightning. The remaining tower holds five bells including the Golden Bell (cast in Cuncolim in 1652). The vast interior, divided into the barrel-vaulted nave with clerestory and two side aisles, has a granite baptismal font. On each side of the church are four chapels along the aisles; on the right, these are dedicated to St Anthony, St Bernard, the Cross of Miracles and the Holy Spirit, and on the left, starting at the entrance, to Our Lady of Virtues, St Sebastian, the Blessed Sacrament and Our Lady of Life. The clerestory windows are protected by a shield crowned by a balustrade to keep out the sun. The main altar is superbly gilded and painted, with six further altars in the transept. The marble-top table in front of the main altar is where, since 1955, St Francis Xavier's remains have been held during their exposition. The main *reredos* has four panels illustrating the life of St Catherine. There is also an **art gallery** ⓘ *Mon-Thu, Sat 0900-1230, Sun 0900-1030, closed during services, Rs 5*.

Around the cathedral Southwest of the cathedral's front door are the ruins of the **Palace of the Inquisition**, where over 16,000 cases were heard between 1561 and 1774. The Inquisition was finally suppressed in 1814. Beneath the hall were dungeons. In Old Goa's heyday this was the town centre.

There are two churches and a museum in the same complex as the Cathedral. The **Church and Convent of St Francis of Assisi** is a broad vault of a church with two octagonal towers. The floor is paved with tombstones and on either side of the baroque high altar are paintings on wood depicting scenes from St Francis' life while the walls above have frescoes with floral designs. The original **Holy Spirit Church** in the Portuguese Gothic (manueline) style was begun by Franciscan friars in 1517; everything except the old doorway was replaced by the larger present structure in the 1660s (itself restored 1762-1765). The convent now houses the **Archaeological Museum and Portrait Gallery** ⓘ *T0832-228 6133, 1000-1230, 1500-1830 (closed Fri), Rs 5*, with sculptures pre-dating the Portuguese, many from the 12th-13th centuries when Goa was ruled by the Kadamba Dynasty. There are 'hero stones' commemorating naval battles, and 'sati stones' marking the practice of widow burning. There is also a rather fine collection of portraits of Portuguese governors upstairs that is revealing both for its charting of the evolution of court dress as well as the physical robustness of the governors inside. Some governors were remarkable for their

ON THE ROAD
Living the dream?

The happy combination of easy living, tropical sun, cheap flights and the innumerable beautiful Portuguese-style houses – big porches, bright white lime walls, window panes of oyster shell and red tile roofs crumbling into disrepair – all across Goa has triggered many a foreigner's fantasy of getting their own tattered toehold in the state.

Renting is commonplace, and for US$300-500 a month you can snare yourself a six-bedroom place so romantically derelict you'd swoon.

For longer term, there are plenty of modern condos set around swimming pools, simplifying the whole process, but setting yourself up in your own 100-year-old house takes graft. Goan houses for rent are likely to be vacant because children, emigrant or living elsewhere in the state, are bickering about how best to divest themselves of the brick and mortar inheritance of their parents' ancestral homes.

This means they are unlikely to be in good decorative order. One missing roof tile opens these old houses to a violent monsoon beating. Mud and lime walls dissolve quickly, wood rots and takes in termites, and shortly the wildlife (animal and vegetable) starts moving in. Initial set up costs as most places are unfurnished could easily set you back US$2000.

Agents are springing up to act as intermediaries in what is still a largely amateurish and deregulated industry, but you will pay pretty high charges to avoid the headache of having to handle things yourself. The best representative is probably the slick **Homes & Estates**, head ofice: Parra-Tinto, Bardez, T0832-247 2338, www.homesgoa.com, which also publishes a quarterly magazine.

Making a longer-term commitment to the Goan property market used to be a breeze, but beware. In 2006, the state government launched a retrospective investigation into some 445 property deals brokered for foreign nationals, on the basis that many foreigners had taken advantage of Goa's decidedly lax enforcement of India's Foreign Exchange Management Act, which dictates that foreigners must be resident in the country for six months before purchases are legal.

Nor are Goan des reses quite the steal they once were: New-build two-bed condos can cost as little as US$34,000 but rise to US400,000.

One thing's for sure: if you are intent on joining the 5000 foreigners with homes in Goa, 3000 of them Brits, it's more important than ever to seek professional legal advice.

---

sickly pallor, others for the sheer brevity of their tenure of office, which must have set the portrait painters something of a challenge. (The ASI booklet on the monuments, *Old Goa*, by S Rajagopalan, is available from the museum, Rs 10.)

To the west is **St Catherine's Chapel**. It was built at the gate of the old city on the orders of Albuquerque as an act of gratitude after the Portuguese defeat of the forces of Bijapur in 1510. The original mud and thatch church was soon replaced by a stone chapel which in 1534 became the cathedral (considerably renovated in 1952), remaining so until Sé Cathedral was built.

On the road towards the Mandovi, northeast from the cathedral compound, lies the **Arch of the Viceroys (Ribeira dos Viceroys)**, commemorating the centenary of Vasco da Gama's discovery of the sea route to India. It was built at the end of the 16th century by his great-grandson, Francisco da Gama, Goa's Viceroy from 1597 to 1600. Its laterite block structure is faced with green granite on the side approached from the river. This was the main gateway to the seat of power: on arrival by ship each new Viceroy would be handed the keys and enter through this ceremonial archway before taking office. The statue of Vasco da Gama above the arch was originally surmounted by a gilded statue of St Catherine, the patron saint of the city. Walking east towards the convent from the arch you pass the **Gate of the Fortress of the Adil Shahs**, probably built by Sabaji, the Maratha ruler of Goa before the Muslim conquest of 1471. The now-ruined palace was home to the Adil Shahi sultans of Bijapur who occupied Goa before the arrival of the Portuguese. It was the Palace of the Viceroys until 1554 after which it served as both the hall of trials for the Inquisition and to house prisoners.

A little further still stands the splendid, domed baroque **Convent and Church of St Cajetan (Caetano)**. Pope Urban III dispatched a band of Italian friars of the Theatine order to spread the Gospel to the Deccani Muslim city of Golconda near Hyderabad but they got a frosty reception so headed back west to settle in Goa. They acquired land around 1661 to build this church, which is shaped like a Greek cross and is partly modelled on St Peter's in Rome. It is the last domed church in Goa.

The crypt below the main altar, where the Italian friars were buried, has some sealed lead caskets that are supposed to contain the embalmed bodies of senior Portuguese officials who never returned home. Next door is the beautiful former convent building which is now a pastoral foundation (closed to the public).

On a hill a good way further east is the modest **Chapel of Our Lady of the Mount**, dating from 1510, which gives you a good idea of how the other churches here must originally have looked. It is a peaceful spot with excellent panoramic views across Old Goa, evocative of the turbulent past when Albuquerque and Adil Shah vied for control of the surrounding area. The altar gilding inside has been beautifully restored. In front of the main altar lies the body of architect Antonio Pereira whose burial slab requests the visitor to say an Ave Maria for his soul.

Holy Hill Between the domineering central monuments of Old Goa's broad tree-lined centre and Panjim stand the cluster of churches of Holy Hill. The first building you reach (on your left) as you leave the central plaza is the **Church and Convent of St John of God**, built in 1685 and abandoned in 1835. The **Museum of Christian Art** ① *everyday 0930-1700, Rs 5*, is to the right, with 150 items gathered from Goa's churches, convents and Christian homes to give a rich cross section of Indo-Portuguese sacred craft in wood, ivory, silver and gold. There is a little outdoor café too.

Next door sits the **Convent of St Monica** (1607-1627), the first nunnery in India and the largest in Asia. A huge three-storey square building, with the church in the southern part, it was built around a sunken central courtyard containing a formal garden. At one time it was a royal monastery, but in 1964 it became a theological institute, the Mater Dei Institute for Nuns. It was here in 1936 that Bishop Dom Frei Miguel Rangel is believed to have had a vision of the Christ figure on the Miraculous Cross opening his eyes, his stigmata bleeding and his lips quivering as if to speak. The vision was repeated later that year in the presence of the Bishop, the Viceroy Dom Pedro de Silva and a large congregation.

It is well worth the effort of the hike, taking the left fork of the road, to reach the **Royal Chapel of St Anthony** (1543) – dedicated to Portugal's national saint and restored by its government in 1961 – and, opposite, the **Tower of St Augustine**. The Augustinians came to Goa in 1572; the church they immediately began, bar the belfry, now lies in ruins. It once boasted eight chapels, a convent and an excellent library and was enlarged to become one of the finest in the kingdom. It was finally abandoned in 1835 because of religious persecution. The vault collapsed in 1842, burying the image; the façade and main tower followed in 1931 and 1938. Only one of the original four towers survives. The large bell now hangs in Panjim's Church of the Immaculate Conception. The Archaeological Survey of India is spearheading extensive repairs.

Behind is the **Chapel of Our Lady of the Rosary** (1526). Belonging to the earliest period of church building, it is called Manueline after Manuel I, the Portuguese king who oversaw a period of great prosperity that coincided with the country's conquest of Goa. The use of Hindu and Muslim craftsmen in building the chapel led to an architectural style that borrowed from Iberian decoration but also absorbed both local naturalistic motifs and Islamic elements (seen on the marble cenotaph). The church here has a two-storey entrance, a single tower and low flanking turrets. It was from here that Albuquerque directed the battle against the Adil Shahi forces in 1510.

AROUND PANJIM
Across the river from Panjim stands the **Fort of Reis Magos**, built by Albuquerque in 1551 to protect the narrowest neck of the Mandovi estuary, its angular 16th-century battlements now overrun with jungle. The nextdoor church is where the village gets its name – this was where the first Mass on Goan soil was celebrated in 1550, and the Hindu temple was promptly turned over into a church to the three Magi Kings – Gaspar, Melchior and Balthazar – whose stories are told on the inside reredos.

Five kilometres north of Panjim is the fascinating **Houses of Goa Museum** ⓘ *www.archgoa.org*, created by architect Gerard da Cunha on a traffic island. It's a beautiful building itself shaped like a ship and looks at traditional Goan architecture and style; it's a collection of doors, tiles, altars, lamps and rare postcards. It offers a unique insight into Goa's heritage.

→ MARGAO AND COASTAL SALCETE

A wide belt of golden sand runs the length Salcete's coast in one glorious long lazy sweep, hemmed on the landward side by a ribbon of low-key beach shacks; tucked inland lie Goa's most imposing and deluxe hotels. The thrumming nightlife of North Goa is generally absent here, but some beaches, Cavelossim in particular, have been on the receiving end of a building boom kept afloat by Russian package tourists, while Colva has gone all out and built itself a line of Baywatch-style lifeguard shacks – buxom blonde lifesavers not included. Inland, in various states of decline, lie the stately mansions of Goa's landowning classes: worn-out cases of homes once fit for princes.

ARRIVING IN MARGAO AND COASTAL SALCETE
Getting there and around The railway station is at the south end of town, 1.5 km southeast of the bus stands and most hotels. Auto-rickshaws and motorcycle taxis are available for the transfer.

Moving on Buses to **Colva** (see page 112), **Benaulim** (see page 113) and points south leave from the local bus stand in the centre. Buses bound for **Panjim** (see page 101) and the north leave from the New Kadamba bus stand, 2 km north of town, with frequent shared rickshaws shuttling between the two. Several trains a day head north for **Mumbai** (see page 35).

Tourist information Goa Tourism Development Corporation (GTDC) ① *Margao Residency, south of the plaza, T0832-271 5204.* Also has a counter at the railway station, T0832-270 2298.

MARGAO (MADGAON)

Margao is a fetching, bustling market town which, as the capital of the state's historically richest and most fertile *taluka*, Salcete, is a shop window for fans of grand old Portuguese domestic architecture and churches. Sadly, in their haste to get to the nearby beaches, few tourists take the time to explore this charming, busy provincial town.

The impressive baroque **Church of the Holy Spirit** with its classic Goan façade dominates the Old Market square, the Largo de Igreja. Originally built in 1564, it was sacked by Muslims in 1589 and rebuilt in 1675. A remarkable pulpit on the north wall has carvings of the Apostles. There are also some glass cabinets in the north aisle containing statues of St Anthony and of the Blessed Joseph Vaz. Vaz was a homegrown Catholic missionary who smuggled himself to Sri Lanka dressed as a porter when the Dutch occupation challenged the island's faith. The church's feast day is in June.

The real gem of Margao is the glut of run-down 18th-century houses especially in and around Abade Faria Road, of which **da Silva House** ① *visits arranged via the GTDC*, is a splendid example. Built around 1790 when Inacio da Silva stepped up to become Secretary to the Viceroy, it has a long façade whose roof was once divided into seven separate cropped 'towers', hence its other name, 'Seven Shoulders'; only three of these have survived. The house's grandeur is also evident in its interiors, featuring lavishly carved dark rosewood furniture, gilded mirrors and fine chandeliers. Da Silva's descendants still live in a small wing of the house.

The **municipal market** (Mercado de Afonso de Albuquerque) is a labyrinthine treat of flower garlands, silks and agricultural yield.

CHANDOR, LOUTOLIM AND QUEPEM

By the late 18th century, an educated middle-class elite had emerged in the villages of the Old Conquests. With newly established rights to property, well-to-do Goans began to invest in large homes and very fine living. West of the Zuari River, the villages of Loutolim and Chandor are two of a number that saw the distinct development of estates and houses built on this grand scale. Their houses were stuffed with tokens of their Europeanization and affluence, mixed with traditions appropriated from their native ancestry, installing personal chapels instead of *devachem kuds*, or Hindu prayer rooms. Driving around inland Goa is simply stunning.

One beautiful example is the **Figuerda Mansion** (Casa Museu Vicente Joao de Figueiredo) in Loutolim and if you are lucky you get shown around by the lady of the house who is now in her 80s and has many a story to share about Goa. Ask for directions by the church in Loutolim as there are no signs. Despite being something of a backwater today, the once-grand village of Chandor nonetheless boasts several fine Portuguese mansions. Foremost among them is the enormous **Menezes Braganza family house** ① *13 km east of Margao, both wings usually open 1000-1730 but confirm by telephone. West Wing: T0832-278 4201, 1300-1400 or early evening after 1830; East Wing: T0832-278 4227; a donation of Rs 100 at the end of the tour is greatly appreciated.* Luis de Menezes Braganza was an influential journalist and politician (1878-1938) who not only campaigned for freedom from colonial rule but also became a champion of the less privileged sections of Goan society. The late 16th-century two-storey mansion he inherited (extended in the 18th and 19th centuries), still complete with much of the family furniture and effects, shows the sheer opulence of the life enjoyed by those old Goan families who established great plantation estates. The two wings are occupied separately by members of the Braganza family who have inherited the property.

The **West Wing**, which is better maintained and has finer antiques, is owned by Aida de Menezes Braganza. The guided tour by this elderly member of the family – when she resides here – is fascinating. She has managed to restore the teak ceiling of the 250-year-old library gallery to its original state; the old *mareta* wood floor survived better since this native Goan timber can withstand water. There is much carved and inlaid antique furniture and very fine imported china and porcelain, some specially ordered, and bearing the family crest.

The faded **East Wing**, occupied by Sr Alvaro de Perreira-Braganza, partly mirrors the West Wing. It also has some excellent carved and inlaid furniture and a similar large salon with fine chandeliers. The baroque family chapel at the back now has a prized relic added to its collection, the bejewelled nail of St Francis Xavier, which had, until recently, been kept guarded away from public view.

The guide from the East Wing of the Braganza House can also show you the **Fernandes House** ① *open daily, phone ahead T0832-278 4245, suggested donation Rs 100*, if he's not too busy. It's another example of a once-fine mansion just to the southeast of the village, on the Quepem road. This too has an impressive grand salon occupying the front of the house and a hidden inner courtyard. Recent excavations have unearthed an underground hiding place for when Christian families were under attack from Hindu raiders.

Back in Chandor village itself, the **Church of Our Lady of Bethlehem**, built in 1645, replaced the principal **Sapta Matrika** (Seven Mothers) **temple**, which was demolished in the previous century.

Chandor is closest to Margao but can also easily be visited from Panjim or the beaches in central Goa. It would be an arduous day trip from the northern beaches. Buses from Margao Kadamba Bus Stand (45 minutes) take you within walking distance of the sights but it is worth considering a taxi. Madgaon Railway Station, with connections to Mumbai and the Konkan coastal route as well as direct trains to Hospet, is close by. Heading south from Chandor to Quepem you can have a tour and a fantastic Portuguese-era lunch at **Palacio do Deao** (Priest's House), opposite Holy Cross Church in Quepem. This house has been lovingly restored by Ruben and Celia Vasco da Gama and has an interesting collection of old Goan stamps, coins and books. Time it so that you can have lunch here on their beautiful veranda – it's a multi-course affair with Indo-Portuguese food. Book in advance (T0832 266 4029, www.palaciododeao.com).

COLVA (COLWA)

Although it's just 6 km from the city and is the tourist hub of the southern beaches, sleepy Colva is a far cry from its overgrown northern equivalent Calangute. The village itself is a bit scruffy, but the beach ticks all the right boxes: powdery white sand, gently swaying palms, shallow crystalline waters and lines of local fishermen drawing their nets in hand over fist, dumping pounds of mackerel which are left to dry out in glistening silver heaps.

Margao's parasol-twirling elite, in their search for *mudanca* or a change of air, were the first to succumb to Colva's charms. They would commandeer the homes of local fisher-folk, who had decamped to their shacks for months leading up to the monsoon. The shacks have now traded up for gaudy pink and turquoise guesthouses and the odd chi-chi resort, but Colva's holiday scene remains a mostly domestic affair, beloved by Indian fun-seekers who'll willingly shell out the cash to go parasailing for 90 seconds.

Out on the eastern edge of town, the large **Church of Our Lady of Mercy** (Nossa Senhora das Merces), dating from 1630 and rebuilt in the 18th century, has a relatively simple façade and a single tower on the south side that is so short as to be scarcely noticeable, and the strong horizontal lines normally given to Goan churches by three of four full storeys is broken by a narrow band of shallow semi-circular arches above the second floor. But the church is much less famous for its architecture than for the huge fair it hosts, thanks to its association with the miraculous **Menino Jesus**. Jesuit Father Bento Ferreira found the original image in the river Sena, Mozambique, en route to Goa, and brought it to Colva where he took up his position as rector in 1648. The image's miraculous healing powers secured it special veneration.

The **Fama of Menino Jesus festival** (Monday of 12-18 October) sees thousands of frantic devotees flock to kiss the statue in hope of a miracle. Near the church, specially blessed lengths of string are sold, as well as replicas of limbs, offered to the image in thanks for cures.

BETALBATIM TO VELSAO

A short walk from Colva, **Betalbatim** is named after the main Hindu temple to Betall that stood here before the deity was moved to Queula in Ponda for safety. This is a pleasant stretch with a mix of coconut palms and casuarinas on the low dunes. At low tide, when the firm sand is exposed, you can cycle for miles along the beach in either direction.

The broad, flat open beaches to the north – **Velsao**, **Arossim**, **Utorda** and **Majorda** – are the emptiest: the odd fishing village or deluxe resort shelters under coconut thicket canopy.

Bogmalo is a small, palm-fringed and attractive beach that's exceptionally handy for the airport (only 4 km, and a 10-minute drive away). **Hollant Beach**, 2 km further on, is a small rocky cove that is fringed with coconut palms. From Bogmalo village you can get to **Santra Beach**, where fishermen will ferry you to two small islands for about Rs 350 per boat.

The quiet back lanes snaking between these drowsy villages make perfect bicycle terrain and Velsao boasts some particularly grand examples of old mansions.

VERNA

The church at Verna (the 'place of fresh air'), inland from the northern Salcete beaches on the NH17, was initially built on the site of the Mahalsa Temple, which had housed the deity now in Mardol (see page 126) and featured exquisite carvings, but was destroyed and marked by the cross to prevent it being re-used for Hindu worship. As a sanctuary for widows who did not commit *sati*, it was dubbed the Temple of Nuns.

Verna was also picked to house the fifth century BC, 2.5-m-high **Mother Goddess figure** from Curdi in Sanguem, which was under threat of being submerged by the Selaulim Dam project in 1988. Two megalithic sites were found in the area. It is surrounded by seven healing springs. Just north towards Cortalim are the popular medicinal **Kersarval springs**.

BENAULIM TO MOBOR

At Colva Beach's southern end lies tranquil **Benaulim**, which, according to the myth of Parasurama, is "where the arrow fell" to make Goa. It is now a relaxed village set under palms, where business centres around toddy tapping and fishing. The hub of village activity is Maria Hall crossing, just over 1 km from the beach. Beaches aside, Benaulim's main attraction is the beautifully created **Goa Chitra Museum** ① *Tue-Sun 0900-1800, Rs 100, www.goachitra.com*, that gives an insight into the day-to-day life of rice farmers, toddy tappers and fishermen of not-so-yesteryear.

On a hill beyond the village is the diminutive **Church of St John the Baptist**, a fine piece of Goan Christian architecture rebuilt in 1596. Although the gable façade, with twin balustraded towers, is striking, the real treat is inside, in its sumptuous altar *reredos* and wonderful rococo pulpit with its depiction of the Lamb of the Apocalypse from the Book of Revelation.

The picturesque lane south from Benaulim runs through small villages and past white-painted churches. Paddy gives way to palm, and tracks empty onto small seaside settlements and deserted beaches. Benaulim Beach runs into **Varca**, and then Fatrade, before the main road finally hits the shoreline amid a sprouting of resorts and restaurants at **Cavelossim**. Farthest south, **Mobor**, about 6 km from Cavelossim, lies on the narrow peninsula where the river Sal joins the sea. The Sal is a busy fishing route, but doubles as a lovely spot for boat rides.

→ NORTH GOA

While Baga and Calangute, the fishing villages first settled by the hippies, now stand as cautionary tales to all that's worst about mass tourism, the stretch of lovely beaches and laterite headlands stretching up towards the Maharashtra border are still where Goa's freak flag flies proudest – albeit somewhat at half mast nowadays.

The all night parties that once made Anjuna a magnet for Goa's trance freaks may have gone by the wayside, but the village's weekly flea market remains a brilliant bazar – like Camden or Portobello but with sacred cows, sadhus, fakirs and snake charmers – and makes it onto every holidaymaker's itinerary. The little stretch of shoreline from the northern end of Anjuna Beach to the Chapora River is beautifully desolate: rust-coloured rugged cliffs covered with scrub interrupt scrappy bays strewn with laterite boulders. Pretty cliff-backed Vagator stands just south of the romantic ruins of Chapora Fort, with its busy fishing jetty, where trawler landings are met by a welcoming committee of kites, gulls and herons wheeling hungrily on high, while further upstream around the pretty village of Siolim young men wade through mangrove swamps to sift the muds for clams, mussels and oysters. Over the Chapora lies Arambol, a warm, hippy backpacker hamlet, and its beach satellites of Mandrem, Asvem and Keri and the wonderful little Catholic enclave clustered around the ancient Tiracol Fort.

ARRIVING IN NORTH GOA
Getting there and around All of North Goa lies within easy reach of the hotels in Panjim or Calangute, but you'd be doing yourself a disservice to visit what are some of Goa's loveliest beaches on a day trip. Better to set up camp in one and make it your base to explore the rest.

The resort strip of Calangute is 16 km from Panjim, and connected to the capital by frequent buses, some of which continue north to Baga. Taxis and motorcycle taxis can get you up and down the coast from here, and there's a boat service from Baga to Anjuna on Wednesdays for the flea market. Mapusa, 14 km north of Panjim, is well connected to Panjim and has buses to Calangute, Anjuna, Chapora, Arambol, and the other northern

ON THE ROAD
Portuguese origins

The name Bardez may have come from the term *bara desh* (12 'divisions of land'), which refers to the 12 Brahmin villages that once dominated the region. Another explanation is that it refers to 12 *zagors* celebrated to ward off evil. Or it could be *bahir des*, meaning 'outside land' – ie, the land beyond the Mandovi River. It was occupied by the Portuguese as part of their original conquest, and bears the greatest direct imprint of their Christianizing inflfluence.

beaches. Once you're installed, every village has at least one place offering scooters and motorbikes for rent – by far the cheapest and most flexible way to zip up and down the coast, though you have to be watchful for speed bumps and other drivers.

Moving on North Goa has two stops on the Konkan Railway route between Goa and **Mumbai** (see page 35): Thivim, 10 km northeast of Mapusa, and Pernem, half an hour inland from Arambol. If you're flying, allow 1½ to two hours for the taxi ride from Arambol.

BAGA TO FORT AGUADA

Some 40 years ago, the faultless fawn shoreline of Bardez taluka was a string of fishing villages. Now the 9 km unbroken strand that stretches from Baga down through Calangute, Candolim and Sinquerim to the rocky promontory of Fort Aguada acts as sandpit to the bulk of Goa's travel trade. Chock full of accommodation, eateries, travel agents, money changers, beggars and under-dressed, over-sunned charter tourists, unchecked development has turned Calangute in particular into a largely concrete conurbation of breezeblock hotels and mini markets. Screw up your eyes and you can still see what brought the hippies here – wonderful coconut-fringed sands backed by plump dunes, occasionally broken by rocky headlands and coves – but it's only in the far south around Fort Aguada that this stretch of coast retains traces of its former wild appeal.

As the epicentre of beer-and-chips tourism in Goa, there's little to draw you to **Calangute** other than ATMs, nightlife and a smattering of genuinely excellent restaurants. If you find yourself in town, it's worth strolling up to look at the quirky hexagonal *barbeiria* (barber's shop) at the northern roundabout, while the striking gold and white **Church of St Alex** just outside town is a good example of Goan rococo. **Kerkar Art Complex** ① *Gaurawaddo, T0832-227 6017, www.subodhkerkar.com*, is a beautiful art space showcasing local notable Subodh Kerkar's paintings and installation work.

Baga is basically Calangute North: there's continuity in congestion, shops, shacks and sun loungers. Here though, there are also paddy marshes, water tanks and salt pans, the beach is still clean, and the river that divides this commercial strip of sand from Anjuna in the north brings fishermen pulling in their catch at dawn, and casting their nets at dusk. The north bank, or Baga River, is all thick woods, mangroves and birdlife; it has quite a different, more villagey feel, with a few classy European restaurants looking out across the river. You can take an hour to wade across the river at low tide, then walk over the crest of the hill and down into Anjuna South, or detour inland to reach the bridge.

South of Calangute, the wide unsheltered stretch of beach through **Candolim** and **Sinquerim** offers unusual visual stimulus courtesy of the unlovely rusting wreck of the

Sea Princess tanker. Press on south to reach **Fort Aguada**, built on the northern tip of the Mandovi estuary in 1612. The strongest coastal fort ever built by the Portuguese colonizers, with 200 guns along with two magazines, four barracks, several residences for officers and two prisons, it was intended to stop the Dutch from gaining a foothold in Goa, but saw most of its action in the Maratha raids on Bardez of 1741, its ramparts proving time and again impregnable. The main fortifications (laterite walls nearly 5 m high and 1.3 m thick) are still intact, and the buildings at sea level now house Goa's **Central Jail**, whose 142 male and 25 female inmates are incarcerated in what must be one of the world's prettiest lock-ups.

MAPUSA

Standing in the nape of one of Goa's east–west ridges lies Bardez's administrative headquarters: a buzzy, unruly market town filled with 1960s low-rise buildings set on former marshland on the banks of the Mapusa River; (Maha apsa' means 'great swamps, a reference to Mapusa's watery past). Mapusa town won't find its way onto many tourist postcards, but it's friendly, small and messy, is an important transport hub and has an excellent daily **municipal market**, worth journeying inland for, especially on its busiest day, Friday. Open from early morning Monday to Saturday, it peters out 1200-1500, then gathers steam again till night, and has giant rings of *chourica* sausage, tumbles of spices and rows of squatting fruit and vegetable hawkers.

Walk east for the small 16th-century St Jerome's Church, or 'Milagres', Our Lady of Miracles (1594), rebuilt first in 1674 then again in 1839 after a candle sparked a devastating fire. In 1961 the roof was badly damaged when the Portuguese blew up a nearby bridge in their struggle with the liberating Indian army. The church has a scrolled gable, balconied windows in the façade, a belfry at the rear and an interesting slatted wood ceiling. The main altar is to Our Lady, and on either side are St John and St Jerome: the *retables* (shelves behind the altar) were brought from Daugim. The church is sacred to Hindus as well as Catholics, not only because it stands near the site of the Shanteri Temple but also because 'Our Lady of Miracles' was one of seven Hindu sisters converted to Christianity. Her lotus pattern gold necklace (kept under lock and key) may also have been taken from a Hindu deity who preceded her.

The **Maruti Temple** ① *west of the market opposite taxi stand*, was built on the site of a firecracker shop where Rama followers in the 1840s would gather in clandestine worship of first a picture, then a silver image, of monkey god Hanuman after the Portuguese destroyed the local Hindu temples.

Barely 5 km east of Mapusa lies **Moira**, deep in the belly of a rich agricultural district that was once the scene of Portuguese mass baptisms. The town is ancient – some say it was the site of a sixth or seventh century AD Mauryan settlement – and until the arrival of the Portuguese it must have been a Brahmin village. A total of seven important temples were destroyed during the Inquisition and six idols moved to Mulgaon in Bicholim district (immediately east).

Today the village is dominated by the unusual **Church of Our Lady of the Immaculate Conception**. Originally built of mud and thatch in 1619, it was rebuilt during the 19th century with square towers close to the false dome. The balustrades at the top of the first and second floors run the length of the building and the central doorways of the ground and first floors have Islamic-looking trefoil arches that contrast with the Romanesque flanking arches. There is an interesting exterior pulpit. Inside, the image of the crucifixion is unusual in having its feet nailed apart instead of together. A Siva *lingam* recycled here as the base of the font after its temple was razed is now in the Archaeological Museum at Old Goa. Moira's famous long red bananas (grown nearby) are not eaten raw but come cooked with sugar and coconuts as the cavity-speeding sweet *figada*.

ANJUNA AND AROUND

When the freaks waded across the Baga River after the squares got hip to Calangute, Anjuna was where they washed up. The village still plays host to a large alternative community: some from that first generation of hippies, but the latest influx of spiritual Westerners has brought both an enterprising spirit and often young families, meaning there's fresh pasta, gnocci, marinated tofu or chocolate brownies to be had, cool threads to buy, great, creative childcare, amazing tattoo artists, alternative therapists and world-class yoga teachers. For the beautiful life lived cheap Anjuna is still hard to beat; the countryside here is hilly and lush and jungly, the beaches good for swimming and seldom crowded. A state crackdown has made for a hiatus in the parties for which Anjuna was once synonymous, but as you head south along the shore the beach shack soundtracks get progressively more hardcore, until Curlies, where you'll still find arm-pumping techno and trance.

The **Flea Market** ① *Dandovaddo, south Anjuna, Oct-Apr Wed 0800 till sunset, water taxis (from Baga) or shared taxis from anywhere in Goa*, is a brilliant hullabaloo with over 2000 stalls hawking everything from Gujarati wooden printing blocks to Bhutanese silver and even Burberry-check pashminas. The trade is so lucrative by the subcontinent's standards that for six months a year several thousand Rajasthani, Gujaratis, Karnatakans and Tibetans decamp from their home states to tout their wares. The flea had very different origins, and was once an intra-community car boot-style bric-a-brac sale for the freaks. Anjuna's links with trade pre-date the hippies though – the port was an important Arab trading post in the 10th and 12th centuries.

Saturday Night Bazar ① *Arpora Hill, 1630-2400*, is a more sanitized and less headlong version of the flea. There's no shortage of dazzling stall fronts draped with glittering saris and the beautiful Rajasthani fare, but while there are fewer stalls there's more variety here; expats who've crafted everything from organic yoga clothes and designer mosquito nets to handmade leather goods are more likely to pitch up here than at the Wednesday event. But there's no need to shop at all – the live music and huge range of food stalls make the Night Bazaar the weekly social event for tourist and long-stayer alike. You'll find most of North Goa out for the evening, and many businesses shut up shop for the night as a result of the bazar's magnetic appeal. Bring cash and an appetite.

The Anjuna area is also home to two of Goa's best contemporary yoga schools. **Brahmani** ① *www.brahmaniyoga.com*, housed in in the grounds of Tito's **White House**, runs workshops and drop-in classes, from excellent *ashtanga*, Mysore-style, to more free-flowing movement like dance yoga, and *Scaravelli*. Packages with unlimited yoga are offered, but accommodation is not on site or specifically for yoga students. Some 10 minutes away in the neighbouring village of **Assagao**, the **Purple Valley Yoga Retreat** ① *T0832-226 8364, www.yogagoa.com, offer retreat packages including yoga and meals (see box, page 120)*, runs two-week *ashtanga* retreats with leading teachers like Sharath Rangaswamy, grandson of Sri K Pattabhi Jois, David Swenson and Nancy Gilgoff, two of the first to introduce *ashtanga* to the West in the 1970s. Lessons are held in a lovely *shala* in delightful gardens, food is vegetarian and the atmosphere collegiate.

VAGATOR

Vagator's beaches are possibly Goa's most dramatic: here, muddied sand bays upset by slabs of gray rock, quite different from the bubblings of porous laterite in Anjuna, fall at the bottom of terraced red cliffs planted with coconut trees that lean out towards the crashing waves, some of their trunks painted bright neon from past parties.

Big Vagator Beach is a long sweep of beach to the right of the main access road, behind which stands the profile of the wide outer rim of the ruined **Chapora Fort** against a stunning backdrop of India's western coastline, stretching beyond Goa's northern borders and into Maharashtra. The factory you can just pick out in the distance marks the border.

To your left, running inland, is **Little Vagator Beach**, its terracing lorded over by **Nine Bar**, a giant venue with an unswerving musical loyalty to trance. Just out of sight is **Ozran Beach**, christened 'Spaghetti Beach' by English settlers for its Italian community. Though a bit scrappy and dogged by persistent sarong sellers, **Spaghetti** is more sheltered, more scenic and more remote than the other beaches, ending in tumbled rocks and jungle, with excellent swimming spots. To get straight to Spaghetti from Vagator follow the signposts to Leoney Resorts, then when you reach the headland turn off the tarmac road onto one of the gravel tracks following the sign for Shiva Place shack; coming from Anjuna, take the path that starts just inland from Zoori's and thread your way down the gravelly terracing.

CHAPORA FORT

Looming over the north end of Big Vagator Beach, there's little left of Chapora Fort but crumbling blocks of black rock overgrown with tawny grasses and a general air of tranquil ruination. Built by Adil Shah (hence the name, Shah pura), the remaining ramparts lead out to a jutting promontory that affords spectacular sunset views across the mouth of the Chapora River, where fishing boats edge slowly out of harbour and seabird flocks settle on the sand spits across from Morjim.

Chapora village itself may be too feral for some tastes. At dusk the smoke from domestic fires spreads a haze through the jungle canopy between which Portuguese houses stand worn and derelict. Down by the river's edge men lean to mend their fuzzy nets while village boys saunter out to bat on threshed fields, and Enfields and Hondas hum along the potholed roads bearing long-stayers and Goan village folk home – many of them toting fresh catch from the buzzing fish market (ignore the stern 'No Entry' signs and ride on in) held every sunset at the harbour. Along the village's main street the shady bars are decked with fairy lights and the internationals (who call Chapora both 'home' and, in an affectionate nod to its less savoury side, 'the Bronx') settle down to nurse their drinks.

The flat arc of the estuary here is perfect for cycling: the rim-side road will take you all the way out to the bridge at **Siolim** where you can loop back to take a look at the **Church of St Anthony**. Built in 1606, it replaced an earlier Franciscan church dating from 1568. Both Goa's Hindu and Catholic communities pray to St Anthony, Portugal's patron saint, in the hope of good fishing catches. The high, flat-ceilinged church has a narrow balustraded gallery and Belgian glass chandeliers, with statues of Jesus and St Anthony in the gabled west end.

Splendid Portuguese houses stand scattered about the village's shadows in varying degrees of disrepair; it's worth walking around to take in some of the facades. You can even stay in one which has been refurbished, the lovely Siolim House, see page 132. The ferry that once crossed the Chapora River at the northern end of the village no longer runs (there's a bridge instead) but it's worth heading up this way for the little daily fish market and the handful of food stalls selling fresh grilled catch. The village also has a basic bar, **Mandola**, on the coast road heading back towards Chapora, selling European snacks and cold beer.

ARAMBOL, KERI, MORJIM, ASVEM, MANDREM

The long bridge that spans the Chapora River joins Bardez to the last – and thus most heavily Hindu – of the new conquests, hilly Pernem *taluka*. This is the gateway to a series of pretty and quiet beaches that hug the coastal road in a nearly unbroken strip up to the Maharashtra border, where a tiny pocket of Catholicism squats in the shadow of the pretty pride of the district, Tiracol Church and Fort. Haphazard and hippy Arambol has a warm community feel and is rightly popular with open-minded travellers of all ages, who are drawn to its live music, the dolphins that fin along its beaches and its famous saltwater lake. Sunset takes on the magnitude of a ritual in Arambol: people gather to sing, dance, juggle, do *capoeira* or find a silent spot for meditation and contemplation. To the south, Mandrem and Asvem are more chic and less busy, and will suit those less prepared to compromise on their accommodation. With construction of a new airport near Pernem and a large road bridge over the Tiracol to Maharashtra finally open, Northern Goa is becoming more accessible, and there will be increased development no doubt.

Arriving in Arambol, Keri, Morjim, Asvem, Mandrem There are regular buses to the villages from Mapusa and from Chopdem. The beaches are about 10 minutes apart. If you are crossing the bridge at Siolim on a motorbike turn left off the new main road immediately after the bridge to use the smaller, more scenic coastal roads.

Arambol (Harmal) Arambol, which you reach when the plateau road noses down through paddy fields and cashew trees, is a beautiful long stretch of sand at the bottom of a bumpy dirt track that's fringed with stalls selling brightly coloured, heavily embroidered clothes and pretty *lungis*. This is the creative and holistic hub of Goa – many Western designers, artists, performers, yogis and healers have been inspired to make the area home, and because people have put down roots here, the village is abuzz with industriousness. Flyers advertise *satsang* with smiling Western gurus: there's also *tabla* classes and drumming circles, yoga teacher training, reiki and belly dancing. Arrive at the right time of year and you might catch the International Juggling Convention in full swing, or stumble across a phenomenal fire-dancing show by performers who work their magic on the stages of Vegas. Arambol is also synonymous with live music, with everything from Indian classical to open mike, Sufi musicians and psychedelic metal bands playing in rotation at the beach bars. Inevitably, though, Arambol's ever-growing popularity means both long and short-term accommodation get more expensive by the year.

You have to skirt the beach's northern cliff and tiny basalt rocky bays by foot to reach the real lure: a second bay cut off from the roads and a **natural 'sweet water' lake** that collects at the base of a jungle spring. The lagoon collects just metres from the high tide line where the lush forest crawls down to the water's edge. You can walk up the spring's path to reach a belt of natural mineral clay: an idyllic spot for self-service **mud baths**. Further into the jungle is the famous **banyan tree**, its branches straddling 50 m, which has long been a point of Hindu and hippy pilgrimage. Or clamber over the boulders at

ON THE ROAD
Sun salutations

It's one of those funny ironies that yoga, now at the zenith of its international popularity, is given a resounding thumbs down by your average metropolitan Indian, who's much more likely to pull on Lycra and go jogging or pump iron down the gym than pursue the perfect *trikonasana*. They look with curiosity at the swarms of foreign yogis yearning to pick up extreme postures from the various *guru-jis* scattered about the subcontinent. "For them, it's the equivalent of having hoards of middle-class Indians rocking up in Yorkshire to study something we see as outmoded as morris dancing," admits Phil Dane, who runs Yogamagic Canvas Ecotel.

While some Indians look askance at the vast numbers of *firangi* yogis, others are making the most of it. Yoga is a good line of work on the subcontinent. In some places, there are certainly a fair few yoga teachers to choose from. Some are put off by the commercialization by those who see *ashtanga* yoga for example as the lowliest building block towards the greater endeavour of advanced Hindu consciousness. Asana CDs, featuring cameos from students such as Sting, only serve to irk these traditionalists.

Similarly, yoga teacher Lalit Kumar, who runs Himalaya Yoga Valley in Goa, was often told that he should grow his hair, ditch his Western garb and grab a white kurta – live up to the image. He said, "Why? I'm just a yoga teacher." Many don the spiritual uniform and aim for the pedestal, both the teachers and the students reinforce their spiritual ego by telling everyone just how fit/spiritual/holistic they are. There is business to be had in selling enlightenment, it turns out. At one place you can even pay US$2000 for your course – enlightenment guaranteed and a certificate to prove it. Naturally India has its fair share of spiritual wisdom and compassionate gurus, but there is also a percentage of dodgy dealers and predatory gurus. Be aware of the showmen. Some might baulk at seeking out a Western teacher in India, but often Western teachers have a better understanding of the needs of their students. And it's important that we remember, "the guru is a finger pointing to the moon. If you hold on to the finger, you'll never get to the moon."

India remains, nevertheless, one of the best places to study the ancient art, and many people who have embarked on yoga courses purely for its physical benefits also end up reaping some mental and emotional rewards. Yoga done with awareness can give you a taste of the bigger picture. Just keep asking around to find the right teacher. As Viriam Kaur, who runs the Kundalini Yoga Roof Garden, says, "Maybe even more than finding the yoga that you most resonate with, it is essential that you find a teacher that you resonate with. You want a teacher that inspires you. But you also want a teacher that pushes your limits and makes you grow into your potential. The mantra for the Kundalini Yoga teacher as decried by Yogi Bhajan, is 'to poke, provoke, confront and elevate'!"

The large alternative communities settled around Arambol and Anjuna make good starting points if you are looking for some ad hoc teaching, but if you are travelling to India specifically to practice it's worth doing your homework first. Here are some places that are recommended. Going furthest north first, where there is more yoga than you can shake a yoga mat at, there are two places of special mention. **Samata Holistic Retreat Centre** (www.samatagoa.com) is 10 minutes inland from Arambol proper on a beautiful swathe of land. Bringing hints of Bali and using reclaimed wood from Indonesia this exceptional place focuses on retreats and has accommodation for 40 people with a beautiful pool surrounded by nature and an organic farm. There is also a drop-in space, **Samata and Tamarind Cafe**, with two great restaurants, a delightful swimming pool and drop-in yoga, dance classes and workshops. **Samata** keeps on inspiring as its profits also go to the **Dunagiri Foundation**, set up by the founder and working to preserve Himalayan herbs and ayurvedic plants. Another good option is **Kundalini Yoga Rooftop Garden and Healing Centre** (www.organickarma.co.uk), close to the beach on the way out of Arambol. This is one of the few places in India where you can study Kundalini Yoga as taught by Yogi Bhajan. It's a wonderful space for yoga, meditation, in-depth courses, therapeutic bodywork and they offer popular courses in Ayurvedic Yoga Massage.

Travelling south to Mandrem, you will find the beautiful **Ashiyana** (www.ashiyana-yoga-goa.com), which has had a recent revamp and offers yoga holidays and detox retreats. Many rooms have river views and are stacked with Rajasthani furniture and heaps of character. It's a peaceful place with large grounds, two yoga shalas, spa and natural swimming pool. In the very peaceful beach area of Mandrem you will also find **Himalaya Yoga Valley** (www.yogagoaindia.com), which holds great drop-in classes (morning and late afternoon) at an elevated *shala* at **Beach Street**. But the main focus here is exceptional Yoga Teacher Training with talented team headed up by Lalit Kumar. They run regular trainings throughout the season just outside Mandrem and then head to Europe and Thailand for the summer months. If you want to take your practice to the next level, this place is inspirational.

On Aswem Beach, the lovely **Yoga Gypsys** (www.yogagypsys.com) hosts yoga holidays, trainings and satsangs. There are terracotta bungalows, charming floppy-fringed bamboo huts and tipis in a palm grove right on the beach and close to a Hindu temple.

In Anjuna, you will find excellent drop-in classes, workshops and their own-brand teacher trainings at **Brahmani** (www.brahmaniyoga.com). There is also Mysore-style self practice and excellent *ashtanga*, as well as a smattering of free-flowing movement yoga classes and *Scaravelli*. Close by is **Yogamagic Canvas Ecotel** (www.yogamagic.net), which hosts a whole range of yoga classes and holidays in their stunning yoga temple and you can stay like a Maharani in a suite or Rajasthani hunting tents. This is a very special place. Some 10 minutes away in the neighbouring village of Assagao you find the renowned **Purple Valley Yoga Retreat** (www.yogagoa.com), which hosts the heavyweights of the yoga world like Sharath Rangaswamy, grandson of Sri K Pattabhi Jois, David Swenson and Nancy Gilgoff. Lessons are held in a lovely *shala* in delightful gardens, food is vegetarian and the atmosphere collegiate. Travel a little further into inland Goa to find **Satsanga Retreat** (www.satsangaretreat.com), a beautiful space with two inspiring *shalas*, a lovely pool and great accommodation. This is often where **Brahmani** host their longer trainings.

Skipping to South Goa, you will find two inspiring centres in Patnem Beach. **Harmonic Healing Centre** (www.harmonicingoa.com) have an enviable location high above the north end of the beach with superlative views so that you can perform your *asanas* while looking out to sea. There is drop-in yoga and holistic treats of all varieties. Nearby **Lotus Yoga Retreats** (www.lotus-yoga-retreat.com) focuses on yoga holidays and retreats with guest teachers from Europe, including the fantastic Dynamic Yoga teacher Dina Cohen.

Seek out different schools in the four corners of India: in Pune (BKS Iyengar), Mysore (Pattabhi Jois), Neyyar Dam (Sivananda), Anandapur Sahib (Yogi Bhajan – Kundalini Yoga) and Bihar (Paramahamsa Satyananda). There is also the International Yoga Festival in Rishikesh every year in February or March.

Good books include: BKS Iyengar's *Light On Yoga*, *Asana, Pranayama, Mudra, Bandha*, from the Bihar school, and anything by Georg Feuerstein.

the north to join the scrappy dirt track over the headland for the half-hour walk it takes to reach the achingly lovely and reliably empty **Keri Beach**.

Keri (Querim) and Tiracol Fort Goa's northernmost beach is uniquely untouched. The drive towards Keri (Querim) along the banks of the Tiracol River from Pernem passes through some stunning rural areas untouched by any tourist development.

Walk across deep dunes to a casuarina thicket and out onto empty sand that stretches all the way from the mouth of the Tiracol river to the highland that splits it from Arambol. **Querim** gets busy on weekends with Indian tourists and occasionally hosts parties, but remains a lovely spot of sand. You can reach the beach from the north on foot from the Tiracol ferry terminal, or from the south by walking round the headland from Arambol. The Tiracol ferry runs every 30 minutes 0600-2130 taking 15 minutes, depending on the tides. The ferry is still charming, but more redundant now the bridge is open.

Tiracol (Terekhol), at the northernmost tip of Goa, is a tiny enclave of just 350 Catholics on the Maharashtra border just 3.5 km across where *feni* production is the biggest business. Its name probably comes from *tir-khol* ('steep river bank') and it's a jungly little patch of land full of cashew trees, banyans, orange blossoms, black-faced monkeys and squirrels.

The small but strategic **fort** ① *0900-1800, cross Tiracol river by ferry (every 30 mins 0600-2130) and walk the remaining 2 km; ferries take cars and motorbikes*, stands above the village on the north side of the Tiracol River estuary on a rugged promontory with amazing views across the water. Its high battlement walls are clearly visible from the Arambol headland. Built by the Maharaja Khem Sawant Bhonsle in the 17th century, it is protected from attacks from the sea, while the walls on the land side rise from a dry moat. It was captured in 1746 by the Portuguese Viceroy Dom Pedro Miguel de Almeida (Marques de Alorna), who renamed it Holy Trinity and had a chapel built inside (now St Anthony's). You can explore the fort's battlements and tiny circular turrets that scarcely seem fit for slaying the enemy. The views south are magnificent. Steps lead down to a terrace on the south side while the north has an open plateau.

St Anthony's Church ① *open on Wed and Sun for Mass at 1730*, inside the tiny fort, was built in the early 1750s soon after the Portuguese takeover. It has a classic Goan façade and is just large enough to cater for the small village. In the small courtyard, paved with laterite blocks, stands a modern statue of Christ. The **Festival of St Anthony** is held here at the beginning of May (usually on the second Tuesday) instead of on the conventional festival day of 13 June.

Morjim (Morji) to Asvem Morjim, which stands on the opposite side of the estuary from Chapora, has two wide sweeping beaches that both sit at the bottom of separate dead end streets. This inaccessibility means that, development-wise, it has got away relatively unscathed. The southern, protected, turtle beach appears at the end of the narrow track that winds along the north bank of the Chapora rivermouth. Loungers, which are mostly empty, are strewn haphazardly north of the official-looking **Turtle Nesting Control Room**.

The wide shoreline with its gentle incline (the water is hip height for about 100 m) is washed by easy rolling breakers, making it one of North Goa's best swimming beaches. The northern beach, or **Little Morjim**, a left turn off the main coast road is, by comparison, an established tourist hamlet with guesthouses and beach huts. The road from Morjim cuts inland over the low wooded hills running parallel to the coast. After a few kilometres the road drops down to the coast and runs along the edge of northeast tilting **Asvem Beach**. (Morjim faces Chapora to the south and west.) The northern end of this peaceful palm-fringed beach is divided by a small river. It's a great stretch of beach and gaining in popularity with increasing development alas.

Mandrem Mandrem creek forces the road to feed inland where it passes through a small commercial centre with a few shops and a bank. Mandrem village has the **Shri Bhumika Temple** housing an ancient image. In the **Shri Purchevo Ravalnatha Temple** there is a particularly striking medieval image of the half-eagle, half-human Garuda, who acts as the *vahana* (carrier) of Vishnu.

A little further on, a lane off to the left leads down towards the main beach and a secluded hamlet in a beautifully shaded setting. The **beach** is one of the least developed along this stretch of coast; for the moment it is managing to tread that fine line between having enough facilities for comfort and enough isolation to guarantee idyllic peace. Further north there is a lagoon fringed by palm trees and some simple rooms, virtually all with sea view.

MOVING ON
To Mumbai

From Goa you can fly or take the train back to Mumbai (page 35) for an international flight home. For further information see page 96.

GOING FURTHER
Bhagwan Mahaveer and Goa's Hindu heartland

→PONDA AND INTERIOR SANGUEM

There is enough spirituality and architecture in the neighbouring districts of Ponda and Salcete to reverse even the most cynical notions of Goa as a state rich in beach but weak on culture. Once you've had your fill of basking on the sand you'll find that delving into this geographically small area will open a window on a whole new, and richly rewarding, Goa.

Also hidden away in the hinterland are a sprinkling of superb isolated nature resorts, and the state's best wildlife sanctuaries: remnants of the hugely biodiverse forests of the Western Ghats which offer particularly rich pickings for birdwatchers.

→PONDA AND AROUND

Ponda, once a centre of culture, music, drama and poetry, is Goa's smallest *taluka*. It is also the richest in Goan Hindu religious architecture. A stone's throw from the Portuguese capital of Old Goa and within 5 km of the district's traffic-snarled and fume-filled town centre are some of Goa's most important temples including the Shri Shantadurga at Queula and the Nagesh Temple near Bandora. Ponda is also a pastoral haven full of spice gardens and wonderfully scenic views from low hills over sweeping rivers. The Bondla Sanctuary in the east of the *taluka*, though small and underwhelming in terms of wildlife, is a vestige of the forest-rich environment that once cloaked the entire foothills of the Western Ghats.

ARRIVING IN PONDA
Getting there and around Ponda town is an important transport intersection where the main road from Margao via Borlim meets the east–west National Highway, NH4A. Buses to Panjim and Bondla via Tisk run along the NH4A, which passes through the centre of town. The temples are spread out so it's best to have your own transport: take a bike or charter an auto-rickshaw or taxi; you'll find these around the bus stand.

BACKGROUND
The Zuari River represented the stormy boundary between the Christianized Old Conquests and the Hindu east for two centuries. St Francis Xavier found a dissolute band of European degenerates in the first settlers when he arrived in the headquarters of Luso-India and recommended the formation of an Inquisition. Founded in 1560 to redress the failings within their own community, the Portuguese panel's remit quickly broadened as they found that their earliest Goan converts were also clinging clandestinely to their former faith. So the inquisitors set about weeding out these 'furtive Hindus', too, seeking to impose a Catholic orthodoxy and holding great show trials every few years with the public executions of infidels. Outside those dates set aside for putting people to death, intimidation was slightly more subtle: shrines were desecrated, temple tanks polluted and landowners threatened with confiscation of their holdings to encourage defection. Those unwilling to switch religion instead had to look for places to flee, carrying their idols in their hands.

When the conquistadors (or *descubridores*) took to sacking shrines and desecrating temples, building churches in their place, the keepers of the Hindu faith fled for the broad river banks and the Cumbarjua creek to its west, to build new homes for their gods.

PONDA

Ponda wasn't always the poster-boy for Goa's Hindu identity that it is today. The **Safa Mosque** (Shahouri Masjid), the largest of 26 mosques in Goa, was built by Ibrahim 'Ali' Adil Shah in 1560. It has a simple rectangular chamber on a low plinth, with a pointed pitched roof, very much in the local architectural style, but the arches are distinctly Bijapuri. Because it was built of laterite the lower tier has been quite badly eroded. On the south side is a tank with *meherab* designs for ritual cleansing. The gardens and fountains were destroyed under the Portuguese, today the mosque's backdrop is set off by low rising forest-covered hills.

KHANDEPAR

Meanwhile, for a picture of Goa's Buddhist history, travel 4 km east from Ponda on the NH4A to Khandepar to visit Goa's best-preserved cave site. Believed to be Buddhist, it dates from the 10th or 11th century. The first three of the four laterite caves have an outer and an inner cell, possibly used as monks' living quarters. Much more refined than others discovered in Goa, they show clear evidence of schist frames for doors to the inner cells, sockets on which wooden doors would have been hung, pegs carved out of the walls for hanging clothing, and niches for storage and for placing lamps. The site is hidden on the edge of a wooded area near a tributary of the Mandovi: turn left off the main road from Ponda, look for the green and red archaeological survey sign, just before the bridge over the river. Turn right after the football pitch then walk down the track off to the right by the electric substation.

FARMAGUDI

On the left as you approach Farmagudi from Ponda is a **Ganesh temple** built by Goa's first chief minister, Shri D Bandodkar, back in the 1960s. It is an amalgam of ancient and modern styles. Opposite is a statue of Sivaji commemorating the Maratha leader's association with **Ponda's Fort**. The fort was built by the Adil Shahis of Bijapur and destroyed by the Portuguese in 1549. It lay in ruins for over a century before Sivaji conquered the town in 1675 and rebuilt it. The Portuguese viceroy attempted to re-take it in October 1683 but quickly withdrew, afraid to take on the Maratha King Sambhaji, who suddenly appeared with his vast army.

VELINGA

Lakshmi-Narasimha Temple ① *just north of Farmagudi at Velinga, from the north take a right immediately after crossing a small river bridge*, is Goa's only temple to Vishnu's fourth avatar. The small half-man, half-lion image at this 18th-century temple was whisked away from the torches of Captain Diogo Rodrigues in 1567. Its tower and dome over the sanctuary are markedly Islamic. Inside there are well-carved wooden pillars in the *mandapa* and elaborate silverwork on the screen and shrine.

PRIOL

Shri Mangesh Temple ① *Priol, northwest of Ponda on a wooded hill, on the NH4A leading to Old Goa*, is an 18th-century temple to Siva's incarnation as the benevolent Mangesh is one of the most important temples in Goa. Its Mangesh *lingam* originally belonged to an ancient temple in Kushatali (Cortalim) across the river. The complex is typical of Goan Hindu temple architecture and the surrounding estate provides a beautiful setting. Note the attractive tank on the left as you approach, which is one of the oldest parts of the site. The complex, with its *agrashalas* (pilgrims' hostel), administrative offices and other rooms set aside for religious ceremonies, is a good representative of Goan Hindu temple worship: the temple is supported by a large community who serve its various functions. February 25 is **Jatra**.

MARDOL

Two kilometres on from Shri Mangesh, the early 16th-century **Mahalsa Narayani Temple** is dedicated to Mahalsa, a Goan form of Vishnu's consort Lakshmi or, according to some, the god himself in female form *Mohini* (from the story of the battle between the *devas* and *asuras*). The deity was rescued from what was once a fabulous temple in Verna at around the same time as the Mangesh Sivalinga was brought to Priol. The entrance to the temple complex is through the arch under the *nagarkhana* (drum room). There is a seven-storeyed *deepstambha* and a tall brass Garuda pillar which rests on the back of a turtle, acting as an impressive second lamp tower. The half-human half-eagle *Garuda*, Vishnu's vehicle, sits on top. A stone 'cosmic pillar' with rings, next to it, signifies the axis along which the temple is aligned. The new *mandapa* (columned assembly hall) is made of concrete, but is hidden somewhat under the red tiling, finely carved columns and a series of brightly painted carvings of the 10 *avatars*, or incarnations, of Vishnu. The unusual dome above the sanctuary is particularly elegant. A decorative arched gate at the back leads to the peace and cool of the palm-fringed temple tank. A palanquin procession with the deity marks the February **Mardol Jatra**, **Mahasivaratri** is observed in February/March and **Kojagiri Purnima** celebrated at the August/September full moon.

BANDORA

A narrow winding lane dips down to this tiny hamlet and its **temple ⓘ** *head 4 km west from Ponda towards Farmagudi on the NH4A, looking for a fork signposted to Bandora*, to Siva as Nagesh (God of Serpents). The temple's origin is put at 1413 by an inscribed tablet here, though the temple was refurbished in the 18th century. The temple tank, which is well stocked with carp, is enclosed by a white-outlined laterite block wall and surrounded by shady palms. The five-storey lamp tower near the temple has brightly coloured deities painted in niches just above the base, the main *mandapa* (assembly hall) has interesting painted woodcarvings illustrating stories from the epics *Ramayana* and *Mahabharata* below the ceiling line, as well as the *Ashtadikpalas*, the eight Directional Guardians (Indra, Agni, Yama, Nirritti, Varuna, Vayu, Kubera and Ishana). The principal deity has the usual *Nandi* and in addition there are shrines to Ganesh and Lakshmi-Narayan and subsidiary shrines with *lingams*, in the courtyard. The **Nagesh Jatra**, normally in November, is celebrated at full moon to commemorate Siva's victory.

In a valley south of the Nagesh Temple lies the **Mahalakshmi Temple**, thought to be the original form of the deity of the Shakti cult. Mahalakshmi was worshipped by the Silaharas (chieftains of the Rashtrakutas, AD 750-1030) and the early Kadamba kings. The sanctuary has an octagonal tower and dome, while the side entrances have shallow domes. The stone slab with the Marathi inscription dating from 1413 on the front of the Nagesh Temple refers to a temple to Mahalakshmi at Bandora. The *sabhamandap* has an impressive gallery of 18 wooden images of Vishnu. Mahalakshmi is special in that she wears a *lingam* in her headdress and is believed to be a peaceful, 'Satvik', form of Devi; the first temple the Portuguese allowed at Panjim is also dedicated to her.

QUEULA (KAVALE)

Just 3 km southwest from Ponda's Central Bus Stand is one of the largest and most famous of Goa's temples; dedicated to Shantadurga (1738), the wife of Siva as the Goddess of Peace. She earns the Shanti (Sanskrit for peace) prefix here because, at the request of Brahma, she mediated in a great quarrel between her husband and Vishnu, and restored peace in the universe. In the sanctuary here she stands symbolically between the two bickering gods. The temple, which stands in a forest clearing, was built by Shahu, the grandson of the mighty Maratha ruler Sivaji, but the deity was taken from Quelossim well before then, back in the 16th century. It is neoclassical in design: the two-storey octagonal drum, topped by a dome with a lantern, is a classic example of the strong impact church architecture made on Goan temple design. The interior of polished marble is lit by several chandeliers. Steps lead up to the temple complex which has a large tank cut into the hillside and a spacious courtyard surrounded by the usual pilgrim hostels and administration offices.

Shri Sausthan Goud Padacharya Kavale Math, named after the historic seer and exponent of the Advaita system of Vedanta, was founded between Cortalim and Quelossim. This Hindu seminary was destroyed during the Inquisition in the 1560s and was temporarily transferred to Golvan and Chinar outside Goa. After 77 years, in the early 17th century, the Math regrouped here in Queula, the village where the Shantadurga deity (which had also originated in Quelossim) had been reinstalled. There is a temple to Vittala at the Math. The foundation has another Math at Sanquelim.

→ NORTH OF PONDA

SPICE HILLS

There are a number of spice plantations in the foothills around northeast Ponda that have thrown open their gates to offer in-depth tours that detail medicinal and food uses of plants during a walk through these cultivated forests. These are surprisingly informative and fun. Of these, Savoi Spice Plantation is probably the most popular and the guide is excellent. Taxis from the coastal resorts cost around Rs 700 return from Candolim, but it's better value to ask a travel agent as many offer competitive rates including entrance fees.

Savoi Spice Plantation ① *6 km from Savoi, T0832-234 0272, www.savoiplantation.com, 1030-1730, tour Rs 350, 1 hr, awkward to reach by public transport, ask buses from Ponda or Banastari heading for Volvoi for the plantation*, now over 200 years old, covers 40 ha around a large irrigation tank. Half the area is wetland and the other half on a hillside, making it possible for a large variety of plants and trees to grow. The plantation was founded by Mr Shetye and is now in the hands of the fourth generation of his family, who regularly donate funds to local community projects such as the school and temple. All plants are grown according to traditional Goan methods of organic farming. The tour includes drinks and snacks on arrival, and concludes with the chance to buy packets of spices (good gifts to take home) and a tot of *feni* to 'give strength' for the return journey to your resort. You will even be offered several cheap, natural alternatives to Viagra, whether you need them or not.

Pascoal Spice Plantation ① *signposted 1.5 km off the NH4A, near Khandepar between Ponda and Tisk, T0832-234 4268, 0800-1800, tours Rs 300*, is pleasantly located by a river and grows a wide variety of spices and exotic fruit. A guided tour takes you through a beautiful and fascinating setting. Spices can be bought directly from the plantation.

Sahakari Spice Farm ① *on the Ponda–Khandepar road, Curti, T0832-231 1394*, is also open to the public. The spice tour includes an authentic banana-leaf lunch.

Tropical Spice Plantation ① *Keri, clearly signposted off the NH4A (just south of the Sri Mangesh Temple), T0832-234 0625, tours Rs 300, boats for hire Rs 100*, is a very pleasant plantation situated in a picturesque valley. Guides are well informed and staff are friendly. It specializes in medicinal uses for the spices, the majority of which seem to be good for the skin. At the end of the tour an areca nut picker will demonstrate the art of harvesting by shinning up a tall palm with his feet tied together in a circle of rope. The demonstration ends with the equally impressive art of descent, a rapid slide down the trunk like a fireman. After the tour a delicious lunch is served in the shade overlooking a lake where there are a couple of boats for hire. Visitors arriving in the early morning will find the boats an excellent opportunity for viewing the varied birdlife around the lake.

BONDLA WILDLIFE SANCTUARY

ⓘ *20 km northeast of Ponda, mid-Sep to mid-Jun, Fri-Wed 0930-1730. Rs 5, camera Rs 25, video Rs 100, 2-wheelers Rs 10, cars Rs 50. Buses from Ponda via Tisk and Usgaon stop near the sanctuary where you can get taxis and motorcycle taxis. KTC buses sometimes run weekends from Panjim. During the season the Forest Department minibus runs twice daily (except Thu) between Bondla and Tisk: from Bondla, 0815, 1745; from Tisk, 1100 (Sun 1030) and 1900. Check at the tourist office. If you are on a motorbike make sure you fill up with petrol; the nearest pumps are at Ponda and Tisk. Bondla is well signposted from the NH4A east of Ponda (5 km beyond Usgaon, a fork to the right leads to the park up a winding steep road).*

Bondla is the most popular of Goa's three sanctuaries because it is relatively easily accessible. The 8-sq-km sanctuary is situated in the foothills of the Western Ghats; sambar, wild boar, gaur (Indian bison) and monkeys live alongside a few migratory elephants that wander in from Karnataka during the summer. The mini-zoo here guarantees sightings of 'Goa's wildlife in natural surroundings', although whether the porcupine and African lion are examples of indigenous species is another matter. Thankfully, the number of animals in the zoo has decreased in recent years and those that remain seem to have adequate space compared to other zoos in India. The small **Nature Education Centre** has the facility to show wildlife videos, but is rarely used. Five-minute elephant rides are available 1100-1200 and 1600-1700. A deer safari (minimum eight people), 1600-1730, costs Rs 10. The park also has an attractive picnic area in a botanical garden setting and a 2.4-km nature trail with waterholes, lake and treetop observation tower.

→ CENTRAL AND SOUTHERN INTERIOR

Sanguem, Goa's largest *taluka*, covers the state's eastern hill borderland with the South Indian state of Karnataka. The still-forested hills, populated until recently by tribal peoples practising shifting cultivation, rise to Goa's highest points. Just on the Goan side of the border with Karnataka are the Dudhsagar Falls, some of India's highest waterfalls, where the river, which ultimately flows into the Mandovi, cascades dramatically down the hillside. Both the Bhagwan Mahaveer Sanctuary and the beautiful, small Tambdi Surla Temple can be reached in a day from the coast (about two hours from Panaji).

ARRIVING IN CENTRAL AND SOUTHERN INTERIOR

Getting there Buses running along the NH4A between Panjim, Ponda or Margao and Belgaum or Bengaluru (Bangalore) in Karnataka stop at Molem, in the north of the *taluka*. Much of the southeastern part of Sanguem remains inaccessible. Trains towards Karnataka stop at Kulem (Colem) and Dudhsagar stations. Jeeps wait at Kulem to transfer tourists to the waterfalls. If you are travelling to Tambdi Surla or the falls from north or central Goa, then the best and most direct route is the NH4A via Ponda. By going to or from the southern beaches of Salcete or Canacona you can travel through an interesting cluster of villages, only really accessible if you have your own transport, to see the sites of rock-cut caves and prehistoric cave art.

Getting around There is no direct public transport between Molem and the sites, but the town is the start of hikes and treks in December and January.

BHAGWAN MAHAVEER SANCTUARY

ⓘ *29 km east of Pondon on NH4A, T0832-260 0231, or contact Forest Dept in Canacona, T0832-296 5601. Open 0700-1730 except public holidays. Rs 5, 2-wheelers Rs 10, cars Rs 250. Or check Goa Tourism (www.goa-tourism.com) Entrance to Molem National Park, within the sanctuary, 100 m east of the Tourist Complex, is clearly signed but the 14 km of tracks in the park are not mapped. Tickets at the Nature Interpretation Centre, 100 m from the police check post in Molem.*

Goa's largest wildlife sanctuary holds 240 sq km of lush moist deciduous to evergreen forest types and a herd of gaur (*bos gaurus*, aka Indian bison). The **Molem National Park**, in the central section of the sanctuary, occupies about half the area with the **Dudhsagar Falls** located in its southeast corner; the remote **Tambdi Surla Temple** is hidden in the dense forest at the northern end of the sanctuary. Forest department jeeps are available for viewing within the sanctuary; contact the Range Forest Officer (Wildlife), Molem. Motorbikes, but not scooters, can manage the rough track outside the monsoon period. In theory it is possible to reach Devil's Canyon and Dudhsagar Falls via the road next to the Nature Interpretation Centre, although the road is very rough and it may require a guide. Make sure you have a full tank of petrol if attempting a long journey into the forest. You can stay overnight.

Sambar, barking deer, monkeys and rich birdlife are occasionally joined by elephants that wander in from neighbouring Karnataka during the summer months, but these are rarely spotted. Birds include the striking golden oriole, emerald dove, paradise flycatcher, malabar hornbill and trogon and crested serpent eagle.

DUDHSAGAR FALLS

ⓘ *There are train daytrips organized though Goa Tourism (www.goa-tourism.com) on Wed and Sun. It's a spectacular journey worth taking in its own right, as the railway tracks climb right across the cascades, but trains no longer stop at the falls themselves; to get to the pools at the bottom you can take a road from Kulem, where jeep owners offer 'safaris' through the jungle to the base of the falls. If taking the train simply for the view, it's best to travel through to Belgaum in Karnataka, from where there are good bus and train services back to Goa.*

The Dudhsagar Falls on the border between Goa and Karnataka are the highest in India and measure a total drop of about 600 m. The name, meaning 'the sea of milk', is derived from the white foam that the force of the water creates as it drops in stages, forming pools along the way. They are best seen just after the monsoon, between October and December, but right up to April there is enough water to make a visit worthwhile. You need to be fit and athletic to visit the falls. It's no longer possible to visit Dudhsagar by train, but we have retained the following description in case the station re-opens in the near future.

From the train station, a rough, steep path takes you down to a viewing area which allows you a better appreciation of the falls' grandeur, and to a beautifully fresh pool which is lovely for a swim (take your costume and towel). There are further pools below but you need to be sure-footed. The final section of the journey is a scramble on foot across stream beds with boulders; it is a difficult task for anyone but the most athletic. For the really fit and adventurous the arduous climb up to the head of the falls with a guide, is well worth the effort. Allow three hours, plus some time to rest at the top.

By road, motorbikes, but not scooters, can get to the start of the trail to the falls from Molem crossroads by taking the road south towards Kulem. From there it is 17 km of rough track with at least two river crossings, so is not recommended after a long period of heavy rain. The ride through the forest is very attractive and the reward at the end spectacular, even in the dry season. A swim in the pool at the falls is particularly refreshing after a hot and dusty ride. Guides are available but the track is easy to follow even without one.

TAMBDI SURLA

ⓘ *There is no public transport to Tambdi Surla but it is possible to hike from Molem. From the crossroads at Molem on the NH4A, the road north goes through dense forest to Tambdi Surla. 4 km from the crossroads you reach a fork. Take the right fork and after a further 3 km take a right turn at Barabhumi village (there is a sign). The temple is a further 8 km, just after Shanti Nature Resort. Make sure you have enough petrol before leaving Molem. It is also possible to reach the site along minor roads from Valpoi. The entrance to the temple is a short walk from the car park.*

This Mahadeva (Siva) Temple is a beautifully preserved miniature example of early Hindu temple architecture from the Kadamba-Yadava period. Tucked into the forested foothills, the place is often deserted, although the compound is well maintained by the Archaeology Department. The temple is the only major remaining example of pre-Portuguese Hindu architecture in Goa; it may well have been saved from destruction by its very remoteness.

WHERE TO STAY

$$$$ Avanilaya, on the island of Corjuem, 9 km east of Mapusa, T0832-248 4888, www.avanilaya.com. Just 4 elegant rooms in this stunning secluded house overlooking the Mapusa River, potentially by time of reading there will be more rooms available in neighbouring properties. Not much to do here except laze in bliss with Ayurvedic massages and facials, amazing food and mesmerizing views.
$$$ Wildernest, www.wildernestgoa.com. Amazing eco resort tucked into the border of Goa with Maharashtra and Karnataka – it's 1½ hrs from Mapusa. This eco-hotel sprung up as a protest – the land was to

be sold to a big mining company and in order to save it **Wildernest** was created. So this place is the real deal, they are concerned with the local wildlife and there is a research centre on-site and for guests there are birdwatching tours and waterfall treks. The luxe log cabins hug the valley with amazing views of the ghats and there is an infinity swimming pool hanging just above the horizon. Working closely with 6 local villages from all three states, they offer up delicious home-cooked food. This is a totally alternative view of Goa. Whole-heartedly recommended.

GOA LISTINGS

WHERE TO STAY

South Goa

$$$-$$ Dunhill Beach Resort, towards south end of the beach, T(0)832-264 7328, www.dunhillbeachresort.in. Having had a bit of a facelift, Dunhill offers up the most stylish accommodation on the beach with 6 chic wooden cabanas on the beach and then cheaper, but large and comfortable rooms at the back. There is a good restaurant serving up all of the usual favourites too.

$$$-$ Shanti Village, towards south end of the beach, T(0)9823-962154, www.shantiagonda.com. With lovely views and chic huts, Shanti has chic black huts on the beach and an intimate vibe. It's good value and they have another outpost towards the north end of the beach near **Simrose**, where there are some cheaper huts, although still very nice with tribal masks and textiles to decorate.

$$ Hidden Gourmet, Colomb, T(0)9923-686185, www.gourmetpatnem.com. As the name suggests this place is off the beaten track, or at least through the village and tucked away on the promontory overlooking Patnem Beach. Beautifully decorated stone rooms all with a stunning ocean view and 2 mango wood and bamboo huts with stylish open-roofed bathrooms. Recommended.

$$-$ Ordo Sounsar extreme north end of the beach, over a small bridge, T(0)9822-488769, www.ordosounsar.com. Simple yet stylish beach huts nestling north of the estuary away from the business and busyness of Palolem Beach. Exceptional location, amazing restaurant serving up traditional Goan tastes. Highly recommended.

$ Kaama Kethna, 5 km south of Agonda off Palolem Rd. www.kaamakethna.net, phone reception patchy so email kaamakethna@ymail.com. Beautiful bamboo huts with open-air bathrooms

perched in the jungle. Part of an enterprising organic farm there are 5 stylish huts and 2 treehouses and a lot more land to play with for creating new accommodation – really you feel your only neighbour is the jungle itself with just a mosquito net and swaying sari between you and Nature. You will find beautiful land, inspiring people, a yoga platform and a great and nourishing restaurant using the produce from the farm. There is an annual yoga festival, art projects and if you want to get your hands dirty there are opportunities for volunteering. You can walk through the jungle to Agonda Beach in 30 mins and to the neighbouring Butterfly Beach in 40 mins. Wholeheartedly recommended.

Central Goa

$$$$ Alila Diwa Goa, Adao Waddo, Majorda, T0832-274 6800, www.alila diwagoa.com. The latest of the lush hotels to open its doors in the Majorda area, it has already racked up a host of awards. Stunning lobby and beautiful infinity pool – beyond that the rooms are stylish and have lovely balconies.

$$$$-$$$ Vivenda Dos Palhacos, Costa Vaddo, Majorda, T0832-322 1119, www.vivendagoa.com. One of the most charming places you can lay your hat in Goa. Stunning renovation of old Portuguese mansion – all rooms are different: Madras has a beautiful outdoor bathroom so you can shower under the stars, The Chummery is a lovely cottage with its own veranda, there is the Darjeeling with a mezzanine floor and you can stay in a huge luxe tent beyond the pretty swimming pool. Dinners are a fantastic communal affair, although obviously you can opt out. Run by the hosts with the most Simon and Charlotte Hayward who come from the lineage of

Haywards 5000 and their bar is dedicated to the tipple. Wholeheartedly recommended.

$$$ Casa Susegad, T0832-264 3477, www.casasusegad.com. This is a special gem of a place tucked away in sleepy Loutolim village – you will find just 5 rooms here in a converted 300-year-old Portuguese house. There is a beautiful swimming pool, an enormous games room and delicious food, sometimes even home-smoked mackerel pâté or mango pie from the enormous mango trees. Norman and Carole have done a remarkable job restoring this place and are very happy to share their little bit of paradise with you.

$$$ The Panjim Peoples, opposite **Panjim Inn**, www.panjiminn.com. The latest heritage project from the Sukhija family, this one is genuinely top end with just 4 rooms, antique 4-poster beds and bathtubs, plus internet access. Changing art exhibitions on the ground floor.

$$ Panjim Inn, E212, 31 January Rd, T0832-222 6523, www.panjiminn.com. Goa's first heritage hotel is idiosyncratic, even in the context of the historic Fontainhas district. 14 rooms of varying size all fitted with 4-poster beds, a/c for an extra Rs 250.

$$-$ Afonso, near San Sebastian Chapel, Fontainhas, Panjim, T0832-222 2359. Atmospheric family-run guesthouse, obliging and friendly, 8 clean rooms with bath, shaded roof terrace for breakfast. It's first come first served, though, as the owners don't take advance bookings. Recommended.

$$-$ Art Escape Vaddi Beach, south Benaulim, T(0)989-228 6666, www.art escape.in. Lovely place to stay with wood and bamboo huts. There is lots of live music including a *Qawalli Sufi* music festival, art and holistic therapy workshops. It's a great place close to the beach to relax or be inspired.

North Goa
$$$$ Elsewhere's Beach House, Mandrem, T(0)9326-020701, www.asea scape.com. **Elsewhere** is 4 lovingly restored 19th-century houses, just a sigh from the beach. Some are closer to the sea while others have views of the saltwater creek. Facilities include maid service, day- and nightwatchman, but extra for cook. Minimum rental period 1 week at US$2000-4000. There are also the beautiful **Otter Creek Tents** with 4-poster beds Rajasthani-style close to the creek.

$$$$ Fort Tiracol Heritage Hotel, Tiracol, T0236-622 7631, www.forttiracol.com. In 2003 the owners of Nilaya in Arpora, took over Fort Tiracol to create an outpost of isolated, personalized luxury with unbroken views of the Arabian Sea. Just 7 exquisite rooms, all with giant en suite, set in the fort walls that surround the Catholic Church, which is still used by the 350 villagers of the wholly Christian Tiracol. This is Goa's most romantic hotel. Prices include breakfast and delicious dinners. Highly recommended.

$$$$-$$$ Siolim House, opposite Vaddy Chapel, Siolim, T0832-227 2138, www.siolimhouse.com. Lovingly restored 300-year-old house. This is a stunning property once owned by the governor of Macau. 4-poster beds, epic bathrooms and fantastic large windows. Restored in 1999, it had a further facelift in 2009 and the pool is outstandingly beautiful. Great food, chilled atmosphere. There is a sister property – **Little Siolim** – with just 3 rooms in another beautifully crafted house. And further up on the Arpora Hill there is a new development for rent aimed at yoga groups. Highly recommended.

$$$ Beach Street, Mandrem, T(0)9423-882600, www.beachstreet.in. Summer house of the Deshprabhu family built in the early 1920s, this interesting building has had many incarnations including a prawn hatchery and nightclub, now the family have transformed it into a beautiful resort with a courtyard swimming pool, restaurant and chic beach cabanas. There is also a yoga space here with regular drop-in classes and workshops run by the highly recommended **Himalaya Yoga Valley** team.

$$$ Yab Yum Eco Resort, Asvem Beach, T0832-651 0392, www.yabyumresorts. com. 10 deluxe 'eco-domes' made of local materials – blue painted lava rocks make up the bases, woven palm leaves and mango wood the roofs, spread across a huge shady expanse of coconut and banana grove tucked behind a row of trees from the sand dunes. These pods come in 2 sizes – family or single – but both have living areas, and en suite bathrooms. It's classy, discreet and bohemian. There are also some cottages on-site. There's a reading room over the sea, a yoga *shala*, swimming pool and a children's teepee crammed with toys. The price includes breakfast and papers. Also now new chic accommodation at their villa, **Artists' House**, which is absolutely stunning.

$$-$ O'Saiba, Junasvaddo, Mandrem, T(0)9552 997440/(0)8308-415655, sunnymehara@yahoo.com. **O'Saiba** offers a range of coco huts, bungalows and nicely decorated rooms. Also has a good restaurant by the beach.

$ Thalassa Huts, Vagator, T(0)9850-033537, www.thalassagoa.com. Tucked behind popular atmospheric Greek restaurant, great huts with attached bathrooms – a couple have their own rooftop chill-out area. It's a short walk down the cliff to the beach.

RESTAURANTS

South Goa

$$ Blue Planet, Palolem–Agonda road, 5 km before Agonda, T0832-264 7448, www.blueplanet-cafe.com. This Palolem institution has taken a risk and moved into the countryside just outside Agonda – but it's a beautiful risk to take. Great drive and lovely view from their new abode. On the menu, you will find an array of vegetarian and organic healthy treats.

$$ Home, Patnem. Great range of salads, pastas, and veggie specials, such as beetroot and vodka risotto – make sure you leave room for their legendary desserts like chocolate brownie and sharp lemon tart – with a very chilled chic beachfront vibe.

$$ Magic View, Colomb, in front of **Hidden Gourmet**, T(0)9960-917287. Remarkably popular Italian restaurant delivering fantastic pizzas served up on tree trunks, deliciously decadent pastas such as gorgonzola and fish specials.

$$ Ourem 88, close to Art Resort in Ourem area, T(0)869-882 7679. New player on the Palolem scene offering up exceptional food. With Jodi in the kitchen and Brett out front, there is a relaxed vibe and delicious food with specials like sea bass with rucola mash and great steaks on a menu that changes weekly. And leave room for deserts such as espresso brûlée and an awe-inspiring lemon tart. Booking essential. Highly recommended.

Central Goa

$$$ Martin's Corner, Betalbatim (coming from the south, look for sign on left after village), T0832-648 1518. Huge place in front of an old house, serving great seafood including lobster, tiger prawns and crab. As cricket superstar Sachin Tendulkar has bought a house here, it's become the hangout of choice for holidaying cricket stars and media types.

$$$ Zeebop, Utorda Beach, follow signs to Kenilworth resort, www.zeebopbythe sea.com. Lovely beachfront restaurant offering up a delicious range of seafood, try the crab *papads* and great Goan specialities. Recommended.

$$ Venite, 31 Janeiro Rd, T0832-222 5537. Mon-Sat 0800-2200, closes in the afternoon. The most charming of Panjim's eateries has 1st-floor balconies overlooking the San Thome street life and good music. Specializing in fish, this place has a great atmosphere.

$$ Viva Panjim, house no 178, signposted from 31 Janeiro Rd, T0832-242 2405.

This family-run joint in the atmospheric Fontainhas quarter spills out of the restaurant and into a courtyard, and dishes up Goan specials such as *xacuti* and *cafreal* along with seafood, plus takeaway parcels of Indian, Chinese and continental.

$ Anandashram, opposite **Venite**, 31 Janeiro Rd. Serving up platters of fish and veg *thali*, this is a great place to break *pao* (local bread) with the locals. Recommended.

North Goa

$$$ Bomras, Candolim towards Sinquerim, T(0)9822-10 6236, bawmra@yahoo.com. Mouth-watering Burmese and Asian fusion food, such as seared rare tuna, mussel curry and Nobu-esque blackened miso cod. Fantastic vegetarian dishes and curries too, washed down with quite possibly the best cocktail in the world, spiced with lemongrass and ginger. Beautiful chic setting amidst the bright lights of Candolim, you could almost blink and miss it. Highly recommended.

$$$ La Plage, Asvem, T(0)9822-121712. Hidden slightly from the beach, you can still feel the breeze in this lovely laid-back restaurant. The food is excellent and changes seasonally; you might discover seared rare tuna with wasabi mash, calamari risotto, or sage butter ravioli. Regulars daydream about the chocolate *thali*, and they do a good selection of wines and cocktails, including a fabulous peppery Bloody Mary with mustard seeds and curry leaves. Bookings essential.

$$$ Sublime, Morjim Beach. T(0)9822-484051. **Sublime** is a Goa institution – exceptional food guaranteed. Chris Saleem Agha Bee has opened up the latest incarnation of **Sublime** on Morjim Beach and it's a chic spin on the beachshack, offering a punchy Asiatic beef, delicious rare tuna with anchovy sauce, the renowned mega-organic salad and delicious melt-in-

the-mouth pesto and mozzarella parcels, to name but a few. The cocktails go down very easily and it's a laid back-vibe – the perfect combination for balmy Goan nights. Booking essential.

$$$-$$ Café Nu, Junnaswaddo, Mandrem Beach, T(0)9850-658568. Another helping from **Sublime** guru Chris Saleem Agha Bee – great food in laid-back locale. Mustard-encrusted fish, the non-yogi burger (Mandrem does cater to a large yogi clientele), the phenomenal mega-organic salad for the aforementioned yogis and the legendary chocolate bon-bons. Good food to linger over. Highly recommended.

$$ Anand, Siolim Rd, Anjuna. Roadside shack that looks like any other, except for the queue of people waiting for a table. This place has a devoted following from here to Mumbai and serves up the freshest seafood with every type of masala and all the Goan favourites.

$$ Gunpowder, Mapusa road, Assagao, T0832-226 8091, www.gunpowder.in. Inland from Anjuna, **Gunpowder** offers up more unusual South Indian food and dishes from Andhra Pradesh. They have an acclaimed sister restaurant in Delhi and they stay open during the monsoon. Another Delhi institution, **People Tree**, is on-site offering up fair trade clothes and recycled products.

$$ Matsya, Temple Rd, Arambol, www.samatagoa.com. This beautiful restaurant is inspired by the organic garden of **Samata Retreat**, the fresh seafood of Goa fused with delights from Israeli chef Gome. Breakfasts are a lazy affair and dinners draw a crowd of Westerners that call north Goa home – take their word for it, the food is amazing. If you get a chance, ask to visit their organic farm. And you can always work off the calories by taking a drop-in yoga or dance class here too. Highly recommended.

DREAM TRIP 2
Chennai → Madurai → Trivandrum 21 days

Chennai 2 nights, page 137

Mahabalipuram 1 night, page 149
Bus from Chennai 1½ hrs

Puducherry and Auroville 2 nights, page 156
Bus or taxi from Mahabalipuram (3 hrs)

Chidambaram 1 night, page 164
Bus from Puducherry (1½ hrs)

Gangaikondacholapuram en route, page 167

Kumbakonam 1 night, page 167
Taxi from Chidambaram (half day with stops)

Thanjavur 1 night, page 169
Bus from Kumbakonam (1 hr)

Tiruchirappalli en route, page 172

Chettinad 2 nights, page 174
Bus or train from Tiruchirappali (1½-2 hrs)

Madurai 2 nights, page 176
Bus or train from Karaikudi (2-3 hrs)

Kodaikkanal 2 nights, page 186
Bus from Madurai (3½-4 hrs); or train from Madurai to Kodai Road station then taxi to Kodaikkanal (2½ hrs)

Thekkady (Periyar National Park) 2 nights, page 188
Epic bus battle or taxi from Kodaikkanal (5-6/4 hrs)

Varkala 3 nights, page 191
Bus from Thekkady to Kottayam then train to Varkala (6 hrs ish) or taxi (5 hrs)

Thiruvananthapuram (Trivandrum) or Kovalam
2 nights, pages 193 and 195

GOING FURTHER

Gingee and Tiruvannamalai page 161
Bus from Pondicherry to Tiruvannamalai (3½ hrs) via Gingee (2 hrs); or direct bus from Chennai (5 hrs).

Rameswaram page 182
Bus (4½ hrs) or day tour from Madurai

Kanyakumari page 197
Train or bus from Thiruvanathapuram (2½-3 hrs)

DREAM TRIP 2
Chennai→Madurai→Trivandrum

Like a good Bollywood film, this journey through southernmost Tamil Nadu and Kerala sucks you in with a vivid burst of colour and noise, builds to a crescendo amidst the ash-smeared intensity of the Tamil temple trail, then takes a half-time plot twist and re-emerges with a new cast of characters – leopards and langurs in place of priests and pilgrims.

The story opens in Chennai, a deeply traditional city with a vibrant cultural scene. Allow a day to explore the Brahminical suburb of Mylapore, then head south for chilled-out Mahabalipuram, with its beaches and superb stone sculptures, and Puducherry, a French colonial outpost of colonnaded mansions, quirky cafés and expat-run boutiques.

Heading inland, you enter the delta of the great Kaveri River, amongst whose paddy fields and winding backwaters the Chola kings raised thousands of superbly wrought temples. The temple trail takes you through a string of spiritual citadels – Chidambaram, Thanjavur, Srirangam – each one battling to out-do the last in artistry and spiritual fervour. Things reach a giddy peak in Madurai, a city as old as Rome, whose mesmerizing temple to the 'fish-eyed' goddess Meenakshi towers above the concentric streets that funnel pilgrims into its towering god-strewn gateways.

From Madurai the route climbs to Kodaikkanal, a bracing highland refuge of woodland walks and glittering lakes. Westwards across the Kerala border lies Periyar National Park, home to tiger, wild elephant, and an innovative project that's turning yesterday's poachers into the tour guides of tomorrow.

After a couple of long days in the saddle, unwind on the pleasantly touristy beach of Varkala before the credits roll in Kerala's busy capital Thiruvananthapuram – a handy base from which to visit the holy toe-tip of India at Kanyakumari.

CHENNAI AND AROUND

Chennai (Madras), South India's sprawling chief metropolis and India's fourth largest city, is dubbed 'India's Detroit' thanks to its chiefly automotive industrial revolution. The analogy is apt in more ways than one. Chennai's beautiful Indo-Saracenic buildings now stand like islands of elegance in a sea of concrete sprawl, and seen from the back of a taxi crawling along Anna Salai in the rush hour, the city can seem to be little more than a huge, sweltering traffic jam.

Nevertheless, modern Chennai remains the de facto capital of Indian high culture – complex dances such as Bharatnatyam are still widely taught and practised here – and the city retains an air of gentility that's missing from the other Indian metros. Despite attempts to carpet-bomb the southern suburbs with IT parks and malls, you'll find little here of the boom of Mumbai or the overheated dynamism of Bengaluru. Chennai's urban elite of textile magnates, artists and web entrepreneurs still maintain their networks around the bars and walking tracks of the city's Raj-era clubs, where chinos and loafers rule and churidars and lungis are checked at the door.

Outside the gates of these green refuges, Chennai can be a hard city to love. It's polluted, congested, tricky to negotiate and lacks anything resembling a centre. Nevertheless, there are reasons to stick around for more than the customary pre- or post-flight overnight stay, particularly if you base yourself near the old Brahmin suburb of Mylapore, which with its beautiful temple towers, old-time silk emporia and dingy cafés, makes a worthy introduction to the Tamil temple circuit.

→ ARRIVING IN CHENNAI

GETTING THERE

Chennai's international and domestic air terminals are next to each other about 15 km south of the city. You'll find exchange facilities and ATMs that accept overseas cards after you pass through customs. Air-conditioned buses run from outside the international terminal to the main CMBT bus station at Koyambedu, via several of the main hotels and Egmore Station, roughly once an hour. Otherwise, it's best to take a prepaid taxi to your hotel. For the cheaper non-air-conditioned taxis head for the busiest counter you can see, state your destination and check for the licence number written on your receipt, then proceed into the scrum of waiting drivers outside. The other counters are for more comfortable and more expensive private cabs. If you come by train from further north in India you'll arrive at Central Station, in the northern part of the city centre. There are plenty of hotels nearby, and prepaid taxis and auto-rickshaw counters.

MOVING ON

Buses to **Mahabalipuram** (see page 149) leave every hour from from the vast CMBT bus terminal at Koyambedu. If you're staying in southern Chennai it's more logical to catch one from outside the bus stand at Thiruvanmiyur, in the far south of the city. Most efficient and least crowded are the air-conditioned buses that run down the East Coast Road to Pondicherry, leaving roughly once an hour.

GETTING AROUND

Chennai is very spread out and walking is usually uncomfortably hot so it's best to find an auto-rickshaw. Most refuse to run their meter, so ask your hotel for an approximate rate to your destination. Taxis are comparatively rare and a bit more expensive, but there's an efficient system of radio taxis which can be yours for as little as Rs 120 per hour if you book one for a day (try **Fast Track** ① *T044-6000 6000*). The bus network is extensive with frequent services, but it's often very crowded. A new Metro system connecting the airport, bus and railway stations with the main hotel clusters is slated to open in 2015.

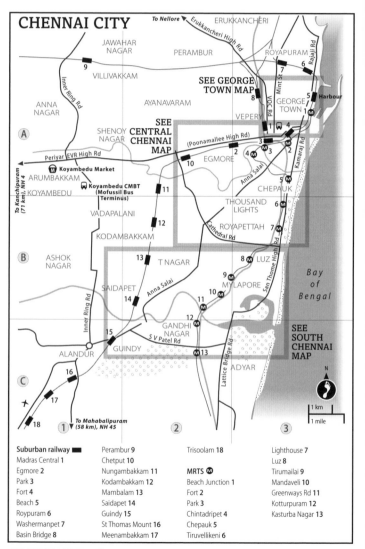

Suburban railway ▰	Perambur **9**	Trisoolam **18**	Lighthouse **7**
Madras Central **1**	Chetput **10**		Luz **8**
Egmore **2**	Nungambakkam **11**	**MRTS** Ⓜ	Tirumailai **9**
Park **3**	Kodambakkam **12**	Beach Junction **1**	Mandaveli **10**
Fort **4**	Mambalam **13**	Fort **2**	Greenways Rd **11**
Beach **5**	Saidapet **14**	Park **3**	Kotturpuram **12**
Roypuram **6**	Guindy **15**	Chintadripet **4**	Kasturba Nagar **13**
Washermanpet **7**	St Thomas Mount **16**	Chepauk **5**	
Basin Bridge **8**	Meenambakkam **17**	Tiruvellikeni **6**	

ON THE ROAD
Screen gods

Tamil Nadu's lively temple society also keeps aflame sculpture and the arts, and makes for a people singularly receptive to iconography. Tamil film-making is every bit as prolific and profitable as its closest rival, Hindi-language Bollywood. The state's industry is famous for its dancing and choreography and the super-saturated colour of its film stock. Film stars too, are massive here; worshipped like demigods, their careers often offering them a fast track into politics, where they are singularly well placed to establish personality cults. Two such figures who have hopped from the screen into the state's political driving seat as chief minister are the cherished MGR – MG Ramachandran, the film star and charismatic chief minister during the 1980s – and Jayalalitha, his one-time girlfriend and contentious successor, three times chief minister since 1991 despite being the figure of multiple corruption scandals.

ORIENTATION

Chennai is far from an 'organized' city. The main harbour near the old British military zone of **George Town** is marked by cranes for the cargo business. Nearby is the **fort**, the former headquarters of the British and now the Secretariat of the Tamil Nadu Government, and the High Court. The **Burma bazar**, a long line of pokey shops, runs between the two near Parry's Corner, while the two main rail stations lie to the west of George Town. From the fort, **Anna Salai** (Mount Road of old) cuts a southwestward swathe through the city, passing through or near to most areas of interest to visitors: **Triplicane**, where most of Chennai's cheap accommodation can be found; **Thousand Lights** and **Teynampet**, where ritzier hotels and malls dominate; and the commercial free-for-all of **T Nagar**. Just south of the central area between Anna Salai and the long sweep of Marina Beach lies **Mylapore**, older than Chennai itself and the cultural heart of the city. Further south still, industrial and high-tech sprawl stretches down the coast almost as far as **Mahabalipuram**.

TOURIST INFORMATION

Most tourist offices are located in the the new **Tourism Complex** ① *2 Wallajah Rd, near Kalaivanar Arangam*. Tamil Nadu Tourism (TN) ① *T044-2536 8358, www.tamilnadutourism.org*, also has offices opposite Central station (T044-2535 3351), in Egmore (T044-2819 2165), and at the Domestic and International airports. Tamil Tourist Development Corporation (TTDC) ① *T044-2538 9857, www.ttdconline.com*. Kerala Tourism ① *T044-2538 2639*; Andhra Pradesh Tourism ① *T044-6543 9987*; Andaman and Nicobar Islands Tourism ① *T044-2654 9295*.

Possibly the best organized office is **Government of India Tourism** ① *154 Anna Salai, T044-2846 0205, Mon-Fri 0915-1745, Sat until 1300*. India Tourism Development Corporation (ITDC) ① *29 Ethiraj Salai, T044-2821 1782, Mon-Sat 0600-2000, Sun 0600-1400*, organizes tour packages and car rental. For city information see also www.chennaionline.com.

→BACKGROUND

Armenian and Portuguese traders had settled the San Thome area before the arrival of the British. In 1639, **Francis Day**, a trader with the East India Company, negotiated the grant of a tiny plot of sandy land to the north of the Cooum River as the base for a warehouse or factory. The building was completed on 23 April 1640, St George's Day. The site was chosen partly because of local politics – Francis Day's friendship with Ayyappa Nayak, brother of the local ruler of the coast country from Pulicat to the Portuguese settlement of San Thome – but more importantly by the favourable local price of cotton goods.

By 1654 the patch of sand had grown into Fort St George, complete with a church and English residences – the 'White Town'. To its north was 'Black Town', referred to locally as Chennaipatnam, after Chennappa Nayak, Dharmala Ayyappa Nayak's father. The two towns merged and Madraspatnam grew with the acquisition of neighbouring villages of Tiru-alli-keni (meaning Lily Tank, and Anglicised as Triplicane), in 1676. In 1693, Governor Yale (founder of Yale University in the USA) acquired Egmore, Purasawalkam and Tondiarpet from Emperor Aurangzeb, who had by then extended Mughal power to the far south. In 1746 Madras was captured by the French, to be returned to British control as a result of the Treaty of Aix-la-Chapelle in 1748. Villages like Nungambakkam, Ennore, Perambur, San Thome and Mylapore (the 'city of the peacock') were absorbed by the mid-18th century with the help of friendly Nawabs. In 1793, the British colonial administration moved to Calcutta, but Madras remained the centre of the East India Company's expanding power in South India.

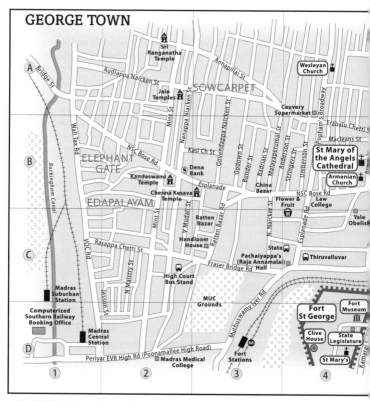

It was more than 150 years after they had founded Fort St George at Madras (in 1639) before the East India Company could claim political supremacy in South India. Haidar Ali, who mounted the throne of Mysore in 1761, and his son Tipu Sultan, allied with the French, won many battles against the English. The 1783 Treaty of Versailles forced peace. The English took Malabar in 1792, and in 1801 Lord Wellesley brought together most of the south under the Madras Presidency.

The city continues to grow, although many services, including water and housing, are stretched to breaking point. Since Independence an increasing range of heavy and light goods industries, particularly automotive, has joined the long-established cotton textiles and leather industries.

→ PLACES IN CHENNAI

Apart from anomalous little pockets of expats, such as Chetpet's Jamaican and South African communities, life in Chennai continues much as it always has done: brahminical neighbourhoods still demand strict vegetarianism of all tenants; and flat sharing, a commonly accepted practice among the young in other major cities, remains taboo in the most staid quarters of Chennai. Superstition is important here too: rents are decided according to vasthu, India's equivalent of feng shui, and a wrong-facing front door can slash your payments.

You have to squint hard today to picture the half-empty grandeur that was the Madras of the East India Presidency. Triplicane has some of the finest architectural remains but the derelict district is better known today as 'bachelors' neighbourhood' due to its popularity with young men who come to make their fortune in the city.

The long expanse of Marina Beach, just seaward of Triplicane, made Chennai's residents tragically vulnerable to the 2004 tsunami, which devastated this public land – the city's cricket pitch, picnic ground and fishing shore. There's no trace of the ferocity of the waves today, but here alone it took about 200 lives.

THE FORT AND PORT: ST GEORGE AND GEORGE TOWN

Chennai began as nothing more than a huddle of fishing villages on the Bay of Bengal, re-christened Madras by British

17th-century traders after they built the Factory House fortifications on the beach. The present fort dates from 1666. The 24 black **Charnockite pillars**, were reclaimed by the British in 1762 after the French had carried them off to Puducherry in 1746. Now the site of state government, the **State Legislative Hall** has fine woodwork and black and white stone paving. You can also see the old barracks and officers' quarters including Lord Clive's house, which he rented from an Armenian merchant. One room, Clive's Corner, has small exhibits. The house once occupied by Arthur Wellesley, the future Duke of Wellington, is 100 m further along.

The fort's governor Streynsham Master was responsible for the most interesting building in the compound, **St Mary's Church** ① *T044-2538 2023*. Built between 1678 and 1680, it ranks as the first English church in India and the oldest British building to survive. It's unusually well fortified for a house of God – all solid masonry with semi-circular cannon-proof roofs and 1.3-m-thick walls – so that in times of siege it could function as a military dormitory and storehouse, and had to be almost entirely rebuilt in 1759 after military action in a siege. **Governor Elihu Yale** and **Robert Clive** were both married in the church. Yale, an American (born to English parents), who worked as a writer for the East India Company from the ages of 24 to 39, rose to become governor; his son David is buried under the Hynmers Obelisk in the old burial ground. The famous missionary **Schwartz**, at one time the intermediary between the British and Haidar Ali, is also celebrated here for his role just "going about doing good". Job Charnock is commemorated for carrying a Hindu widow from the funeral pyre she was about to burn herself on and whereupon he took her as his wife. You can also learn the unhappy end of poor Malcolm McNeill, a colonel of the Madras Light Cavalry, who died at Rangoon in 1852 from neither battle nor disease but from a case of sunstroke. Nor is he alone: many Britishers appear to have fallen "a martyr to an ungenial climate".

The original black font, made from 3000-million-year-old Charnockite from Pallavaram, has been in continuous use since the church was consecrated. Outside the west entrance lies one of the oldest British inscriptions in India: the tombstone of Elizabeth Baker.

Also in the compound is an 18th-century building housing the **Fort Museum** ① *Sat-Thu 0900-1700, US$2, photography prohibited*, with exhibits from 300 years of British Indian history including brilliant portraits of Madras governors. It includes prints, documents, paintings, sculpture, arms (medieval weapons with instructions on their use) and uniforms. The Indo-French gallery has some Louis XIV furniture and clocks. Clive Corner, which includes letters and photographs, is particularly interesting. The building itself was once an exchange for East India Company merchants, becoming an officers' mess later.

Within walking distance of the compound, to the north, is the city's long-standing commercial centre, **George Town**. The area was renamed after the future King George V when he visited India in 1905. You first reach the grand Indo-Saracenic complex of the **High Court** ① *Mon-Sat 1045-1345, 1430-1630, contact registrar for visit and guide, Rs 10*, developed in the style of the late 19th-century architects like **Henry Irwin**, who was also responsible for the National Art Gallery. You are allowed to visit the courtrooms by using the entrance on the left. A fine example is Court No 13 which has stained glass, fretted woodwork, carved furniture, silvered panels and a painted ceiling. The huge red central tower, nearly 50 m tall (you can climb to the top), built like a domed minaret to serve as a lighthouse, can be seen 30 km out at sea. It was in use from 1894 until 1977. The original **Esplanade Lighthouse**, southeast of the High Court, is in the form of a large Doric pillar and took over from the Fort lighthouse in 1841.

Cross NSC Bose Road from the High Court's north gate to walk up Armenian Street for the beautiful Armenian **Church of the Holy Virgin Mary** (1772) ① *0930-1430, bells rung on Sun at 0930*. Solid walls and massive 3-m-high wooden doors conceal the pleasant open courtyard inside, which contains a pretty belltower and many Armenian tombstones, the oldest dating from 1663. The East India Company praised the Armenian community for their 'sober, frugal and wise' lifestyle and they were given the same rights as English settlers in 1688. Immediately north again is the Roman Catholic Cathedral, **St Mary of the Angels** (1675). The inscription above the entrance – 1642 – celebrates the date when the Capuchin monks built their first church in Madras.

Popham's Broadway, west from the St Mary cathedral, takes its name from Stephen Popham, a solicitor (in Madras 1778-1795) who was keen to improve the city's sanitation, laying out what was to become Madras's main commercial street. Just off Popham's Broadway in Prakasham Road is the **Wesleyan Church** (1820).

In the 18th century there was major expansion between what is now First Line Beach (North Beach Road) and **Mint Street** to the west of George Town. The Mint was first opened in 1640, and from the late 17th century minted gold coins under licence for the Mughals, but did not move to Mint Street until 1841-1842.

The 19th-century growth of Madras can be traced north from **Parry's Corner. First Line Beach**, built on reclaimed land in 1814 fronted the beach itself. The **GPO** (1844-1884) was designed by Chisholm. The completion of the harbour (1896), transformed the economy of the city.

CENTRAL CHENNAI AND THE MARINA

Triplicane and **Chepauk** contain some of the finest examples of late 19th-century Indo-Saracenic architecture in India, concentrated in the area around the University of Madras. The Governor of Madras, Mountstuart Elphinstone Grant-Duff (1881-1886), decided to develop the Marina as a promenade, since when it has been a favourite place for thousands of city inhabitants to walk on a Sunday evening.

Until the harbour was built at the end of the 19th century the sea washed up close to the present line of Kamaraj Salai (South Beach Road). However, the north-drifting current has progressively widened **Marina Beach**, which now stands as one of the longest urban beaches in the world – a fact that fills Chennai with great pride, if little sense of urgency about keeping the beach itself clean. The area just south of the malodorous mouth of the River Cooum is dedicated to a series of memorials to former state governors: **Anna Park** is named after the founder of the DMK party, CN Annadurai, while pilgrims converge on the **MGR Samadhi** to celebrate **MG Ramachandran** – the charismatic 1980s filmstar-turned-chief minister (see box, page 139). **Chepauk Palace**, 400 m away on South Beach Road, was the former residence of the Nawab of the Carnatic. The original four-domed Khalsa Mahal and the Humayun Mahal with a grand *durbar* hall had a tower added between them in 1855. The original building is now hidden from the road by the modern Public Works Department (PWD) building, Ezhilagam. Immediately behind is the Chepauk **cricket ground** where test matches are played. Further south, opposite the clunky sculpture entitled 'the Triumph of Labour', the elegant circular **Vivekenanda Illam** was Madras' first ice house, and now hosts a **museum** ① *Thu-Tue 1000-1200, 1500-1900, Rs 10,* devoted to the wandering 20th-century saint, Swami Vivekananda. There are weekend yoga classes at the ice house (weekends, 0630-0830) and regular meditation classes (T044-2844 6188, Wednesday at 1900) run by the Sri Ramakrishna Math.

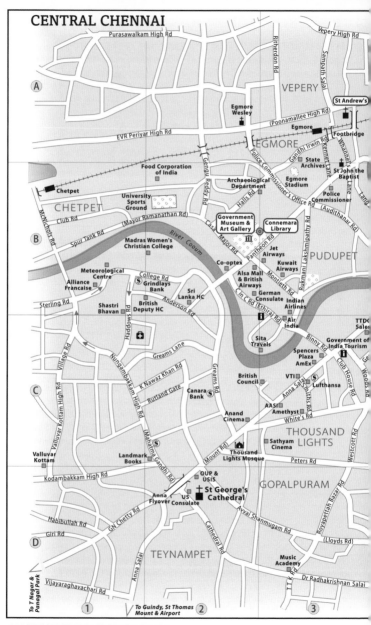

CENTRAL CHENNAI

Purasawalkam High Rd

Vepery High Rd

Ritherdon Rd

Sampath Salai

A

VEPERY

St Andrew's

Egmore Wesley

(Poonamallee High Rd)

Egmore

EVR Periyar High Rd

EGMORE

Footbridge

Wharnel

Gandhi Irwin Rd

Kennet Lane

Police Commissioner's Office Rd

State Archives

St John the Baptist

Food Corporation of India

Venu Reddy Rd

Archaeological Department

Egmore Stadium

Police Commissioner

Lane

Chetpet

Halls Rd

(Audithanar Rd)

CHETPET

Club Rd

(Mayor Ramanathan Rd)

Casa Major Rd

Government Museum & Art Gallery

Pantheon Rd

Connemara Library

McNichols Rd

Spur Tank Rd

River Cooum

Madras Women's Christian College

Jet Airways

PUDUPET

Co-optex

Kuwait Airways

Ruknani Lakshmipathy Rd

Meteorological Centre

College Rd

Grindlays Bank

Sri Lanka HC

Alsa Mall & British Airways

Monteith Rd

Alliance Francaise

German Consulate

Indian Airlines

Sterling Rd

Anderson Rd

British Deputy HC

Cin C Rd (Ethiraj Rd)

Air India

Shastri Bhavan

Haddows Rd

Binny Rd

TTDC Sales

Village Rd

Greams Lane

Sita Travels

Government of India Tourism

Nungambakkam High Rd

Greams Rd

Spencers Plaza

Club House Rd

AmEx

Woods Rd

C

K Nawaz Khan Rd

British Council

VTI

Lufthansa

Valluvar Kottam High Rd

Rutland Gate

Canara Bank

Anna Salai

South Blvd Rd

AASI

Amethyst

Anand Cinema

White's Rd

Westcott Rd

Valluvar Kottam

Mahatma Gandhi Rd

THOUSAND LIGHTS

Landmark Books

Sathyam Cinema

Kodambakkam High Rd

Thousand Lights Mosque

Peters Rd

GOPALPURAM

Habibullah Rd

OUP & USIS

Anna Flyover

St George's Cathedral

GN Chetty Rd

US Consulate

Giri Rd

Avvai Shanmugam Rd

Royapettah Bazar Rd

Cathedral Rd

(Lloyds Rd)

TEYNAMPET

Music Academy

To T Nagar & Panagal Park

Vijayaraghavachari Rd

To Guindy, St Thomas Mount & Airport

Dr Radhakrishnan Salai

1   **2**   **3**

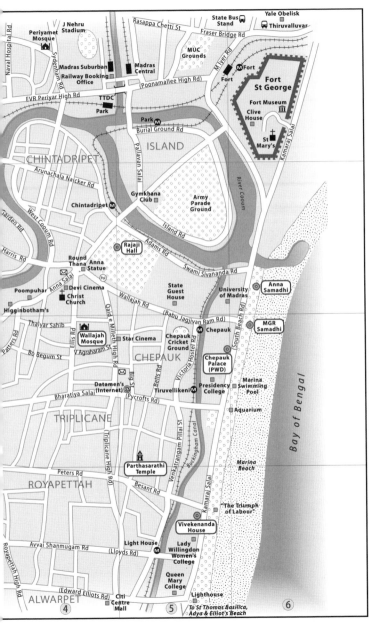

Inland from here lies the **Parthasarathi Temple** ① *0630-1300, 1500-2000,* the oldest temple structure in Chennai. It was built by eighth-century Pallava kings, then renovated in the 16th by Vijayanagara rulers. Dedicated to Krishna as the royal charioteer, it shows five of Vishnu's 10 incarnations, and is the only temple dedicated to Parthasarathi. Further north in the heart of Triplicane, the **Wallajah Mosque** ① *0600-1200, 1600-2200,* or 'Big Mosque', was built in 1795 by the Nawab of the Carnatic. There are two slender minarets with golden domes on either side. North again, near the Round Thana which marks the beginning of Anna Salai, is the Greek temple style banqueting hall of the old Government House, now known as **Rajaji Hall** (1802), built to mark the British victory over Tipu Sultan.

EGMORE

A bridge across the Cooum at Egmore was opened in 1700, and by the late 18th century, the area around Pantheon Road became the fulcrum of Madras's social and cultural life, a

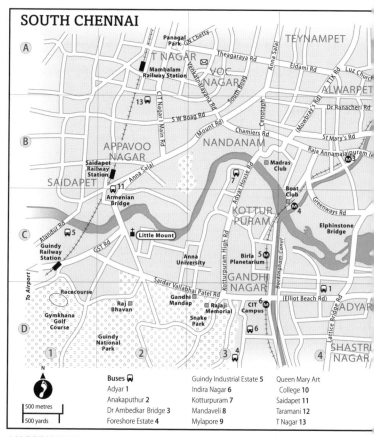

SOUTH CHENNAI

Buses 🚌	Guindy Industrial Estate 5	Queen Mary Art
Adyar 1	Indira Nagar 6	College 10
Anakaputhur 2	Kotturpuram 7	Saidapet 11
Dr Ambedkar Bridge 3	Mandaveli 8	Taramani 12
Foreshore Estate 4	Mylapore 9	T Nagar 13

'place of public entertainment and balls'. Egmore's development, which continued for a century, started with the building of Horden's garden house in 1715. The original pantheon (public assembly rooms) was completely replaced by one of India's National Libraries. The **Connemara Library** (built 1896) began in 1662, when residents exchanged a bale of Madras calico for books from London. At the southwest corner of the site stands Irwin's Victoria Memorial Hall, now the **Government Museum and Art Gallery** ① *486 Pantheon Rd, T044-2819 3238, Sat-Thu 0930-1700, closed Fri, foreigners Rs 250, Indians Rs 15, camera Rs 500*. The red brick rotunda surrounded by an Italianate arcade was described by Tillotson as one of "the proudest expressions of the Indo-Saracenic movement". There are locally excavated Stone and Iron Age implements and striking bronzes including a 11th-century Nataraja from Tiruvengadu, seated images of Siva and Parvati from Kilaiyur, and large figures of Rama, Lakshmana and Sita from Vadak-kuppanaiyur. Buddhist bronzes from Nagapattinam have been assigned to Chola and later periods. The beautiful Ardhanariswara statue here is one of the most prized of all Chola bronzes: Siva in his rare incarnation as a hermaphrodite. There are also good old paintings including Tanjore glass paintings, Rajput and Mughal miniatures and 17th-century Deccan paintings. Contemporary art is displayed at the **Gallery of Modern Art** ① *Government Museum, T044-2819 3035*.

Egmore has other reminders of the Indo-Saracenic period of the 19th and early 20th centuries, the station itself being one of the last to be built, in the 1930s. Northeast of the station on Poonamalle High Road is the splendid **St Andrew's Church**, consecrated in 1821, with a façade like that of London's St Martin-in-the-Fields and a magnificent shallow-domed ceiling.

MYLAPORE AND SOUTH CHENNAI

Mylapore, which is technically older than Chennai and is the seat of city's urban elite, is more charming than the city centre. The present **Basilica of San Thomas** (1898) ① *24 San Thome High Rd, T044-2498 5455*, surrounded now by the tenement rehousing scheme of a fishermen's colony, is claimed as one of the very few churches to be built over an apostle's tomb. St Thomas Didymus (Doubting Thomas) is believed to have come to India in AD 52. According to one legend, he crossed the

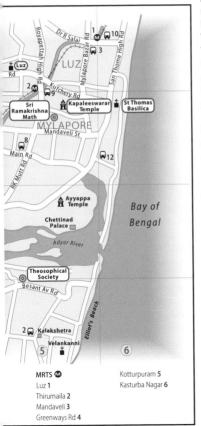

MRTS ⓜ
Luz **1**
Thirumaila **2**
Mandaveli **3**
Greenways Rd **4**

Kotturpuram **5**
Kasturba Nagar **6**

peninsula from his landing on the west coast to reach Mylapore (the 'town of peacocks') where he proceeded to live and preach, taking shelter from persecution in Little Mount (see below). An alternative story argues King Gondophernes invited him to Taxila, where he converted the king and his court before moving to South India. Some claim that his body was ultimately buried in the Italian town of Ortona. Marco Polo in his travels in 1293 recorded the chapel on the seashore and a Nestorian monastery on a hill to the west where the apostle was put to death. In 1523, when the Portuguese started to rebuild the church they discovered the tomb containing the relics consisting of a few bones, a lance head and an earthenware pot containing bloodstained earth. The church was replaced by the neo-Gothic structure which has two spires and was granted the status of a basilica in 1956. The relics are kept in the sacristy and can be seen on request. There are 13th-century wall plaques, a modern stained glass window, a 450-year-old Madonna brought from Portugal and a 16th-century stone sundial. A meticulous restoration carried out in 2002-2004 has repaired the damaged tiled roof, refreshed the stained-glass windows in the shrine and peeled back paint to reveal the original teak roof beams, and added a new underground chapel next to the tomb; there's a well-attended Mass here each morning at 1100.

Kapaleeswarar Temple ① *0600-1300, 1600-2200*, to the west, is a 16th-century Siva temple with a 40-m *gopuram* (gateway), built after the original was destroyed by the Portuguese in 1566. Sacred to Tamil Shaivites, non-Hindus are only allowed in the outer courtyard, but it's absolutely worth a visit, especially at sunset when worshippers gather for the evening *puja*, conducted amidst plumes of incense smoke and swirling pipe music.

The nearby **Sri Ramakrishna Math** ① *31 Ramakrishna Mutt Rd, www.sriramakrishna math.org, 0500-1145, 1500-2100*, is one of the city's more appealing quiet corners, with a spectacular multi-faith temple, a quieter memorial to Ramakrishna in a prettily tiled Chettinad-style house, and a bookshop packed with writings by Ramamkrishna and notable devotees, including Swami Vivekananda.

The diminutive Portuguese **Luz Church**, 1547-1582 (the 1516 date in the inscription is probably wrong), is possibly the oldest church in Chennai. Its Tamil name, *Kattu Kovil*, means 'jungle temple'. Legend has it that Portuguese sailors lost at sea in a storm followed a light to the shore, where it disappeared. In gratitude they built the church. There are a number of 19th-century marble plaques to wives of the Madras civil service in the church and an ornate crypt.

To the south of Elphinstone Bridge, the **Theosophical Society** ① *Mon-Fri 0830-1000, 1400-1600, Sat 0830-1000, bus 5 from Central Chennai, ask taxi for Ayappa Temple on San Thome High Rd*, is set in large and beautifully quiet gardens. There are several shrines of different faiths and a Serene Garden of Remembrance for Madame Blavatsky and Colonel Olcott who founded the society in New York in 1875 and moved its headquarters to Madras in 1882. There's a huge 400-year-old banyan past the kitchen garden, a library and a meditation hall. The brackish river attracts waders and seabirds.

Tucked away near Saidapet is the **Little Mount** area. The older of the two churches (1551), with its small vaulted chapel, was built by the Portuguese. The modern circular church was built in 1971. St Thomas is believed to have been martyred and bled to death in AD 52 on the **Great Mount**, though others believe he was accidentally killed by a hunter's arrow. On top of the 90-m-high 'mount' is the **Church of Our Lady of Expectation**. The altar marks the spot where, according to legend, Thomas fell. Some legends suggest that after St Thomas had been martyred on the Little Mount, near Saidapet Bridge, his body was brought back to the beach which had been his home and was buried there.

→ MAHABALIPURAM (MAMALLAPURAM)

Mahabalipuram's mix of magnificent historic rock temples, exquisite alfresco bas-reliefs and inviting sandy beach bestows a formidable magnetism, and it has matured into a buzzing backpacker hamlet, complete with all the hotel touts and high-power Kashmiri salesmanship that such a role implies. Though the beach and ocean are dirty enough to make you think twice about swimming, the craftsmanship that built the temples continues today and the whole place echoes with the sound of chisels tapping industriously on stone.

If travelling from Chennai, there are three good stop-off points before Mahabalipuram. The first is 19 km from Chennai at **Cholamandal Artists' Village** ① *East Coast Rd, Enjampakkam, T044-2449 0092, 0900-1900, free*. The artists' community, started in 1969, gives living, working and exhibition space for artists creating sculptures, pottery and batik. They sometimes hold dance performances in a small open-air theatre, and there are some simple cottages for hire if you want to stick around for a workshop or residency.

The second stop is the **Madras Craft Foundation**'s model village, **Dakshinchitra** ① *East Coast Rd, T044-2747 2603, www.dakshinachitra.net, Wed-Mon 1000-1800, foreigners Rs 175, Indians Rs 50*, which showcases the rich cultural heritage of the four southern states against

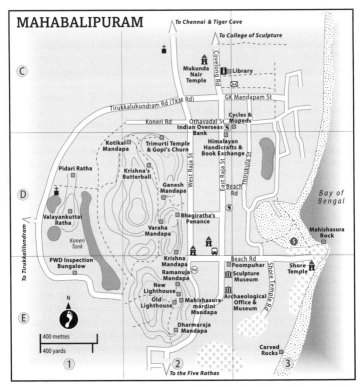

a backdrop of 17 authentic buildings, each relocated piece by piece from their original homes around South India. There's a regular programme of folk performances, including puppet shows, plus a small textile museum, a restaurant and a fortune-telling parrot.

Finally, 14 km before Mahabalipuram, is Romulus Whitaker's **Madras Crocodile Bank** ① *Tue-Sun 0830-1730, Rs 20, camera Rs 10, video Rs 75*, established by the American-born herpetologist (known as the Snake Man of India) as a captive breeding centre for Indian crocodilians. You can now see several rare species from India and beyond, including Siamese and African dwarf crocodiles, basking around the open pools. There's a small extra charge to visit the snake venom bank, where snakes donate small quantities of poison for use in antivenins before being released back to the wild.

ARRIVING IN MAHABALIPURAM

Getting there Buses from Chennai take around 1½ hours to the bus stand in the centre of the small village; some express buses will drop you at the crossroads on East Coast Road, from where auto-rickshaws should charge Rs 50 for the short hop into town, or Rs 50-100 to the resorts north of Mahabalipuram. Arriving by car, you may have to pay a Rs 20 toll at the booth near the post office on Kovalam Road.

Moving on You can pick up buses for **Puducherry** (see page 156) from the crossroads on East Coast Road. Ordinary buses, though more frequent, tend to be crowded, but the more expensive (and frankly less interesting) a/c express bus is more likely to have spare seats.

Getting around The town is small enough to explore on foot, but hiring a bike can get you further afield.

Tourist information Tamil Nadu Tourist Office ① *Kovalam Rd, 300 m north of Othavadai St, T044-2744 2232, Mon-Fri 0945-1745*, can arrange guides, car and cycle hire. The best time to visit is early morning, for the best light on Bhagiratha's Penance. Allow two hours for a circuit. It's hard to get lost but the paths on the top of the rock are not always clear. Mahabalipuram has two ATMs, but these often run out of cash; stock up in Chennai to avoid punitive exchange rates.

BACKGROUND

The coastal temple town Mahabalipuram is officially known as Mamallapuram after 'Mamalla' ('great wrestler'), the name given to Narasimhavarman I Pallavamalla (ruled AD 630-668). The Pallava ruler made the port famous in the seventh century and was largely responsible for the temples. There are 14 cave temples and nine monolithic *rathas* (shrines in the shape of temple chariots), three stone temples and four relief sculptured rock panels.

The **Dravida** or Dravidian style underwent several changes over the course of the different dynasties that ruled for about 1000 years from the time of the Pallavas who laid its foundations. In Mahabalipuram, rock-cut cave temples, *mandapas* (small excavated columned halls), and *rathas* were carved out by the early Pallavas. These were followed by structural temples and bas-relief sculptures on giant rocks. The Ekambaresvara Temple in Kanchipuram shows the evolution of the Dravidian style – the shrine with its pyramidal tower and the separate *mandapa* (pillared portico) all within the courtyard with its high enclosure wall made up of cells. Six centuries later the two separate structures were

ON THE ROAD
Stone temple pilot

When the British Council sponsored Bristol-born artist Stephen Cox to scout India for a place to make his huge-scale stone works for the national art prize, the Indian Triennale, he chose not the country's best art schools, but a little fishing village on the Coromandel coast of Tamil Nadu. It may sound bloody minded, until you arrive in Mahabalipuram, where the whole air clatters with the sound of chisel on rock. It must be the most industrious seat of Hindu idol-making the world over; everywhere you look masons sit on their haunches hammering away at the local dolerite rock.

As Cox explains: "I didn't go to India to work with like-minded contemporary artists, I wanted people who could work with great big blocks of stone without fear. Mahabalipuram is totally unique in having this unbroken, living tradition of making idols for people to pray to, and that means that they are also used to working with huge monolithic stone so no-one's daunted by making my 14-tonne sculptures." Although he has kept a studio there from that first year, 1986, you won't find any of his sculpture in the town itself – these are mainly kept for cities: the British High Commission at Delhi, the British Council's office in Chennai and dotted about London's Square Mile. Indeed his work – too minimalist for Hindu temple carving purists – has been received with something less than gusto by some of the local craftsman, and journalist Mark Tully branded Cox's use of Indian labour a form of 'neo-colonialism'. One sculpture alone can take up to a year to make and will have passed through, on average, 20 pairs of Indian hands before being shipped for exhibition. "At the end of the day of course, I wouldn't be working in India over Carrara in Italy if it wasn't economically viable," Cox concedes, but he also says "my raison d'être for working in India is because, in working amongst and with the temple carvers, I can immerse myself in a living antique tradition. It is not just the cost factor. The hand skills of the silpies have been lost to the rest of the world."

The town has changed dramatically since he arrived in 1986, but Cox spares the burgeoning tourist industry infrastructure to reserve his criticism for the Architectural Survey of India's maintenance of the monuments themselves. "Since it was declared a World Heritage Site, they've buggered the Shore Temple up; it's not a shore temple anymore, instead it sits in a bijou plot of grassland, while the five *rathas* are fenced off, destroying the whole beauty of these wonderful monuments in a natural environment."

And his favourite piece of sculpture in a town teeming with them? It's the Pallava's flair for observation that still gets him: "the naturalism that Giotto was supposed to have invented you find in a ninth-century relief carving here. It is amazing. I only hope fewer and fewer people come."

joined by the *antarala* (covered hall). A large subsidiary shrine, which took the place of an entrance gateway, also hinted at the later *gopuram*.

A characteristic feature of the temples here was the system of water channels and tanks, drawn from the **Palar River**, which made it particularly suitable as a site of religious worship. The *naga*, or serpent cult associated with water worship, can be seen to be given prominence at Bhagiratha's Penance.

Carving in stone is still a living art; stone masons can be heard chipping away from dawn to dusk along the dusty roadsides, while students at the **Government School of Sculpture** ① *near the bus stand, Wed-Mon 0900-1300, 1400-1830,* continue to practise the skills which flourished centuries ago.

PLACES IN MAHABALIPURAM

Bhagiratha's Penance *Descent of the Ganga*, also called **Arjuna's Penance**, is a bas-relief sculpted on the face of two enormous adjacent rocks, 29 m long and 7 m high. It shows realistic life-size figures of animals, gods and saints watching the descent of the river from the Himalaya. Bhagiratha, Rama's ancestor, is seen praying to Ganga. A man-made waterfall, fed from a collecting chamber above, issues from the natural crack between the two rocks. Some see the figure of an ascetic (to the top left-hand side of the rock, near the cleft) as representing Arjuna's penance when praying for powers from Siva, though this is disputed. There are scenes from the fables in the *Panchatantra* and a small shrine to Vishnu.

A path north goes to the double-decker rectangular **Ganesh** *ratha* with a highly decorative roof and two pillars with lions at their base – an architectural feature which was to become significant. The Ganesh image inside is mid-20th century. To the west are the **Valayankuttai** and twin **Pidari** *rathas*. The path continues past the precariously balanced **Krishna's Butterball** through some huge boulders at the north end of the hillock to the **Trimurti Temple** caves that hold three shrines to Brahma, Vishnu and Siva, the last with a lingam.

Mandapas The 10 *mandapas* are shallow, pillared halls or porticos in the rocky hillside which hold superb sculptures from mythological tales, and illustrate the development of the Dravidian (South Indian) temple style.

On the south is a **Durga niche** (AD 630-660), while next door is the **Gopi's Churn**, a Pallava cistern. Walk back along the ridge, passing Krishna's Butterball on your left and boulders with evidence of incomplete work. The **Varaha Mandapa** (AD 640-674) on the left of the ridge shows two incarnations of Vishnu – Varaha (boar) and Vamana (dwarf) – among scenes with kings and queens. The base forms a narrow water pool for pilgrims to use before entering the temple. From here you can walk to the top of Bhagiratha's Penance.

Krishna Mandapa (mid-seventh century) has a bas-relief scene of Krishna lifting Mount Govardhana to protect a crowd of his kinsmen from the anger of the Rain God, Indra. The cow licking its calf during milking is remarkably realistic.

Kotikal Mandapa (early seventh century) may be the earliest of the *mandapas*, roughly carved with a small shrine with no image inside. **Ramanuja Mandapa** was originally a triple-cell Siva temple, converted later into a Vaishnava temple.

South of the new lighthouse the simple **Dharmaraja cave** (early seventh century) contains three empty shrines. To its west is **Isvara Temple** (or Old Lighthouse), a truncated Siva temple still standing like a beacon on the highest summit, with a view for miles around. (To the south, across the Five Rathas, is the nuclear power station of Kalpakkam; to the west is the flat lagoon and the original port of Mahabalipuram.)

Mahishasuramardini Mandapa (mid-seventh century) is immediately below. It has fine bas-relief and carved columns with lion bases. The main sculpture shows the goddess Durga slaying the buffalo demon Mahishasura while another relief shows Vishnu lying under Adishesha, the seven-hooded serpent.

Pancha Rathas ⓘ *Rs 250, Indians Rs 10.* These mid-seventh-century monolithic temples, 1.5 km south of the Old Lighthouse, were influenced by Buddhist architecture as they resemble the *vihara* (monastery) and *chaitya* (temple hall). They imitate in granite temple structures that were originally built of wood and are among the oldest examples of their type.

The five *rathas* to the south of the hill are named after the Pancha Pandava (five Pandava brothers) in the epic *Mahabharata* and their wife Draupadi. The largest is the domed **Dharmaraja** with many images including an interesting Ardhanarishvara (Siva-Parvati) at the rear. The barrel-vaulted **Bhima** nearby has a roof suggestive of a thatched hut, while next to it the dome-shaped ratha **Arjuna** imitates the Dharmaraja. **Draupadi ratha** is the smallest and simplest and is again in the form of a thatched hut. The base, now covered by sand, conceals a lion in front which appears to carry it, which suggests that it may be a replica of a portable shrine. Immediately east is a large unfinished *Nandi*. To its west is the apsidal **Nakula-Sahadeva ratha** with a freestanding elephant nearby. The Bhima and Nakula-Sahadeva follow the oblong plan of the Buddhist *chaitya* hall and are built to two or more storeys, a precursor to the *gopuram*, the elaborate entrance gateway of the Dravidian temple.

Shore Temple ⓘ *0900-1730, foreigners Rs 250, Indians Rs 10, video Rs 25, includes Panch Rathas if visited on same day.* This beautiful sandstone World Heritage Site, built in the seventh century by King Rajasimha, is unusual for holding shrines to both Siva and Vishnu. Its gardens have been laid out to ape their ancient antecedents. Its base is granite and it has a basalt *kalasha* at its top. Its position on the water's edge, with an east-facing altar designed to catch the rising sun and a stone pillar to hold the beacon for sailors at night, meant that there was no space for a forecourt or entrance gateway, but two additional shrines were built to the west. The second smaller spire adds to the temple's unusual structure. The outer parapet wall has lines of *Nandi* (Siva's sacred bull) and lion pilasters.

Saluvankuppam Five kilometres north of Mahabalipuram, on the coast, is the temple at Saluvankuppam. It holds the **Tiger Cave** *mandapa* with carvings of tiger heads. The cave, not signposted from the beach, is secluded and peaceful – perfect for a picnic. On the way you will see the **Mukunda Nayar Temple**.

Beaches Mahabalipuram's beach is far from pristine, particularly north of the temples towards the **Ashok** and in the rocky area behind the Descent of the Ganga where it serves as an open latrine. To sunbathe undisturbed by hawkers pay Rs 200 to use the small pools at **Crystal Shore Palace** or **Sea Breeze**, or the bigger pool, 1 km north at **Tamil Nadu Beach Resort**.

AROUND MAHABALIPURAM

Tirukkalukundram is a small Siva temple dedicated to Vedagirishvara on top of the 3000-million-year-old rock 14 km west of Mahabalipuram. About 400 steps take you to the top of the 160-m hill which has good views, plus money-conscious priests and 'guides'. Be prepared for a hot barefoot climb, 'donations' at several shrines and Rs 10 for your shoes. At midday, two Neophran vultures (Pharaoh's chickens) sometimes fly down to be fed by the priests. The Bhaktavatsleesvara in town with its *gopuram* (gateway) stands out like a beacon. The tank is considered holy and believed to produce a conch every 12 years. Small shops in the village sell cold drinks. Buses from Mahabalipuram take 30 minutes or you can hire a bike.

Sriperumbudur, 44 km from Chennai on National Highway 4, is the birthplace of the 11th-century Hindu philosopher Ramanuja, and is where Rajiv Gandhi was assassinated on 21 May 1991. There is a memorial at the site in a well-kept garden.

CHENNAI LISTINGS

WHERE TO STAY

Chennai

$$$$ Taj Connemara, Binny Rd (off Anna Salai), T044-6600 0000, www.tajhotels.com. The oldest and most elegant of Chennai's 5-star hotels, with 148 renovated rooms that retain splendid art deco features. Excellent restaurants, bar and good **Giggles** bookshop – so heavily stocked you can't get in the door. Heavily booked Dec-Mar.

$$$ Footprint Bed and Breakfast, behind **Park Sheraton**, off TTK Rd, T044-3255 7720, T(0)9840-037383, www.footprint.in. Beautifully cool, peaceful and intimate retreat from the city, with 9 stylish but unfussy rooms, decorated with handmade paper from Auroville, spread over 2 floors of a residential apartment block. Indian and continental breakfasts come with fresh newspapers, and there's a small library, free internet and Wi-Fi. Owner, Rucha, pops in every day to check on things, and will negotiate weekly and monthly rates if you want to stay longer. Highly recommended.

$$$ Radisson Blu, 531 GST Rd, Saint Thomas Mount, T044-2231 0101, www.radissonblu.com. Excellent value if rather anonymous rooms just 2 km from the airport. With amenable staff and a good variety of restaurants and bars, plus free airport pickup, this is a good choice if you just want to flop for a night off the plane.

$$$ Residency, 49 GN Chetty Rd, T044-2825 3434, www.theresidency.com. 112 very comfortable spacious rooms, 4th floor upwards have good views (9th floor, plush suites). Excellent **Ahaar** restaurant (good buffet lunches), exchange, car hire with knowledgeable drivers. Better rooms and service than some more expensive hotels. Highly recommended, book ahead.

$$ Oriental Inn, 71 Cathedral Rd, T044-2811 4941, www.orientalgroup.in. The older rooms here come with crisp sheets and unusually fragrant bathrooms, but the studio apartments in the new wing are the real steal, with huge amounts of space and designer fittings. Wi-Fi available in both wings, and a slew of good restaurants right downstairs. Price includes breakfast.

$ Karpagam International, 41 South Mada St, Mylapore, T044-2495 9984. Basic but clean rooms amid the Mylapore temple madness; the best ones face straight across the lake. Book 2 weeks in advance.

$ Paradise, 17/1 Vallabha Agraharam St, Triplicane, T044-2859 4252, paradisegh@hotmail.com. Spacious clean rooms with fans (some with 2), shower, good value, very friendly and helpful owners. A firm budget-traveller favourite.

Mahabalipuram

$$$$ Fisherman's Cove (Taj), Kovalam Rd, 21 km north, T044-6741 3333, www.tajhotels.com. A beautiful resort, recently expanded and given a sleek and thoroughly modern makeover. Pick of the rooms are the beachfront cottages with private sit-outs and open-air showers.

$$$-$$ Sea Breeze, Othavadai Cross, T044-2744 3035, www.hotelseabreeze.in. Clean, spacious, well-furnished rooms set around a large swimming pool (non-residents can use it for Rs 200) with steps leading from the palm-shaded grounds down to the beach. Rooms in the next-door annexe are cheaper and more basic, with iffy hot water and mediocre upkeep.

$ Greenwoods Beach Resort, 7 Othavadai Cross St, T044-2744 2212, greenwoods_resort@yahoo.com. Basic but good and clean rooms with mosquito nets in a rambling building lushly shaded by banana and mango trees. The family owners are genuinely welcoming, and there's a well-regarded Ayurvedic clinic on-site.

$ Sri Harul Guest House, 181 Bajanai Koil St, T(0)93846-20173, lings6@rediffmail.com. Friendly little guesthouse right on the beach, with interesting views over the fishermen's colony. Rooms on the ground floor have private balconies.

RESTAURANTS

Chennai

$$$ 601, The Park Hotel, Anna Salai, T044-4267 6000. Possibly the best choice in town for a night out, with fantastic fusion food in a super elegant setting. Also at The Park, **Aqua**, serves excellent Mediterranean dishes and cocktails in poolside cabanas, and lays on a barbeques with live music on Wed nights.

$$$ Copper Chimney, Oriental Inn (see Where to stay). Rich Mughlai and tandoori offerings in very clean setting. In the same building you can eat Chinese at **Chinatown** and good Spanish tapas at **Zara**.

$$$ Dakshin, ICT Park Sheraton Hotel, T044-2499 4101. High on the list of the best South Indian restaurants in the city, with Kanchipuram silk draped everywhere and a huge range of veg and non-veg choices. Book ahead.

$$$ Hotel Savera, 146 Dr Radhakrishnan Rd, T044-2811 4700. Atmospheric rooftop restaurant with superb views, excellent Indian food, friendly service and live Indian music in the evenings. The hotel pool is open to non-residents, Rs 150.

$$ Annalakshmi, 18/3 Rukmani Lakshmipathy Rd, Egmore, T044-2852 5109. Wholesome, health-restoring offerings, run by volunteers with profits to charity. Closed Mon. Recommended.

$$ Benjarong, 537 TTK Rd, Alwarpet, T044-2432 2640. Upscale Thai restaurant, doing very passable renditions of *tom kha* and *pad thai* amid a collection of Buddhas in glass cases. Plenty of veg options.

$ Mathsya, Udipi Home, 1 Hall's Rd (corner of Police Commissioner's Rd). Chennai's night-owl haunt par excellence has been burning the midnight oil (the kitchen stays open until 0200) by government order since the Indo-Chinese war. It also happens to serve some of the city's best pure veg food; their Mathsya *thali* comes with tamarind and sweetened coconut *dosas* and will keep you going all day. Recommended.

$ Saravana Bhavan, branches all over the city including Cathedral Rd opposite **Savera Hotel**, both railway stations, **Spencer Plaza Mall** and **Pondy Bazar**. Spotlessly clean Chennai-based chain restaurant, serving excellent snacks and 'mini tiffin', fruit juices (try pomegranate), sweetmeats, all freshly made.

Mahabalipuram

$$$ The Wharf, Radisson BLU Temple Bay Resort, just north of town on Kovalam Rd, T(0)99404-22999. Set in Mahabalipuram's poshest resort, **The Wharf** pulls a miraculous hat trick by managing to serve both reasonably authentic Chinese and first-rate Indian and Continental food, all to a hypnotic backdrop of palm-framed ocean. Emphatically worth the extra money over Mahab's other mostly lacklustre attempts at French food.

$$ Golden Palate, Mamallaa Heritage Hotel, 104 East Raja St, T(0)919380-126188. Excellent fresh North Indian vegetarian food, with rich buttery paneer and lentil dishes.

$ Mamalla Bhavan, opposite bus stand. This archetypal South Indian diner is a surprise treat, with rattling fans dangling from the high ceiling, barefoot boys scurrying back and forth carrying dirty plates, and grey-uniformed waiters who dole out plates of fresh, hot and incredibly cheap *idli-sambar*, *vada* and *dosa*, washed down with milky sweet coffee.

PUDUCHERRY AND AUROVILLE

Pretty little Puducherry (still widely known by it's old name of Pondicherry) has all the lazy charm of a former French colony: its stately whitewashed 18th-century homes froth with bright pink bougainvillea and its kitchens still smack gloriously of Gaul – excellent French breads, hard cheese and ratatouilles that run with olive oil, accompanied by real French wines. The primly residential French quarter contrasts wonderfully with the dog-eared heritage houses of the Tamil districts, whose streets were built to tilt towards Mecca, while the scores of pristine grey mansions indicate the offices of the Sri Aurobindo Ashram, headquarters of one of India's liveliest spiritual schools of thought. Up the road is the 1960s Westernized branch of Sri Aurobindo's legacy, Auroville, the 'City of Dawn', which was conceived as "a place where human beings could live freely as citizens obeying one single authority, that of the supreme Truth". This is the industrious fulcrum of people seeking an alternative lifestyle – a place of spirulina, incense and white cotton weeds – and while many tourists visit Auroville on a rushed day trip from Puducherry, if you're of a meditative mindset and can forgo your fix of Gallic good cheer, it's far more interesting to do it the other way round.

→ PUDUCHERRY (PONDICHERRY)

Puducherry is the archetypal ambling town: cleaved in two with the **French quarter** along the beach, boasting pretty high-ceilinged wood-slatted residential houses with walled gardens and bougainvillea, and with the markets, mess, businesses and 'talking streets' of the **Tamil** ('black') town to its west. While the French area, with 300 heritage buildings, is well maintained (the majority owned by the ashram), the Tamil area, despite its 1000 homes now classified as heritage, is dangerously dilapidated. The European Commission has funded the restoration of Calve Subraya Chettiar (Vysial) street (between Mission and Gandhi streets), while Muslim domestic architecture is clearly visible in the streets of Kazy, Mulla and Tippu Sultan, in the southern part of the Tamil quarter.

Many people come to Puducherry to visit the campus-like ashram of **Sri Aurobindo Ghosh** and his chief disciple Mirra Alfassa ('The Mother'). Ghosh was an early 20th-century Bengali nationalist and philosopher who struggled for freedom from British colonial power and wrote prodigiously on a huge variety of subjects, particularly Integral Yoga and education. In his aim to create an ashram utopia he found a lifelong *compadre* in the charismatic Frenchwoman Alfassa, who continued as his spiritual successor after his death in 1950. It was Alfassa who pushed into practice Sri Aurobindo's ideas on integral schooling, the aim of which is to develop all aspects of the student's being – "mind, life, body, soul and spirit". In the ashram school, class sizes are limited to eight students, and both pupils and teachers enjoy an extraordinary freedom to alter classes according to individual needs. Alfassa died in 1973 at the age of 93. Both Sri Aurobindo and Alfassa live on as icons, their images gazing down from the walls of almost every building in Puducherry.

ARRIVING IN PUDUCHERRY

Getting there Buses from Mahabalipuram arrive into Pondicherry from the north via the East Coast Road. The main bus stand is just west of the centre, within walkable distance if it's not too hot, or a short auto-rickshaw ride from most hotels. If you're heading straight for Auroville, gather up your courage and ask the driver to let you off at Periyamudaliarchavadi – the Auroville turn-off – from where it's a 15- to 20-minute ride by auto-rickshaw to the village centre. A taxi from Pondicherry to Auroville costs around Rs 300 one way.

Moving on Frequent buses to **Chidambaram** (see page 164) leave from Puducherry's main bus stand, taking 1½ hours.

Getting around Puducherry is lovely to explore on foot, but hiring a bike or moped will give you the freedom to venture further along the coast.

Tourist information Puducherry Tourism ① *40 Goubert Salai, T0413-233 9497, www.tourism.puducherry.gov.in, 0845-1300, 1400-1700*, is well run with maps, brochures, and tours. The **Indian National Trust for Art and Cultural Heritage (INTACH)** ① *62 rue Aurobindo St, T0413-222 5991, http://intach pondicherry.org*, is particularly active in Puducherry and runs heritage walks from its offices. La **Boutique d'Auroville** ① *38 JL Nehru St, T0413-233 7264*, provides information on visiting Auroville.

BACKGROUND

Ancient Vedapuri was where the sage **Agastya Muni** had his hermitage in 1500 BC and in the first century AD Romans traded from nearby Arikamedu. The French renamed the area Puducherry in 1673. In 1742, Dupleix, newly named Governor of the French India Company, took up residence. In 1746 the British lost Fort St George in Madras to Dupleix but in 1751 Clive counter-attacked by capturing Pondicherry in 1761. Puducherry was voluntarily handed over to the Indian government in 1954 and became the Union Territory of Pondicherry.

PLACES IN PUDUCHERRY

The **French Quarter**, which extends from the seafront promenade inland to the canal, contains most of Puducherry's sights, and wandering the quiet streets, stopping into antique shops and colonial mansions, is a pleasure in itself.

The **Sri Aurobindo Ashram** ① *rue de la Marine, 800-1200, 1400-1800, free, meditation Mon-Wed, Fri 1925-1950*, has its main centre in Rue de la Marine. Painted in neat grey and white like most of the ashram's buildings, it contains the flower-bedecked marble Samadhi (resting place and memorial) of both Sri Aurobindo and the Mother.

The **French Institute** ① *rue St Louis*, was set up in 1955 for the study of Indian culture and the 'Scientific and Technical Section' for ecological studies. There's a French and English library looking over the sea, and the colonial building is an architectural treat in its own right.

Puducherry Museum ① *next to the library, rue St Louis, Tue-Sun 0940-1300 and 1400-1720, closed public holidays, free,* has a good sculpture gallery and an archaeological section with finds discovered at the Roman settlement at Arikamedu. The French gallery charts the history of the colony and includes Dupleix's four-poster bed. Another place worth seeking out is the grand whitewashed **Lycée Français** ① *rue Victor Simonel*, with its lovely shady courtyard and balconies.

The French Catholic influence is evident in a number of churches, notably the **Jesuit Cathedral** (Notre Dame de la Conception, 1691-1765). The attractive amber

PUDUCHERRY

To Serenity Beach,
Auroville & Chennai

Cinema

Sangara Dass St

Thiyagaraja St   Bharatidasan
                 Museum   Siva
Sri   Sakthi
Varadaraja   Travels   Handmade
Temple   Paper
         Sri   Aroma
         Vedapuriswarar Clinic   Perumal Koil St
         Temple   Muttu Mariamman
Eswaran Dharmaraja Koil St   Koil St

Kamatchi Amman Koil St

Sri Aurobindo St (Arvindar St)   Bharati
                                              Museum
Calve Supraya Chettiar St   Rue des Bassyins de Richemo

Caltisvaran Koil St   Vysial St

                                              Red
Amballattadavar Madam St Bike Hire   Courtyard

Poompuhur   Jail   Chemist
          India   Bazar   La Boutique
Raju   Overseas Jawaharlal Nehru St   d'Auroville
Moped Thiaga St Bank
                  Grand   Chemist   Auro
Ananda Rangapillai St Bazar   Travels

Vellaja St
                  Maison Ananda
Nidarajapayer St (Big Brahmin St) Rangapillai

St Theresa St   Cathedral Focus
Chinna Vaikal St   Books

Savaricayalu St (Small Brahmin St) Saint Theresa St
                                    Chinna Vaikal St
La Porte St

Rue Montorsier

Candappa St   (Anna Salai)   Coffee.com

Kamban   Lal Bahadur Shastri St
Kalaiarargam
Kailash   Ignas Mestry St   (Rue Bussy)
City Bus French
Stand   Bookshop
Yanam Vangadasala Pillar St
Botanical   LKP
Gardens Thillai Mestry St   Forex

         Jeevandam St
                               Kuthpa
         VOC St   Mosque

         Badar Sahib St   French
                                              Bookshop
Eglise de   Pondy
Sacre Coeur Rajasingh St   Cre'Art
de Jesus
             Ramaraja St
             Subbaiyah Salai   Water   (South
                                    Tower   Boulevard)

To Tindivanam & Chennai

Anna Salai (West Boulevard)

To Botanical Gardens & Main Bus Stand

Chinna Subraya Billa St

Bharati St

Mahatma Gandhi Rd

Ellaman Koil St

Cathedral St Mission St

Canteen St

Marius Xavier St

Ambur Salai

Rue Victor Simonel

Lycée
Français

Surcouf St

Mulla St

Calvary St

Chanda Sahib St

Canal

Rue Labourdonnais

Gingee Salai

Suffren St

Bazar

A B C D E F
1 2 3 4

and pink **Church of Our Lady of Angels** (1855) holds an oil painting of Our Lady of Assumption given to the church by King Louis Napoleon III.

The **Government (Puducherry) Park**, laid out with lawns, flower beds and fountains (one at the centre is of the Napoleon III period), lies in front of the Raj Niwas, the residence of the lieutenant governor. This was the original site of the first French garrison, Fort Louis, which was destroyed in Clive's raid of 1761.

→ AUROVILLE

ⓘ *Visitor centre, International Zone, T0413-262 2239, www.auroville.org, Mon-Sat 0900-1300 and 1400-1730, Sun 1000-1200 and 1400-1730. All visitors are expected to report here first. Passes for visits to Matrimandir gardens and Amphitheatre are issued here (Mon-Sat 0930-1230 and 1400-1600, Sun 0930-1230; gardens open daily 1000-1250 and 1400-1630), and a 5-min video about the Matrimandir is shown according to demand. Visitors may enter the Inner Chamber for 10 mins' silent 'concentration' with at least 1 day's notice; apply in person at the Visitor Centre 1000-1100 or 1400-1500 any day except Tue. A useful information booklet,* The Auroville Handbook, *is available here and at La Boutique d'Auroville, 38 JL Nehru St, Puducherry.*

Futuristic Auroville, 'City of Dawn', was founded in 1968 by the Mother as a tribute to Sri Aurobindo, and remains a fascinating experiment in communal living and spiritual evolution. The founding charter reads: "To live in Auroville one must be a willing servitor of the Divine Consciousness," and describes it as belonging "to humanity as a whole ... the place of an unending education, of constant progress ... a bridge between the past and the future ... a site of material and spiritual researches for a living embodiment of actual human unity".

A baked and desolate plateau when the first residents moved here, Auroville has been transformed into a lush forest, among which are scattered 100 distinct hamlets, housing a permanent population of 2200 people plus a regular throughflow of international eco-warriors, holistic therapists and spiritually inclined intellectuals. It's a place where concepts that would be deemed too flakey to fly in the outside world are given free rein: the town plan is based on the shape of a spiralling galaxy, with the **Matrimandir** – an extraordinary 30-m-high globe-shaped meditation chamber clad in shimmering discs of gold leaf, with a lotus bud shaped foundation urn and a centrepiece crystal said to be the largest in the world – at its spiritual and geographic fulcrum. The main buildings are based on principles espoused in Sri Aurobindo's philosophical tracts. And a town that can't provide enough housing to accommodate all its would-be residents has found the money to build a gleaming pavilion dedicated to study of Aurobindo's epic poem Savitri. Yet there's a great deal of serious and earnest work going on here, in the fields of sustainable architecture, reforestation, education, organic agriculture, renewable energy and self-development.

Residents are quick to point out that Auroville is not a tourist attraction, and a casual day trip here can be as much an exercise in frustration as inspiration. Tours from Puducherry visit the Matrimandir gardens for a view of the dome, but to experience the unforgettable womb-like interior and spend 10 minutes in silent 'concentration' you have to request permission in person at the Matrimandir office, at least 24 hours in advance.

On the other hand, the community welcomes visitors who have a genuine interest in its philosophy – all the more so if you can find a project you'd like to work on – and an extended stay here makes a very pleasant retreat. An ideal way to get to know the place is to take the three-day orientation tour, which guides you around many of Auroville's "villages" by bike and provides a good opportunity to interact with Aurovilians.

GOING FURTHER
Gingee and Tiruvannamalai

GINGEE

Inland from Puducherry off the NH45, Gingee (pronounced *Senjee*) has a remarkable 15th-century Vijayanagar fort with much to explore. It is well off the beaten track, very peaceful and in beautiful surroundings. Spend the night here if you can. Lovers come here at the weekends; it's on the domestic tourist map because it is often used as a film location. The landscape is made up of man-sized boulders, like Hampi, piled on top of each other to make mounds the texture of cottage cheese.

The fort ① *0900-1700, allow 2½ hrs for Rajagiri, and 2 hrs for Krishnagiri (if you have time), foreigners Rs 100, Indians Rs 20, camera Rs 50, video Rs 250, includes both forts*, was intensely contested by successive powers before being captured by an East India Company force in 1762, by the end of the century, however, it had lost its importance. Although it had Chola foundations, the 'most famous fort in the Carnatic' was almost entirely rebuilt in 1442. It is set on three strongly fortified Charnockite hills: Krishnagiri, Chakklidrug and Rajagiri. In places the hills on which the fort stands are sheer cliffs over 150 m high. The highest, Rajagiri ('King's Hill'), has a south-facing overhanging cliff face, on top of which is the citadel. The inner fort contains two temples and the Kalyana Mahal, a square court with a 27-m breezy tower topped by pyramidal roof, surrounded by apartments for the women of the governor's household. On top of the citadel is a huge cannon and a smooth granite slab known as the Raja's bathing stone. An extraordinary stone about 7 m high and balanced precariously on a rock, surrounded by a low circular brick wall, it is referred to as the Prisoner's Well. There are fine Vijaynagara temples, granary, barracks and stables and an 'elephant tank'. A caretaker may unlock a temple and then expect a tip.

The Archaeological Survey of India Office is just off the main road towards the fort. They may have guides to accompany you to the fort. Carry provisions, especially plenty of drinks; a few refreshments are sold, but only at the bottom of the hill. The climb is only for the fit and healthy; it's cooler in the morning and the views are less hazy.

TIRUVANNAMALAI

At the foot of rocky Arunachala Hill, revered by Hindus across South India as the physical manifestation of Siva, Tiruvannamalai is one of Tamil Nadu's holiest towns. It is a major pilgrimage centre, focused around the enormous and fascinating Arunachaleshwar Temple whose tall *gopurams* stand dazzling white against the blue sky, and for the first half of the 20th century was home to one of India's most beloved saints, the clear-eyed Sri Ramana Maharishi.

One of the largest temples in South India, the 16th- and 17th-century **Arunachala Temple** was built mainly under the patronage of the Vijayanagar kings and is dedicated to Siva as God incarnate of Fire. Its massive bright white *gopurams*, the tallest of which is 66 m high, dominate the centre of the town. The temple has three sets of walls forming nested rectangles. Built at different periods they illustrate the way in which many Dravidian temples grew by accretion. The east end of each is extended to make a court, and the main entrance is at the east end of the temple. The lower parts of the *gopurams*, built of granite, date from the late Vijayanagar period but have been added to subsequently. The upper 10 storeys and the decoration are of brick and plaster. There are some remarkable carvings on the *gopurams*. On the outer wall of the east *gopuram*, for example, Siva is shown in the south corner dancing, with an elephant's skin. Inside the east doorway of the first courtyard is the 1000-pillared *mandapa* (hall, portico) built in the late Vijayanagar period. To the south of the court is a small shrine dedicated to Subrahmanya. To the south again is a large tank. The pillars in the *mandapa* are typically carved vigorous horses, riders and lion-like *yalis*. The middle court has four much earlier *gopurams* (mid-14th century), a large columned *mandapa* and a tank. The innermost court may date from as early as the 11th century and the main sanctuary with carvings of deities is certainly of Chola origin. In the south is Dakshinamurti, the west shows Siva appearing out of a lingam and the north has Brahma. The outer porch has small shrines to Ganesh and Subrahmanya. In front of the main shrine are a brass column lamp and the *Nandi* bull.

Two kilometres southwest of the centre, the **Sri Ramanasramam** ① *T04175-237292, www.sriramanamaharshi.org*, was founded by Sri Ramana Maharishi, the Sage of Arunachala (1879-1950). Aged 16, he achieved spontaneous self-realization and left his family to immerse himself in *samadhi* at the foot of the holy mountain. He spent 20 years in caves, steadily accumulating followers, one of whom was his own mother, who died at the base of the mountain in 1922. Recognized as a saint herself, Sri Ramana chose his mother's shrine as the site for his ashram.

The peacock-filled ashram grounds, which attract a sizeable community of Westerners between December and April, contain a library with 30,000 spiritual books and many photos of Maharishi, the last of which were taken by Henri Cartier-Bresson, who photographed him when he was alive and also the morning after his death in April 1950. Apart from the two daily *pujas* (1000 and 1815) the ashram organizes few daily programs; the focus here is on quiet self-enquiry and meditation. Foreigners wishing to stay need to write to the ashram president with proposed dates.

A gate at the back of the ashram gives access to the hillside, from where you can begin the 14-km *pradakshina* (circuit) of Arunachala. (At the time of going to press the inner circuit path was closed to walkers, ostensibly due to concerns about wild fires. It may reopen in the future, so we've kept the following text in the book. Check locally for the current situation.) The hike is done barefoot – no shoes should be worn on the holy mountain – and takes four to five hours; on full moon nights, particularly during the annual Karthikai Deepam festival (November-December), the trail fills with crowds of pilgrims who chant the name of Siva and make offerings at the many small temples along the way. Another track, branching off to the right shortly after the ashram gate, climbs to Skandasramam, a shady hermitage dug into the rock at which Sri Ramana lived from 1916 to 1922. From here there's a wonderful view over the town, best at sunrise when the temples rise out of the haze like a lost Mayan city. The challenging trek to the summit of Arunachala continues beyond Skandasramam (allow six hours up and down).

WHERE TO STAY

$ Arunachala, 5 Vadasannathi St, Tiruvannamalai, T04175-228300. 32 clean, rooms, 16 a/c, TV, hot water, best away from temple, can get noisy during festivals, great vegetarian food downstairs.
$ Arunachala Ramana Home, 70 Ramana Nagar, off Chengam Rd near ashram, Tiruvannamalai, T04175-236120. Friendly

place with clean, good-value rooms. The owners can arrange bike hire and taxis, and also hand out a home-made map of the ashram area and mountain circuit.
$ Shivasand, M Gandhi Rd, opposite bus stand, Gingee, T04145-222218. Good views of fort from roof, 21 clean rooms with bath, some a/c, veg restaurant, a/c bar, helpful manager.

PUDUCHERRY AND AUROVILLE LISTINGS

WHERE TO STAY

Puducherry

$$$$-$$$ The Dune, 15 km north of Puducherry, T0413-265 5751, www.the dunehotel.com. Funky beachside eco-hotel with 36 themed villas and 15 colourful, clean and comfortable rooms spread amongst 12 ha of landscaped grounds. Yoga, reflexology, Ayurvedic massage, organic food and optional detox programmes are on offer, along with a pool, tennis and free bike hire.

$$$ Ajantha Sea View, 1C 50 Goubert Salai, T0413-234 9032, www.ajanthaseaview hotel.com. The best-value sea views in town. Not the most modern rooms, but they're clean, bright and have huge balconies gazing straight out into the Bay of Bengal. .

$$$-$$ Hotel de l'Orient, 17 Romain Rolland St, T0413-234 3067, www. neemranahotels.com. Beautifully renovated 19th-century school now a small exclusive hotel, with 16 tastefully decorated rooms in colonial style with objets d'art. Mixed reviews of the restaurant (French/Creole) and service, but achingly beautiful location. Recommended

$ Ram Guest House, 546 MG Rd, 278 Avvai Shanmugham (Lloyds) Rd, T0413-222 0072, ramguest@hotmail.com. 20 excellent rooms set back from the main road, maintained to European standards, spotless, good breakfast from clean kitchen. Recommended.

Auroville

For a complete list of guesthouses within Auroville see www.aurovilleguesthouses.org.

$ Centre Guest House, T0413-262 2155. Most short-stay visitors are accommodated here ("welcomes those who wish to see and be in Auroville, but not to work there"), in a lovely setting under a huge banyan tree. There are bikes and scooters for rent and famous weekly pizza.

RESTAURANTS

Puducherry

$$$ Lighthouse, on the roof of Promenade Hotel, 23 Goubert Salai, T0413-222 7750. Superb barbecue fare, including some quite adventurous veg options alongside the expected seafood and meat options, served on a glassed-in terrace with front-row sea views. Good cocktails, too.

$$ Rendezvous, 30 Suffren St, T0413-222 7677. Closed Tue. French and Continental. Attractive, modern, reasonable food but overpriced wine, nice roof terrace, pleasant atmosphere: the owner worked for a wealthy American family for 20 years and so his continental grub is first rate.

$$ Salad Bar, 13 rue Surcouf. Delivers what it promises: fresh, hygienic and delicious salads, as well as falafel wraps, burgers and crepes. There's free Wi-Fi too.

$ Ashram Dining Hall, north of Govt Pl. Indian vegetarian. Simple, filling, meals (Rs 30 per day) in an unusual setting, seating on cushions at low tables, farm-grown produce, non-spicy and non-greasy. Buy a ticket (from Ashram guesthouses or Central Bureau), then turn up at 0640, 1115, 1745 or 2000. Recommended, though non-ashramites can expect a grilling before being sold a ticket.

$ Le Space, 2 rue de la Bourdonnais. Sociable hippy-chic roof terrace hideaway strung with lanterns. Serves pastas and snacks, cheap drinks and plays music that's not too loud to talk over. Draws a mixed crowd of backpackers, Chennai hipsters and Pondy's young and beautiful.

CHOLA HEARTLAND AND KAVERI DELTA

Chidambaram, Thanjavur, Trichy and Madurai together represent the apotheosis of Tamilian temple architecture: the great temples here act as tirthas, or gateways, linking the profane to the sacred. This pilgrim's road boasts the beautiful Nataraja Temple at Chidambaram, with its two towers given over to bas-reliefs of the 108 mudras, or gestures, of classical dance; the bare granite Big Temple in the charming agricultural town of Thanjavur, which was for 300 years the capital of the Cholas; Trichy's 21-gopuram, seven-walled island city of Srirangam, a patchwork quilt of a temple built by successive dynastic waves of Cholas, Cheras, Pandyas, Hoysalas, Vijayanagars and Madurai Nanaks; and the swirling spiritual vortex of Madurai's Meenakshi Temple, where pilgrims and pipers jostle with prostrating devotees amid billowing clouds of incense smoke.

→ ARRIVING IN CHOLA HEARTLAND AND KAVERI DELTA

GETTING THERE
Buses from Puducherry will drop you at the grim fly-blown bus stand to the east of the centre, a five minute walk from the temple and hotels.

MOVING ON
Frequent buses and several daily trains connect Chidambaram with **Thanjavur** (see page 169), a beautiful trip through soft countryside of paddy fields and winding rivers. Most trains and all buses stop at **Kumbakonam** (see page 167) on the way. However, the best way to visit all the places of interest in this temple-rich section of Tamil Nadu is to hire a car and driver for the day; travel agents charge around Rs 3500-4500 for the one-way trip, though you might persuade local drivers to do it cheaper.

→ CHIDAMBARAM

The capital of the Cholas from AD 907 to 1310, the scruffy temple town of Chidambaram is one of Hinduism's most important holy sites. Rarely visited by foreigners, its main attraction is the hugely atmospheric temple, a sprawling collection of shrines held by Hindus to represent Shiva in the element of ether. There's a potent magic here at dusk, when lamps flare in the towering gateways and bells clang through the narrow passageway that leads to the inner sanctum of Nataraja – the famous idol of Shiva in the form of creator, preserver and destroyer of the universe, dancing wildly within a flaming halo.

The **Nataraja Temple** ① *0400-1200, 1630-2200, visitors may be asked for donations, entrance into the inner sanctum Rs 50, men must remove their shirts*, was the subject of a supreme court battle that ended in Delhi, where it was decided that it should remain as a private enterprise. All others fall under the state, with the Archeological Survey of India's sometimes questionable mandate to restore and maintain them. The unique brahmin community, with their right forehead shaved to indicate Siva, the left grown long and tied in a front top knot to denote his wife Parvati, will no doubt trot this out to you. As a private temple, it is unique in allowing non-Hindus to enter the sanctum (for a fee);

however, the brahmins at other shrines will ask you to sign a book with other foreign names in it, supposedly having donated Rs 400. The lack of state support does make this temple poorer than its neighbours, but if you want to give a token rupee coinage instead then do so. The atmosphere of this temple more than compensates for any money-grabbing tactics, however. Temple lamps still hang from the hallways, the temple music is rousing and the *puja* has the statues coming alive in sudden illumination. The brahmins themselves have a unique, stately presence too. The evening *puja* at 1800 is particularly interesting. At each shrine the visitor will be daubed with *vibhuti* (sacred ash) and paste. It is not easy to see some of the sculptures in the interior gloom. You may need patience and persuasive powers if you want to take your own time but it is worth the effort.

There are records of the temple's existence before the 10th century and inscriptions from the 11th century. One legend surrounding its construction suggests that it was built by 'the golden-coloured emperor', Hiranya Varna Chakravarti, who suffered from leprosy. He came to Chidambaram on a pilgrimage from Kashmir in about AD 500. After bathing in the temple tank he was reputed to have recovered from the disease and in gratitude offered to rebuild and enlarge the temple.

On each side are four enormous *gopurams*, those on the north and south being about 45 m high. The east *gopuram* (AD 1250), through which you enter the temple, is the oldest. The north *gopuram* was built by the great Vijayanagar king **Krishna Deva Raya** (1509-1530). Immediately on entering the East Gate is the large **Sivaganga** tank, and the **Raja Sabha**, a 1000-columned *mandapa* (1595-1685). In the northwest of the compound are temples dedicated to Subrahmanya (late 13th century), and to its south the 12th-century shrine to

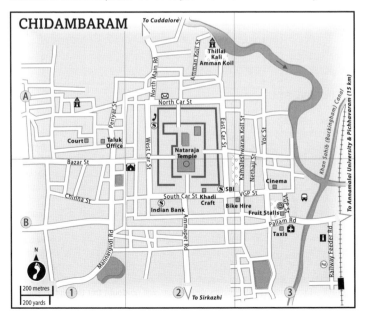

CHIDAMBARAM

Sivakumasundari or Parvati (circa 14th century). The ceiling paintings are 17th century. At the southern end of this outer compound is what is said to be the largest shrine to **Ganesh** in India. The next inner compound has been filled with colonnades and passageways. In the innermost shrine are two images of Siva, the Nataraja and the lingam. A later Vishnu shrine to Govindaraja was added by the Vijayanagar kings. The **inner enclosure**, the most sacred, contains four important *Sabhas* (halls), the **deva sabha**, where the temple managers hold their meetings; the **chit sabha** or *chit ambalam* (from which the temple and the town get their names), meaning the hall of wisdom; the **kanakha sabha**, or golden hall; and the **nritta sabha**, or hall of dancing. Siva is worshipped in the *chit ambalam*, a plain wooden building standing on a stone base, in his form as Lord of the Dance, Nataraja. The area immediately over the deity's head is gold plated. Immediately behind the idol is the focus of the temple's power, the Akasa Lingam, representing the invisible element, 'space', and hence is itself invisible. It is known as the Chidambaram secret.

AROUND CHIDAMBARAM

The Danish king Christian IV received permission from Raghunath Nayak of Thanjavur to build a fort at **Tranquebar** (Tharangampadi) in 1620. The Danish Tranquebar Mission was

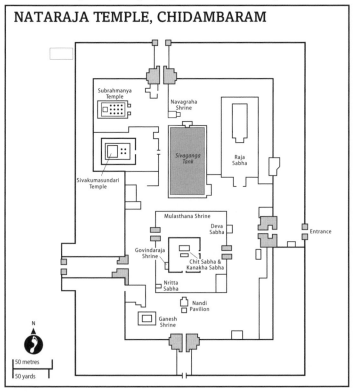

NATARAJA TEMPLE, CHIDAMBARAM

founded in 1706 and the Danesborg **fort** and the old **church** still survive. The Danes set up the first Tamil printing press, altering the script to make the casting of type easier and the Danish connection resulted in the National Museum of Copenhagen today possessing a remarkable collection of 17th-century Thanjavur paintings and Chola bronzes. There is a **museum** and a good beach, plus the evocatively ruined 14th-century Masilamani Nathar temple on the seashore. From Chidambaram most transport requires a change at Sirkazhi. From Thanjavur there are some direct buses; other buses involve a change at Mayiladuthurai (24 km).

→ GANGAIKONDACHOLAPURAM

Once the capital of the Chola king Rajendra (1012-1044), this town (whose name means 'The city of the Chola who conquered the Ganga') has now all but disappeared. The temple and the 5-km-long 11th-century reservoir embankment survive.

The **temple** ① *0700-1200, 1600-2100,* that Rajendra built was designed to rival the Brihadisvara temple built by Rajendra's father Rajaraja in Thanjavur. Unlike the *Nandi* in Thanjavur, the huge *Nandi* facing the *mandapa* and sanctuary inside the compound by the ruined east *gopuram* is not carved out of one block of stone. As in Thanjavur, the *mandapa* and sanctuary are raised on a high platform, orientated from west to east and climbed by steps. The whole building is over 100 m long and over 40 m wide. Two massive *dvarapalas* (doorkeepers) stand guard at the entrance to the long closed *mandapa* (the first of the many subsequent *mandapas* which expanded to 'halls of 1000 pillars'); the plinth is original. A *mukha-mandapa* (narrow colonnaded hall) links this hall to the shrine. On the east side of this hall are various carvings of Siva for example bestowing grace on Vishnu, who worships him with his lotus-eye. On the northeast is a large panel, a masterpiece of Chola art, showing Siva blessing Chandikesvara, the steward. At the centre of the shrine is a huge *lingam* on a round stand. As in Thanjavur there is a magnificent eight-tiered, pyramidal *vimana* (tower) above the sanctuary, nearly 55 m high. Unlike the austere straight line of the Thanjavur Temple, however, here gentle curves are introduced. Ask the custodian to allow you to look inside (best for light in the morning). Immediately to the north of the *mandapa* is an excellently carved shrine dedicated to Chandikesvara. To north and south are two shrines dedicated to Kailasanatha with excellent wall sculptures. The small shrine in the southwest corner is to Ganesh.

→ KUMBAKONAM

This very pleasant town was named after the legend in which Siva was said to have broken a *kumbh* (water pot) after it was brought here by a great flood. The water from the pot is reputed to have filled the Mahamakam Tank. Kumbakonam and its surrounding villages are renowned centres of bronze sculpture, some still practising the traditional *pancha loha* (five metals – gold, silver, lead, copper and iron) technique reserved for casting temple idols. You can visit workshops in Kumbakaonam itself, and in Swamimalai to the west and Nachiyar Koil to the southeast. High-quality betel vines, used for chewing paan, are grown here.

ARRIVING IN KUMBAKONAM
Getting there The bus stand and railway station are both east of the town centre, within walking distance of hotels and temples. If you're coming by car from Chidambaram/

Gongaikondacholapuram, consider turning left off the NH45C at Thiruppanandal and taking the back roads leading south to visit the wonderful Nataraja temple at Konerirajapuram; like other temples in the area, it closes 1200-1600.

Moving on Frequent buses (one hour) and trains (30 minutes to one hour) go south to **Thanjavur** (see page 169), 54 km away.

PLACES IN KUMBAKONAM

The temples in this region contain some exceptional pieces of jewellery – seen on payment of a small fee. There are 18 **temples** ⓘ *closed 1200-1630, no photography,* in the town centre and a monastery of the Kanchipuram Sankaracharya. The oldest is the **Nagesvara Swami Temple**, a Shaivite temple begun in AD 886. The small Nataraja shrine on the right before you reach the main sanctum is designed to look like a chariot being pulled by horses and elephants. Superb statues decorate the outside walls of the inner shrine; Dakshinamurti (exterior south wall), Ardinarisvara (west facing) and Brahma (north) are in the central panels, and described as being among the best works of sculpture of the Chola period. The temple has a special atmosphere and is definitely worth a visit.

Sarangapani is the largest of Kumbakonam's shrines. Dedicated to Vishnu (one of whose avatars is Krishna the cowherd), it is also one of the few temples in Tamil Nadu where you will see devotees actively paying reverence to cows. Beyond the 11-storey main *gopuram* that towers above the entrance lies a cattle shed, where visitors can offer gifts of leaves before tiptoeing in (barefoot, naturally) to touch the hindquarters of the closest

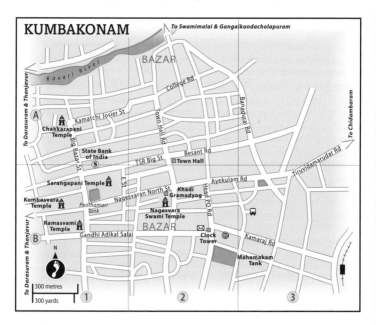

cow. The Nayaka *mandapa*, with huge beams of beautifully carved stone, leads through a second, smaller *gopuram* to a further *mandapa* carved in the form of a chariot, towed by horses and elephants.

The **Kumbesvara Temple** dates mainly from the 17th century and is the largest Siva temple in the town. It has a long colonnaded *mandapa* and a magnificent collection of silver *vahanas* (vehicles) for carrying the deities during festivals. The **Ramasvami Temple** is another Nayaka period building, with beautiful carved rearing horses in its pillared *mandapa*. The frescoes on the walls depict events from the *Ramayana*. The Navaratri Festival is observed with great colour.

The **Mahamakam Tank** is visited for a bathe by huge numbers of pilgrims every 12 years, when 'Jupiter passes over the sign of Leo'. It is believed that on the day of the festival nine of India's holiest rivers manifest themselves in the tank, including the Ganga, Yamuna and Narmada.

DARASURAM

About 5 km south of Kumbakonam is Darasuram with the **Airavatesvara Temple** ① *open 0600-1200,1600-2000*, the third of the great Chola temples after Thanjavur and Gangaikondacholapuram, built during the reign of **Rajaraja II** (1146-1172). The entrance is through two gateways. A small inner gateway leads to a court where the mainly granite temple stands in the centre. The *gopuram* is supported by beautifully carved *apsaras*. Inside, there are friezes of dancing figures and musicians. The *mandapa* is best entered from the south. Note the elephant, ridden by dwarfs, whose trunk is lost down the jaws of a crocodile. The pillars illustrate mythological stories for example 'the penance of Parvati'. The five gods Agni, Indra, Brahma, Vishnu and Vayu in the niches are all shown paying homage to Siva. The **main mandapa**, completely enclosed and joined to the central shrine, has figures carved in black basalt on the outside. The ceilings are also richly decorated and the pillars have the same flower emblems as in the outer *mandapa*. The main shrine has some outstanding sculptures; the guardians on the north are particularly fine. Sculpted doorkeepers with massive clubs guard the entrance to the main shrine, which has a *Nandi* at the entrance. Some of the niches inside contain superb early Chola sculptures of polished black basalt, including a unique sculpture of Ardhanarisvara with three faces and eight arms, a four-armed Nagaraja and a very unusual sculpture of Siva destroying Narasimha. The **outer walls** are also highly decorative. Siva as Dakshinamurti on the south wall, Brahma on the north wall and Siva appearing out of the lingam on the west wall. The inner wall of the *prakara* (encircling walkway) is divided into cells, each originally to house a deity. The corners of the courtyard have been enlarged to make four *mandapas*, again with beautiful decoration.

→ THANJAVUR (TANJORE)

Thanjavur's mathematically perfect Brihadisvara Temple, a World Heritage Site, is one of the great monuments of South India, its huge Nandi bull washed each fortnight with water, milk, turmeric and gingelly in front of a rapt audience that packs out the whole temple compound. In the heart of the lush, rice-growing delta of the Kaveri, the upper echelons of Tanjore life are landowners, rather than industrialists, and the city itself is mellow in comparison with Trichy, especially in the old town surrounding the Royal Palace.

ARRIVING IN THANJAVUR

Getting there Buses from Kumbakonam pull into the State (SETC) bus stand, a couple of blocks east of the Brihadisvara Temple in the town centre. The train station is at the south end of the town centre, about a 20-minute walk from the temple. Both are surrounded by cheap and mostly dismal hotels.

Moving on Frequent buses to **Tiruchirappali** (see page 172), Karaikudi (for Chettinad, see page 174) and points south leave from the New Bus Stand, 4 km south of the centre by local bus or auto-rickshaw. Trains leave for Trichy roughly every hour from 0530-1000 and 1230-2330 (1½ hours). However, to cover Trichy and Srirangam temple and reach Chettinad by nightfall a taxi is the most efficient means of transport.

Getting around Most hotels are within a 15-minute walk of the temple. Auto-rickshaws charge Rs 40-50 for trips around town.

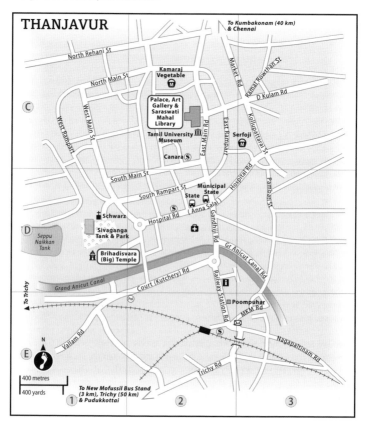

ON THE ROAD
The terrifying guardian deities

Many Hindu villagers in Tamil Nadu believe in guardian deities of the village – Ayyanar, Muneeswaram, Kaliamman, Mariamman and many more. Groups of larger-than-life images built of brick, wood or stone and covered in chunam (brightly painted lime plaster) guard the outskirts of several villages. They are deliberately terrifying, designed to frighten away evil spirits from village homes, but villagers themselves are also very frightened of these gods and try to keep away from them. The deities are supposed to prevent epidemics, but if an epidemic does strike, special sacrifices are offered, mainly of rice. Firewalking, often undertaken in fulfilment of a vow, is a feature of the special festivals at these shrines. Disease is also believed to be held at bay by other ceremonies, including piercing the cheeks and tongue with wire and the carrying of *kavadis* (special carriages or boxes, sometimes designed like a coffin).

Tourist information ⓘ *In the grounds of Hotel Tamil Nadu, Railway Station Rd (aka Gandhiji Rd), T04362-230984.*

PLACES IN THANJAVUR

Brihadisvara Temple ⓘ *0600-2030, inner sanctum closed 1230-1600*, known as the Big Temple, was the achievement of the Chola king Rajaraja I (ruled AD 985-1012). The magnificent main temple has a 62-m-high *vimana* (the tallest in India), topped by a dome carved from an 80-tonne block of granite, which needed a 6.5-km-long ramp to raise it to the top. The attractive gardens, the clean surroundings and well-lit sanctuaries make a visit doubly rewarding, especially in the evening. The entrance is from the east. After crossing the moat you enter through two *gopurams*, the second guarded by two *dvarapalas* typical of the early Chola period, when the *gopurams* on the outer enclosure walls were dwarfed by the scale of the *vimana* over the main shrine. An enormous Nandi, carved out of a single block of granite 6 m long, guards the entrance to the sanctuary. According to one of the many myths that revolve around the image of a wounded Nandi, the Thanjavur Nandi was growing larger and larger, threatening the temple, until a nail was driven into its back. The temple, built mainly with large granite blocks, has superb inscriptions and sculptures of Siva, Vishnu and Durga on three sides of the massive plinth. Siva appears in three forms, the dancer with 10 arms, the seated figure with a sword and trident, and Siva bearing a spear. The carvings of dancers showing the 81 different Bharat Natyam poses are the first to record classical dance form in this manner. The main shrine has a large lingam. In the inner courtyard are Chola frescoes on walls prepared with lime plaster, smoothed and polished, then painted while the surface was wet. These were hidden under later Nayaka paintings. Since music and dance were a vital part of temple life and dancing in the temple would accompany the chanting of the holy scriptures which the community attended, Rajaraja also built two housing colonies nearby to accommodate 400 *devadasis* (temple dancers). Subsidiary shrines were added to the main temple at different periods. The Vijayanagara kings built the Amman shrine, the Nayakas the Subrahmanya shrine and the Marathas the Ganesh shrine.

The Palace ⓘ *1000-1700, foreigners Rs 50, Indians Rs 5, camera Rs 30*, built by the Nayakas in the mid-16th century and later completed by the Marathas, is now partly in ruins, its walls used as makeshift hoardings for the latest Tamil movie release or political campaign. Still, there's evidence of its original splendour in the ornate Durbar Hall. The towers are worth climbing for a good view; one tower has a whale skeleton which was washed up in Chennai. The **art gallery** ① *0900-1300, 1500-1800, foreigners Rs 20, Indians Rs 5, camera Rs 30*, with bronze and granite sculptures, **Sangeeta Mahal** (the Hall of Music, where musicians and dancers performed before the Chola kings) with excellent acoustics, and the **Tamil University Museum** are here, together with some government offices. The pokey **Saraswati Mahal Library** ① *Thu-Tue 1000-1300, 1330-1700*, is brilliant: among its 40,000 rare books are texts from the medieval period, beautiful botanical pictures from the 18th century, palm leaf manuscripts of the Ramayana, intricate 250-year-old miniatures, and splendid examples of the gaudy Tanjore style of painting. It also has old samples of dhoti cloth design, and 22 engravings illustrating methods of torture from other oriental cultures in the 'Punishments of China'.

AROUND THANJAVUR

A visit to **Thiruvaiyaru**, 13 km away, with the Panchanatheswara Siva temple, known for its **Thyagaraja Music Festival**, gives a glimpse of South Indian rural life. Hardly visited by tourists, music connoisseurs arrive in large numbers in January. Performances vary and the often subtle music is marred by loud amplification. There is a **Car Festival** in March. Catch one of the frequent, crowded buses from the old bus station in Thanjavur, taking 30 minutes.

Point Calimere (Kodikkarai) Wildlife and Bird Sanctuary ① *open throughout the year, best season mid-Dec to Feb, Rs 5, camera Rs 5, video Rs 50*, is 90 km southeast of Thanjavur. The coastal sanctuary, half of which is tidal swamp, is famous for its migratory water birds. The Great Vedaranayam Salt Swamp (or 'Great Swamp') attracts one of the largest colonies of flamingos in Asia (5000-10,000) especially in December and January. Some 243 different bird species have been spotted here. In the spring green pigeons, rosy pastors, koels, mynahs and barbets can be seen. In the winter vegetables and insects attract paradise flycatchers, Indian pittas, shrikes, swallows, drongos, minivets, blue jays, woodpeckers and robins among others. Spotted deer, black buck, feral horses and wild boar are also found, as well as reptiles. The swamp supports a major commercial fishing industry. Jeeps can be booked at reception. Exploring on foot is a pleasant alternative to being 'bussed'; ask at reception for a guide.

→ TIRUCHIRAPPALLI (TRICHY) AND AROUND

Trichy, at the head of the fertile Kaveri Delta, is an industrial city and transport hub of some significance, with its own international airport connecting southern Tamil Nadu to Singapore and the Gulf. Land prices are high here, and houses, as you'll see if you climb up to its 84-m-high rock fort, are densely packed, outside the elegant doctors' suburbs. If you're ticking off sights on the temple circuit you'll want to stop here to visit the huge Srirangam temple – worth half a day en route to Chettinad – but if temple fatigue is starting to take hold you may prefer to bypass the city, which has little else to offer by way of easily accessed charms.

ARRIVING IN TIRUCHIRAPPALLI

Getting there Trains from Thanjavur arrive at Tiruchirappalli Junction, in the busy commercial centre, while buses pull in at the Central Bus Stand on Rockins Road nearby.

Srirangam is 10 km north: jump on the 1A or 1B bus from the bus stand, which runs in a circuit via the Rock Fort, or take an auto-rickshaw.

Moving on Plenty of trains and buses head south for Karaikudi and Pudukottai, jumping-off points for the villages of **Chettinad** (see page 174). An appealing alternative is to go by one of the handful of trains that call at little-used Chettinad Station, close to the mansion-hotel hotspot of Kanadukathan; there's a handy train that leaves Trichy at around 1545 (daily except Sunday). This is a non-standard way of reaching Chettinad, and you'll need to let your hotel know to pick you up.

Tourist information Tourist office ① *New Central Bus Stand, T0431-246 0136.* Also counters at the railway station and airport.

BACKGROUND
Trichy was mentioned by Ptolemy in the second century BC. A Chola fortification from the second century, it came to prominence under the Nayakas from Madurai who built the fort and the town, capitalizing on its strategic position. In legend its name is traced to a three-headed demon, Trisiras, who terrorized both men and the gods until Siva overpowered him in the place called Tiruchi. Cigar making became important between the two world wars, while the indigenous *bidis* continue to be made, following a tradition started in the 18th century. Trichy is the country's largest artificial diamond manufacturing centre. Jaffersha Street is known as Diamond Bazar. The town is also noted for its high-quality string instruments, especially veenas and violins.

PLACES IN TIRUCHIRAPPALLI
Rock Fort, 1660, stands on an 84-m-high rock. **Ucchi Pillayar Koil (Vinayaka Temple)** ① *Tue-Sun 0600-1200, 1600-2100, camera Rs 10, video Rs 50,* approached from Chinna Bazar, is worth climbing for the stunning panoramas but don't expect much from the temple. At the top of the first flight of steps lies the main 11th-century defence line and the remains of a thousand-pillared hall, destroyed in 1772. Further up is a hundred-pillared hall where civic receptions are held. At the end of the last flight is the **Tayumanasvami Temple**, dedicated to Siva, which has a golden *vimana* and a lingam carved from the rock itself. There are further seventh-century Pallava cave temples of beautiful carved pillars and panels.

Try to make time to explore the atmospheric old city, particularly **Big Bazar Street** and **Chinna Bazar**. The Gandhi Market is a colourful vegetable and fruit market.

Among the dozen or so mosques in the town, the **Nadir Shah Mosque** near the city railway station stands out with its white dome and metal steeple, said to have been built with material taken from a Hindu temple. **St Joseph's College Church** (Church of our Lady of Lourdes), one of several Catholic churches here, was designed as a smaller version of the Basilica at Lourdes in France. It has an unusual sandalwood altar but is rather garish inside. The grounds are a peaceful spot. The 18th-century **Christ Church**, the first English church, is north of the Teppakulam, while the early 19th-century **St John's Church** has a memorial plaque to Bishop Heber, one of India's best known missionary bishops, who died in Trichy in 1826.

SRIRANGAM
The temple town on the Kaveri, just north of Trichy, is surrounded by seven concentric walled courtyards, with magnificent gateways and several shrines. On the way to

Srirangam is an interesting river *ghat* where pilgrims take their ritual bath before entering the temple. The countryside to the west of the temple is an excellent place to sample rural Indian life and a good way to spend a couple of hours.

Sri Ranganathasvami Temple ① *0700-1300, 1400-1800, camera Rs 50, video Rs 100 (Rs 10 for the rooftop viewing tower), allow about 2 hrs, guides will greet you on arrival (their abilities are highly variable; some tell you that the staircase to the viewpoint will close shortly, which is usually a scam to encourage you to use their services),* is one of the largest in India and dedicated to Vishnu. It has some fine carvings and a good atmosphere. The fact that it faces south, unlike most other Hindu temples, is explained by the legend that Rama intended to present the image of Ranganatha to a temple in Sri Lanka but this was impossible since the deity became fixed here, but it still honours the original destination. The temple, where the Vaishnava reformer **Ramanuja** settled and worshipped, is famous for its superb sculpture, the 21 impressive *gopurams* and its rich collection of temple jewellery. The 'thousand' pillared hall (904 columns) stands beyond the fourth wall, and fifth enclosure there is the unusual shrine to Tulukka Nachiyar, the God's Muslim consort. Non-Hindus are not allowed into the sanctuary but can enter the fourth courtyard where the famous sculptures of *gopis* (*Radha's* milk maids) in the Venugopala shrine can be seen.

Nearby, on the north bank of the Kaveri, **Amma Mandapam** is a hive of activity. The *ghats*, where devotees wash, bathe, commit cremated ashes and pray, are interesting to visit, although some may find the dirt and smell overpowering.

So named because a legendary elephant worshipped the lingam, **Tiruvanaikkaval** is located 3 km east of Srirangam. It has the architecturally finer **Jambukesvara Temple** ① *200 m east off the main Tiruchi–Chennai road, a short stroll from Srirangam or easily reached by bus, officially 0600-2045, camera Rs 10, non-Hindus are not allowed into the sanctuary,* with its five walls and seven splendid *gopurams* and one of the oldest and largest Siva temples in Tamil Nadu. The unusual lingam under a *jambu* tree always remains under water.

→ CHETTINAD

The magnificent palaces of South India's old merchant and banking classes rise from the hot and dusty plains to stand as strong as fortresses and as gaudy as a packet of French Fancies. As the merchants, bankers and money-lenders of the British Empire, the Nattukottai Chettiars raked in enormous riches on their postings to places such as Burma, Sri Lanka, Indochina and South Africa, wealth they ploughed into these glorious architectural pastiches that explode in a profusion of colour in the arid desert-scape. It's been estimated that the Burma teak and satinwood pillars in a single Chettiar house weigh 300 tonnes. The plaster on the walls is made from a mixture of lime, egg white, powdered shells and myrobalan fruit (the astringent fruit of the tree *Phyllantles emblica*), mixed into a paste which, when dried, gives a gleaming finish. Most houses have the goddess of wealth, Lakshmi, made of stucco over the main arch.

Now their monumental arches and long processional corridors open onto empty halls, the bats are more at home here than princes and shafts of light break on empty, cobwebbed dining rooms. The Nattukottai Chettiars saw their riches contract with the Second World War and the wanton palaces they built turned into tombstones, the series of south Indian villages they stand in left as virtual ghost towns. Architectural salvage merchants in the main town of Karaikkudi now sell off the portraits and granite pillars this proud caste have been forced to surrender to stave off financial hardship, while Bollywood crews invade the old mansions, propping up the owners with *lakhs* of studio rupees in return for the right to daub their chosen colour scheme across the walls.

Karaikkudi is in the heart of Chettinad, and has several typical mansions, particularly along the back lanes leading off busy Sekkalai Road (ask for the Thousand Window House, a well-known landmark). From here you can walk south to the local *santhai* (market), where you can find gold and silversmiths in their workshops, as well as antique and textile shops and several colourful temples.

Devakottai, 18 km south of Karaikkudi, is Chettinad's second largest town and offers similarly rich pickings in the way of old mansions and palaces: look out for the particularly grand Periya Minor's *veedu*.

Kanadukathan, 12 km north of Karaikkudi, has a number of magnificent mansions, – some still inhabited by friendly owners (who'll let you have a look around for a Rs 100 donation), others are empty except for bats, monkeys and antique dealers. It has been estimated that the Burma teak and satinwood pillars in a single Chettiar house weighs 300 tonnes, often superbly carved. The plaster on the walls is made from a mixture of lime, egg white, powdered shells and myrobalan fruit (the astringent fruit of the tree *Phyllantles emblica*), mixed into a paste which, when dried, gives a gleaming finish. Most houses have the goddess of wealth, Lakshmi, made of stucco over the main arch.

The **Raja of Chettinad's Palace** ⓘ *0930-1630, free, caretakers provide brief free tours*, is an amazing place overlooking the town's pond and full of sepia, larger-than-life-size portraits of stern family members, the frames garlanded with heavy yellow flowers. Next door is **Visalakshi Ramaswamy's house**, with a museum of local crafts, artefacts and handlooms upstairs. The raja's waiting room at the railway station is also pretty special.

Athangudi, 9 km away, is renowned for its tiles, which grace the floors of most Chettiar mansions; ask locally if you want to visit one of the 30-40 workshops in town. Nearby is Pillaiyarpatti, one of the most important temples in Chettinad, dedicated to Ganesh (known as Pillaiyaru in Tamil Nadu) and with an inner sanctum carved out of a natural boulder.

At **Avudayarkoil**, 30 km northeast of Karaikkudi, the **Athmanathar Temple** has one of the most renowned sites in Tamil history. A legend tells that Manickavaskar, a Pandyan prime minister, redirected money intended for the purchase of horses to build the temple. However, his real fame lies as author of the *Thiruvasakam* ('Holy Outpourings'), one of the most revered Tamil poetic texts. Completely off the beaten track, the temple has superb sculptures, and is noted for the absence of any images of Siva or Parvati, the main deities, whose empty pedestals are worshipped. The woodcarvings on the temple car are notable too.

PUDUKKOTTAI AND AROUND

Pudukkottai, on the northern edge of Chettinad, 50 km south of Trichy, was the capital of the former princely state ruled by the Tondaiman Rajas, founded by Raghunatha Raya Tondaiman in 1686. At one entrance to the town is a ceremonial arch raised by the raja in honour of Queen Victoria's jubilee celebrations. The town's broad streets suggest a planned history; the temple is at the centre, with the old palace and a tank. The new palace is now the District Collector's office.

Thirukokarnam, 5 km north of the railway station, is the site of the rock-cut **Sri Kokarnesvarar Temple** ⓘ *closed 1200-1600,* dates from the Pallava period. The natural rock shelters, caves, stone circles, dolmens and Neolithic burial sites show that there was very early human occupation. The local **museum** ① *Big St, open daily except except Fri, 2nd Sat of the month, public holidays, 0930-1700, free, allow 40 mins, recommended,* has a wide range of exhibits including sections on geology, zoology and the economy as well as sculptures and the arts. The archaeology section has some excellent sculptures from nearby temples. There is a notable carving of Siva as *Dakshinamurti* and some fine bronzes from Pudukkottai itself.

Sittannavasal, 13 km away, has a Jain cave temple (circa eighth century) with sculptures, where monks took shelter when they fled from persecution in North India. In a shrine and veranda there are some fine frescoes in the Ajanta-style and bas-relief carvings. You can also see rock-hewn beds of the monks. The *Brahmi* inscriptions date from the second century BC.

→MADURAI AND AROUND

Madurai is a maddening whirl of a temple town: the red-and-white striped sanctuary of the 'fish-eyed goddess' is a towering edifice crested by elaborate gaudy stucco-work gopurams, soundtracked by tinny religious songs, peopled by 10,000 devoted pilgrims prostrating themselves at shrines, lighting candles and presenting flower garlands to idols, seeking blessings from the temple elephant or palmistry on the shores of the Golden Lotus tank. Even the city's town planning reflects the sanctity of the spot: surrounding streets radiate like bicycle spokes from the temple in the mandala architectural style, a sacred form of geometry. There is the usual combination of messy crumbling buildings harking back to times of greater architectural aspirations, modern glass-and-chrome palaces, internet cafés, flower sellers, tailors and tinkers and Kashmiri antique and shawl dealers. The centre seems all dust and cycle-rickshaws, but Madurai, as the second biggest city in Tamil Nadu, is also a modern industrial place that never sleeps. The fertile agricultural land surrounding the city is dotted with exotically shaped granite mountain ranges such as Nagamalai (snake hills) and Yanaimalai (elephant hills).

ARRIVING IN MADURAI
Getting there Buses from Karaikudi and elsewhere in Chettinad will drop you at the Mattuthavani Bus Stand 6 km northeast of the centre; local buses and auto-rickshaws can take you to the centre. The railway station is right in the centre of the city, and – no matter what predatory rickshaw drivers may try to tell you – it's only a five-minute walk to the temple and many budget hotels.

Moving on There are several morning buses to **Kodaikkanal** (see page 186; 3½ hours) from the Arapalayam bus stand, 3 km northwest of the city. It's a long and winding road up the mountain, and even if you're not prone to carsickness on the hairpin bends your fellow passengers probably will be. Alternatively, take a taxi from Madurai, or jump on a Chennai-bound train to Kodai Road station (30 minutes) and hail a local taxi from there; the price will drop if you cross the road and look determined to catch a bus.

Getting around The city centre is compact and the temple is within easy walking distance of most hotels. There's a useful and non-intimidating network of city buses that can get you to the long-distance bus stands, and the ever-present cycle- and auto-rickshaws trying to drum up a fare.

Tourist information ⓘ *W Veli St, T0452-233 4757, Mon-Fri 1000-1745*, has useful maps, tours (arranged through agents), guides for hire. Also at **Madurai Junction Railway Station** ⓘ *Main Hall, 0630-2030*.

BACKGROUND

According to legend, drops of nectar fell from Siva's locks on this site, so it was named Madhuram or Madurai, 'the Nectar City'. The city's history goes back to the sixth century

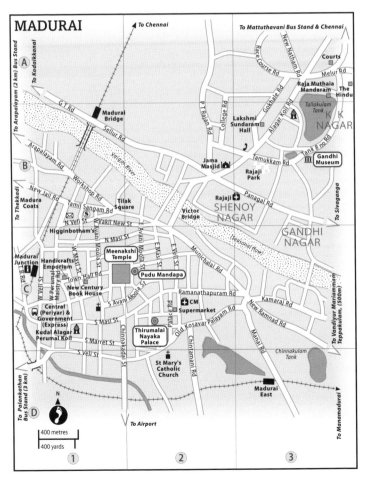

BC. Ancient Madurai, which traded with Greece and Rome, was a centre of Tamil culture, famous for its writers and poets during the last period of the three *Sangam* (Tamil 'Academies') nearly 2000 years ago.

By the fourth century, Madurai, Tirunelveli and a part of southern Kerala were under the **Pandiyas**, a major power from the sixth to the early 10th century. The Pandiyas made Madurai their capital and remained here for 300 years, staying on even during the rule of the **Cholas**; after Chola power declined in the late 12th century the Pandiyas regained control of Madurai, and they presided over a period of flourishing international trade until Malik Kafur destroyed the city in 1310.

For a period Madurai became a sultanate, but Muslim rule in Tamil Nadu proved as short-lived as it was tenuous. In 1364 the city was recaptured by the Hindu Vijayanagar kings (see Hampi, page 90), who remained until 1565, when the defeat of the Vijayanagar Empire by a confederacy of Muslim states forced their leaders to take refuge in Madurai. As the **Nayaka** kings, they continued to rule well into the 17th century. The Nayakas have been seen essentially as warriors, given an official position by the Vijayanagar rulers, but in Sanskrit the term applied to someone of prominence and leadership. Burton Stein comments, "the history of the Vijayanagara is essentially the history of the great Telugu Nayakas" from Madurai.

The Vijayanagar had been great builders, preserving and enriching the architectural heritage of the town, and the Nayakas held true to their legacy. They laid out the old town in the pattern of a lotus, with narrow streets surrounding the Meenakshi Temple at the centre, and took up the Vijayanagar predilection for building temple complexes with tall *gopurams*. These increased in height to become dominating structures covered profusely with plaster decorations. The tall *gopurams* of Madurai were built by Thirumalai (ruled 1623-1655), the greatest of the Nayaka rulers, and may have served a strategic purpose as they moved away from the earlier Chola practice of giving the central shrine the tallest tower. The *kalyana mandapa* or marriage hall with a 'hundred' or 'thousand' pillars, and the temple tank with steps on all four sides, were introduced in some southern temples, along with the *Nandi* bull, Siva's vehicle, which occupies a prominent position at the entrance to the main Shaivite shrine.

In 1840, after the Carnatic Wars, the British destroyed the fort, filling in the surrounding moat; its original course is now followed by the four Veli streets. The inner streets encircling the central temple are named after the festivals which take place in them and give their relative direction: South 'Chitrai Street, East 'Avani Moola' Street and West 'Masi Street'.

PLACES IN MADURAI

Meenakshi Temple ① *Inner Temple 0500-1230, 1600-2130, foreigners Rs 50, camera Rs 50, tickets from counters near South Entrance and Thousand-Pillared Hall (valid for multiple entries on same day); art museum 0600-2030, Rs 5, camera fee Rs 50. Metal detectors and body searches at entrance gates. Sanctuaries of Meenakshi and Sundareswarar are open only to Hindus. Offers of good viewpoints made by helpful bystanders will invariably turn out to be from the roofs of nearby shops.* This is an outstanding example of Vijayanagar temple architecture and an exact contemporary of the Taj Mahal in Agra. Meenakshi, the 'fish-eyed goddess' and the consort of Siva, has a temple to the south, and Sundareswarar (Siva), a temple to the west. Since she is the presiding deity the daily ceremonies are first performed in her shrine and, unlike the practice at other temples, Sundareswarar plays a secondary role. The temple's nine towering *gopurams* stand out with their colourful stucco images of gods, goddesses and animals which are renewed and painted every 12 years – the most recent touch-up having been completed in February 2009. There are about 4000 granite sculptures on the lower levels. In addition to the Golden Lotus tank and various pillared halls there are five *vimanas* over the sanctuaries.

The temple is a hive of activity, with a colourful temple elephant, flower sellers and **musical performances** ① *1800-1930, 2100-2130*. There is an evening ceremony (arrive by 2100), when an image of Sundareswarar is carried in procession, to a heady accompaniment of whirling pipe and drum music and clouds of incense, from the shrine near the east *gopuram* to Meenakshi, to 'sleep' by her side; he is returned first thing the next morning. The procession around the temple is occasionally led by the elephant and a cow. During the day the elephant is on continual duty, 'blessing' visitors with its trunk and then collecting a small offering.

The main entrance is through a small door of the **Ashta Sakthi Mandapa (1)** (Porch of the Eight Goddesses) which projects from the wall, south of the eastern *gopuram*. Inside to the left is the sacred **Tank of the Golden Lotus (2)**, with a lamp in the centre, surrounded by pillared cloisters and steps down to the waters. The Sangam legend speaks of the test that

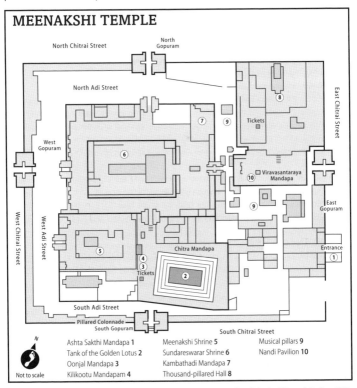

MEENAKSHI TEMPLE

Ashta Sakthi Mandapa **1**
Tank of the Golden Lotus **2**
Oonjal Mandapa **3**
Kilikootu Mandapam **4**
Meenakshi Shrine **5**
Sundareswaar Shrine **6**
Kambathadi Mandapa **7**
Thousand-pillared Hall **8**
Musical pillars **9**
Nandi Pavilion **10**

Not to scale

ancient manuscripts had to undergo: they were thrown into the sacred tank, and only if they floated were they considered worthy of further study. The north gallery has murals (under restoration at the time of writing) relating 64 miracles said to have been performed by Siva, and the southern has marble inscriptions of the 1330 couplets of the *Tamil Book of Ethics*. To the west of the tank is the **Oonjal Mandapa (3)**, the pavilion leading to the Meenakshi shrine. Here the pillars are carved in the form of the mythical beast *yali* which recurs in temples throughout the region. Golden images of Meenakshi and Sundareswarar are brought to the *oonjal* or swing each Friday evening where they are worshipped. Cages with parrots, Meenakshi's green bird that brings luck, hang from the ceiling of the neighbouring **Kilikootu Mandapam (4)**, which is flanked by finely carved columns. The **Meenakshi shrine (5)** with the principal image of the goddess, stands in its own enclosure with smaller shrines around it.

To the north of the tank is another enclosure with smaller *gopurams* on four sides within which is the **Sundareswarar shrine (6)** guarded by two tall *dwarapalas*. In the northeast corner, the superb sculptures of the divine marriage of Meenakshi and Sundareswarar being blessed by Vishnu and Brahma, and Siva in his 24 forms are in the 19th-century **Kambathadi Mandapa (7)**, around the golden flagstaff.

The mid-16th century **Thousand-pillared Hall (8)** is in the northeast corner of the complex. The 985 exquisitely carved columns include a lady playing the *vina*, a dancing Ganesh, and a gypsy leading a monkey. The art museum here exhibits temple art and architecture, fine brass and stone images, friezes and photos (the labelling could be improved). Just inside the museum to the right is a cluster of five **musical pillars (9)** carved out of a single stone. Each pillar produces a different note which vibrates when tapped. Nayaka musicians could play these as an instrument.

The **Nandi pavilion (10)** is to the east and is often packed with market stalls peddling flowers, trinkets and coconuts. The long *Pudu Mandapa* (New Mandapa), across the road from the East Tower, is lined with yet more beautiful sculptures of *yalis*, Nayaka rulers and elephants, and during the day Beyond lies the base of the unfinished *Raya Gopuram* which was planned to be the tallest in the country.

Northeast of the Meenakshi Temple, off N Avani Moola Street, is the **flower market**, a profusion of colour and activity at its best 0500-0730. It is a two-storey hall with piles of jasmine of all colours, lotuses, and huge jumbles of floral prettiness amid a sea of decomposing mulch of flowers trampled underfoot.

Thirumalai Nayaka Palace ① *0900-1300, 1400-1700, bus 17, 17A, 11, 11A.* Built in 1636 in the Indo-Mughal style, its 15 domes and arches are adorned with stucco work while some of its 240 columns rise to 12 m. Its *Swarga Vilasam* (Celestial Pavilion), an arcaded octagonal structure, is curiously constructed in brick and mortar without any supporting rafters. Special artisans skilled in the use of traditional lime plaster and powdered seashell and quartz have renovated parts. The original complex had a shrine, an armoury, a theatre, royal quarters, a royal bandstand, a harem, a pond and a garden but only about a quarter survives since Thirumalai's grandson removed sections to build another palace in Tiruchirappalli, and the original *Ranga* Vilasam was destroyed by Muslim invaders. It is a bit run down.

Vandiyur Mariammam Teppakulam ① *Buses 4 and 4A take 10 mins from the bus stand and railway station.* To the southeast of town, this has a small shrine in its centre where the annual **Float Festival** takes place in January/February.

Gandhi Museum ⓘ *1000-1300, 1400-1730, free.* Located in the 300-year-old Rani Mangammal Palace, this is Madurai's best museum: informative, interesting and well laid out. It contains an art gallery, memorabilia (including the *dhoti* Gandhi was wearing when he was shot) and traces the history of the Independence struggle and the Quit India movement. It also has sections for Khadi and Village Industries and some stunning examples of South Indian handicrafts. Yoga classes are held daily (though only in Tamil) at 0630. Excellent bookshop.

GOING FURTHER
Ramesvaram

The conch-shaped island of Ramesvaram is normally lapped by the limpid blue waters of the Gulf of Mannar, but cyclones can whip the sea here into ferocious stormy waves. This is where Rama is believed to have worshipped Siva, making it sacred to both Shaivites and Vaishnavites, and so a pilgrim to Varanasi is expected to visit Ramesvaram next if he is to reach salvation. The great Ramalingesvara temple, which forms the core of the scrappy town, is one of India's most memorable, as much for the sight of priests spattering pilgrims with holy water from each of 22 sacred wells as for its cavernous, echoing corridors.

ARRIVING IN RAMESVARAM
Getting there and around Ramesvaram is connected to Madurai and other centres by regular bus and train services. It's a very long and tiring day trip, but manageable (and actually quite good fun) on one of the guided tours offered by every hotel in Madurai. The bus stand is 2 km from the centre, the railway station 1 km southwest of the great temple. Local buses and auto-rickshaws link the bus and train stations to the temple, where there are a few places to stay.

Tourist information Tourist office ① *14 East Car St, T04573-221371, 1000-1700*. Also at the **Railway Station** ① *T04573-221373, open (with some breaks) 0700-2030*. The **Temple Information** is on the east side of the temple.

BACKGROUND
The *Ramayana* tells how the monkey king Hanuman built the bridges linking Ramnad to Pamban and Danushkodi (a spot where Rama is believed to have bathed) to help Rama rescue Sita from the demon king Ravana. When Rama returned he was told by the *rishis* that he must purify himself after committing the sin of murdering a Brahmin, for *Ravana* was the son of a Brahmin. To do this he was advised to set up a *lingam* and worship Siva. The red image of Hanuman north of the main East Gate illustrates this story.

The original shrine long predates the present great Ramesvaram temple. It is one of India's most sacred shrines and is visited by pilgrims from all over India. The temple benefited from huge donations from the 17th-century *Setupatis* (the so-called guardians of the causeway), who derived their wealth from the right to levy taxes on crossings to the island. The temple stands on slightly higher ground, surrounded by a freshwater lake.

Having bathed in the Ganga at Varanasi, Hindu pilgrims head straight for Ramesvaram, where a bath in the 22 *theertham* (holy wells) dotted within and around the Ramalingesvara temple promise a final release from the chains of *karma*.

The *theertham* circuit is a festive event for the pilgrims, complete with much cheering and song as buckets are emptied over heads, and as a visitor it can offer one of the most atmospheric and memorable temple experiences in Tamil Nadu, especially if you can get yourself adopted by a group of Indian visitors. The locals tend to bring along a change of clothes and submit to a thorough drenching, but if you come overdressed it is possible to request a light sprinkle. It's also traditional, but not obligatory, to taste of the waters; each apparently has a distinct flavour.

Brahmin priests wait at the train and bus stations and along the shoreline east of the temple to greet new arrivals, but he haggling of old has now been replaced by a standard charge of Rs 51 per person, which includes a dunking in each of the wells and access to the inner sanctum. Non-Hindus are traditionally prevented from entering the sanctum, but if you dress appropriately and arrive with a group (day tours from Madurai are an all-but-guaranteed way to join one) there's a good chance the priests will allow you in. If you do the circuit alone, it's best to leave valuables outside the temple: bystanders who offer to watch your bags are not all trustworthy.

RAMESVARAM

Ramalingesvara (or **Ramanathasvami**) **Temple** was founded by the Cholas but most of the temple was built in the Nayaka period (16th-17th centuries). It is a massive structure, enclosed by a huge rectangular wall with *gopurams* in the middle of three sides. Entrances through the east wall are approached through columned *mandapas* and the east *gopuram* is on the wall of the inner enclosure rather than the outer wall. Over 45 m high, it was begun in 1640 but left incomplete until recently. On entering, you see the statue of Hanuman, then the *Nandi* flanked by statues of the Nayaka kings of Madurai, Visvanatha and Krishnama. The north and south *gopurams* were built by Keerana Rayar of the Deccan in about AD 1420; the west *gopuram* is comparatively new.

The most remarkable feature of the temple is its pillared *mandapas*, the longest of which is over 200 m long. The pillars lining the four corridors, nearly 4 m tall, give an impression of almost unending perspective: those on the north and south sides are particularly striking. Tragically, however, the original stone pillars, decorated with scrollwork and lotus motifs, are being progressively phased out in favour of graceless grey concrete facsimiles. You're only likely to see the original versions lying on the ground in piles.

There are two gateways on the east side which give access to the Parvati and Ramalinga shrines at the centre; the masonry shrine is probably the oldest building on the site, going back to 1173. Non-Hindus are generally turned away, but you might be able to enter if you can tag along with a group of pilgrims doing the holy well circuit (see above).

A popular place to stay is the **Hotel Tamil Nadu** (**$**) (TTDC, 14 East Car Street, T04573-221064) which has sea-facing balconies, 53 clean rooms (with two to six beds), some are air conditioned, and a grubby restaurant (breakfast from 0700). There's also a bar, sea bathing nearby and exchange. Book well in advance.

GANDHAMADANA PARVATAM

Gandhamadana Parvatam, 2 km north of Ramesvaram, takes its name from the Sanskrit words *gandha* (fragrance) and *mad* (intoxicate), 'highly fragrant hill'. Dedicated to Rama's feet, this is the spot from which Hanuman is believed to have surveyed the area before taking his leap across the narrow Palk strait to Sri Lanka. You can get an excellent view from the top of the *mandapa*.

DHANUSKODI

Dhanuskodi ('the end of the bow') is the island's toe-tip where the Bay of Bengal meets the Indian Ocean, so named because Rama, at the request of Vibishana, his friend, destroyed the bridge to Sri Lanka with the end of his bow. Some 20 km to the east of Ramesvaram island, it is considered particularly holy. There is a good beach, on which pilgrims will be making *puja*, and beautiful flat turquoise waters in which they take their holy bath, not to mention excellent views. A trip across the scrappy sand dunes is only recommended for the really hardy – get a local person to go with you. Travel by bus, and then join a pilgrim group on a jeep or lorry for the last desolate few miles (this should cost Rs 50 for a round trip but establish the price up front). Alternatively, take an auto to Adam's Bridge; insist on going as far as the radio mast for beach and fishing shack photos.

CHOLA HEARTLAND AND KAVERI DELTA LISTINGS

WHERE TO STAY

Chidambaram
$ Akshaya, 17-18 East Car St, T04144-220192, www.hotelakshaya.com. Comfortable small hotel right in the centre (can be noisy) with 24 well-swept rooms and a rooftop overlooking the temple grounds.

Kumbakonam
$$-$ Raya's Annexe, 19 Head PO Rd, near Mahamaham tank, T0435-242 3270, www.hotelrayas.com. The shiny exterior conceals the best and cleanest rooms in town: 'Standard' rooms are a/c, light and spacious with good bathrooms; 'Elite' and 'Studio' rooms offer extra space and dining/sitting areas. Interesting views across temple roofs from upper floor lobbies.

Thanjavur
$$$ Ideal River View Resort, Vennar Bank, Palli Agraharam, 6 km north of centre, T04362-250533, www.idealresort.com. Clean, comfortable cottages (some a/c) in large grounds overlooking a branch of the Kaveri. A peaceful alternative to staying in Thanjavur, with boating, a big pool, restaurant and shuttles into town.
$$ Gnanam, Anna Salai (Market Rd), T04362-278501, www.hotelgnanam.com. The best mid-range choice in town, with 30 sparkling a/c rooms, some with balcony, a vegetarian restaurant and free Wi-Fi in the lobby.

Chettinad
$$$$ Visalam, Kanadukathan, T04565-273302, www.cghearth.com. Romantic and supremely comfortable high-celinged rooms, sparely furnished with Chettiar writing desks and 4-posters, in a beautifully restored art deco mansion – the only one in Chettinad built for a girl. The chef serves banana leaf lunches and does cooking demonstrations, good local guides are available for walking and bike tours, plus there's a huge pool and lawns.
$$$ The Bangala, Senjai, T04565-220221, www.thebangala.com. 8 bright and spacious a/c rooms with period colonial furniture, in restored 1916 bungalow, a heritage guesthouse of character set amidst orchards and palms, serves full-on, totally authentic Chettinad feasts for a fair whack at Rs 800 per meal (must be booked in advance). The family here wrote the (coffee table) book on Chettinad architecture.
$$$ Chettinadu Mansion, behind the Raja's Palace, Kanadukathan, T04565-273080; book through **Deshadan Tours and Travels**, T0484-232 1518, www.chettinadumansion.com. Dating back to 1902, this stunning house takes up half the block, with courtyard after courtyard stretching back from the street. Huge rooms, with a quirky green-brown colour scheme, heavy painted shutters and private rooftop sit-outs, encircle the upper floor. Simple Chettinad-style meals, served in the colonnaded dining room or under stars in the courtyard, cost Rs 700, and the charming Mr Chandramouli, who was born in the house, is often on hand to share stories or sharp business advice.

Madurai
$$$ Gateway (Taj), Pasumalai Hills, 7 TPK Rd, 5 km southwest of centre on NH7, T0452-663 3000, www.thegateway hotels.com. A real oasis, great views over surrounding country, 30 rooms (some in old colonial house) sheltered by the shade of trees, gardens full of peacocks, outdoor dining, good bookshop, lovely pool.
$$$-$$ Royal Court, 4 West Veli St, T0452-435 6666, www.royalcourtindia.com. 70 extremely clean a/c rooms with bath, satellite TV and great views from rooftop (open 1900-2300), good value.

$ YMCA International Guest House, Main Guard Sq, near temple, T0452-234 0861, www.ymcamadurai.com. A great option within spitting distance of the temple. The double rooms here are simple but spacious and clean, the staff are friendly, and profits go to worthwhile projects.

RESTAURANTS

Vegetarians and those prepared to consume *idli-sambar* for breakfast and vast mounds of rice at lunch will have no trouble finding food on the temple trail; just pick the busiest place you can find and dive in. Other food choices tend to be limited to hotel restaurants.

Kumbakonam
$ Sri Venkkatramana Hotel, 40 Gandhi Park North St. Simple but clean place serving great veg *thalis* on banana leaves.

Chettinad
Chettinadu food is famously fiery and exported all over India. You'll find that most high-end hotels serve dampened-down versions made friendly for foreign palates, though **The Bangala** (see Where to Stay) keeps true to tradition – and elsewhere you can always ask your waiter to instruct the chef not to spare the chilli powder.

Tiruchirappalli
Shree Sangeetas, 2 VOC Rd. Popular pan-Indian vegetarian place, close to the bus stand and station.

Thanjavur
$ Sathars, Gandhiji Road. Tandoori. Excellent for biryani and tandoori, both vegetarian and meat variants. Recommended.

Madurai
$$ Surya, Hotel Supreme. Open 1600-2400. 7th-floor rooftop restaurant with international as well as Indian menu. Excellent Andhra *thalis*, very busy Sun evenings.
$ Sri Sabarees, corner of W Perumal Maistry St and Town Hall Rd. Serves simple South Indian fare – *thalis* (lunchtime only), *pongal*, *iddli* and *dosai* – but the 2 dining halls are perpetually packed, as is the coffee stall out front.

KODAIKKANAL TO THE COAST

West of Madurai, the cool Palani Hills rear up from the plains, promising a blissful respite from the heat of the Tamil Nadu flatlands. Established by American missionaries, the hill station of Kodaikkanal sits high and pretty around a glittering lake, with excellent walks along quiet roads. A day's meandering drive to the west takes you across the Western Ghats watershed and into the lush and prosperous climes of Kerala, where Periyar National Park awaits with some of the best wildlife spotting opportunities in India's far south. After some tough travel days, rest up in Varkala, an appealingly low-key beach town set atop red cliffs that has, thus far proven immune to mass commercialisation.

→ KODAIKKANAL

The climb up the Palanis starts 47 km before Kodaikkanal (Kodai) and is one of the most rapid ascents anywhere across the ghats. The views are stunning. In the lower reaches of the climb you look down over the Kambam Valley, the Vaigai Lake and across to the Varushanad Hills beyond, while higher up the scene is dominated by the sawn-off pyramid of Perumal Malai. Set around a small artificial lake, the town has crisply fresh air, even at the height of summer, and the beautiful scent of pine and eucalyptus make it a popular retreat from the southern plains. Today Kodai is a fast growing resort, yet it retains a relatively low-key air that gives it an edge over its more populist cousin Ooty.

ARRIVING IN KODAIKKANAL
Getting there and around Buses make the long climb from Madurai and Kodaikkanal Road station to the Central Bus Stand, which is within easy walking distance of most hotels. Kodai is small enough to walk around – indeed it's one of the chief pleasures of being here – but for some of the more far-flung sites it's worth getting an unmetered taxi.

Moving on Getting anywhere from Kodaikkanal takes a long time, and crossing the mountains into Kerala especially so. The marathon trip to **Kumily** (Periyar National Park; see page 188) involves two to three buses: first back down the hill to Vathalakkundu, then to Theni, and finally to Kumily. Much easier to hire a taxi, which allows you to stop and enjoy the beautiful mountain scenery along the way.

Tourist information There's a Tamil Nadu tourist office ① *Hospital Rd next to bus stand, T04542-241675, 1000-1745 except holidays*, with helpful staff and maps available.

BACKGROUND
The **Palani Hills** were first surveyed by British administrators in 1821, but the surveyor's report was not published until 1837, 10 years after Ooty had become the official sanatorium for the British in South India. A proposal to build a sanatorium was made in 1861-1862 by Colonel Hamilton, who noted the extremely healthy climate and the lack of disease, but the sanatorium was never built because the site was so inaccessible. So it was that Kodaikkanal became the first hill station in India to be set up not by heat-sick Britons but by American missionaries.

The American Mission in Madurai, established in 1834, had lost six of their early missionaries within a decade. The missionaries had been eyeing a site in the Sirumalai Hills, at around 1300 m, but while these were high enough to offer respite from the heat of the plains they were still prone to malaria. Isolated Kodai, almost 1000 m higher, proved to be the ticket, and the first two bungalows were built by June 1845. Kodai's big transformation came at the turn of the 20th century with the arrival of the car and the bus. In 1905 it was possible to do the whole journey from Kodai Road station to Kodai within the hours of daylight. The present road, up Law's Ghat, was opened to traffic in 1916.

PLACES IN KODAIKKANAL

Star-shaped **Kodaikkanal Lake** covers 24 ha and is surrounded by gentle wooded slopes. The walk around the lake takes about one hour; you can also hire pedal boats and pedal boats and horses. Fishing and swimming are best avoided owing to mercury pollution in the lake. The International School, established in 1901, has a commanding position on the lakeside, and provides education for children from India and abroad between the ages of five and 18. The view over the plains from Coaker's Walk, built by Lieutenant Coaker in the 1870s, can be magnificent; on a rare clear day you can see as far as Madurai. It is reached from a signposted path just above the bazar, 1 km from the bus stand.

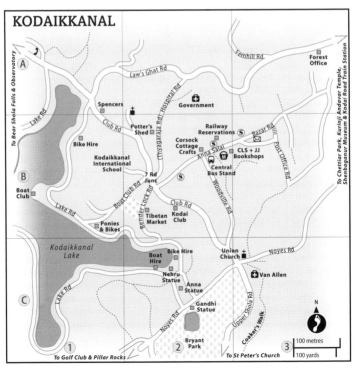

Kurinji Andavar Temple, northeast of the town past Chettiar Park, is dedicated to Murugan and associated with the Neelakurinji flower that carpets the hills in purple flowers once every 12 years (the next mass flowering is due in 2018). There are excellent views of the north and southern plains, including Palani and Vaigai dams.

The small but interesting **Shenbaganur Museum** ① *5 km down Law's Ghat Rd, open 1000-1130, 1500-1700*, at the Sacred Heart College seminary, is the local flora and fauna museum, exhibiting 300 orchid species as well as some archaeological remains. It's an attractive walk downhill from the town passing a number of small waterfalls. Some 4 km west of the bus stand at a height of 2347 m, the **Solar Physical Observatory** ① *T04542-240588, Fri 1000-1230, 1900-2100*, is one of the oldest in the world, established in 1899.

Bear Shola Falls, named because it once attracted bears, is a favourite picnic spot about 2 km from the bus stand. The falls, like most others around Kodai, have been reduced to a trickle outside monsoon season. A pleasant walk or bike/scooter ride leads southwest from the lake along leafy avenues, past the golf course where wild deer and gaur are sometimes seen, to the striking viewpoint at Valley View; a further 3 km away are **Pillar Rocks**, a trio of impressive granite formations over 120 m high.

→ AROUND KODAIKKANAL

If you're in the mood for an adventure there's a popular semi-official trekking route that links Kodaikkanal to Munnar (see page 220), roughly following the now-overgrown Escape Road built by the British Army in anticipation of a Japanese invasion in 1942. The route follows the Pillar Rocks road, then descends to beautiful **Berijam Lake**, 21 km southwest of Kodaikkanal, where there's an adequate Forest Rest House. You can visit the lake on a day trip with permission from the **Forestry Department Office** ① *Law's Ghat Rd, Kodaikkanal, T04542-240287*; only 10 permits are granted a day so arrive at the office before 1000. The next day you continue through pine and eucalypt plantations, patches of shola forest and the occasional village to **Top Station** in Kerala (five to six hours), where there is a Forest Hut and shops and tea stalls selling snacks. From here you can catch a bus or jeep to **Munnar**, 41 km away. You'll need permission from the Forestry Department in both Kodai and Munnar to complete the trek, and cross-border bureaucratic wrangling can make this hard to come by. Local guides can help with permits and transport at a charge: try **Raja** ① *T(0)98421 88893*, or the semi-legendary **Kodai Mani** ① *T(0)98940 48493*, who knows the trails well and charges accordingly.

→ THEKKADY (PERIYAR NATIONAL PARK, KUMILY TOWN)

Covering 930 sq km of montane forest and grassland and centred on an attractive lake, **Periyar National Park**, may not throw up many tiger sightings nowadays, but still attracts more than 300,000 visitors a year for its beautiful setting and unique range of soft adventure activities. Elephants, *gaur* and wild boar, though by no means guaranteed, are regularly spotted from the lake cruise boats, while sloth bear, porcupine and Malabar giant squirrel also haunt the woods.

The sanctuary was established by the old Travancore State government in 1934 and brought under the umbrella of Project Tiger in 1973, but Periyar's finest hour came in 1998 when the Kerala Forest Department, in partnership with the World Bank and the Thekkady

Wildlife Society (a local NGO), set up a project to deploy a band of reformed cinnamon poachers from the surrounding villages as tour leaders and forest rangers in remote parts of the park. The camo-clad members of the **Ex-Vayana Bark Collectors Eco Development Committee** now earn a steady income from tourism, not to mention new-found respect within their communities, and their hard-won knowledge of the terrain and sharp instincts for animal behaviour makes them skilled, if not exactly chatty, forest guides. Trekking with them for a day represents your best chance of getting up close with elephants.

The centre of activities in the park is the boat jetty on pretty **Lake Periyar**, 3 km down a beautiful forest road from the tourist village of **Kumily**, which was created in 1895 by a dam that inundated 55 sq km of rich forest. A 180-m-long tunnel now leads the water eastward into the Suruli and Vaigai rivers, irrigating extensive areas of Ramanathapuram and Madurai districts in Tamil Nadu. Hidden away in the hills to the south is Sabarimala, the focus of what some say is the world's biggest annual pilgrimage: 55 million pilgrims a year, almost all men, trek through the forest to the shrine, which is where the god Ayyappan is believed to have meditated after slaying a demoness.

ARRIVING IN THEKKADY

Getting there and around With the exception of a couple of government-run hotels down by the lakeside, everything that happens in Periyar happens in the busy little tourist trap of Kumily. The bus stand is at the north end of the main street, a 10-minute walk from most hotels. Buses run down to the lake jetty, or you can hire a bike (a tough ride back up the hill without gears), take an auto-rickshaw, share a jeep, or take the pleasant walk through the woods.

Moving on To get to **Varkala** (see page 191), first take a 'town-to-town' express bus from Kumily to Kottayam (three hours), then a southbound train to Varkala (2½ hours). The 0800 bus, followed by a 2-km auto-rickshaw dash, gets you to Kottayam station in time to catch the Kanyakumari Express at 1130, and you can be in Varkala by 1500. A taxi to Varkala will cost around Rs 4000, and allows you to stop off along the beautiful road to Kottayam.

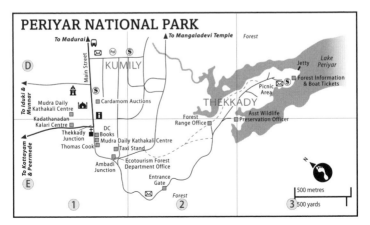

ON THE ROAD

A modern mass pilgrimage

Sabarimala pilgrims are readily visible in many parts of South India as they wear black *dhotis* as a symbol of the penance they must undergo for 41 days before they make the pilgrimage. In addition to the black dress, pilgrims must take two baths daily and only eat food at home during this period. The pilgrimage, which begins at Deepavali, is only for males and prepubescent and post-menstrual females, to avoid the defilement believed to be associated with menstruation.

The pilgrimage in January is deliberately hard, writes KR Vaidyanathan in *Pilgrimage to Sabari*, because "the pilgrimage to the shrine symbolizes the struggle of the individual soul in its onward journey to the abode of bliss and beatitude. The path of the spiritual aspirant is always long, arduous and hazardous. And so is the pilgrimage to Sabarimala, what with the observance of severe austerities and trekking up forested mountains, risking attacks from wild animals".

Tourist information Eco Tourism Office ① *Ambady Junction, Kumily, T0486-922 4571, www.periyartigerreserve.org*, has information and books tickets for treks and tours in the park. District Tourism Information Office ① *T0486-922 2620*, runs plantation tours to Abraham's Spice Garden (4 km) and Vandiperiyar (18 km). Entry to the park costs Rs 300 per day, Rs 150 for children; Indians pay Rs 25/Rs 5. The best time to visit is December to April, when dry weather brings animals closer to the lake. Dawn and dusk are best for wildlife, so stay overnight (winter nights can get quite cold). Avoid weekends and holidays, and especially the **Makaravilakku** festival in mid-January, which brings pilgrims by their millions to the Sabarimala shrine (see above).

VISITING PERIYAR NATIONAL PARK

The standard way to see Periyar is to take a trip across the lake on a **motor launch** ① *depart 0730, 0930, 1115, 1345 and 1530, Rs 150; tickets on sale 90 mins before departure, no advance reservation required*. You can get good wildlife sightings on the first trip of the morning – elephants, gaur, wild boar, sambar and Barking deer are regularly spotted browsing on the banks, and packs of dhole (wild dog) very occasionally seen – but noisy boats (and their occupants) and the heat soon drive animals away from the shore. Jeeps begin queueing at the park entrance gate from 0500 to get on the first launch of the morning, and there's a mad sprint to the ticket office once you reach the lake's edge.

From the same office you can book a three-hour **forest trek** ① *maximum 5 people, depart 0700, 0730, 1000, 1030, 1400, 1430, Rs 300, no advance reservations so get to office early to queue; carry water and beware of leeches*. There are good chances of seeing Malabar giant squirrel and Nilgiri langur, but much depends on your guide and not everybody comes face to face with a herd of elephants; some return very disappointed. Guides may also offer to arrange unofficial private walking tours in the park periphery in the afternoon (not the best time for spotting wildlife); try to assess the guide before signing up.

A more rewarding option is to sign up for one of the longer adventures into the park offered by the Ex-Vayana Bark Collectors Eco Development Committee. If you only have a day to spend in the park, spend it on the **Bamboo Rafting trip** (Rs 2000) – a full-day odyssey on land and water, trekking through a mosaic of grasslands, dense forest and rocky lakeshore, and navigating a long stretch of the lake on rickety rafts. Bird sightings are fabulous, with Malabar giant hornbill a real possibility, and the ex-poacher guides have been known to change the route to pursue – in a strictly non-violent sense – herds of elephant. A rifleman accompanies every group to ward off the threat of a charge.

If you've got longer, the **Tiger Trail** covers much the same ground but offers a chance to trek deeper into the forest, camping out for one or two nights (Rs 5000/7000 per person, maximum of six guests). Other activities include the **Jungle Patrol** (an exciting three-hour night trek, where you might spotlight porcupine and nightjars), the full-day **Border Hiking** trail to a peak overlooking the Kambam Valley, and bullock cart rides to a traditional farming village.

AROUND THEKKADY

There are a number of attractions within easy reach of Thekkady. These include the traditional Keralite-style **Mangaladevi Temple**, set amongst dense woodland on the peak of a 1337 m hill, 15 km northeast. Permission to visit the area must be obtained from the Wildlife Warden in Thekkady, though the temple itself is only open during the **Chithra Pounami** holiday. Other picturesque spots around Thekkady include **Pandikuzhi** (5 km) and **Chellarkovil** (15 km).

An hour west of Thekkady on the Kottayam road is **Peermade**, named after Peer Mohammed, a Sufi saint and crony of the royal family of Travancore. The fertile country here nourishes countless spice plantations growing cardamom, pepper, turmeric, nutmeg, cloves, ginger and vanilla. From here the road dives down towards the coastal plain, the air becoming thick with humidity as you drop lower. Tea bushes and forest give way to a dense monoculture of rubber plantations, and if you have a night to spare there's one wonderful plantation retreat hidden away off the main road, where you can see rubber being tapped and dried and wander the country lanes of a little-visited corner of Kerala (see Where to stay, page 199).

→ VARKALA

Like Gokarna in Karnataka (see page 100), Varkala is a pilgrimage centre for both backpackers and Hindus. The former come for the ruddy beach which lies at the bottom of the dramatic drop of a laterite cliff, the latter for the Vaishnavite **Janardhanaswamy Temple** and the Sivagiri Mutt of social reformer Sree Narayana Guru. The sea is far from calm (it has lifeguards for good reason), and the main beach, **Papanasam**, accessed by steep steps hacked in the cliffs, is shared between holidaymakers and fishermen. Along the cliff path, particularly along the **North Cliff**, is the tourist village high street; sizeable concrete hotels, travel agents, internet cafés, tailors stitching out endless pairs of fisherman's trousers and a huge preponderance of Kashmiri and Tibetan salespeople pushing their customary turquoise, silverware and carpets. Further north, the tourist shacks bleed into fishing village life around the **Alimood Mosque** (dress modestly). Watch your step around the cliff, particularly at night; carry a torch after dark.

The south, bordered by a golden beach, has a lovely village feel, with traditional houses built around the 13th-century temple dedicated to Vishnu. The **Arratu festival** in March-April draws thousands of visitors.

Opposite is the **Sri Rama Hanuman Temple**, whose large temple tank three-wheeler drivers splash through in the morning, while women thwack their lungis clean on its steps. The main 'town' area (including the train station) is a further 2 km inland from Temple Junction.

A two-hour excursion takes you to **Golden Island** for a glimpse of local backwaters; there's a small temple here but it's the type of visit you'd make for the atmosphere more than anything else. A boat round the island should cost Rs 50 for the hour.

Lullaby@Varkala, www.lullabyatvarkala.in, runs tours to introduce tourists to *anganwadis*, childcare centres for underprivileged families. The project helps feed, clothe and educate its beneficiaries.

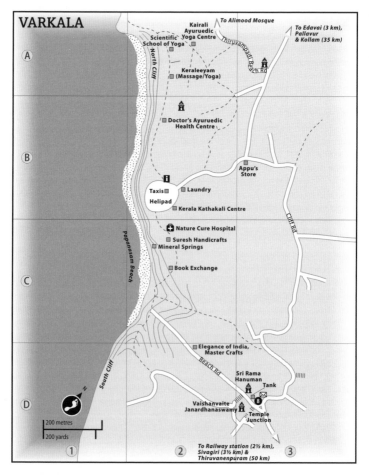

VARKALA

To Alimood Mosque
To Edavai (3 km), Pallavur & Kollam (35 km)
Kairali Ayuruedic Yoga Centre
Scientific School of Yoga
Thiruvambadi Beach Rd
Keraleeyam (Massage/Yoga)
North Cliff
Doctor's Ayuruedic Health Centre
Appu's Store
Taxis
Laundry
Helipad
Kerala Kathakali Centre
Cliff Rd
Nature Cure Hospital
Suresh Handicrafts
Mineral Springs
Papanasam Beach
Book Exchange
Elegance of India, Master Crafts
Beach Rd
Sri Rama Hanuman
Tank
South Cliff
Vaishanvaite Janardhanaswamy
Temple Junction
200 metres
200 yards
To Railway station (2½ km), Sivagiri (3½ km) & Thiruvanenpuram (50 km)

ARRIVING IN VARKALA

Getting there Varkala's railway station and bus stand are next to each other, 3 km inland from the beach and a 10-minute ride by auto-rickhaw from most hotels.

Moving on Dozens of trains a day shuttle down the coast to **Thiruvananthapuram** (see below), an hour away. If you're heading straight for the airport a taxi costs around Rs 1000.

→ THIRUVANANTHAPURAM (TRIVANDRUM)

A pleasant city built over gently rolling coastal land, Thiruvananthapuram is very much a village as soon as you step away from the crowded centre. There's none of the throb, bustle and boom-time of Ernakulam, its opposite city up north, and no one could accuse it of being cosmopolitan; you'll be pushed to find a bar or a club, or even any traffic on the roads after midnight. It is, however, a stone's throw from here to the white sands of Kovalam, still a working fishing village, albeit one that survives under the lengthening shadow cast by unchecked tourist development.

ARRIVING IN THIRUVANANTHAPURAM

Getting there Trains from Varkala sweep through a number of small suburban stations on their way into Trivandrum Central, which stands at the south end of the town centre across the road from the long distance bus stand. There are a rash of decent budget hotels within easy reach, and the usual band of auto-rickshaws to ferry you further afield.

Moving on Thiruvanathapuram's airport is 6 km west of the town centre, and is well served by international airlines; you can fly via the Gulf to Europe with the likes of **Emirates**, **Etihad** and **Qatar Airways**, and to Singapore with **Silk Air**. To return to Chennai, take a 1½-hour flight or a 16-hour overnight train. Alternatively, take any northbound train through the Backwaters to Ernakulam to connect with our third and final Dream Trip.

Getting around Trivandrum is a small city and most things you'd want to see are within walking distance. Crowded town buses buzz up and down MG Road, connecting the railway and bus stations with the Napier Museum. Buses to Kovalam leave from the local bus stand at East Fort south of the railway line; an auto to Kovalam should cost Rs 150-200.

PLACES IN THIRUVANANTHAPURAM

According to legend, the **Sri Padmanabhaswamy Temple** ① *East Fort, T0471-245 0233, 0330-0445 (Nirmalya Darshanam), 0630-0700, 0830-1000, 1030-1110, 1145-1200, 0500-0615, 0645-0720*, was built in stages to house the statue of Vishnu reclining on the sacred serpent *Ananta*, which was found in the forest. It was rebuilt in 1733 by Raja Marthanda Varma, king of Travancore, who dedicated the whole kingdom, including his rights and possessions, to the deity. The full significance of this gift came to light in July 2011, after Kerala's High Court ordered the Travancore royal family to hand over control of the temple and its assets to the State. Upon opening the six *kallaras* (vaults) hidden beneath the temple, a team of archaeologists discovered a hoard of gold and jewel-encrusted idols estimated to be worth at least US$22 billion by weight alone. The find instantly propelled the temple to the head of the list of India's richest religious institutions. Meanwhile, in a twist fit for Indiana Jones, a sixth vault, guarded by an iron door emblazoned with images

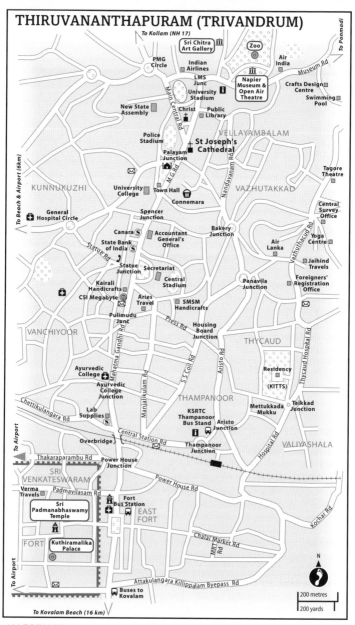

THIRUVANANTHAPURAM (TRIVANDRUM)

To Kollam (NH 17)

To Ponmadi

Sri Chitra Art Gallery

Zoo

Air India

To Ponmadi

Museum Rd

PMG Circle

Indian Airlines

LMS Junc

University Stadium

Napier Museum & Open Air Theatre

Crafts Design Centre

Swimming Pool

New State Assembly

Christ

Public Library

VELLAYAMBALAM

Police Stadium

St Joseph's Cathedral

Main Central Rd

Nandavanam Rd

Tagore Theatre

Palayam Junction

M.G. Rd

KUNNUKUZHI

University College

Town Hall

Connemara

VAZHUTAKKAD

Central Survey Office

General Hospital Circle

Spencer Junction

Bakery Junction

Yoga Centre

Vazhuthacaud Rd

Air Lanka

Canara

Accountant General's Office

Jaihind Travels

State Bank of India

Statue Rd

Statue Junction

Secretariat

Panavila Junction

Foreigners' Registration Office

Kairali Handicrafts

CSI Megabyte

Central Stadium

Aries Travel

SMSM Handicrafts

VANCHIYOOR

Pulimudu Junc

Mahatma Gandhi Rd

Manjalikulam Rd

Pless Rd

Housing Board Junction

THYCAUD

Aristo Rd

Residency (KITTS)

Ayurvedic College

S.S.Coil Rd

Thycaud Hospital Rd

Ayurvedic College Junction

THAMPANOOR

Mettukkada Mukku

Taikkad Junction

Chettikulangara Rd

Lab Supplies

KSRTC Thampanoor Bus Stand

Aristo Junction

VALIYASHALA

To Airport

Central Station Rd

Overbridge

Thampanoor Junction

Hospital Rd

Kochar Rd

Thakaraparambu Rd

Power House Junction

Power House Rd

SRI VENKATESWARAM

Verma Travels

Padmavilasam Rd

Sri Padmanabhaswamy Temple

Fort Bus Station

EAST FORT

FORT

Kuthiramalika Palace

Chalai Market Rd

MRT Rd

To Airport

Attakulangara Killippalam Byepass Rd

N

To Kovalam Beach (16 km)

Buses to Kovalam

200 metres

200 yards

of cobras, remains sealed while the Supreme Court and temple astrologers wrestle over legends of a powerful curse set to be unleashed if the door is ever prised open.

Unusually for Kerala, the temple is built in the Dravidian style associated with Tamil Nadu, with beautiful murals, sculptures and 368 carved granite pillars which support the main pavilion or *Kulashekhara Mandapa*. You can see the seven-storeyed *gopuram* with its sacred pool from outside; otherwise to get a closer look you first have to persuade the famously strict Kerala Brahmins to waive the Hindus-only entry restriction. It becomes easier to do so if men have donned a crisp white *dhoti*, women a sari and blouse.

The Travancore king, Maharajah Swathi Thirunal Balarama Varma, was a musician, poet and social reformer, and his palace, just next door to the temple, **Kuthiramalika (Puthenmalika) Palace** ① *Temple Rd, East Fort, T0471-247 3952, Tue-Sun 0830-1230 and 1530-1730, Rs 20, camera Rs 15*, is a fine reflection of his patronage of the arts. On the upper level a window gives an angle on scores of fine wood-carved horses that look like a huge cavalry charge, and among the portraits painted in the slightly unsettling Indian/European classical hybrid style is one from an artist who trumped his rivals by painting not just eyes that follow you around the room, but also feet. Sadly, it is ill maintained, but a gem nonetheless.

Napier Museum ① *North Park Grounds, city north, T0471-231 8294, Tue-Sun 1000-1645, Wed morning only, closed public holidays*, is a spectacular landmark. The structure designed by RF Chisholm in traditional-Kerala-meets-Indo-Saracenic style, was completed in 1872. Today, it houses a famous collection of eighth to 18th-century South Indian bronzes, mostly from Chola, Vijayanagar and Nayaka periods, a few Jain and Buddhist sculptures and excellent woodcarvings. **Sri Chitra Art Gallery** ① *just north of the museum, 1000-1645, closed Mon and Wed mornings, Rs 5*, has a fine catalogue of Indian art from early to modern schools: works by Raja Ravi Varma, 20th-century pioneer of the radical post-colonial school of painting, sit among paintings from Java, Bali, China and Japan, Mughal and Rajput miniatures. The Tanjore paintings are studded with semi-precious stones. The **Zoological Park** ① *entrance at southwest corner of park, Tue-Sun 0900-1815, Rs 5, cameras Rs 15*, is a hilly woodland of frangipani and jacaranda with a wide collection of animals and a well-labelled botanical garden.

→KOVALAM AND NEARBY RESORTS

Local fishermen's boats still sit on Kovalam's narrow strip of sand right next to sunbathing tourists, but the sleepy Lakshadweep seaside village of old has now been almost completely swallowed up by package tourist infrastructure: Ayurveda parlours, trinkets, tailoring shops and tour operators line every inch of the narrow walkways behind the shore. In peak season it's something of an exotic god's waiting room, popular with pensioners, and it's safe and sedate enough for families.

North and south of Kovalam are four main stretches of beach, about 400 m long, divided by a rocky promontory on which sits the Charles Correa-designed **Leela**. The area to the north of the promontory, known as **Samudra Beach** and **Pozhikara Beach**, 5 km away offers the most sheltered bathing and the clearest water. The southern beaches, **Lighthouse Beach** and **Eve's Beach**, are more crowded and lively. Lighthouse Beach is far and away the most happening and has a long line of bars screening pirated Hollywood films, cafés selling muesli and pastries and hawkers peddling crafts or drugs. Further south still is where the classy resorts are clustered. **Pulinkudi Beach** and **Chowara Beach**, respectively 8 km and 10 km to the south, is where to go for hand-and-foot attentiveness, isolation, heritage-style villas and Ayurveda in luxurious surrounds. Chowara Beach has security staff but some sunbathers still feel plagued by hawkers. **Poovar Island**, 20 km south, is accessible only by boat (Rs 200). There are now lifeguard patrols but you still need to be careful when swimming. The sea can get rough, particularly between April and October with swells of up to 6 m. From May the sea level rises, removing the beach completely in places, and swimming becomes very dangerous.

Within easy walking distance of Kovalam, sandwiched in between Lighthouse and Poovar beaches but scarcely visited by tourists, is **Vizhinjam**, a scruffy town with a low-rise string of bangle shops, banana stalls, beauticians and seamstresses sewing jasmine buds onto strings for garlands. It's hard to believe it today but Vizhinjam was once the capital of the Ay rulers who dominated South Travancore in the ninth century AD. In the seventh century they had faced constant pressure from the Pandiyans who kept the Ay chieftains under firm control for long periods. There are rock-cut sculptures in the 18th-century cave temple here, including a rough sculpture of Vinandhara Dakshinamurthi in the shrine and unfinished reliefs of Siva and Parvati on the outer wall. Today Vizhinjam is the centre of the fishing industry and is being developed as a major container port. The traditional boats are rapidly being modernized and the catch is sold all over India, but you can still see the keen interest in the sale of fish, and women taking headloads off to local markets.

AROUND KOVALAM

South of Kovalam in Tamil Nadu, is **Padmanabhapuram** ① *Tue-Sun 0900-1300, 1400-1630 (last tickets 1600), Rs 200, child Rs 50 (accredited guide included, but expects a 'donation' after the tour), camera Rs 25, video Rs 1500; best at 0900 before coach parties arrive*, the old wooden palace of the Rajas of Travancore. Enclosed within a cyclopean stone wall, the palace served as the capital of Travancore from 1490-1790, and is a beautiful example of the Kerala school of architecture, with fine murals, floral carvings and black granite floors. It makes a great day trip, or a neat stopover on the route to Kanyakumari, see page, opposite.

MOVING ON

From Thiruvanathapuram you can either fly or take an overnight train to Chennai (page 137) for your international flight home, or you can you can head north to connect with Dream Trip 3 (page 201). See also Moving on, page 193.

GOING FURTHER
Kanyakumari

Kanyakumari's grubby streets come alive in the hour before dawn, as thousands throng the shoreline to witness the sunrise over the southern tip of India. This important pilgrimage site is centred on worship of the Goddess Kumari, 'the protector of India's shores'. The new day is heralded in by the scent of jasmine garlands, the wail of temple music and the whoops and applause of excited children as the sun finally crawls its way over the sea. It's an early-morning party that everyone is invited to join. The view offshore is dominated by India's answer to the Statue of Liberty: a 133-ft sculpture of the Tamil poet Thiruvalluvar. Just behind is a memorial to the philosopher Swami Vivekananda, a spiritual leader inspired by the Devi. Both can be reached by a quick ferry ride. In April, at full moon, special *chithra pournami* celebrations are held at sunset and the town heaves with crowds who come to see the simultaneous setting and rising of the sun and moon.

PLACES IN KANYAKUMARI

The **Kanyakumari Temple** ① *0400-1200, 1600-2000, non-Hindus are not allowed into the sanctuary, shoes must be left outside and men must wear a dhoti to enter*, overlooks the shoreline. The Devi Kumari, an incarnation of Parvati, vowed to remain a virgin to her dying day after meddling gods prevented her marriage to Siva. Legend tells that the exceptionally brilliant diamond in the deity's nose ring is visible even from the sea, and the sea-facing temple door is kept closed to prevent ships being misguided by the gem's shimmer.

The **Vivekananda Memorial** ① *0800-1600, Rs 10, ferry Rs 20, 15 mins, allow 1 hr for the visit, smoking and eating prohibited, take off shoes before entering*, stands on one of two rocks, about 500 m from the mainland. The Bengali religious leader and philosopher Swami Vivekananda swam out here when a simple monk and devotee of the Devi, to sit in long meditation on this rock in 1892. He left convinced that religion could be a powerful instrument of social regeneration and individual development and was inspired to speak on Hinduism at the Parliament of Religions in Chicago, preaching that "the Lord is one, but the sages describe Him differently". On his return, he founded the Ramakrishna Mission in Chennai, which now has spread across the world. The rock was renamed Vivekananda Rock and a memorial was built in 1970. The design of the *mandapa* incorporates different styles of temple architecture from all over India and houses a statue of Vivekananda. People also come to see Sri Pada Parai, where the 'footprint' of the Devi has been enshrined on the rock.

The massive **Thiruvalluvar Statue** ① *0800-1600, free, ferry Rs 20, 15 mins*, immortalizes the writer of the Tamil classic, *Thirukkural*. The statue is exactly 133 ft (40 m) tall, to correspond with the 133 chapters of his most famous work. Stairs allow visitors to stand at his giant feet.

In 1948 some of Mahatma Gandhi's ashes were brought here for public display before being immersed in the sea. The **Ghandi Mandapam** ① *0700-1900, free*, was built as a memorial to this event. At midday on Gandhi's birthday, 2 October, the sun shines on the spot where his ashes were placed.

The **Wandering Monk Museum** ① *Main Rd, 0830-1200, 1600-2000, Rs 5*, has an informative exhibition on the life and work of Vivekananda. There is also a photo exhibition, in **Vivekanandapuram**, 1 km north, which can be reached by an easy walk along the beach though there is no access from the north side. The **Yoga Kendra** there runs courses from June to December. Further north there is a pleasant sandy beach, 3.5 km along Kovalam Road.

AROUND KANYAKUMARI

Suchindram Temple ① *open to non-Hindus, priests acting as guides may expect donations*, was founded during the Pandiyan period but was expanded under Thirumalai Nayaka in the 17th century. It was also used later as a sanctuary for the rulers of Travancore to the west and so contains treasures from many kingdoms. One of the few temples dedicated to the Hindu Trinity, Brahma, Vishnu and Siva, it is in a rectangular enclosure that you enter through the massive ornate seven-storeyed *gopuram*. North of the temple is a large tank with a small shelter in the middle while round the walls is the typically broad street used for car festivals. Leading to the entrance is a long colonnade with musical pillars and sculptures of Siva, Parvati, Ganesh and Subrahmanya on the front and a huge Hanuman statue inside. The main sanctuary, with a *lingam*, dates from the ninth century but many of the other structures and sculptures date from the 13th century and after. There are special temple ceremonies at sunset on Friday.

Nagercoil, 19 km from Kanyakumari, is set with a stunning backcloth of the Western Ghats, reflected from place to place in the broad tanks dotted with lotuses. The landscape begins to feel more like Kerala than Tamil Nadu. It is an important railway junction and bus terminal. It is often a bottleneck filled with lorries so be prepared for delays. The old town of **Kottar**, now a suburb, was a centre of art, culture and pilgrimage. The **temple** ① *0630-0900, 1730-2000,* to Nagaraja, after which the town is named, is unique in that although the presiding deity is the Serpent God Naga, there are also shrines to Siva and Vishnu as well as images of Jain *Tirthankaras*, Mahavira and Parsvanatha on the pillars. The temple is alive with snakes during some festivals. Christian missionaries played an important part in the town's development and left their mark in schools, colleges, hospitals and churches of different denominations. There is also a prominent Muslim community in Kottar, reflected in the shops closing on Fridays and remaining open on Sunday.

WHERE TO STAY

$$$ Seaview, East Car St, T04652-247841, www.hotelseaview.in. Plush, central hotel with spotlessly clean, a/c rooms. Helpful staff, restaurant, bar. Recommended.
$$-$ Hotel Tamil Nadu (TTDC), Beach Rd, T04652-246257, www.ttdconline.com.

Acceptably decrepit rooms in a superb location, with terraces looking out to sea and a nice garden setting, in a quiet spot away from the centre. Popular with Indian families.

RESTAURANTS

$ Seashore Hotel, East Car St, T04652-246704. The top-floor restaurant in this swish new hotel offers good Indian and seafood dishes, accompanied by wonderful ocean views.

$ Annapoorna, Sannathi St. Excellent vegetarian food in clean, bright surroundings. Very popular with families.

KODAIKKANAL TO THE COAST LISTINGS

WHERE TO STAY

Kodaikkanal and around

$$$ Carlton, Boat Club Rd, T04542-248555, carlton@krahejahospitality.com. Fully modernized but colonial-style hotel with 91 excellent rooms, many with private terraces overlooking the lake. Excellent restaurant, billiards, tennis, golf and boating, often full in season. Recommended.

$$$ Elephant Valley, Ganesh Puram village (20 km from Kodai off Palani road), T0413-265 5751, www.elephantvalley hotel.com. This tranquil eco-resort comprises 13 cute rustic stone cottages (some in converted village houses) dotted across a 30-ha organic farm on either side of a rocky river, visited by wild boar, gaur and elephants (best sightings Apr–Jun). Restaurant serves good food based on home-grown veg and herbs, fantastic salads, plus superb coffee which is grown, roasted and ground entirely on-site. Highly recommended.

$ Hilltop Towers, Club Rd, T04542-240413, www.hilltopgroup.in. 26 modern, properly cleaned and comfortable rooms, some noise from passing buses and limited hours for hot water, but the management are very obliging and the complex contains a slew of good restaurants. Recommended.

Thekkady (Periyar National Park)

$$$$ Lake Palace, Lake Periyar, T0486-922 3887, www.lakepalacethekkady.com. 6 rooms in interesting building inside the reserve. Idyllic island setting with superb views and wildlife spotting. Access by free ferry (20 mins) from jetty (last trip 1600). Relaxed and informal.

$$$$ Spice Village (CGH Earth), Thekkady– Kumily Rd, T0486-922 4514, www.cghearth.com. Cottages with elephant grass thatch (cool and dark with wide eaves), spice garden, badminton, tennis, good pool, yoga centre. Excellent restaurant, lunch and dinner buffets (Rs 500), chilled beer. Good cookery demonstrations, great Ayurvedic massage and forest walks to see smaller wildlife. Luxurious, quiet, restful, friendly, with superb service. Discounts Apr-Sep.

$$-$ Claus Garden, Rosapukandam, 10 mins' uphill from bus stand behind PO, 3rd turn right, T0486-922 2320, claus. hoppe@web.de. Spacious rooms in a peaceful house surrounded by jungle. Funky communal area, book exchange, friendly chilled-out vibe.

Around Thekkady

$$$$ Serenity Kanam, at Kanam Estate, 25 km east of Kottayam off Kumily Rd, T0481-245 6353, www.malabarhouse.com. This wonderful villa hotel has just 6 huge rooms, decorated with quality art and sculpture, set in a gently restored 1920s bungalow surrounded by rubber plantations and spice gardens. There's a big pool, spa and excellent food, and you can spend a morning exploring the quiet lanes from the back of Lakshmi, the estate elephant. Far from any sights, but it's worth building in an extra night or 2 just to stay here.

Varkala

$$$ Villa Jacaranda, Temple Rd West, South Cliff, T0470-261 0296, www.villa-jacaranda.biz. A delightful guesthouse, home with 5 huge rooms elegantly but sparely decorated. Jasmine, birds of paradise and magnolia blossoms are tucked into alcoves, there's a lotus-filled pond and tropical garden and everything is immaculately maintained. Guests have their own keys and entrance. Really special.

$$$-$ Marine Palace, Papanasam Beach, T0470-260 3204, www.varkalamarine.com. 12 rooms in total with 3 lovely old-style wooden rooms with balconies and a sea

view. The honeymoon suite has a truly gigantic bed. Good service and nice *tandoori* restaurant on the beach. Recommended.
\$\$-\$ Akshay Beach Resort, Beach Rd (about 200 m from beach), T0470-260 2668. Wide variety of bright, clean rooms. Quiet location away from the cliff. Restaurant, TV lounge, good value.

Trivandrum
\$\$\$-\$\$ Residency Tower, Press Rd, T0471-233 1661, www.residencytower.com. Top-quality a/c rooms in a business hotel, with full facilities. Highly efficient, good.

restaurants, bar, rooftop pool (non-residents Rs 350). A bit swish.
\$\$-\$ Wild Palms Homestay, Mathrubhoomi Rd, Vanchiyoor, 10 mins' walk from Statue Junction or ask for pickup, T0471-247 1175, wildpalms@vsnl.net. Modern welcoming guesthouse set in pretty tropical garden in the leafy suburbs. Spacious rooms, some a/c. Price includes breakfast.
\$ Greenland, Aristo Junction, T0471-232 3485. Great-value rooms in quiet, immaculate, freshly renovated hotel, perfectly located within a couple of mins of both bus and railway stations. Best budget choice in town.

RESTAURANTS

Kodaikkanal and around
\$\$ Royal Tibet Hotel, J's Heritage Complex, for noodle soup and *momos*.

Thekkady (Periyar National Park)
\$\$ Coffee Inn, Thekkady Rd. Open 0700-2200. International dishes served at tables outside under the palms, bonfire in the evening, relaxed and peaceful. Friendly but very slow service.

Varkala
\$\$\$ The Gateway, Gateway Hotel, near Government Guest House. Sun 1230-1530 (Rs 300, includes pool use). Good-value eat-all-you-want buffet, delicious rich vegetarian cuisine.
\$\$ Sri Padman, near Hanuman Temple, T0472-260 5422. Sri Padman's terrace overlooking the temple tank offers the best non-beachfront position in town. Come here for South Indian vegetarian breakfasts served in big stainless steel *thali* trays, and oily *parathas* to sop up spicy curries and coconut chutneys.
\$ The Juice Shack, cliffside Varkala, turn off at Tibetan market. Shady little spot with healthy juice, good coffee and excellent toasted sandwiches. Brilliant for breakfast – they even have Marmite.

\$ Oottupura, cliffside Varkala, near helipad, T0472-260 6994. A Varkala institution. Excellent 100% vegetarian with 60 vegetarian curries and everything from Chinese to macaroni cheese. Breakfast can be *iddlies* or toasted sandwiches, all served under a giant pistachio tree covered in fairy lights.

Trivandrum
\$\$\$ Villa Maya, Airport Rd, Subash Nagar, Enchakkal Westfort Rd, T0471-257 8901. One of the most beautiful restaurants in this book, set in a restored 18th-century Dutch villa surrounded by tinkling fountains. Dishes span a broad range of cuisines, from trad Kerala curries to Israeli and Moroccan specials. It's pricey and they don't serve alcohol, but this is a superb choice for a last-night splurge.
\$ Arul Jyoti, MG Rd, opposite Secretariat. South Indian vegetarian. With a/c family room, clean, wide choice of good-value dishes, try jumbo *dosas*. Great Tamil Nadu *thalis*.
\$ Indian Coffee House, 2 on MG Rd, with others near YWCA, north of the Secretariat, and near KSRTC Bus Stand (the latter designed by the English architect Laurie Baker). Worth seeing, excellent value coffee and snacks.

DREAM TRIP 3
Kochi➔Backwaters➔Ooty➔Bengaluru 21 days

Fort Kochi 2 nights, page 203

The Backwaters 3 nights, page 210
Taxi from Fort Kochi (2 hrs)
Prebooked houseboat trip

Munnar 2 nights, page 218
Taxi from Allapuzha (5 hrs)

Ooty, Coonoor and Mettupalayam
3 nights, pages 229, 231 and 232
Taxi or bus from Munnar to Mettupalayam
(5-7 hrs); overnight stay
Toy train to Coonoor or Ooty

Wayanad 3 nights, page 235
Taxi from Ooty (2 hrs)

Nagarhole National Park 3 nights,
page 236
Taxi from Wayanad (2-3 hrs)
Prebooked jungle safaris

Mysore 2 nights, page 237
Taxi from Nagarhole National Park (2 hrs)

Western Plateau 1 night, page 243
Taxi from Mysore to Hassan
via Sravanabelagola (5-7 hrs
including sightseeing)

Bengaluru 2 nights, page 250
Taxi from Hassan via temples
at Belur and Halebid (8 hrs)

GOING FURTHER

River Nila and Palakkad page 223
Train from Kochi to Shoranur, 2-3 hrs,
or Palakkad, 3½-4 hrs

Coorg page 246
Bus from Nagarhole (4½ hrs)
or Mysore (3 hrs)

DREAM TRIP 3
Kochi → Backwaters → Ooty → Bengaluru

Sheltered under the lush canopies of its spreading raintrees, the sleepy colonial outpost of Fort Kochi sets the tone for a journey through some of the country's softest and most luxuriant landscapes.

South of Kochi lie Kerala's fabled Backwaters, a watery web of lagoons and slow-flowing rivers palisaded by swaying palms and peppered with clusters of grey-timbered Chinese fishing nets. Life ebbs by at a snail's pace here, and once you settle into the nothing-to-do-ness of it all, the shaded deck of your houseboat might just become the most relaxing place you've ever been.

Next comes a highland fling through South India's favourite hill stations: Munnar, where an emerald ocean of tea bushes laps at black rock peaks; 'snooty Ooty', once a den of monocles and fox hunts, now a wild mess of a resort town reached by the glorious Raj-era Nilgiri Mountain Railway; and the magical highland plateau of Wayanad, where you can wake up in the boughs of a towering jungle tree to the cheery calls of the Asian fairy bluebird. Things get even wilder as you head north into the pristine forests of Nagarhole National Park, which offers the best tiger spotting in South India and excellent birding on the Kabini River.

From here the route turns east to Mysore, whose majestic, kitschy palace glows in the glimmer of 96,000 fairy lights during the Dasara festival. The countryside to the north is littered with echoing temples, culminating in the exquisitely carved Hoysala temples of Belur and Halebid.

Journey's end is Bengaluru, an icon of India's tech revolution and the conspicuous consumption of 'India Shining'. Yet for all its nouveau riche trappings of malls and trendy bars, even this most frantically flashy city still offers glimpses of the past through its thronged bazaars and genteel Victorian gardens.

FORT KOCHI AND ERNAKULAM

Charming Fort Kochi (Cochin) is a true one-off in modern Kerala: a layer cake of colonial India, where British parade grounds overlay Portugese forts, where Dutch palaces slowly crumble into the soil alongside synagogues, where every turn takes you down some romantically fossilized narrow winding street. Despite a tourist invasion that's flooded the lanes with antique shops, internet cafés and shops flogging fisherman trousers, parts of the ramshackle island still feel frozen back in the 15th and 16th centuries, and the huge trees here are so old that their parasitic aphids are as tall as trees themselves. In the southern quarter of Mattancherry, row upon row of wood-fronted doors give glimpses of rice and spice merchants sitting sifting their produce into small 'tasting' bowls. The iconic batwing Chinese fishing nets, first used in the 14th century, stand on the shores of the north fort area, silhouetted against the lapping waters of one of the world's finest natural harbours: a wide bay interrupted by narrow spits of land and coconut-covered islands.

All of which does little to prepare you for arriving into Kochi via the city's modern centre of gravity – grubby, dynamic Ernakulam, a Rs 5 ferry ride and half a world away across the harbour. While Fort Kochi languishes dreamily in the past, its ambitious sibling is expanding outwards and upwards at breakneck pace, propelled by the vast new container terminal on Vallarpadam Island. The first port in India capable of handling the huge container ships that until now have had to berth in Colombo or Singapore, Kochi stands poised to transform India's logistical landscape, and over the next decade this hitherto sleepy southern city will undoubtedly assume a front-and-centre seat in the future of the Indian economy.

→ ARRIVING IN FORT KOCHI AND ERNAKULAM

GETTING THERE

Kochi's mellow little International Airport is at Nedumbassery, 36 km northeast of the city centre. The smoothest way into town is to arrange a pickup from your hotel – around Rs 900-1500 depending on type of car and what your hosts feel the market will support. Alternatively, hire a prepaid taxi from the booth after Customs; a transfer to Fort Kochi costs around Rs 800, a little less to downtown Ernakulam. Air-conditioned buses leave the airport for Fort Kochi bus stand, dead-centre next to the Chinese fishing nets, between 0500 and 1900, taking 1½ hours.

MOVING ON

Frequent trains leave Ernakulam Junction station bound for the **Backwaters** (see page 210), some following the coastal line through Alappuzha (two hours), others the inland line via Kottayam (2½-3½ hours); the two lines join north of Kollam (spelled Quilon by Indian Railways' booking system; three to four hours). A taxi from Fort Kochi to Alappuzha or Kumarakom costs around Rs 1500. If you're heading for Kumarakom on public transport, either take a train to Kottayam and a bus or taxi (14 km, around Rs 400), or an express bus from Kochi's Vyttila bus stand (5km east of Ernakulam Jn) to Cherthala, which has frequent buses to Kumarakom.

GETTING AROUND

Fort Kochi has all the sights and a huge number of hotels, and many visitors never leave its cozy bubble. The quiet roads are easy to explore on foot or by bicycle, with an occasional

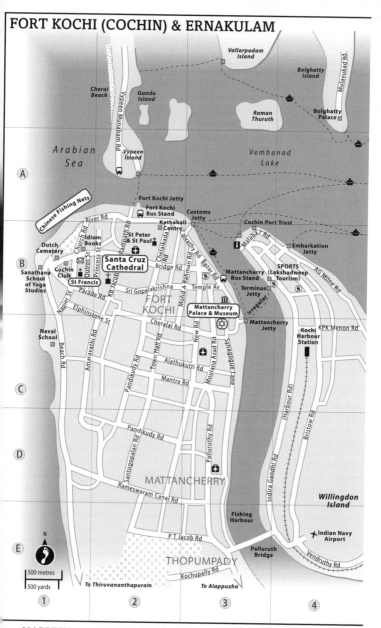

FORT KOCHI (COCHIN) & ERNAKULAM

Vallarpadam
Island

Bolghatty
Island

Cherai
Beach

Gundu
Island

Raman
Thuruth

Bolghatty
Palace

Arabia
Sea

Vypeen Munamban Rd

Vypeen
Island

Vembanad
Lake

A

Chinese Fishing Nets

Fort Kochi Jetty

Fort Kochi
Bus Stand

Customs
Jetty

Cochin Port Trust

River Rd

Kathakali
Centre

Malabar Rd

Church St

Dutch
Cemetery

Idiom
Books

Princess St

St Peter
& St Paul

Chelakada

Calvathy Rd

Bazar Rd

Embarkation
Jetty

AG Mine Rd

B

Cochin
Club

Quiros St

Santa Cruz
Cathedral

Rampart Rd

Bridge Rd

Mattancherry
Bus Stand

SPORTS
(Lakshadweep
Tourism)

Sanathana
School
of Yoga
Studies

St Francis

Parade Rd

Sri Gopalakrishna

Mohd A Rahman Rd

Temple Av

Terminus
Jetty

Napier St

Elphinstone St

FORT
KOCHI

Mattancherry
Palace & Museum

Mattancherry
Jetty

Naval
School

Cheralai Rd

New Rd

Synagogue Lane

Irregular

Kochi
Harbour
Station

KPK Menon Rd

Beach Rd

Amaravathi Rd

Town Hall Rd

Alathukutti Rd

Moulana Azad Rd

Harbour Rd

C

Pandikudy Rd

Mantra Rd

Bristow Rd

Indira Gandhi Rd

D

Pandikudy Rd

Palluruthy Rd

MATTANCHERRY

Willingdon
Island

Rameswaram Canal Rd

Fishing
Harbour

Indian Navy
Airport

E

N

500 metres

500 yards

P T Jacob Rd

Palluruth
Bridge

Vendruthy Rd

THOPUMPADY

Kochupally Rd

To Thiruvananthapuram

To Alappuzha

1   **2**   **3**   **4**

cameo from an auto-rickshaw. If you need to get across to Ernakulam for non-touristy shopping or to catch a train, there are two routes: a circuitous trip by bus, taxi or auto-rickshaw (around Rs 250-500), or one of the cheap and cheerful ferries that chug across the harbour to Ernakulam's Main Jetty – an enjoyably breezy 30-minute trip that's most atmospheric around sunset (ferries run 0600 to 2130). From the jetty you can catch a rickshaw to the railway station or bus stand for around Rs 40. Leave plenty of spare time if you need to travel during peak hours.

TOURIST INFORMATION

Kerala Tourism Development Corporation (KTDC) ⓘ *Shanmugham Rd, Ernakulam, T0484-235 3234, 0800-1800.* Tourist Desk ⓘ *Main Boat Jetty, Ernakulam, T0484-237 1761, and on Tower Rd in Fort Kochi, T0484-221 6129, www.touristdesk.in, 0900-1800.* This travel agent, with good maps and local information, runs daily Backwater tours, has information on more than 2000 temple festivals in Kerala.

→ BACKGROUND

"If China is where you make your money," declared Italian traveller Nicolas Conti in the Middle Ages, "then Kochi surely is the place to spend it." Kochi has acted as a trading port since at least Roman times, and was a link in the main trade route between Europe and China. From 1795 until India's Independence the long outer sand spit, with its narrow beach leading to the wide bay inland, was under British political control. The inner harbour was in Kochi State, while most of the hinterland was in the separate state of Travancore. The division of political authority delayed development of the harbour facilities until 1920-1923, when the approach channel was dredged so ships that could get through the Suez Canal could dock here, opening the harbour to modern shipping.

ON THE ROAD
Kerala's social underbelly

Although you'll get the sense of living under one long coconut palm thicket, locals have good reason to call Kerala the city state; the ratio of people per square metre outstrips that of anywhere else in India. And don't let the socialist rhetoric of their political parties fool you – in the main, Keralites are a prosperous bunch and money and status certainly matters. Kerala is where the marketing people come to test their advertising campaigns, and the state boasts of how highly it scores in all quality of life indicators. But relative affluence brings with it social problems: Kerala also has both the highest suicide rate and one of the highest rates of alcohol consumption per capita on the subcontinent, and huge swathes of agricultural land go uncultivated as high literacy creates a class with loftier ambitions than tilling the soil.

→ PLACES IN FORT KOCHI AND ERNAKULAM

If you land at the Customs Jetty, a plaque in nearby Vasco da Gama Square commemorates the landing of Vasco da Gama in 1500. Next to it is the **Stromberg Bastion**, "one of the seven bastions of Fort Emanuel built in 1767", named after the Portuguese king. Little is left of the 1503 Portuguese fort except ruins. Along the seafront, between the Fort Kochi Bus Stand, the boat jetty and the Dutch cemetery, run the cantilevered Chinese fishing nets. These are not unique to Kochi, but are perhaps uniquely accessible to the short-stay visitor.

Mattancherry Palace and **Parikshith Thampuran Museum** ⓘ *Mattancherry, daily 1000-1700 except Fri and national holidays, Rs 2, photography not allowed*, was first built by the Portuguese around 1557 as a sweetener for the Raja Veera Kerala Varma of Kochi bestowing them trading rights. In 1663, it was largely rebuilt by the new trading power, the Dutch. The layout follows the traditional Kerala pattern known as *nalukettus*, meaning four buildings, which are set around a quadrangle with a temple. There are display cases of the Rajas of Kochi's clothes, palanquins, etc, but these are no match for the amazing murals. The royal bedroom's low wooden walls squeezes the whole narrative of the *Ramayana* into about 45 late 16th-century panels. Every inch is covered with rich red, yellow, black and white. To the south of the Coronation Hall, the *kovinithilam* (staircase room) has six large 18th-century murals including the coronation of Rama. Vishnu is in a room to the north. Two of the women's bedrooms downstairs have 19th-century murals with greater detail. They relate Kalidasa's *Kumarasambava* and themes from the *Puranas*. This stuff is triple x-rated. If you are of a sensitive disposition avert your eyes from panel 27 and 29, whose deer, birds and other animals are captioned as giving themselves up to 'merry enjoyment', a coy way of describing the furious copulation and multiple penetration in plain view. Krishna, meanwhile, finally works out why he was given so many limbs, much to the evident satisfaction of the gopis who are looking on.

The **synagogue** ⓘ *Mattancherry, Sun-Thu 1000-1200, 1500-1700, cameras have to be left in the cloakroom and shoes removed; no shorts, short skirts or sleeveless shirts*, dating from 1568 (rebuilt in 1662), is near Mattancherry Palace at the heart of what is known as Jew Town, which is a fascinating mixture of shops (some selling antiques), warehouses and spice auction rooms. Stepping inside the synagogue is an extraordinary experience of light and airiness, partly due to the 18th-century blue Cantonese ceramic tiles, hand painted and each one different, covering the floor. There are original glass oil lamps. For several centuries there were two Jewish communities. The earlier group (often referred to as 'black' Jews), according to one source, settled here as early as 587 BC. The earliest evidence of their presence is a copper inscription dated AD 388 by the Prince of Malabar. Those referred to as 'white' Jews came much later, when, with Dutch and then British patronage, they played a major role as trading agents. Speaking fluent Malayalam, they made excellent go-betweens for foreigners seeking to establish contacts. The community has shrunk to six families, with many now settled at Moshav Nevatim in Israel's Negev desert. The second Jewish synagogue (in Ernakulam) is deserted.

St Francis' Church ① *Fort Kochi, Mon-Sat 0930-1730, Sun afternoon, Sun services in English 0800 (except for the 3rd Sun of each month)*, was originally dedicated to Santo Antonio, the patron saint of Portugal and is the first church to reflect the new and European-influenced tradition. The original wooden structure (circa 1510) was replaced by the present stone building (there is no authority for the widely quoted date of 1546). Vasco da Gama died on the site in 1524 and was originally buried in the cemetery. Some 14 years later his body was removed to Portugal. The church was renamed St Francis in 1663, and the Dutch both converted it to a Protestant church and substantially modified it. They retained control until 1795, adding the impressive gable façade at the entrance. In 1804, it became an Anglican church. In 1949 the congregation joined the Church of South India. Note the old string-pulled *punkahs* (fans) and the Dutch and Portuguese gravestones that now line the walls.

Santa Cruz Cathedral, near St Francis' Church, originally built in 1557 by the Portuguese, and used as a warehouse by the British in the 18th century, was rebuilt in the early 20th century. It has lovely carved wooden panels and pulpit, and an interesting graveyard.

AROUND FORT KOCHI AND ERNAKULAM

Bolghatty Island has the 'palace' (circa 1745), set in large gardens and converted into a hotel. It was originally built by the Dutch and then became the home of the British Resident at the court of the Raja of Kochi after 1799. There is still some atmosphere of colonial decay which haunted the old building in its pre-modernized form and gave it much of its charm.

Vypeen Island lies on the northwestern fringe of the harbour. There are quiet beaches here, along with the Portuguese Azhikotta Fort, built around 1503. You can see cannon holes on the walls of the octagonal fort, which was garrisoned by 20 soldiers when it guarded the entrance to the Backwaters. Vehicle ferries make the crossing from Fort Kochi.

Our Lady's Convent ① *Palluruthy, Thoppampady, 14 km south, by appointment, T0484-223 0508*, specializes in high-quality needlework lace and embroidery. The sisters are very welcoming and it is an interesting tour with items for sale.

Hill Palace Archaeological Museum ① *Thirpunithura, 12 km east of Ernakulam, Tue-Sun 0900-1230, 1400-1630, small entry fee*, has a huge number of historical records and artefacts of the old royal state of Cochin, with portraits, ornaments, porcelain, palm leaf records and ancient musical instruments.

Some 45 km northeast of Kochi is the town of **Kalady**, on the bank of the Periyar River. This popular pilgrimage site was the birthplace of one of India's most influential philosophers, **Sankaracharya**, who lived in the eighth century. He founded the school of *advaita* philosophy, see page 127, which spread widely across South India. The **Adi Sankara Kirti Stambha Mandapam** ① *0700-1900, small entry fee*, is a nine-storeyed octagonal tower, 46 m high, and details Sri Sankara's life and works and the Shan Maths, or six ways to worship. Inside the **Shankara Temple** (Hindus only), are two shrines, one dedicated to Sankaracharya and the other to the goddess Sarada. The management of the shrines is in the hands of the Math at Sringeri in Karnataka. Kalady can easily be visited in an afternoon from Kochi.

FORT KOCHI AND ERNAKULAM LISTINGS

WHERE TO STAY

Fort Kochi

$$$$ Malabar House, 1/268 Parade Rd, near St Francis' Church, T0484-221 6666, www.malabarhouse.com. Fort Kochi's original boutique hotel, and still one of its best. Big and beautiful high-ceilinged rooms in a sensitively restored 18th-century mansion, set around a flagstoned courtyard with an excellent restaurant and small swimming pool. Helpful staff, reliable airport pickups and a funky bar make this a perfect if pricey first place to hang your hat.

$$$ Old Courtyard, 1/371 Princess St, T0484-221 6302, www.oldcourtyard.com. Beautiful, comfortable rooms, superbly styled with old wooden furniture, overlooking large, breezy courtyard of pretty pot plants and sit-outs. The suite is easily the most romantic with a 4-poster bed and white cotton. Attentive liveried staff, breakfast included, average food but excellent cakes and Turkish coffee, and lovely calm atmosphere. Recommended.

$$ Caza Maria Hotel, 6/125 Jew Town Rd, Mattancherry, T(0)98460-50901, cazamaria@rediffmail.com. Just 2 huge and wonderful rooms in beautiful converted house, with tiled floors, wooden furniture and antiques: isolated (the only hotel in Jew Town), romantic and shabbily elegant. Fan only. Breakfast is included, at French/Indian restaurant of same name (on the opposite side of the street).

$$-$ Delight Homestay, Parade Ground, Ridsdale Rd, T0484-221 7658, www.delightfulhomestay.com. This lovingly restored Portuguese homestay provides a welcoming, peaceful haven. Airy, spotlessly clean rooms open onto a wide terrace, budget rooms are great value. The garden is a riot of colourful blooms. Breakfast is served at the family table. A home away from home. Highly recommended.

RESTAURANTS

Fort Kochi

$$$ Fort House, 2/6A Calvathy Rd, T0484-221 7103, www.hotelforthouse.com. For a city surrounded by water, Fort Kochi is surprisingly short on sea-view restaurants. **Fort House** is a standout exception, serving excellent seafood on candlelit tables arranged along an open jetty that juts out into the harbour; they also have a handful of clean and modern (if slightly spartan) rooms (**$$$**). The immediate neighbourhood is fast becoming a culinary hotspot, with art gallery/restaurant **Pepper House** next door, and well-regarded **Dosas and Pancakes** across the street.

$ Dal Roti, 1/293 Lilly St, T0484-221 7655. Firmly established favourite for pukka North Indian food – delicious *khati* rolls, huge stuffed *parathas* – served up by the affable Ramesh and his family. Don't arrive starving as queues often stretch out the door.

$ Kashi, Burgher St, Kochi, T0484-221 5769, www.kashiartgallery.com. If you've been away a while, Kashi is the type of place you'll fall on in wonder. The first 2 rooms are the art gallery, the rest is a restaurant where you can drink coffee fresh from your own cafetière, or indulge in a perfect cappuccino. There's a handful of excellently made sweets and 1-2 dishes they make for breakfast or lunch.

Ernakulam

$$ Sri Krishna Inn, Warriom Rd, next to Chinmaya Vidya Peeth, T0484-236 6664. One of the best pure-veg places in a city of seafood, with great North and South Indian options.

THE BACKWATERS

Kerala is synonymous with its lyrical Backwaters: a watery cat's cradle of endlessly intersecting rivers, streams, lagoons and tanks that flood the alluvial plain between the Indian Ocean and Western Ghats. They run all the way from Kollam via Alappuzha and Kottayam to Kochi to open up a charming slow-tempo window onto Keralite waterfront life: this is the state's lush and fertile Christian belt, Arundhati Roy country, with lakes fringed by bird sanctuaries, idyllic little hamlets, beside huge paddy ponds rustling in the breeze.

The silent daybreak is best, as boats cut through mists, geese and ducks start to stir along banks, plumes from breakfast fires drift out across the lagoons. As the hamlets and villages wake, Kerala's domestic scene comes to life: clothes are pounded clean, teeth brushed, and smartly turned out primary school children swing their ways to class.

Luxury houseboats are the quintessential way of seeing the waterfront, but they can be shocking polluters, and if your budget or attention span won't stretch that far the state-operated ferries will give you much the same access for a fraction of the fee. Alternatively, borrow a bicycle or move around by car; the roads and canals are interchangeable, both threading their way through flood plains the size of football pitches, brown lakes with new shoots prodding out and netted fields that protect prawns and fish from snooping white egrets. At dusk the young men sit about on bridges or congregate by teashops made of corrugated iron, as men shimmy up coconut palms to tap a fresh supply of sour moonshine toddy, and kids catch fish with poles.

ARRIVING IN THE BACKWATERS

Getting there The chief embarkation point for houseboat trips through the Backwaters is Alappuzha (Alleppey), 64 km south of Kochi. Trains pull in at the station 3 km west of the town centre, while the bus stand is right on the waterfront a short walk from several budget hotels and the main houseboat jetty. The other main centres are Kumarakom, a short taxi ride from the railway station at Kottayam, and Kollam, where the railway station is 1.5 km from the main boat jetty. As always, throngs of taxis and auto-rickshaws wait around the stations.

Moving on The easiest way to reach **Munnar** (see page 218) by public transport is to backtrack to Ernakulam and catch a bus from the Vyttila bus stand. A taxi is a good option on this route, and allows you to visit Thattekad bird sanctuary on the way.

Getting around Buses, trains and taxis link the main Backwaters towns, but the most appealing ways to explore are by bike and boat. A cheap alternative to the full houseboat experience is to spend a few hours riding the ferries that ply across Lake Vembanad and south to Kollam. The 'tourist boat' from Alappuzha to Kollam gives you eight hours on the water at a bargain price of Rs 300, but it's a long day and lacks the peace of the best houseboats.

Tourist information In Alappuzha: KTDC ① *Motel Araam, T0477-224 4460*; ATDC ① *Komala Rd, T0477-226 4462, info@atdcalleppey.com*; DTPC ① *KSRTC bus station near jetty, T0477-225 3308, 0830-2000*, is helpful and offers Backwaters trips. In Kottayam: KTDC ① *Kavanattinkara T0481-252 5861*. In Kumarakom: **Responsible Tourism Travel**

Desk ① *T0481-252 4343*, books tours to meet local craftsmen; **KTDC** ① *T0481-252 5864*. In Kollam: **District Tourism Promotion Council (DTPC)** ① *Govt Guest House Complex, T0474-275 0170; also at DTPC bus station, T0474-274 5625, train station and ferry jetty, www.dtpckollam.com*, offers cruises, coach tours, and details of Kathakali performances.

→ALAPPUZHA (ALLEPPEY)

Alappuzha (pronounced *Alappoorra*) has a large network of canals, choked with the blue flowers of water hyacinth, passing through the town. It's the chief departure point for cruises into the Backwaters and the venue for the spectacular **snake boat races** in July and August, when as many as 40 highly decorated boats rowed by several dozen oarsmen race along the canals before huge crowds. **Houseboat trips** can be arranged at any of the numerous tour operators in town or directly, by heading to the boat dock just off VCNB Road. Although the town itself doesn't have many tourist sites, it's a pleasant, bustling place to walk around and there's a lovely stretch of undeveloped beach as well.

Mararikulam, 15 km north of Alappuzha on the coast, is a quiet, secluded beach which, until recently, was only known to the adjoining fishing village. The main village has a thriving cottage industry of coir and jute weaving.

Some 16 km southeast of Alappuzha is the hushed backwaters' village of **Champakulam** where the only noise pollution is the odd squeak of a bicycle and the slush of a canoe paddle. The Syrian Christian church of **St Mary's Forane** was built in 1870 on the site of a previous church dating from AD 427. The English-speaking priest is happy to show visitors round. Nearby the **St Thomas Statuary** makes wooden statues of Christ for export round

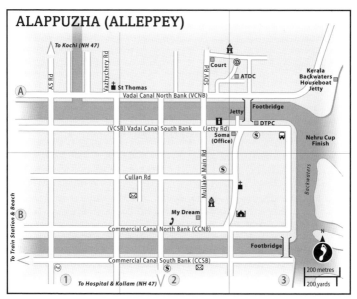

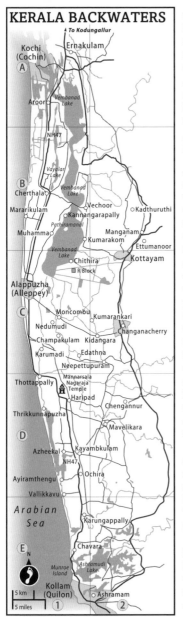

KERALA BACKWATERS

To Kodungallur

Kochi (Cochin)

Ernakulam

Aroor

Vembanad Lake

NH47

Vayalar Lake

Cherthala

Vembanad Lake

Mararikulam

Vechoor

Kannangarapally

Kadthuruthi

Muhamma

Pathiramanal

Manganam

Kumarakom

Ettumanoor

Vembanad Lake

Chithira

Kottayam

R Block

Alappuzha (Alleppey)

Moncombu

Kumarankari

Nedumudi

Changanacherry

Champakulam

Kidangara

Karumadi

Edathna

Neepettupuram

Thottappally

Mannarsala Nagaraja Temple

Haripad

Chengannur

Thrikkunnapuzha

Mavelikara

Azheekal

Kayambkulam

NH47

Ayiramthengu

Ochira

Vallikkavu

Arabian Sea

Karungappally

Chavara

Munroe Island

Ashtamudi Lake

Kollam (Quilon)

Ashramam

5 km
5 miles

1   2

the world: a 2-m-tall Jesus will set you back US$450. To get there, take the Alappuzha–Changanacherry bus (every 30 minutes) to Moncombu (Rs 4), then an auto-rickshaw to Champakulam. Alternatively the Alappuzha–Edathna ferry leaves at 0615 and 1715 and stops at Champakulam. In the backwater village of **Edathna**, you can visit the early Syrian **St George's Church**.

→KOTTAYAM AND KUMARAKOM

Around Kottayam lies some of the lushest and most beautiful scenery in the state, with hills to its east and Backwaters to its west. Kottayam itself is the capital of Kerala's Christian community, which belonged to the Orthodox Syrian tradition up till the Portuguese arrival. Two churches of the era survive 2 km north of town, in the 450-year-old **Cheria Palli** ('Small' St Mary's Church), which has beautiful vegetable dye mural paintings over its altar, and the **Valia Palli** ('Big' St Mary's Church), from 1550, with two Nestorian crosses carved on plaques behind two side altars. One has a Pallavi inscription on it, the other a Syriac. The cross on the left of the altar is the original and may be the oldest Christian artefact in India; the one to the right is a copy. By the altar there is an unusual small triptych of an Indian St George slaying a dragon. Note the interesting Visitors' Book (1898-1935); a paper cutting reports that "the church has attracted many European and native gentlemen of high position". Mass at Valia Palli at 0900 on Sunday, and Cheria Palli at 0730 on Sunday and Wednesday. The Malankara Syrian Church has its headquarters at Devalokam.

Ettumanoor, just north of Kottayam, has possibly the wealthiest temple in Kerala. The present Mahadeva temple was constructed in 1542, and is famous for its murals depicting scenes from the *Ramayana* and the Krishna legends, both

ON THE ROAD
Preserving the Backwaters for the future

The Backwaters are lagoons fed by a network of perennial rivers with only two permanent outlets to the sea. The salts are flushed out between May and September, but sea waters rush inland by up to 20 km at the end of the monsoon and the waters become increasingly brackish through the dry season. This alternation between fresh and salt water has been essential to the Backwaters' aquatic life. However, as land value has rocketed and reclamation for agriculture has reduced the surface water area, the Backwaters' fragile ecology has been put at risk. Many of the original swamps have been destroyed and the waters are becoming increasingly saline.

Tourism, too, is taking its toll. Exploring the Backwaters in a traditional *kettuvallam* is the ultimate Kerala experience but the popularity of these trips is having an adverse effect on the waterways. However, there are ways to help prevent further degeneration.

The trend so far has been for houseboat operators to offer larger, more luxurious boats (some even equipped with plunge pools) to meet the demands of tourists. The powerful outboard motors contribute heavily to pollution levels in the canals. Opting for a smaller boat not only helps ease environmental damage but also allows you to venture into the many narrower and less visited lagoons that the larger boats are unable to access.

Some operators are becoming aware of the damage being caused and are putting responsible travel practices in place. Support these efforts by checking that your houseboat is equipped with a chemical toilet (to prevent your waste being dumped into the canals) and if possible, opting for a solar-powered boat. Alternatively consider hiring a hand-propelled thoni or canoe as an entirely carbon-neutral way of discovering this unique region.

inside and outside the *gopuram*. The typical circular shrine with a copper-covered conical roof encloses a square sanctuary. The **Arattu festival** in March draws thousands of pilgrims when gold elephant statues are displayed. They weigh 13 kg each.

Tucked among the waterways of Vembanad Lake, in mangrove, paddy and coconut groves with lily-studded shores, is **Kumarakom**, 16 km from Kottayam. Here are stacks of exclusive hotels where you can be buffed and Ayurvedically preened, bent into yoga postures, peacefully sunbathe or take to the water: perfect honeymoon territory.

The tourism department has developed an old rubber plantation set around the Vembanad Lake into a **bird sanctuary** ① *1000-1800*. A path goes through the swamp to the main bird nesting area. **Pathiramanal** ('midnight sands') **Island** in the middle of the lake can be reached by boat. The best season for birdlife is June to August; try to visit early in the morning.

ALAPPUZHA TO KOLLAM

Some 32 km south of Alappuzha, the village of Haripad has one of Kerala's oldest and most important Subrahmanya temples. The four-armed idol is believed to have been found in a river, and in August the three-day Snake Boat Race at nearby Payipad commemorates its rescue and subsequent building of the temple. Just north of Haripad, Mannarsala has a tremendously atmospheric Nagaraja Temple buried deep in a dense jungle forest. Traditionally naga (serpent) worshippers had temples in serpent groves. Mannarsala is the largest of these in Kerala with '30,000 images' of snake gods lined up along the path and among the trees, and many snakes living around the temple. Childless women come for special blessing and also return for a 'thanksgiving' ceremony afterwards when the child born to the couple is placed on special scales and gifts in kind equalling the weight are donated. The temple is unusual for its chief priestess.

About 28 km further south at Vallikkavu, sandwiched between the Backwaters and the sea, is the great pink skyscraper of the **Mata Amritanandamayi Ashram** ① *accessible by the Alappuzha-Kollam tourist boat or by road through Kayambkulam or Karungappally, www.amritapuri.org, Rs 150 per day*, the home of 'Amma' (the hugging 'Mother'). Thousands, Western and Indian alike, attend daily *darshan* in hope of a hug. She has hugged over thirty million people so far: in the early days these used to last for minutes; now she averages one hug every 1½ seconds, so she can happily hug 30,000 in a day. The ashram has shops, a bank, library and internet, but check before visiting whether Amma is in residence as the ashram becomes somewhat lacklustre when she's out on tour. Smoking, sex and alcohol are forbidden.

→ KOLLAM (QUILON)

Kollam (population 361,400) is a busy shaded market town on the side of the Ashtamudi Lake and the headquarters of India's cashew nut trading and processing industry. It is congested and there's little reason to linger, but its position at the south end of Kerala's Backwaters, where the waterways are less crowded than those further north, make it a good alternative starting point for boat trips up the canals.

Known to Marco Polo as *Koilum*, the port saw trading between Phoenicians, Persians, Greeks, Romans and Arabs as well as the Chinese. Kollam became the capital of the Venad Kingdom in the ninth century. The educated king Raja Udaya Marthanda Varma convened a special council at Kollam to introduce a new era. After extensive astronomical calculations the new era was established to start on 15 August AD 825. The town was associated with the early history of Christianity.

From the **KSWTC** boat jetty in the city centre you can hire houseboats or sightseeing boats (a houseboat by appearances but with large seating areas instead of bedrooms) to explore the palm-fringed banks of Ashtamudi Lake. You might see Chinese fishing nets and large-sailed dugouts carrying the local crops of coir, copra and cashew. Munroe Island is a popular destination for tours, with coir factories, good birdwatching and narrow canals to explore.

THE BACKWATERS LISTINGS

WHERE TO STAY

Alleppey and around

$$$$ Marari Beach, Mararikulam, T0478-286 3801, www.cghearth.com. Well-furnished, comfortable, local-style cottages (garden villas, garden pool villas and 3 deluxe pool villas) in palm groves – some with private pool. Good seafood, pool, Ayurvedic treatment, yoga in the morning, *pranayama* in the evening, shop, bikes, badminton, beach volleyball, boat cruises (including overnight houseboat), farm tours, friendly staff, discounts Apr-Sep.

$$$$ Purity, Muhamma, Aryakkara (8 km from Alappuzha town), T0484-221 6666, www.malabarhouse.com. This beautiful Italianate villa, set on an acre of tropical grounds overlooking Lake Vembanad, is the most elegant lodging for miles around, with coolly minimalist decor and a smattering of rare antiques. Huge rooms on the ground floor open out to a grassy lawn, but for the ultimate splurge check in to the huge turquoise-toned suite upstairs, with arched windows hoovering up views of the glassy lake. There's a pool and a discreet spa offering Ayurvedic treatments and yoga classes, and high class dinners, which the chef can tailor to your wishes, are served around a pond in the courtyard. Superb in every respect and thoroughly recommended.

$$$ Pooppally's Heritage Homestay, Pooppally Junction, Nedumudy, T0477-276 2034, www.pooppallys.com. Traditional wooden cottage (water bungalow) and rooms, with open-air bathrooms, in 19th-century family farmhouse, shaded by a mango tree, set in a garden stretching

Kerala's finest circuit of villa hotels & spas, enter our world of personalised experiences

Malabar escapes

www.malabarescapes.com | t +91 484 221 6666 | f 221 7777

down to the River Pampa. Great home-cooked food. Catch the ferry to Alappuzha for 90 mins of free houseboat.

$$-$ Cherukara Nest, just around the corner from KSRTC bus station, Alappuzha, T0477-225 1509, www.cherukaranest.com. Airy, cool, spotlessly clean rooms in a peaceful traditional family home. Very helpful and friendly. Meals available on request.

$ Johnson's The Nest, Lal Bagh Factory Ward (West of Convent Sq), Alappuzha, T0477-224 5825, www.johnsonskerala.com. Friendly family-run guesthouse in a quiet street away from the town centre. 6 rooms, each with balcony. A popular backpacker choice, and a good place to connect with solo travellers looking to share the cost of a houseboat.

Kumarakom

$$$$ Philipkutty's Farm, Pallivathukal, Ambika Market, Vechoor, Kottayam, T0482-927 6530, www.philipkuttysfarm.com. 5 immaculate waterfront villas sharing an island on Vembanad Lake. The delightful working farm boasts coconut, banana, nutmeg, coca and vanilla groves. Delicious home cooking and personal attention from all the family. No a/c or TV. Cooking and painting holidays.

$$$$ Privacy at Sanctuary Bay, Kannamkara, opposite Kumarakom, T0484-221 6666, www.malabarhouse.com. The little twin sister of Purity, Privacy offers absolute lakeside isolation in a fully staffed but fully self-contained 3-bedroom bungalow. Modern opulent interiors hide behind the old Keralite facade, and there's a stunning veranda looking out across the lake.

$$ GK's Riverview Homestay, Valliadu, Aymanam, T0481-259 7527, www.gk homestay-kumarakom.com. Set amid paddy fields in the heart of God of Small Things country, George and Dai's lovely house offers home comforts in the shape of simple immaculate rooms, hammocks lazily overlooking the river, and superb Kerala cooking. Consummate hosts, they're always on hand to share secrets of the area, and arrange excellent tours.

RESTAURANTS

Alleppey and around
$$$ Chakara, Raheem Residency, Beach Rd, T0477-223 0767. Across the road from Alappuzha's long beach, this restaurant in a superbly restored heritage hotel offers excellent Kerala seafood dishes, attentive service and wonderful views from the romantic corner table in the low-lit rooftop restaurant (book ahead to snag the best spot). Pricey, but among the best in town.

Kumarakom
$$$$ Baker's Gourmet House, Vivanta by Taj Kumarakom, T0481-252 5711. Set amid the miniature canals and manicured grounds of the swish Taj resort, the beautiful Baker's House is a literary celebrity – the History House of Arundhati Roy's *The God of Small Things*, looking out across a tree-fringed lagoon in the heart of its own 5-star 'Heart of Darkness'. The 120-year-old bungalow now serves as a venue for pan-global high-end dining, the food at its best when not straying too far from Kerala seafood; come at dusk, when hundreds of brass lamps twinkle around the lagoon.

Alappuzha and around
Houseboat cruises

Some find cruising the Backwaters utterly idyllic and restful, while for others the sluggish pace of the houseboats – combined with the heavy crowding of the waterways close to Alappuzha – a form of slow torture. Most first-time visitors go for an overnight tour, which is in some ways the worst of all worlds: you're often moored alongside a raft of other boats, you get trotted through the standard tourist 'village' visits (read: shopping trips), and you simply don't have time to get away from the crowds. If you can spare an extra night or more, longer cruises let you get away into the deeper reaches of the Backwaters where canal life still continues more or less unmolested by tourism. On the other hand, if you just want a taste of the scenery, a day cruise – or even one of the cheap ferries that ply the lakes and canals – might satisfy you at a fraction of the price of a night on a houseboat.

It's always worth booking in advance during high season, when the theoretical government-set rates (which are printed and displayed in the DTPC booking office at the jetty in Alappuzha) go out the window, and houseboat owners jack the prices up by 50-80%. Houseboats vary widely – by number of bedrooms, facilities (some come with a/c, flatscreen TVs and DVD players), quality of food and the crew's level of English – and booking ahead gives you some degree of certainty about getting the level of luxury you require; it also allows you to circumvent the persistent dockside touts, whose commissions mean that any discount you can negotiate comes at the cost of corners cut on the trip. If you're coming outside peak season, and don't mind spending a morning scouting around, making a booking on the spot gives you a chance to inspect a number of boats before agreeing on a price.

The following companies are generally at the top end of the market, but offer reliably good (in some cases superb) service:
CGHEarth, T0484-301 1711, Kochi, www.cghearth.com. Runs 'spice boat' cruises in modified *kettuvallams*, which are idyllic if not luxurious: shaded sit-outs, modern facilities including solar panels for electricity, 2 double rooms, limited menu. US$325.
Discovery 1, T0484-221 6666, www.malabarhouse.com. **Malabar Escapes'** take on the houseboat is silent, pollutant-free, and bright turquoise. Because it's nimble and trips are for a minimum of 2 nights, Discovery can take you far from the wider watery motorways bigger rice boats ply. 1 bedroom, large bathroom and sitting room plus sun deck. Food and service are to the Malabar House's customary high standard.
Lakes and Lagoons Tour Co, Punnamada, T0477-2266842, www.lakeslagoons.com. Solar-powered 2-bed boats. Consistently recommended operator.

Kollam

Southern Backwaters, opposite KSRTC bus station, Jetty Rd, T(0)94959-76037, www.southernbackwaters.com. Offers 1- to 5-night packages, with longer journeys travelling from Kollam to Kumarakom or Alappuzha. Also run motoroboat cruises and tours to Munroe Island.

KOCHI TO MUNNAR

High in the hills five hours inland from Kochi, Munnar is chai central: a surreal rippling mosaic of yellow-green tea bushes etched with red dust roads, lapping at the feet of stark grey granite peaks. At 1600 m, Munnar gets genuinely cold, a virtue that made it a favourite summer bolthole for officer of the Raj. Antique tea bungalows and a rash of new resorts scattered among the plantations now provide pre Munnar's pre-monsoon rush, Wildlife tourists flock to nearby Eravikulam National Park for a glimpse of the endangered but semi-tame Nilgiri thar, a variety of ibex that grazes the subalpine meadows, while further to the north are the forests and deeply carved ravines of magnificent Chinnar Wildlife Sanctuary, home to elephants and leopards.

THE ROAD TO MUNNAR

The route from the Backwaters to Munnar backtracks north, bypassing Kochi and turning inland at Muvattupula. This is one of South India's most attractive ghat roads, rubber plantations gradually giving way to open forest as you corkscrew up the valley of the Periyar river. The one sight of note here is the **Salim Ali Bird Sanctuary** ① *Thattekad, 70 km east of Kochi on a side road heading north out of Kothamangalam; open 0600-1800, contact Assistant Wildlife Warden, Thattekad, T0485-258 8302.* A tropical evergreen and semi-evergreen forest with teak and rosewood plantations, the sanctuary is surrounded by the Periyar River, which remains shallow most of the year. It attracts many water birds and an exceptional variety of cuckoos, as well as Malabar grey hornbill, Indian pitta, rose and blue-winged parakeet, greater flameback woodpecker, while rarer birds like the Ceylon frogmouth and rose-billed rollers are also sometimes seen here. Sightings are best early in the morning and late in the afternoon and, if you have time, several good hotels around the sanctuary make staying overnight a worthwhile option.

→ MUNNAR

A major centre of Kerala's tea industry, Munnar sits in the lee of Anaimudi, South India's highest peak at 2695 m, and is the nearest Kerala comes to a genuine hill station. The landscape is European Alpine, minus the snow, plus tea bushes – inestimable millions of them. The town is surrounded by about 30 tea estates, among them the highest in the world at Kolukkumalai, yet despite the increasingly commercial use of the hills you can still find forests that are rich in wildlife, including the endangered Nilgiri tahr. The surrounding hills are also home to the rare Neelakurunji orchid (*Strobilanthes*), which covers the hills in colour for a month once every 12 years (next due 2018). During the monsoon cotton wool swabs of cloud shift and eddy across hillsides sodden as a sponge with fresh rains, and springs burst their banks and surge across the pathways where villagers dressed in ski jackets and woollen hats, swing past on Enfields on their way home from a day on the tea plantations.

ARRIVING IN MUNNAR

Getting there and around Munnar is a great long streak of a town, with a scrappy centre built around the market. Buses from Kochi pull in to the small KSRTC bus stand 1.5 km south of the market. Many of the best places to stay are out of town, and require an auto-rickshaw or jeep. The town itself is small and pleasant for exploring on foot or by bike if you don't mind the hills.

Moving on It's a long haul from Munnar to **Ooty** (see page 229): a day's road travel to Mettupalayam, an overnight stay, and an early start next morning to catch the Nilgiri Mountain Railway. It's worth hiring a taxi for the Munnar–Mettupalayam stretch, which snakes down through the wild mountain scenery of Chinnar Wildlife Sanctuary. The cheaper alternative is a crowded bus from Munnar to Coimbatore (two a day go direct, six hours, others require a change in Udumalaipettai, 3½ hours), a major transport hub that has frequent buses and occasional trains to Mettupalayam (one hour).

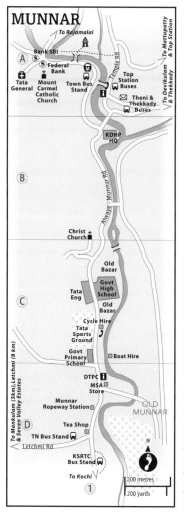

MUNNAR

To Rajamalai
Bank SBI
Federal Bank
Tata General
Mount Carmel Catholic Church
Town Bus Stand
Temple Rd
Top Station Buses
Theni & Thekkady Buses
To Mattupatty & Top Station
To Devikulam & Thekkady
KDHP HQ
Alwaye-Munnar Rd
Christ Church
Old Bazar
Govt High School
Tata Eng
Old Bazar
Cycle Hire
Tata Sports Ground
Govt Primary School
Boat Hire
DTPC
MSA Store
Munnar Ropeway Station
OLD MUNNAR
Tea Shop
TN Bus Stand
To Mankulam (3km), Letchmi (8 km) & Seven Valley Estates
Letchmi Rd
KSRTC Bus Stand
To Kochi
200 metres
200 yards
1

Tourist information DTPC ① *T04865-231516, www.dtpcidukki.com*, runs tours of plantations and rents cycles. Try also the free Tourist Information Service in the Main Bazar opposite the bus stop, run by Joseph Iype, a veritable mine of information. For trekking information, Senthil Kumar of local eco-guiding outfit Kestrel Adventures (see page 228) is hard to beat.

PLACES IN MUNNAR

Tata Tea Museum ① *Nullatanni Estate, T04865-230561, www.keralatourism.org, 0900-1600, Rs 75, tea tastings at 1030 and 1430, Rs 100*, has a heap of artefacts, curios and photographs to help conjure something of the lives of the men who opened up the High Ranges to tea. The crop has grown here for over a century so relics include a rudimentary tea roller from 1905 and a wheel from the Kundale Valley Light Railway that used to transport men and materials between Munnar and Top Station. The museum has descriptions of the fully automated technology of today from the tea factory at Madupatty. The museum can also arrange a visit to this factory, watching tea pickers at work and processing.

In the centre of Old Munnar, set on a hill immediately above the road in the centre of town, is **Christ Church**. Built to serve tea estate managers and workers of the High Ranges, the last English-language service was held in 1981; it is now shared between protestant Tamil and Malayalam worshippers. The exterior is unprepossesing: rather squat and now blackened by weathering, but inside it is a charming small church, and still contains its original 14 rows of wooden pews. Ask to see the diminutive record of births and deaths of the town's founders, the British planters. Immediately behind the church a zigzag path up the hill leads to the small pioneer cemetery that was established long before the church itself as the chosen burial ground of Mrs Eleanor Knight, General Manager Knight's 24-year-old bride who caught cholera after arriving in the High Range in 1894.

Mount Carmel Roman Catholic Church, the first Catholic church in the High Ranges, is in Old Munnar on the road up to the Tata General Hospital. The first chapel on the site was founded in 1898 by Friar Alphonse who arrived in Munnar from Spain in 1854. The present church was built by the then Bishop of Vijayapuram in 1938.

High Range Club ① *T04865-230253*, is a private members' club more relaxed than the famously 'Snooty' Ooty Club. A tradition allowed members to hang their hats on the wall of the bar after 30 years of belonging to the club – the last was hung in 1989 to make 51 hats in all. Saturday is strictly jacket and tie only and you'll need to scrub up well to get in any day of the week. "We like scholars and researchers, professionals and club people," says the club secretary, "they know how to move in a club." It's a wonderful place with teak floors, squash courts, library and fascinating planters to chat to if you're interested in the planters' social history. The easiest way in is to stay in the elegant, rooms and cottages; book 30 days in advance at www.highrangeclubmunnar.com.

AROUND MUNNAR

There are some excellent **cycle rides** around Munnar, not all of them steep. One ride goes up a gentle slope through a beautiful valley 8 km to the Letchmi Estate. There is a *chai* stall at the estate and the road continues to the head of the valley for views down to the forest. A second ride (or walk) leaves Munnar by the south road for 3 km, turning left at the Head Works Dam, then takes a right turn past Copper Castle, then left to a tea stall, viewpoint, tea and cardamom plantations, again with superb views. Continue to the next tea pickers' village for a tea stall. A shorter option for this route is to cross the dam and turn left, taking the quiet road north to the High Range Club and Munnar.

Mattupetty Lake ① *13 km from Munnar, T04865-230389, visits between 0900-1100, 1400-1530, Rs 5*, at an altitude of 1700 m, is flanked by steep hills and woods. It was created by the small hydro-electricity dam. To its south is the Kerala Livestock Development Board's research and cattle breeding centre, formerly the Indo-Swiss dairy project. In a beautiful semi-Alpine setting surrounded for much of the year by lush green fields, the centre offers interesting insights into the practical realities and achievements of cattle breeding in India today.

Top Station, 34 km from Munnar on the Tamil Nadu border, at an altitude of 2100 m, has some of the highest tea estates in India. It is an idyllic spot, with superb views over the Tamil Nadu plains and the edge of the Western Ghats. Stalls serve tea and soft drinks. Top Station took its name from a ropeway that connected it via Middle Station to Lower Station at the valley bottom. The small town of **Bodinayakkanur**, which can be reached on the Devikulam road, lies in the valley. Buses leave from the shelter north of Munnar post office four times a day bound for Kovilor, passing Mattupetty Lake and Kundala Dam. If you get off at Top Station, the return bus comes past after about an hour.

Across the valley from Top Station, and around 40 km east of Munnar, the small plantation of **Kolukkumalai** officially claims to pick the highest tea leaves in the world. The drive to the ridgetop at 2175 m takes two hours (the last section on a plantation road so bad it might be quicker to get out and walk) but the effort is repaid by astonishing

ON THE ROAD
Body language

Ayurveda, a Sanskrit word meaning 'the knowledge (*veda*) of life (*ayur*)', is an Indian holistic system of health dating back over 5000 years. Indians see it as a divine gift from Lord Brahma, their Hindu creator God, which has been developed by sages and holy men over the centuries. In contrast to the Western system of medicine, which is geared to treating an already diseased body or mind, Ayurveda seeks to help the individual strengthen and control both mind and body in order to prolong life and prevent illness. In today's world, it's a brilliant complement to Western medicine and, as well as detoxing the body and mind and relieving stress, has been used to treat ME, high blood pressure, allergies, asthma, back pain, rheumatism, skin diseases, migraines and insomnia, and is used as an effective follow-up treatment to chemotherapy.

How it works In essence, Ayurveda combines body treatments and detoxification therapies with a balanced diet, gentle exercise and meditation to promote wellbeing. The type of treatments and therapies are dictated by an individual's constitution, defined by a balance of three bodily energies or *doshas*: *vata*, *pitta* and *kapha*. Composed of the five elements – earth, water, fire, air and ether (or space) – these *doshas* govern our bodily processes: *vata* controls circulation and the nervous system; *pitta* the metabolism and digestion; *kapha* bodily strength and energy. When we feel out of kilter, our *doshas* are likely to be out of balance, which a course of Ayurvedic treatments will seek to remedy.

An experienced Ayurvedic doctor will diagnose your *dosha* type by taking your pulse, and observing such things as how quickly you speak and move, your build, the colour of your eyes and the quality of your skin. You'll also be asked lots of questions about your preferences – on anything from climate to the spiciness of food. The more open and honest you are, the more accurate a judgement will be, though it's uncanny how the best doctors will read you just right, whatever you tell them.

What you do Any programme of Ayurveda will include preparation treatments and elimination (or detox) therapies. The former include soothing, synchronized oil applications and massages, and *swedana* (purifying steam and herbal baths), while the latter involve ingesting or retaining herbal medicines, medicated oils and ghee (or clarified butter), inhalations, *bastis* (or oil enemas), therapeutic vomiting and bloodletting. Preparation treatments often include sleep-inducing *shirodara*, when a wonderful continuous stream of warm oil is poured across your forehead; *choornaswedana*, where hot herbal or lemon poultices are massaged all over you to induce sweating; and the supremely nourishing four-handed *abhyanga* and *marma* massage. *Pizhichil* is often regarded as the 'Marmite' of Ayurveda. Gallons of cleansing sesame oil are poured continuously over your body and massaged in by two therapists as the oil increases in heat. You'll slip about like a sardine in a tin, but this treatment is very effective. Look at the oil afterwards, and you'll be shocked at just how dirty you were. If you're a smoker, it's likely to be black.

Any hotel or retreat venue that offers only Ayurvedic massages is offering only a part of what Ayurveda is all about. You need time for Ayurveda treatments to have any real effect. A proper course of Ayurveda needs at least two weeks to be effective and offer any real lasting benefit, and rest between treatments is vital. Most people who undertake a course of Ayurveda have a *panchakarma* – which literally translates as 'five therapies', and which also refers to a general Ayurveda detox lasting two weeks or more.

views across misty valleys and distant peaks. It's worth being here for sunrise; set off by 0400 and wrap up warm for the journey. A path through the tea bushes leads down to the 1930s factory, where you can sample the local product and watch the antique processing equipment in action. As the plantation is privately owned you need to join a tour to get in; **Kestrel Adventures** (see What to do, page 228) is the main operator.

Eravikulam/Rajamalai National Park ① *21 km northeast of Munnar, www.eravikulam. org, closed Feb-Mar and during the monsoons, Rs 200, camera Rs 25, video Rs 200,* was set up in 1978 to preserve the endangered Nilgiri tahr (Nilgiri ibex). The conservation programme has resulted in the park now supporting the largest population of the species in the world, of nearly 2000. The sure-footed wild goats live in herds on the steep black rocky slopes of the Anaimudi mountains. They are brownish, have short, flat horns with the male carrying a thick mane, and can be easily seen around the park entrance. There are also elephants, sambars, gaurs, macaques and the occasional leopard and tiger. The scenery is magnificent, though the walks into the forest are steep and strenuous. There is an easier paved path from the park entrance following the road immediately below the bare granite outcrop of the Naikundi Hill to the Rajamalai Gap. The Forest Department issues a limited number of permits to trek through the park on the **Goldsbury Track**.

Adjoining Eravikulam to the north, and spreading down the eastern slope of the ghats into Tamil Nadu, the rarely visited **Chinnar Wildlife Sanctuary** ① *contact the Forest Information Office in Munnar, T04865-231587,* offers near-guaranteed sightings of elephant and bison, and has treehouses and log huts to stay in.

GOING FURTHER
River Nila and Palakkad

The blue thread of the River Nila, Kerala's equivalent of the Ganges and the crucible of much of the state's rich cultural heritage, stitches together a collection of fascinating sights and experiences in the rarely explored central belt of Kerala between Kochi and Kozhikode. Busy Thrissur, the state's cultural capital, is unmissable in April and May when it holds its annual Pooram festival and millions pack into the city's central square, sardine-style, to watch the elephant procession and fireworks display. Coastal Guruvayur, meanwhile, is among Kerala's most sacred Hindu pilgrimage spots; it is home to one of India's wealthiest temples as well as an elephant yard where huge tuskers and their mahouts relax before they hit the road for the next festival. Inland, the Palakkad Gap cuts a broad trench through the Western Ghats, the only natural break in the mountain chain, providing a ready conduit for roads, railway lines, innumerable waves of historical migrants, and blasts of scorching air from the roasted plains of Tamil Nadu.

ARRIVING IN RIVER NILA AND PALAKKA

Getting there Trains on the main north–south line stop in Thrissur and Shoranur Junction, a handy jumping-off point for the River Nila. Trains from Kerala to Coimbatrore and Chennai call at Palakkad. There are bus connections from these towns to the smaller centres.

Tourist Information Thrissur ① *Palace Rd, T0487-232 0800, www.dtpcthrissur.com.* **Guruvayur** ① *Vyjayanti Building, East Nada, Guruvayur, T0487-255 0400.* **Palakkad DTPC** ① *West Fort Rd, Palakkad, T0491-253 8996, www.dtpcpalakkad.com.*

THRISSUR (TRICHUR) AND AROUND

Thrissur, 80 km north of Kochi, is built around a hill on which stand the Vadakkunnathan Temple and an open green, which form the centre of the earth-shaking festivities. The town's bearings are given in cardinal directions from this raised 'Round'.

The **Vadakkunnathan Temple** ① *0400-1030, 1700-2030, non-Hindus not permitted inside except during the Pooram festival*, a predominantly Siva temple, is also known as the Rishabhadri or Thenkailasam ('Kailash of the South'). At the shrine to the Jain Tirthankara Vrishabha, worshippers offer a thread from their clothing, symbolically to cover the saint's nakedness. The shrine to Sankara Narayana has superb murals depicting stories from the *Mahabharata*. It is a classic example of the Kerala style of architecture with its special pagoda-like roof richly decorated with fine wood carving. The temple plays a pivotal role in the **Pooram** celebrations, held during April and May. This magnificent eight-day cacophony of a festival is marked by colourful processions joined by people of all religious groups irrespective of caste. Platoons of elephants decked out in gold, palm leaves and lamps march to the Vadakkunnathan Temple carrying priests and idols, to the accompaniment of dozens of drums, cymbals and pipes. On the final day temple teams meet on the Tekkinkadu maidan for a showdown of drumming and Kudumattam (the name roughly translates as 'umbrella swapping' – one of Kerala's more surreal spectator sports) before a huge fireworks display brings proceedings to a close. In September and October, there are live performances of Chakyarkothu, a classical art form. There is a small elephant compound attached to the temple.

The **Town Hall** is a striking building housing an art gallery with murals from other parts of the state. In the **Archaeological Museum** ① *Town Hall Rd, Tue-Sun 0900-1500*, ask to see the royal chariot. Next door, the **Art Museum** has woodcarvings, sculptures, an excellent collection of traditional lamps and old jewellery. Nearby, **Thrissur Zoo** ① *Tue-Sun 1000-1700, small fee*, is known for its snake collection. The impressive **Lourdes Church** has an interesting underground shrine.

GURUVAYUR

As one of the holiest sites in Kerala, Guruvayur, 29 km west of Trichur, is a heaving pilgrimage centre, filled with stalls and thronged from 0300 to 2200 with people wanting to take *darshan* of Guruvayurappan. The 16th-century Sri Krishna temple is one of the richest in India, and there is a waiting list for the auspicious duty of lighting its oil lamps that stretches to 2025. On well-augured marriage days there is a scrum in which couples are literally shunted from the podium by new pairs urgently pressing behind them in the queue, and the whole town is geared towards the wedding industry.

The temple's inner sanctum is off limits to non-Hindus, but you can visit the **Guruvayur Devaswom Institute of Mural Painting** ① *Mon-Fri 1000-1600*, a tiny educational institute where you can meet and buy finished works from the next generation of mural painters. As with Kathakali, the age-old decorative arts of temple culture steadily declined during the 20th century under the weakening structure of feudalism and opposition to the caste system. When the temple lost three walls to a fire in 1970 there were hardly any artists left to carry out renovation, prompting authorities to build the school in 1989. Today the small institute runs a five-year course on a scholarship basis for just 10 students. Paintings sell for Rs 500-15,000 depending on size, canvas, wood, etc.

Some 4 km outside the town is the **Sri Krishna Temple**, which probably dates from at least the 16th century has an outer enclosure where there is a tall gold-plated flagpost and a pillar of lamps. The sanctum sanctorum is in the two-storeyed *srikoil*, with the image of the four-armed Krishna garlanded with pearls and marigolds. Photography of the tank is not allowed. Non-Hindus are not allowed inside and are not made to feel welcome.

On the left as you walk towards the temple is the **Guruvayur Devaswom Institute of Mural Painting** ① *Mon-Fri 1000-1600*, a tiny educational institute where you can see the training of, and buy finished works from, the next generation of mural painters. In a similar vein to *Kathakali*, with the weakening structure of feudalism and opposition to the caste system, the age-old decorative arts of temple culture steadily declined during the 20th century. When Guruvayur lost three walls to a fire in 1970 there were hardly any artists left to carry out renovation, prompting authorities to build the school in 1989. Today the small institute runs a five-year course on a scholarship basis for just 10 students. Paintings sell for Rs 500-15,000 depending on size, canvas, wood, etc. Humans are stylized (facial expressions and gestures can be traced back to *Kathakali* and *Koodiyattom*) and have wide-open eyes, elongated lips, over-ornamentation and exaggerated eyebrows and hand gestures.

Punnathur Kotta Elephant Yard ① *0900-1700, bathing 0900-0930, Rs 25, buses from Thrissur (45 mins)*. Temple elephants (68 at the last count) are looked after here and wild ones are trained. There are some interesting insights into traditional animal training but this is not everyone's cup of tea. Though captive, the elephants are dedicated to Krishna and appear to be well cared for by their attendants. The elephants are donated by pious Hindus but religious virtue doesn't come cheap: the elephants cost Rs 500,000 each.

ALONG THE RIVER NILA

North of Thrissur the road and railway cut through lush countryside of paddy fields, quiet villages and craggy red hills mantled with coconut and rubber plantations, before crossing the wide sandy bed of the Bharatapuzha River at Shoranur. Known to the people who populate its banks as Nila, this is Kerala's longest river, rising on the eastern side of the Palakkad Gap and winding lazily through 209 km to spill into the Arabian Sea at the bustling fishing port of Ponnani. Though its flow is severely depleted by irrigation dams and its bed gouged by sand miners, the importance of the river to Kerala's cultural development is hard to overstate: Ayurveda, *kathakali* and the martial art *kalaripayattu* were all nurtured along the banks of the Nila, not to mention the cacophonous classical music that soundtracks festive blow-outs like the Thrissur **Pooram**. Folk tradition too is vibrantly represented: elaborately adorned devotees carry colourful effigies to temple festivals, snake worshippers roam house to house performing ancient rituals to seek blessing from the serpent gods, and village musicians sing songs of the paddy field mother goddess, passed down from generation to generation.

Despite all this, the Nila thus far remains refreshingly untouched by Kerala's tourism boom, and few travellers see more of it than the glimpses afforded by the beautiful train ride between Shoranur and Kozhikode. This is in part because there's little tourist infrastructure, few genuine 'sights', and no easy way for a travellers to hook into the cultural scene. Traditional potters and brass-smiths labour in humble workshops behind unmarked houses, while performers (singers and dancers by night, coolies, plumbers and snack sellers by day) only get together for certain events. With your own transport you can search out any number of beautiful riverside temples, but unless you join one of the superb storytelling tours run by local guiding outfit **The Blue Yonder** (see page 228), **Kerala Kalamandalam** (see below) might be the only direct contact you have with the Nila's rich heritage.

The residential school of **Kerala Kalamandalam** ① *3 km south of river, Cheruthuruthy, south of Shoranur Junction, T04884-262305, www.kalamandalam.org, Mon-Fri 0930-1300, closed public holidays and Apr-May,* is dedicated to preserving the state's unique forms of performance art. Founded in 1930, after the provincial rulers' patronage for the arts dwindled in line with their plummeting wealth and influence, the Kalamandalam spearheaded a revival of *Kathakali* dancing, along with *Ottam Thullal* and the all-female drama *Mohiniyattam*. The school and the state tourism department run a fascinating three-hour tour of the campus, 'A Day With the Masters' (US$25), with in-depth explanations of the significance and background of the art forms, the academy and its architecture, taking you through the various open air *kalaris* (classrooms) to watch training sessions. There are all-night *Kathakali* performances on 26 January, 15 August, and 9 November. *Koodiyattam*, the oldest surviving form of Sanskrit theatre, is enshrined by UNESCO as an 'oral and intangible heritage of humanity'. Frequent private buses from Thrissur's northern bus stand (ask for Vadakkancheri Bus Stand) go straight to Kalamandalam, taking about one hour.

PALAKKAD (PALGHAT)

Kerala's rice cellar, prosperous Palakkad has long been of strategic importance for its gap – the only break in the mountain ranges that otherwise block the state from Tamil Nadu and the rest of India. Whereas once this brought military incursions, today the gap bears tourist buses from Chennai and tractors for the rich agricultural fields here that few educated modern Keralites care to plough using the old bullock carts (although the tradition is kept alive through *kaalapoottu*, a series of races between yoked oxen held in mud-churned paddy fields every January). The whole of Palakkad is like a thick paddy forest, its iridescent old blue mansions, many ruined by the Land Reform Act, crumbling into paddy ponds. There are village idylls like a Constable painting. Harvest hands loll idly on pillows of straw during lunch hours, chewing ruminatively on chapattis.

The annual festival of **Chinakathoor Pooram** (late February to early March) held at the Sri Chinakathoor Bhagavathy Temple, Palappuram, features a 33-tusker procession, plus remarkable evening puppet shows. Bejewelled tuskers can also be seen at the 20-day **Nenmara-Vallangi Vela**, held at the Sri Nellikulangara Bhagavathy Temple in Kodakara (early April): an amazing festival with grander firework displays than Trichur's **Pooram** but set in fields rather than across the city.

The region is filled with old architecture of *illams* and *tharavadus* belonging to wealthy landowners making a visit worthwhile in itself – but chief among the actual sights is **Palakkad Fort**, a granite structure in Palakkad town itself, built by Haider Ali in 1766, and taken over by the British in 1790. It now has a Hanuman temple inside. Ask directions locally to the 500-year-old Jain temple of **Jainimedu** in the town's western suburbs, a 10-m-long granite temple with Jain *Thirthankaras* and *Yakshinis* built for the Jain sage Chandranathaswami. Only one Jain family is left in the region, but the area around this temple is one of the only places in Kerala where remnants of the religion have survived.

Also well worth visiting in the region are the many traditional Brahmin villages: **Kalpathy**, 10 km outside Palakkad, holds the oldest Siva temple in Malabar, dating from AD 1425 and built by Kombi Achan, then Raja of Palakkad. But the village itself, an 800-year-old settlement by a self-contained Tamil community, is full of beautiful houses with wooden shutters and metal grills and is now a World Heritage Site that gives you a glimpse of village life that has been held half-frozen in time for nearly 1000 years. The temple here is called **Kasiyil Pakuthi Kalpathy** meaning Half Banares because its situation on the river is reminiscent of the Banares temple on the Ganges. A 10-day **car festival** in November centres on this temple and features teak chariots tugged by people and pushed by elephants.

Another unique feature of Palakkad is the *Ramassery Iddli* made at the **Sarswathy tea stall** ① *daily 0500-1830, iddli Rs 1.50, chai Rs 2.50*. If you spend any time on the street in South India, your morning meal will inevitably feature many of these tasty steamed fermented rice cakes. Palakkad is home to a peculiar take on the dumpling, one that has been developed to last for days rather than having to be cooked from fresh. The four families in this poky teashop churn out 5000 *iddlis* a day. Originally settlers from somewhere near Coimbatore, in Tamil Nadu, over 100 years ago, they turned to making this variety of *iddli* when there wasn't enough weaving work to sustain their families. They started out selling them door to door, but pretty soon started to get orders for weddings. The *iddlis* are known to have travelled as far afield as Delhi, by plane in a shipment of 300. Manufacturers have started to arrive in order to buy the secret recipe.

WHERE TO STAY

If you're in search of Ayurvedic healing at its most authentic and traditional, this quiet region, far inland from the pore-clogging salt air coming off the Arabian Sea, is the best place in all Kerala to find it. But don't come here expecting 5-star spa masseurs who'll tiptoe around your Western foibles about comfort and bodily privacy. These treatments are administered to you in the almost-raw, on hard wooden beds amid buckets of oil – and when your treatment is over your torturer may accompany you to the shower to make sure you thoroughly degrease.

$$$$-$$$ River Retreat, Palace Rd, Cheruthuruthy, T0488-426 2244, www.riverreatreat.in. Heritage hotel and Ayurvedic resort in the former (and much-extended) home of the maharajas of Kochi. Spacious rooms have a/c, TV and modern baths, great views onto large tree-filled garden that backs onto the Nila. Tours of the local area, restaurant, bar, pool, Wi-Fi.

$$$ Maranat Mana, Old Ooty–Mysore Rd, Pandikkad (an hour's drive north of Pattambi), T0493-128 6252, www.maranat mana.com. Special homestay in a traditional *namboodhiri* (Kerala Brahmin) household. Hosts Praveen and Vidya have sensitively converted the 160-year-old guesthouse attached to their ancestral home into 3 cool and airy rooms, all with fans and modern baths. You can visit the sprawling main family residence, one of the last surviving examples of Keralite *pathinaru kettu* ('four courtyards') architecture, which contains a Ganesh shrine to which devotees flock from far and wide. Delicious vegetarian meals included, and local tours, Ayurvedic treatments, yoga classes, cultural activities can be arranged. Fascinating and highly recommended, reservations essential.

Ayurveda retreats
$$$$ Kalari Kovilakom, Kollengode, T04923-263737, www.kalarikovilakom.com.

Ayurveda for purists. Far from the Ayurveda tourist traps, the Maharani of Palakkad's 1890 palace has been restored to make this very elite retreat. It's extremely disciplined yet very luxurious: the indulgence of a palace meets the austerity of an ashram. Treatments include anti-ageing, weight loss, stress management and ailment healing. Lessons include yoga, meditation, Ayurvedic cookery. For treatments there's a minimum 14-day stay, during which there's no exertion, no sunbathing and no mod cons – a genuine off switch for your mind.

$$$ Ayurveda Mana, Peringode, via Kootanadu, T0466-237 0660, www. ayurvedamana.com. Authentic Ayurveda centre set in a fascinating 600-year-old *illam*, with treatments following the traditional methods of Poomully Aram Thampuran, a renowned expert in the discipline. Quiet airy rooms (all with TV, and some with traditional *attukattil* beds that hang from the ceiling) open onto shady veranda and peaceful manicured grounds. Full range of general health care treatments available and specialized therapies for arthritis, sports injuries, infertility, etc. All treatments include individually assessed diet, massage and medicine.

$$$ Kairali Ayurvedic Health Resort, Kodumbu, T0492-322 2553, www. kairali.com. Excellent resort, beautifully landscaped grounds, own dairy and farm, pool, tennis, extensive choice of treatments (packages of Ayurveda, trekking, astrology, golf, pilgrimage), competent and helpful staff. Recommended.

$$ Arya Vaidya Sala, Kottakal town, T0483-274 2216, www.aryavaidyasala.com. One of the biggest and best Ayurvedic centres in India, with a fully equipped hospital offering 4-week *panchkarma* treatments as well as on-site medicine factory and research department.

KOCHI TO MUNNAR LISTINGS

WHERE TO STAY

The Road to Munnar
$$$ Periyar River Lodge, Anakkayam, Kothamanagalam, T0485-258 8315, www.periyarriverlodge.com. 2-bedroom cottage in a rubber plantation on the banks of Periyar River right next to Thattekad Bird Sanctuary. Bamboo rafting, fishing, forest treks, jeep safaris to 30-m-high waterfalls for swimming, boat and bike tours. Lounge, en suite, river views. Keralite food.

Munnar
$$$$-$$$ Windermere Estate, Pothamedu, T04865-230512, www.windermeremunnar.com. Standalone cottages, an alpine farmhouse with 5 rooms and an elegant and utterly comfortable planters' bungalow with 3 rooms. The whole complex is set around an enormous granite boulder, with sweeping across the tops of clouds from the top, and there's a fantastically light and airy reading room done out with rustic timber furniture and vaulted ceilings. Pricey but recommended.
$$$ NatureZone, Pullipara, 5 km up dirt track off Letchmi Rd, west of TN Bus Stand, bookings on T0484-649 3301, www.thenaturezone.org. Arriving here is like stepping into Jurassic Park – you have to get out of the car and unhook the elephant-repelling electric fence. A leading outward-bound training centre with stunning valley views, the drawcards here are the jungly remoteness and the 2 rustic-chic treehouses, with branches growing right through the room. The safari tents down at ground level are OK but get pretty musty. On-site canteen serves good food.
$$$ The Tea Sanctuary, KDHP House, T04865-230141, www.theteasanctuary.com. 6 quaint old-fashioned bungalows on the working Kanan Devan tea estate, pukka colonial-style atmosphere plus activities like mountain biking, trekking, horse riding, golf and angling, and everything clubbable at the **High Range** and **Kundale** clubs.
$ John's Cottage, MSA Rd, near Munnar Supply Association, T04865-231823. Small bungalow home in a well-tended lawn running down to the river, with 8 clean rooms. Indian/Chinese food or use of kitchen.
$ Theresian Cottages, Cottages, north of town before **Tea County**, T04865-230351. For once, a cottage that's actually a cottage. 3 rooms open off the shared living room of this sweet little 1930s house, and though sizes vary, each has a fireplace, chaise longue and clean bathroom.

RESTAURANTS

Apart from hotel and resort restaurants, Munnar's culinary offerings are generally downmarket.

$ Saravana Bhavan, near market. Clean, cheap and friendly place serving great *dosas* and huge Kerala-style *thalis*.

WHAT TO DO

The Blue Yonder, T080-4115 2218, www.theblueyonder.com. Highly regarded and award-winning sustainable and community tourism operators, active in Kerala, Sikkim, Orissa and Rajasthan.
Kestrel Adventures, PB No 44, KTDC Rd, T094-4703 1040, www.kestreladventures.com. Senthil Kumar leads a team of 9 specialist guides, some expert in birds, others in tea growing and history. Highly recommended for camping and trekking, wildlife spotting in Chinnar Wildlife Sanctuary, and the only company in town that can get you into Kolukkumalai for sunrise. Also offers rock climbing, mountain bike tours/hire and jeep safaris.

OOTY AND THE NILGIRI HILLS

The Nilgiri hills, rising on the border between Kerala, Tamil Nadu and Karnataka, were once shared between shola forest and tribal peoples. But the British, limp from the heat of the plains, invested in expeditions up the mountains and before long had planted eucalyptus, established elite members' clubs and substituted jackals for foxes in their pursuit of the hunt. 'Snooty Ooty' sold its exclusivity long ago, and is now a ferociously populist and overdeveloped tourist trap. Nevertheless, there is still charm to these neatly pleated green hills, particularly in the smaller towns of Coonoor and Kotagiri, and arriving in them by the rack-and-pinion Nilgiri Mountain Railway is an unmissable slice of Indian romance for anyone who gets misty-eyed at the thought of billowing steam trains twisting through tunnels and tea bushes. Ooty also makes a convenient jumping-off point for Mudumalai and Bandipur national parks – enjoyable if less compelling wildlife spotting alternatives to Nagarhole if you're short on time.

ARRIVING IN OOTY AND THE NILGIRI HILLS

Getting there If you're going to Ooty, there's only one way to arrive: aboard one of the pocket-sized carriages pulled by the 'toy train' that puffs its way up the narrow-gauge line from Mettupalayam. Steam trains leave Mettupalayam daily at 0710, arriving at Coonoor by 1030, where the steam train is swapped for a diesel, and pulling into Ooty at 1200; book far in advance to secure a reserved seat, particularly during holidays and the summer high season. If you miss out you can do the trip by bus from Mettupalayam or Coimbatore – much quicker than the train, but inevitably less atmospheric.

Moving on Buses leave from Ooty's bus stand for Sultan Bathery and Kalpetta, the two main transport hubs for **Wayanad** (see page 235).

→ UDHAGAMANDALAM (OOTY)

Ooty has been celebrated for rolling hills covered in pine and eucalyptus forests and coffee and tea plantations since the first British planters arrived in 1818. A Government House was built, and the British lifestyle developed with cottages and clubs – tennis, golf, riding – and tea on the lawn. But the town is no longer the haven it once was; the centre is heavily built up and can be downright unpleasant in the holiday months of April to June, and again around October. It's best to stay either in the grand ruins of colonial quarters on the quiet outskirts where it's still possible to steal some serenity or opt instead for the far smaller tea garden town of Coonoor (see page 231), 19 km down mountain. **Tamil Nadu Tourism** ⓘ *Wenlock Rd, T0423-244 3977*, is not very efficient.

PLACES IN OOTY AND THE NILGIRI HILLS

The **Botanical Gardens** ⓘ *0800-1800, Rs 25, camera, Rs 50, video Rs 500, 3 km northeast of railway station*, house more than 1000 varieties of plant, shrub and tree including orchids, ferns, alpines and medicinal plants, but is most fun for watching giant family groups picnicking and gambolling together among beautiful lawns and glass houses. To the east of the garden in a Toda *mund* is the Wood House made of logs. The **Annual Flower Show** is held in the third week of May. The **Rose Garden** ⓘ *750 m from Charing Cross, 0830-1830*, has over 1500 varieties of roses.

Ooty Lake was built in 1825 as a vast irrigation tank and is now more than half overgrown with water hyacinth, though it is still used enthusiastically for boating and pedalo hire ① *0900-1800, Rs 60-110 per hr.*

Kandal Cross ① *3 km west of the railway station*, is a Roman Catholic shrine considered the 'Jerusalem of the East'. During the clearing of the area to make way for a graveyard in 1927, an enormous 4-m-high boulder was found and a cross was erected. Now a relic of the True Cross brought to India by an Apostolic delegate is shown to pilgrims every day. The annual feast is in May.

St Stephen's Church was Ooty's first church, built in the 1820s. Much of the wood is said to be from Tipu Sultan's Lal Bagh Palace in Srirangapatnam. The inside of the church and the graveyard at the rear are worth seeing.

Dodabetta ① *1000-1500, buses from Ooty, autos and taxis (Rs 200 round trip) go to the summit*, is 10 km east of the railway station off the Kotagiri road. Reaching 2638 m, the 'big mountain' is the second highest in the Western Ghats, sheltering Coonoor from the southwest monsoons when Ooty gets heavy rains. The top is often shrouded in mist. There is a viewing platform at the summit. The telescope isn't worth even the nominal Rs 2 fee.

WALKS AND HIKES AROUND OOTY

Hiking or simply walking is excellent in the Nilgiris. It is undisturbed, quiet and interesting. Climbing Dodabetta or Mukurti is hardly a challenge but the longer walks through the

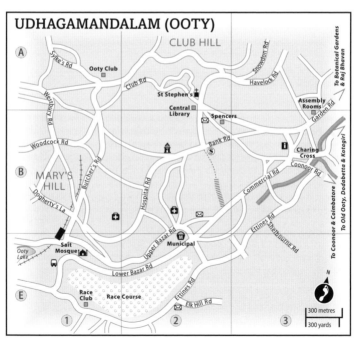

sholas are best undertaken with a guide. It is possible to see characteristic features of Toda settlements such as *munds* and *boas*.

Dodabetta-Snowdon-Ooty walk starts at Dodabetta Junction directly opposite the 3 km road to the summit. It is a pleasant path that curves gently downhill through a variety of woodland (mainly eucalyptus and conifers) back to Ooty and doesn't take more than a couple of hours. For longer treks, contact **Nilgiris Trekking Association** ① *Kavitha Nilayam, 31-D Bank Rd, or R Seniappan, 137 Upper Bazar, T0423-244 4449, sehiappan@yahoo.com*.

Mukurti Peak ① *buses from Ooty every 30 mins from 0630 or you can take a tour, book early as they are popular*, is 36 km away, off the Gudalur road. After 26 km you reach the 6-km-long Mukurti Lake. Mukurti Peak (the name suggests that someone thought it resembled a severed nose), not an easy climb, is to the west. The Todas believe that the souls of the dead and the sacrificed buffaloes leap to the next world from this sacred peak. It is an excellent place to escape for walking, to view the occasional wildlife, to go fishing at the lake or to go boating.

Avalanche ① *24 km from town, buses from Ooty, 1110*, a valley, is a beautiful part of the *shola*, with plenty of rhododendrons, magnolias and orchids and a trout stream running through it, and is excellent for walking. The **Forestry Department Guest House** is clean and has good food. Contact the **Wildlife Warden** ① *1st floor, Mahalingam Building, Ooty T0423-244098*.

The **River Pykara** ① *19 km from Ooty, several buses 0630-2030, or take a car or bicycle*, has a dam and power plant. There is breathtaking scenery. The **waterfalls**, about 6 km from the bridge on the main road, are best in July though it is very wet then, but they are also worth visiting from August to December.

→ COONOOR

① *When you arrive by train or bus (which doesn't always stop at the main bus stand if going on to Ooty), the main town of Lower Coonoor will be to the east, across the river. Upper Coonoor, with the better hotels 2-3 km away, is further east.*

Smaller and much less developed than Ooty, Coonoor (population 50,100) is an ideal starting point for nature walks and rambles through villages. There's no pollution, no noise and very few people. The covered market, as with many towns and cities in South India, is almost medieval and cobblers, jewellers, tailors, pawn brokers and merchants sell everything from jasmine to beetroot. The picturesque hills around the town are covered in coffee and tea plantations.

The real attraction here is the hiking, though there are a couple of sights in town. The large **Sim's Park** ① *0800-1830, Rs 5*, named after a secretary to the Madras Club, is a well-maintained botanical garden on the slopes of a ravine with over 330 varieties of rose but is only really worth the journey for passionate botanists. Contact the **United Planters' Association of South India (UPASI)** ① *Glenview House, Coonoor, T0423-223 0270, www. upasi.org*, to visit tea and coffee plantations.

The **Wellington Barracks**, 3 km northeast of Lower Coonoor, which are the raison d'être for the town, were built in 1852. They are now the headquarters of the Indian Defence Services Staff College and also of the Madras Regiment, which is over 250 years old, the oldest in the Indian Army.

ON THE ROAD
The Blue Mountain Railway

Ever since 15 June 1899, the narrow-gauge steam Mountain Railway, in its blue and cream livery, has chugged from Mettupalayam to Ooty via Coonoor, negotiating 16 tunnels and 31 major bridges and climbing from 326 m to 2193 m. This was the location for the railway scenes of the Marabar Express in the film *A Passage to India*.

It's a charming 4½-hour (46-km) journey through tea plantations and forest, but – outside first class – be prepared for an amiable Indian holidaymakers' scrum. There are rest stops at Hillgrove (17 km) and Coonoor (27 km).

For enthusiasts, the pricier and more spacious Heritage Steam Chariot runs between Ooty and Runneymede picnic area, 23 km away, at weekends (more often in high season). The drawback is that you can be stranded for hours when the engine breaks down; some decide to scramble to the nearest road to flag down a bus.

Lamb's Rock, on a high precipice, 9 km away, has good views over the Coimbatore plains and coffee and tea estates on the slopes. At **Dolphin's Nose** (12 km away, several buses 0700-1615), you can see **Catherine Falls**, a further 10 km away (best in the early morning). **Droog** (13 km away, buses 0900, 1345) has ruins of a 16th-century fort used by Tipu Sultan, and requires a 3-km walk.

Kotagiri (ⓘ *29 km from Ooty, frequent services from Coonoor, Mettupalayam Railway Station and Ooty*), sits on the northeast crest of the plateau overlooking the plains, at an altitude of 1980 m. It has a milder climate than Ooty. The name comes from Kotar–Keri, the street of the *Kotas* who were one of the original hill tribes and who have a village to the west of the town. You can visit some scenic spots from here: **St Catherine Falls** (8 km) and **Elk Falls** (7 km), or one of the peaks, **Kodanad Viewpoint** (16 km) – reached through the tea estates or by taking one of the several buses that run from 0610 onwards – or **Rangaswamy Pillar**, an isolated rock, and the conical Rangaswamy Peak.

→ METTUPALAYAM AND THE NILGIRI GHAT ROAD

Mettupalayam has little going for it other than its status as the lowland terminus of the Nilgiri Mountain Railway, and staying overnight here is a matter of convenience rather than any compelling appeal. The town has become a centre for the areca nut trade as well as producing synthetic gems. The palms are immensely valuable trees: the nut is used across India wrapped in betel vine leaves – two of the essential ingredients of India's universal after-meal digestive, paan. There are magnificent groves of the tall slender trees between Mettupalayam and the start of the ghat road to Coonoor – one of the most scenic mountain journeys in South India, affording superb views over the plains below, and a worthy alternative way to reach the Nilgiris if the trains are booked out.

ⓘ *Minibus safaris 0630-0900, 1530-1800, Rs 45, still camera Rs 25, video Rs 150; Reception Range Office, Theppakadu, T0423-252 6235, open 0630-1800, is where buses between Mysore and Ooty stop. There is a Ranger Office at Kargudi. The best time to visit is Sep-Dec and Mar-May when the undergrowth dies down and it's easier to see animals, especially at dawn when they're on the move. Forest fires can close the park temporarily during Feb-Apr.*

An hour north of Ooty, Mudumalai forms part of the vast Nilgiri Biosphere Reserve – a 5000 sq km necklace of largely intact forest. The Moyar River, its hills (885-1000 m), ravines, flats and valleys being an extension of the same environment. The park is one of the more popular and is now trying to limit numbers of visitors to reduce disturbance to the elephants.

There are large herds of elephant, gaur, sambar, barking deer, wild dog, Nilgiri langur, bonnet monkey, wild boar, four-horned antelope and the rarer tiger and leopard, as well as smaller mammals and many birds and reptiles. **Elephant Camp**, south of Theppakadu, open 0700-0800 and 1600-1700, tames wild elephants. Some are bred in captivity and trained to work for the timber industry. You can watch the elephants being fed in the late afternoon, learn about each individual elephant's diet and the specially prepared 'cakes' of food.

You can hire a jeep for about Rs 10 per km but must be accompanied by a guide. Elephant rides from 0700-0830 and 1530-1700 (Rs 50 per person for 30 minutes); check timing and book in advance in Theppakadu or with the Wildlife Warden, Mount Stuart Hill, Ooty, T0423-244 4098. They can be fun even though you may not see much wildlife. There are *machans* near waterholes and salt licks and along the Moyar River. With patience you can see a lot, especially rare and beautiful birds. Treks and jeep rides in the remoter parts of the forest with guides can be arranged from some lodges, including **Jungle Retreat** (see page 234). You can spend a day climbing the hill and bathe at the impressive waterfalls. The core area is not open to visitors.

BANDIPUR NATIONAL PARK

ⓘ *50 km north of Ooty. 0600-0900, 1530-1830, reception centre 0900-1630; Mysore–Ooty buses stop at the main entrance. Entry fees have increased stratosperically: Rs 1000 per entry for foreigners, Rs 300 for Indians. Except for jeep safaris run by local lodges, the only access is by the Forest Department's uninspiring 1-hr bus safari: foreigners Rs 200, Indians Rs 85, video Rs 150. 30-min elephant 'joy rides', Rs 65. Best times to visit are Nov-Feb to avoid the hot, dry months. For info contact Bandipur Reception Centre, T08229-236051; Deputy Conservator of Forests, T08229-236043, Mysore T0821-248 0901, dcfbandipur@yahoo.co.in.*

Adjoining Mudumalai's northern border, Bandipur was set up by the Mysore maharaja in 1931, and has become one of the richest habitats in India for wild elephants. Large herds are frequently seen crossing the main road between Ooty and Mysore. The park has a mixture of subtropical moist and dry deciduous forests (principally teak and anogeissus) and scrubland in the foothills. The wetter areas support rosewood, silk cotton, sandalwood and jamun. You may spot gaur, chital (spotted deer), sambar, flying squirrel and four-horned antelope; tigers and leopards are rarely seen, but sightings of dhole (wild dog) are reasonably frequent. There's also a good variety of birdlife including crested hawk, serpent eagles and tiny-eared owls.

OOTY AND THE NILGIRI HILLS LISTINGS

WHERE TO STAY

Ooty

$$$$ Savoy (Taj), 77 Sylkes Rd, T0423-222 5500. 40 well-maintained cottage rooms with huge wooden doors, open fires and separate dressing areas. Even if you're not staying it's worth a teatime visit for the building's interesting history and lovely gardens, and the wood-panelled dining room serves excellent takes on traditional Tamil food.

$$ Glyngarth Villa, Golf Club Rd, Fingerpost (2 km from centre), T0423-244 5754, www.glyngarthvilla.com. Just 5 huge double rooms with period furniture plus original fittings including all-teak floors and fireplaces in a Raj building – complete with metal roof – dating from 1853. Modern bathrooms, meals made from fresh garden produce, large grounds, clean, excellent service, tremendously characterful (too much for some) good value. Walking distance to golf course.

$ YWCA Anandagiri, Ettines Rd, T0423-244 2218, www.ywcaagooty.com. It's basic and a little institutional, and the hot water can be iffy, but this is the most atmospheric budget accommodation in Ooty, with high-ceilinged 1920s cottages in an extensive garden complex surrounded by tall pines and superb views.

Coonoor

$$$$-$$$ Gateway Hotel, Church Rd, Upper Coonoor, T0423-223 0021, www.tajhotels.com. 32 spacious and homely cottage-style rooms, many with open fires, set in beautiful gardens. The dining room has some of the best food in the Nilgiris (though service can be slow), and the wood-panelled Hampton bar. There's also a spa offering Ayurvedic treatments, a yoga studio, tennis and table tennis.

$$$ The Tryst, Carolina Tea Estate, Coonoor, T0423-220 7057, www.trystindia.com. The shelves at this homestay groan under years of hoarding. 5 double rooms with well-stocked library, snooker table, games galore and gym, plus a huge cottage that sleeps 10. Unexpected and in an outstanding location away from all other accommodation cradled in the nape of a rolling tea estate. Excellent walking. Book in advance.

Mettupalayam

$ EMS Mayura, 212 Coimbatore Main Rd, T04254-227936. Set back from the main road a 5-min walk from the station, this makes a decent overnight choice with clean rooms, a decent restaurant and bar.

Mudumalai

$$$-$ Jungle Retreat, Bokkapuram, T0423-252 6469, www.jungleretreat.com. This wonderful quiet place offers spectacular mountain views and a wide choice of rooms, including cool stone-walled cottages with private terraces, romantic open-sided treehouses, simple bamboo huts and a well-swept dorm (Rs 700). The friendly owners keep high standards and can arrange safaris, good treks with local guides and elephant rides. There's an excellent swimming pool, and somewhat pricey food.

Bandipur

$$$$ Dhole's Den, Kaniyanapura village, T08229-236062, www.dholesden.com. Lovely small resort, with 2 rooms, a spacious suite and 2 large cottages, done out in modern minimalist style with a minimal-impact ethic: there's no TV or a/c, most electricity comes from wind turbines and solar, and you can pick your own veggies from the organic garden for dinner.

WAYANAD TO WESTERN PLATEAU

The last phase of the journey takes you across the watershed of the Western Ghats into the drier country of the Deccan Plateau. Natural charms abound amid the waterfalls and dense montane forests of Wayanad and tiger-rich Nagarhole National Park, while the country between Mysore and Hassan is dominated by spectacular palaces and finely carved temples.

→ WAYANAD

The forest-shrouded shoulders of Chembra Peak stand guard over Wayanad ('land of paddy fields'), a beguiling highland district of spice farms, tea plantations, waterfalls and weird upwellings of volcanic rock. Compared to Ooty and Munnar Wayanad so far remains delightfully unspoiled, and its cool misty mornings make a refreshing contrast with the sultry coastal plains. It's also prime wildlife spotting territory: elephants patrol the woodlands of Muthanga and Tholpetty sanctuaries, while the dense *shola* forests around Vythiri are home to whistling thrushes, leaping frogs and giant squirrels. Many of the plantation bungalows have thrown open their doors as luxurious, atmospheric homestays, and the vogue for building treehouses makes this the best place in India if you want to wake up among the branches of a fig tree looking out over virgin forest.

ARRIVING IN WAYANAD

Getting there and around Buses from Ooty arrive in Sultan Bathery, which has local connections south to Vaduvanchal (for Edakkal Caves) and west to **Kalpetta** and Vythiri. Jeeps and auto-rickshaws are also available for local transfers. However, hiring a car can save a lot of time and hassle.

Moving on Buses run north from Kalpetta and Sultan Bathery to Mananthavady, where you can pick up occasional buses to Kutta on the western edge of **Nagarhole National Park** (see page 236). If you're heading for the Kabini River Lodge (see page 248) you'll need to organize a car from Mananthavady.

Tourist information DTPC ① *north Kalpetta, T04936-202134, www.dtpcwayanad.com*, is run by the efficient and knowledgeable Dinesh, who is a good source of information on trekking and wildlife.

PLACES IN WAYANAD

At the far western frontier of Wayanad at the crest of the Western Ghats lies **Vythiri**, a popular but low-key weekend getaway set amid stunning forests, with kayaking and nature walks available at **Pookot Lake**. At Chundale (5 km from Vythiri) the road divides: the main route continues to busy **Kalpetta**, which offers plenty of hotels and banks but little in the way of charm, while the more appealing Ooty road leads east to **Meppadi**, the starting point for treks up wild and rugged **Chembra Peak** ① *Forest Range Office, Kalpetta Rd, Meppadi, T04936-282001, trekking Rs 1000 per group including guide; call ahead to check the track is open*, (2100 m) on whose summit lies a heart-shaped lake. Beyond Meppadi the road continues through the rolling teascapes of Ripon Estate, then through cardamom, coffee, pepper tree and vanilla plantations to reach **Vaduvanchal** (18 km). Some 6 km south of here, **Meenmutty Falls** ① *Rs 600 per group including guide (ask for Anoop, who* *speaks English and knows the forest intimately)*, are Wayanad's most spectacular waterfalls, tumbling almost 300 m in three stages. An adventurous forest track leads down to a pool at the base of the second fall; take your swimming things.

Sulthan Bathery (Sultan's Battery), the main town of western Wayanad, was formerly known as Ganapathivattom, or 'the fields of Ganapathi'. In the 18th century Tipu Sultan built a fort here, but not much of it remains. Some 12 km southwest of the town are the **Edakkal Caves**, a natural deep crevice set high on a granite hill on which engravings dating back to the Neolithic era have been discovered. Around 30 km to the east is **Muthanga Wildlife Sanctuary** ① *0700-0900 and 1500-1830 (last entry 1700), Rs 100, Indians Rs 10, guide fee Rs 100 per group, jeep entry Rs 50; jeeps can be hired for Rs 300 per safari*, the least developed section of the Nilgiri Biosphere Reserve. Jeep rides in the sanctuary, noted for its elephants, leave from the entrance gate. Further north on the road to Nagarhole, Tholpetty Wildlife Sanctuary keeps similar hours and offers similar wildlife spotting opportunities.

NAGARHOLE (RAJIV GANDHI) NATIONAL PARK

Getting there and moving on Most of the wildlife resorts are located on the Kabini River, at the end of a rutted dirt road that leads south from the main Wayanad–Mysore highway on Nagarhole's southern fringe; you'll need a car to get here. If you're on a tighter budget, head for the small plantation town of Kutta, which has good-value homestays and shared shuttle buses or taxis to the national park gate, from where you can join government-run safaris.

Occasional buses cross the park from Kutta to Hunsur, from where you can connect to frequent Mysore-bound buses. From the Kabini River resorts it's a two-hour drive to Mysore (see opposite).

Tourist information 0600-0900, 1530-1830. Foreigners Rs 1000, Indians Rs 200, video Rs 1000. Main entrance is near Hunsur on the northern side of the park, T08222-252064, dcfhunsur@rediffmail.com. The southern entrance, with better accommodation, is at Karapur, 5 km from Kabini River Lodge. Arrive during daylight as elephant activity means the roads are closed after dusk. Park-run jeep and open bus safaris leave from Kabini River Lodge daily at around 0600 and 1500; you can also organize your own jeep (slightly cheaper), and pay for the obligatory services of a forest department guide. Most lodges around the park offer an all-inclusive package with park entry fees and jeep safaris included. To maximize your chances of seeing tigers it's worth doing as many safaris as you can afford; ideally two a day for three days.

Visiting the park If you're hoping to come face to face with a wild tiger on your trip through South India, the forests of Nagarhole, across the Karnataka border from Wayanad, represent your best chance – though it's still an outside chance. The biggest and best organized of the Nilgiri Biosphere Reserve national parks, Nagarhole (meaning 'snake streams') was once the maharajas' reserved forest and became a national park in 1955. Covering gentle hills bordering Kerala, it includes swampland, streams, moist deciduous forest, stands of bamboo and valuable timber in teak and rosewood trees. The Kabini River, which is a tributary of the Kaveri, flows through the forest where the upper canopy reaches 30 m. The park is accessible both by road and river. A number of tribesmen, particularly Kurumbas (honey gatherers) who still practise ancient skills, live amongst, and care for, the elephants.

In addition to elephants, the park also has *gaur* (Indian bison), *dhole* (Indian wild dogs), wild cats, four-horned antelopes, flying squirrels, sloth bears, monkeys and sambar deer ("better sightings than at Mudumalai"). Tigers and leopards are sighted very rarely. Many varieties of birds include the rare Malabar trogon, great black woodpecker, Indian pitta, pied hornbill, whistling thrush, green imperial pigeon and also waterfowl and reptiles.

The edge of the dam is the best place to view wildlife, particularly during the dry period from March to June. The Forest Department runs 45-minute bus tours during the morning and evening opening hours; there's a one-hour tour at 1715 with viewing from *machans* near the waterholes. You can also visit the government's Elephant Training Camp at Haballa, and take a 30-minute ride (Rs 75).

→ MYSORE

Mysore centre is a crowded jumble presided over by the gaudy, wondrous kitsch of the Maharaja's Palace, a profusion of turquoise-pink and layered with mirrors. But for some Mysore's world renown is centred less on the palace, its silk production or sandalwood than on the person of Sri Pattabhi Jois and his Mysore-style ashtanga yoga practice (see box, page 240). This all happens outside the chaotic centre, in the city's beautiful Brahmin suburbs, where wide boulevard-like streets are overhung with bougainvillea.

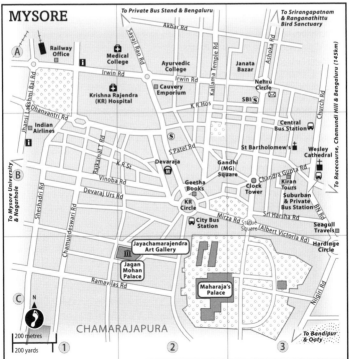

MYSORE

ON THE ROAD
Medieval pageantry at Mysore

The brilliantly colourful festival of Dasara is celebrated with medieval pageantry for 10 days. Although the Dasara festival can be traced back to the Puranas and is widely observed across India, in the south it achieved its special prominence under the Vijayanagar kings. As the Mahanavami festival, it has been celebrated every year since it was sponsored by Raja Wodeyar in September 1610 at Srirangapatnam. It symbolizes the victory of goddess Chamundeswari (Durga) over the demon Mahishasura. On the last day a bedecked elephant with a golden howdah carrying the statue of the goddess processes from the palace through the city to Banni Mantap, about 5 km away, where the Banni tree is worshipped. The temple float festival takes place at a tank at the foot of Chamundi Hill and a car festival on top. In the evening there is a torchlight parade by the mounted guards who demonstrate their keen horsemanship and the night ends with a display of fireworks and all the public buildings are ablaze with fairy lights.

ARRIVING IN MYSORE

Getting there Buses arrive at one of two long-distance bus stands, both on Church Road just north of the Palace and within easy reach of the hotels.

Moving on Buses and trains connect Mysore with Hassan, the capital of the **Western Plateau** (see page 243). However, the ideal way to make this journey is by taxi, stopping off at Srirangapatnam and Sravanabelagola on your way – an excellent day's sightseeing.

Getting around Karnataka's second biggest town, Mysore is still comfortably compact enough to walk around, though there are plenty of autos and buses.

Tourist information Department of Tourism ① *Old Exhibition Building, Irwin Rd, T0821-242 2096, www.mysore.nic.in, 1000-1730.* See also www.karnataka.com/tourism/mysore. There are information counters at the train station and bus stand. **Karnataka State Tourism Development Corporation (KSTDC)** ① *Yatri Nivas, 2 JLB Rd, T0821-242 3652*, is efficient.

PLACES IN MYSORE

The **Maharaja's Palace** ① *enter by south gate, T0821-243 4425, 1000-1730, Rs 200 includes audio guide, cameras must be left in lockers (free, you take the key), allow 2 hrs if you wish to see everything, guidebook Rs 10; go early to avoid the crowds; downstairs is fairly accessible for the disabled,* or 'City Palace' (Amba Vilas) was designed by Henry Irwin and built in 1897 after a fire burnt down the old wooden incarnation. It is in the Indo-Saracenic style in grand proportions, with domes, arches and colonnades of carved pillars and shiny marble floors. The stained glass, wall paintings, ivory inlaid doors and the ornate golden throne (now displayed during Dasara) are remarkable. The fabulous collection of jewels is seldom displayed. Try to visit on a Sunday night, public holiday or festival when the palace is lit up with 50,000 fairy lights.

On the ground floor, visitors are led through the 'Car Passage' with cannons and carriages to the *Gombe thotti* (Dolls' pavilion). This originally displayed dolls during Dasara and today houses a model of the old palace, European marble statues and the golden *howdah* (the maharaja used the battery-operated red and green bulbs on top of the canopy as stop and go signals to the *mahout*). The last is still used during Dasara but goddess Chamundeshwari rides on the elephant. The octagonal *Kalyana Mandap* (marriage hall), or Peacock Pavilion, south of the courtyard, has a beautiful stained glass ceiling and excellent paintings of scenes from Dasara and other festivities on 26 canvas panels. Note the exquisite details, especially of No 19. The Portrait Gallery and the Period Furniture Room lead off this pavilion.

On the first floor, a marble staircase leads to the magnificent Durbar Hall, a grand colonnaded hall measuring 47 m by 13 m with lavishly framed paintings by famous Indian artists. The asbestos-lined ceiling has paintings of Vishnu incarnations. A passage takes you past the beautifully ivory-on-wood inlaid door of the Ganesh Temple, to the Amba Vilas where private audiences (*Diwan-i-Khas*) were held. This exquisitely decorated hall has three doors. The central silver door depicts Vishnu's 10 incarnations and the eight *dikpalas* (directional guardians), with Krishna figures on the reverse (see the tiny Krishna on a leaf, kissing his toes), all done in *repoussé* on teak and rosewood. The room sports art nouveau style, possibly Belgian stained glass, cast iron pillars from Glasgow, carved wood ceiling, chandeliers, etched glass windows and the *pietra dura* on the floors.

The jewel-encrusted Golden Throne with its ornate steps, which some like to attribute to ancient Vedic times, was originally made of figwood decorated with ivory before it was padded out with gold, silver and jewels. Others trace its history to 1336 when the Vijayanagar kings 'found' it before passing it on to the Wodeyars who continue to use it during Dasara.

The **Maharaja's Residence** ① *1000-1730, Rs 20, no photography*, is a slightly under-whelming museum. The ground floor, with a courtyard, displays children's toys, musical instruments, costumes and several portraits. The upper floor has a small weapon collection.

A block west of the palace, housed in the smaller Jagan Mohan Palace, is the **Jaya-chamarajendra Art Gallery** (1861) ① *0800-1700, Rs 25, no photography*, which holds a priceless collection of artworks from Mysore's erstwhile rulers, including Indian miniature paintings and works by Raja Ravi Varma and Nicholas Roerich. There's also an exhibition of ceramics, stone, ivory, sandalwood, antique furniture and old musical instruments. Sadly, there are no descriptions or guidebooks and many items are randomly displayed.

North of KR Circle is the **Devaraja market**, one of India's most atmospheric: visit at noon when it's injected with fresh pickings of marigolds and jasmines. The bigger flowers are stitched onto a thread and wrapped into rolls which arrived heaped in hessian sacks stacked on the heads of farmers.

Immediately to the southeast of the town is **Chamundi Hill** ① *temple 0600-1400, 1530-1800, 1915-2100; vehicle toll Rs 30, City Bus No 185*, with a temple to Durga (Chamundeswari), guardian deity to the Wodeyars, celebrating her victory over the buffalo god. There are lovely views, and a giant Nandi, carved in 1659, on the road down. Walk to it along the trail from the top and be picked up by a car later or catch a return bus from the road. If you continue along the trail you will end up having to get a rickshaw back, instead of a bus.

The **Sandalwood Oil Factory** ① *T0821-248 3651, Mon-Sat 0900-1100, 1400-1600 (prior permission required), no photography inside*, is where the oil is extracted and incense is made. The shop sells soap, incense sticks and other sandalwood items.

At the **Silk Factory** ① *Manathavadi Rd, T0821-248 1803, Mon-Sat 0930-1630, no photography*, weavers produce Mysore silk saris, often with gold *zari* work. Staff will often show you the process from thread winding to jacquard weaving, but they speak little English. The shop sells saris from Rs 3000. Good walks are possible in the Government House if the guard at the gate allows you in.

ON THE ROAD
Power yoga

If you know the primary series, speak fluent ujayyi breath and know about the mulla bandha odds are that you have heard the name of Sri Pattabhi Jois, too. His is the version of yoga that has most percolated contemporary Western practice (it's competitive enough for the type-A modern societies we live in, some argue), and although for most of the years of his teaching he had just a handful of students, things have certainly changed.

Though the Guru left his body in May 2009, a steady flow of international students still make the pilgrimage to his Ashtanga Yoga Nilayam in Mysore, where his daughter Saraswathi and grandson Sharath Rangaswamy continue the lineage.

Saraswathi's classes are deemed suitable for Ashtanga novices, but studying with Sharath is not for dilettante yogis; the Westerners here are extremely ardent about their practice – mostly teachers themselves – and there is a strict pecking order which first-timers could find alienating. Classes start from first light at 0400, and the day's teaching is over by 0700, leaving you free for the rest of the day. The schooling costs US$500 a month.

There's no rule that says you must know the series, but it might be better, and cheaper, to dip a toe in somewhere a bit less hardcore and far-flung, such as Purple Valley in Goa (see page 117).

In a curious side note, the prevalence of foreigners running under-the-table yoga businesses in Mysore has led the local police to institute what may be the world's only city-specific visa. Prospective students heading for Mysore must now apply for a Yoga Visa, essentially a student visa which requires admission papers from a recognized yoga school. Teachers risk a fine if they so much as demonstrate a Surya Namaskar without checking your papers.

Kerala police have been pushing for a similar rule, but as yet, yoga centres outside Mysore seem unaffected by the new rule.

For details and Sharath's teaching schedule, see www.kpjayi.com.

Sri Mahalingeshwara Temple ① *12 km from Mysore, 1 km off the Bhogadi road (right turn after K Hemmanahalli, beyond Mysore University Campus), taxi or auto-rickshaw,* is an 800-year-old Hoysala Temple that has been carefully restored by local villagers under the supervision of the Archaeological Survey of India. The structure is an authentic replica of the old temple: here, too, the low ceiling encourages humility by forcing the worshipper to bow before the shrine. The surrounding garden has been planted with herbs and saplings, including some rare medicinal trees, and provides a tranquil spot away from the city.

→ AROUND MYSORE

SRIRANGAPATNAM

① *The island is over 3 km long and 1 km wide so it's best to hire a cycle from a shop on the main road to get around.*

Srirangapatnam, 12 km from Mysore, has played a crucial role in the region since its origins in the 10th century. Occupying an easily fortified island site in the Kaveri River, it has been home to religious reformers and military conquerors. It makes a fascinating day trip from Mysore; Daria Daulat Bagh and the Gumbaz are wonderful.

The name Srirangapatnam comes from the **temple of Sri Ranganathaswamy** ① *0600-1400, 1600-2030, Rs 10 for shoe stand ,* which stands aloof at the heart of the fortress, containing a highly humanistic idol of Lord Vishnu reclining on the back of a serpent. Dating from AD 894, it is far older than the fort and town, and was subsequently added to by the Hoysala and Vijayanagar kings. The latter built the fort in 1454, and occupied the site for some 150 years until the last Vijayanagar ruler handed over authority to the Hindu Wodeyars of Mysore, who made it their capital. In the second half of the 18th century it became the capital of Haidar Ali, who defended it against the Marathas in 1759, laying the foundations of his expanding power. He was succeeded by his son Tipu Sultan, who also used the town as his headquarters until Colonel Wellesley, the future Duke of Wellington, established his military reputation by defeating the Tiger of Mysore in battle on 4 May 1799. Tipu died in exceptionally fierce fighting near the north gate of the fort; the place is marked by a simple monument.

The fort had triple fortifications, but the British destroyed most of it. The **Jama Masjid** ① *0800-1700*, which Tipu had built, has delicate minarets, and there are two Hindu **temples**, to Narasimha (17th century) and Gangadharesvara (16th century). The **Daria Daulat Bagh** (Splendour of the Sea) ① *1 km east of the fort, Sat-Thu 0830-1730, foreigners Rs 100, Indians Rs 5*, is Tipu's beautiful summer palace, built in 1784 and set in a lovely garden. This social historical jewel has colourful frescoes of battle scenes between the French, British and Mysore armies, ornamental arches and gilded paintings on the teak walls and ceilings crammed with interesting detail. The west wall shows Haidar Ali and Tipu Sultan leading their elephant forces at the battle of Polilur (1780), inflicting a massive defeat on the British. As a result of the battle Colonel Baillie, the defeated British commander, was held prisoner in Srirangapatnam for many years. The murals on the east walls show Tipu offering hospitality to neighbouring princes at various palace durbars. The small museum upstairs has 19th-century European paintings and Tipu's belongings.

Three kilometres east, the **Gumbaz** ① *Sat-Thu 1000-1700, donation collected*, is the family mausoleum, approached through an avenue of cypresses. Built by Tipu in memory of his father, the ornate white dome protects beautiful ivory-on-wood inlay and Tipu's tiger-stripe emblem, some swords and shields. Haider Ali's tomb is in the centre, his wife to the east and Tipu's own to the west.

On the banks of the Cauvery just north of the Lal Bagh Palace is a jetty where six-seater *coracles* are available for river rides.

RANGANATHITTU BIRD SANCTUARY
① *5 km upstream of Srirangapatnam, 0700-1800, foreigners Rs 300, Indians Rs 50, camera Rs 25, video Rs 250. Boats (0830-1330, 1430-1830), foreigners Rs 300, Indians Rs 50. Jun-Oct best. Mysore City Bus 126, or auto-rickshaw from Srirangapatnam.*
The riverine site of this sanctuary was established in 1975. Several islands, some bare and rocky, others larger and well wooded, provide excellent habitat for waterbirds, including the black-crowned night heron, Eurasian spoonbill and cormorants. Some 14 species of waterbird use the sanctuary as a breeding ground from June onwards. There is a large colony of fruit bats in trees on the edge of the river and a number of marsh crocodiles between the small islands. Guided boat trips from the jetty last 15-20 minutes.

SOMNATHPUR
This tiny village boasts the only complete Hoysala temple in the Mysore region. The drive east from Srirangapatnam via Bannur is particularly lovely, passing a couple of lakes through beautiful country and pretty, clean villages. The small but exquisite **Kesava Temple** (1268) ① *0900-1700, foreigners Rs 100, Indians Rs 5, allow 1 hr, canteen, buses from*

Mysore take 1-1½ hrs; via Bannur (25 km, 45 mins) then to Somnathpur (3 km, 15 mins by bus, or lovely walk or bike ride through countryside), is one of the best preserved of 80 Hoysala temples in this area. Excellent ceilings show the distinctive features of the late Hoysala style, and here the roof is intact where other famous temples have lost theirs. The temple has three sanctuaries with the *trikutachala* (triple roof) and stands in the middle of its rectangular courtyard (70 m long, 55 m wide) with cloisters containing 64 cells around it. From the east gateway is a superb view of the temple with an ambulatory standing on its raised platform, in the form of a 16-pointed star. The pillared hall in the centre with the three shrines to the west give it the form of a cross in plan. Walk around the temple to see the fine bands of sculptured figures. The lowest of the six shows a line of elephants, symbolizing strength and stability, then horsemen for speed, followed by a floral scroll. The next band of beautifully carved figures (at eye level) is the most fascinating and tells stories from the epics. Above is the *yali* frieze, the monsters and foliage possibly depicting the river Ganga and uppermost is a line of *hamsa*, the legendary geese.

SIVASAMUDRAM

Here, the Kaveri plunges over 100 m into a series of wild and inaccessible gorges. At the top of the falls the river divides around the island of Sivasamudram, the Barachukki channel on

SRIRANGAPATNAM

the east and the Gaganchukki on the west. The hydro-electricity project was completed in 1902, the first HEP scheme of any size in India. It's best visited during the wet season, when the falls are an impressive sight, as water cascades over a wide area in a series of leaps.

→ WESTERN PLATEAU

The world's tallest monolith – that of the Jain saint Gommateshwara – has stood majestic, 'skyclad' and lost in meditation high on Sravanabelagola's Indragiri hill since the 10th century. It is a profoundly spiritual spot, encircled by long sweeps of paddy and sugar cane plains, and is one of the most popular pilgrimage points for practitioners of the austere Jain religion. Some male Jain followers of the Digambar or skyclad sect of the faith climb the rock naked to denote their freedom from material bonds. Nearby lie the 11th- and 12th-century capital cities of Halebid and Belur, the apex of Hoysala temple architecture whose walls are cut into friezes of the most intricate soapstone. These villages of the Central Maiden sit in the path of one of the main routes for trade and military movement for centuries.

ARRIVING IN THE WESTERN PLATEAU
Getting there Buses from Mysore arrive in the centre of Hassan, within easy walking distance of budget hotels.

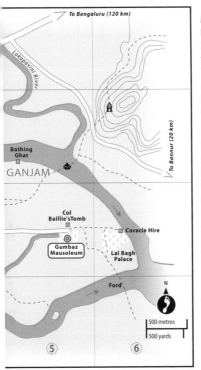

Moving on Frequent buses connect Hassan with **Bengaluru** (4½ hours, see page 250), but if you're hiring a taxi to visit the temples at Belur and Halebid (about Rs 1000 for the day) it's better to get dropped at Arsikere, an hour north of Hassan, from where plenty of trains travel to Bengaluru, avoiding the congested traffic on the way into the capital.

WESTERN PLATEAU TEMPLES
Sravanabelagola, Belur and Halebid can all be seen in a very long day from Bengaluru (Bangalore), but it's far better to stay overnight near the sights themselves or in **Hassan**, a pleasant, busy and fast-developing little town with plenty of hotels a short walk from the bus stand. There are direct buses from Mysore and Bengaluru. The railway station is 2 km to the east.

Sravanabelagola (Shravanabelgola)
The ancient Jain statue of Gommateshwara stands on Vindhyagiri Hill (sometimes known as Indrabetta or Indragiri), 150 m above the plain; Chandragiri to the north (also known as Chikka Betta) is just under

half that height. The 17-m-high Gommateshwara statue, erected somewhere between AD 980 and 983, is of the enlightened prince Bahubali, son of the first Tirthankara (or holy Jain teacher). The prince won a fierce war of succession over his brother, Bharata, only to surrender his rights to the kingdom to take up a life of meditation.

You'll have to clamber barefoot up over 700 hot steep granite steps that carve up the hill to reach the statue from the village tank (socks, sold on-site, offer protection from the hot stone; take water), or charter a *dhooli* (a cane chair tied between two poles and carried), to let four bearers do the work for you. The small, intricately carved shrines you pass on the way up are the **Odeagal Basti**, the **Brahmadeva Mandapa**, the **Akhanda Bagilu** and the **Siddhara Basti**, all 12th-century except the Brahmadeva Mandapa which is 200 years older.

The carved statue is nude (possibly as he is a *Digambara* or 'sky-clad' Jain) and captures the tranquillity typical of Buddhist and Jain art. The depth of the saint's meditation and withdrawal from the world is suggested by the spiralling creepers shown growing up his legs and arms, and by the ant hills and snakes at his feet. Although the features are finely carved, the overall proportions are odd: he has huge shoulders and elongated arms but stumpy legs.

The 'magnificent anointment' (or *Mastakabhisheka*) falls every 12th year when Jain pilgrims flock from across India to bid for 1008 *kalashas* (pots) of holy water that are left overnight at the saint's feet. The next morning their contents, followed with ghee, milk, coconut water, turmeric paste, honey, vermilion powder and a dusting of gold, are poured over the saint's head from specially erected scaffolding. Unusually for India, the thousands of devotees watching the event do so in complete silence. The next celebration is in 2017.

In the town itself is the **Bhandari basti** (1159, with later additions), about 200 m to the left from the path leading up to the Gommateshwara statue. Inside are 24 images of Tirthankaras in a spacious sanctuary. There are 500 rock-cut steps to the top of the hill that take half an hour to climb. It is safe to leave luggage at the tourist office branch at the entrance, which closes 1300-1415. The main **tourist office** ① *Vartha Bhavan, BM Rd, T08172-268862*, is very helpful. There are 14 shrines on Chandragiri and the Mauryan emperor Chandragupta, who is believed by some to have become a Jain and left his empire to fast and meditate, is buried here. The temples are all in the Dravidian style, the **Chamundaraya Basti**, built in AD 982 being one of the most remarkable. There is a good example of a free-standing pillar or *mana-stambha* in front of the Parsvanathasvami Basti. These pillars, sometimes as high as 15 m, were placed at the temple entrance. Here, the stepped base with a square cross section transforms to a circular section and the column is then topped by a capital.

Belur ① *Open daily 0600-2000, but some temples close 1300-1600; free; carry a torch, ASI-trained guides on-site (often excellent), Rs 200 for 4 visitors, though official rate is higher.* Belur, on the banks of the Yagachi River, was the Hoysala dynasty's first capital and continues to be a significant town that is fascinating to explore. The gloriously elaborate Krishna Chennakesavara temple was built over the course of a century from 1116 as a fitting celebration of the victory over the Cholas at Talakad.

At first glance **Chennakesava Temple** (see also Somnathpur, page 241) appears unimpressive because the super-structure has been lost. However, the walls are covered with exquisite friezes. A line of 644 elephants (each different) surrounds the base, with rows of figures and foliage above. The detail of the 38 female figures is perfect. Look at the young musicians and dancers on either side of the main door and the unusual perforated

ON THE ROAD
Temples of Belur and Halebid

The Hoysalas, whose kingdom stretched between the Krishna and Kaveri rivers, encouraged competition among their artisans; their works even bear 12th-century autographs. Steatite meant that sculptors could fashion doily-like detail from solid rock since it is relatively soft when fresh from the quarry but hardens on exposure to air. The temples, built as prayers for victory in battle, are small but superb.

screens between the columns. Ten have typical bold geometrical patterns while the other 10 depict scenes from the *Puranas* in their tracery. Inside superb carving decorates the hand lathe-turned pillars and the bracket-figures on the ceiling. Each stunning filigree pillar is startlingly different in design, a symptom of the intensely competitive climate the sculptors of the day were working in. The **Narasimha pillar** at the centre of the hall is particularly fine and originally could be rotated. The detail is astounding. The jewellery on the figures is hollow and movable and the droplets of water seem to hang at the ends of the dancer's wet hair on a bracket above you. On the platform in front of the shrine is Santalesvara dancing in homage to Lord Krishna. The shrine holds a 3-m-high black polished deity, occasionally opened for *darshan*. The annual **Car Festival** is held in March-April. To the west is the **Viranarayana Temple** with some fine sculpture and smaller shrines around it. The complex is walled with an ambulatory. The entrance is guarded by the winged figure of Garuda, Vishnu's carrier, who faces the temple with joined palms.

Halebid ① *Open daily 0700-1730, free.* The ancient capital of the Hoysala Empire was founded in the early 11th century. It was destroyed by the armies of the Delhi sultanate in 1311 and 1327. The great Hoysalesvara Temple, still incomplete after the best part of a century's toil, survived but the capital lay deserted and came to be called Halebid (ruined village), a name it continues to live up to.

Detour 1 km south to walk around the Basthalli garden filled with remarkably simple 12th-century Jain Bastis. These have lathe-turned and multi-faceted columns, dark interiors and carved ceilings. The smaller **Kedaresvara Temple** with some highly polished columns is on a road going south. There are cycles for hourly hire to visit these quieter sites.

The **Hoysalesvara Temple** set in lawns has two shrines dedicated to Siva with a Nandi bull facing each. The largest of the Hoysala temples, it was started in 1121 but remains unfinished. It is similar in structure to Belur's, but its superstructure was never completed. Belur's real treats are in its interiors, while Halebid's are found on the outside reliefs. Six bands circle the star-shaped temple, elephants, lions, horsemen, a floral scroll and stories from the epics and the Bhagavata Purana. This frieze relates incidents from the *Ramayana* and *Mahabharata*; among them Krishna lifting Mount Govardhana and Rama defeating the demon god Ravana. The friezes above show *yalis* and *hamsa* or geese. There are exceptional half life-size deities with minute details at intervals. Of the original 84 female figures (like the ones at Belur) only 14 remain; thieves have made off with 70 down the centuries.

The **Archaeological Museum** ① *Sat-Thu 0800-1700, Rs 5, no photography*, is on the lawn near the south entrance, with a gallery of 12th- to 13th-century sculptures, wood carvings, idols, coins and inscriptions. Some sculptures are displayed outside. To the west is a small lake.

GOING FURTHER
Coorg (Kodagu)

Coorg, once a proud warrior kingdom, then a state, has now shrunk to become the smallest district in Karnataka. It is a beautiful anomaly in South India in that it has, so far, retained its original forests. Ancient rosewoods jut out of the Western Ghat hills to shade the squat coffee shrubs which the British introduced as the region's chief commodity. Like clockwork, 10 days after the rains come, these trees across whole valleys burst as one into white blossom drenching the moist air with their thick perfume, a hybrid of honeysuckle and jasmine. Although the climate is not as cool as other hill stations, Coorg's proximity by road to the rest of Karnataka makes it a popular weekend bolt hole for inhabitants of Bengaluru (Bangalore). The capital of Coorg District, Madikeri, is an attractive small town in a beautiful hilly setting surrounded by the forested slopes of the Western Ghats and has become a popular trekking destination.

ARRIVING IN COORG
Getting there Frequent buses go to Madikeri from Mysore; there are also services from Hunsur and Hassan.

Tourist information There's a small **tourist office** ⓘ *Mysore Rd south of the Thinmaya statue, T08272-228580.* **Coorg Wildlife Society** ⓘ *2 km further out on Mysore Rd, T08272-223505, www.cws.in,* can help with trekking advice and fishing permits.

BACKGROUND
Although there were references to the Kodaga people in the Tamil Sangam literature of the second century AD, the earliest Kodaga inscriptions date from the eighth century. After the Vjiayanagar Empire was defeated in 1565, many of their courtiers moved south, establishing regional kingdoms. One of these groups were the Haleri Rajas, members of the Lingayat caste whose leader Virarajendra set up the first Kodaga dynasty at Haleri, 10 km from the present district capital of Madikeri.

The later Kodagu rajas were noted for some bizarre behaviour. Dodda Vira (1780-1809) was reputed to have put most of his relatives to death, a pattern followed by the last king, Vira Raja, before he was forced to abdicate by the British in 1834. In 1852 the last Lingayat ruler of Kodagu, Chikkavirarajendra Wodeyar, became the first Indian prince to sail to England, and the economic character of the state was quickly transformed. Coffee was introduced, becoming the staple crop of the region.

The forests of Kodagu are still home to wild elephants, who often crash into plantations on jackfruit raids, and other wildlife. The Kodaga, a tall, fair and proud landowning people who flourished under the British, are renowned for their martial prowess; almost every family has one member in the military. They also make incredibly warm and generous hosts – a characteristic you can discover thanks to the number of plantation homestays in estates of dramatic beauty pioneered here following the crash in coffee prices.

MADIKERI (MERCARA)
The **Omkareshwara Temple**, dedicated to both Vishnu and Siva, was built in 1820. The tiled roofs are typical of Kerala Hindu architecture, while the domes show Muslim influence. On high ground dominating the town is the **fort** with its three stone gateways, built between 1812-1814 by Lingarajendra Wodeyar II. It has a small **museum** ⓘ *Tue-Sun*

0900-1700, closed holidays, in St Mark's Church as well as the town prison, a temple and a chapel while the palace houses government offices. The **Rajas' Tombs** (*Gaddige*), built in 1820 to the north of the town, are the memorials of Virarajendra and his wife and of Lingarajendra. Although the rajas were Hindu, their commemorative monuments are Muslim in style; Kodagas both bury and cremate their dead. The **Friday Market** near the bus stand is very colourful as all the local tribal people come to town to sell their produce. It is known locally as shandy, a British bastardization of the Coorg word *shante*, meaning market. On Mahadevped Road, which leads to the Rajas' tombs, is a 250-year-old **Siva temple** which has an interesting stone façade.

AROUND MADIKERI

Madikeri and the surrounding area makes for beautiful walking but if you want to venture further you'll need to take a guide as paths can soon become indistinct and confusing. **Abbi Falls** is a 30-minute rickshaw ride (9 km, Rs 150 round-trip) through forests and coffee plantations. It is also an enjoyable walk along a fairly quiet road. The falls themselves are beautiful and well worth the visit. You can do a beautiful short trek down the valley and then up and around above the falls before rejoining the main road. Do not attempt it alone since there are no trails and you must depend on your sense of direction along forest paths.

At **Bhagamandala** ① *36 km southwest, half-hourly service from Madikeri's private bus stand from 0630-2000, Rama Motors tour bus departs 0830, with 30-min stop*, the Triveni bathing ghat can be visited at the confluence of the three rivers: Kaveri, Kanike and Suiyothi. Among many small shrines the **Bhandeshwara Temple**, standing in a large stone courtyard surrounded by Keralan-style buildings on all four sides, is particularly striking. You can stay at the temple for a very small charge.

Kakkabe ① *35 km south of Madikeri, bus from Madikeri to Kakkabe at 0630, jeep 1 hr*, is a small town, giving access to the highest peak in Coorg, **Thandiandamole** (1800 m). Nearby, **Padi Iggutappa** is the most important temple in Coorg.

Cauvery Nisargadhama ① *0900-1800, Rs 150, still camera Rs 10*, is a small island reserve in the Kaveri River, 2 km from Kushalnagar, accessed over a hanging bridge. Virtually untouched by tourism, it consists mostly of bamboo thickets and trees, including sandalwood, and is very good for seeing parakeets, bee eaters, woodpeckers and a variety of butterflies. There are tall bamboo treehouses for wildlife viewing.

WHERE TO STAY

Madikeri and around
$$$$ Orange County, Karadigodu Post, Siddapur, T08274-258481, www.orange county.in. The poshest place for miles around, with beautiful red-brick cottages set among 120 ha (300 acres) of coffee plantation. Good bird guides, coracle rides on the river and great food.
$ Palace Estate, 2 km south of Kakkabe (Rs 35 in a rickshaw) along Palace Rd, T08272-238446, www.palaceestate.co.in.

A small, traditional farm growing coffee, pepper, cardamom and bananas lying just above the late 18th-century Nalnad Palace, a summer hunting lodge of the kings of Coorg. 6 basic rooms with shared veranda looking across 180° of forested hills all the way to Madikeri. Isolated and an excellent base for walking; Coorg's highest peak is 6 km from the homestay. Home-cooked local food, English-speaking guide Rs 150.

WAYANAD TO WESTERN PLATEAU LISTINGS

WHERE TO STAY

Wayanad

$$$$-$$$ Vythiri Resort, 6 km up dirt road east of highway, T04936-255366, www.vythiriresort.com. Beautiful resort hidden beside a tumbling forest stream, with a choice of cute *paadi* rooms (low beds and secluded courtyards with outdoor shower), high-ceilinged cottages, or a pair of superb new treehouses in the branches of fig trees, one of which involves being hand-winched up and down. Leisure facilities include spa, pool (swimming and 8-ball), badminton and yoga, and there's a good outdoor restaurant (buffet meals included in price) where you can watch monkeys trying to make away with the leftovers.

$$$ Aranyakam, Valathur (south of Ripon off Meppadi–Vaduvanchal Rd), T04936-280261, T(0)9388-388203, www.aranyakam.com. Atmospheric homestay in Rajesh and Nima's 70-year-old bungalow, set amid a sea of coffee bushes and avocado trees. Huge rooms in the elegant main house come with raked bare-tile ceilings and balconies, or opt for the valley-facing treehouses where you can look out for deer and sloth bear while watching sunset over Chembra Peak. Nima serves genuine home-style Kerala food in the thatched, open sided dining room.

$$$ Edakkal Hermitage, on road before Edakkal Caves, T04936-260123, www.edakkal.com. A sustainable tourism initiative with 5 comfortable cottages and a sweet, simple treehouse, built in, around and on top of a series of huge boulders. Tree frogs inhabit the bamboo-fringed pond, and the sunset views over paddy fields and mountain ranges are magic. The highlight, though, is dinner, served in a natural grotto that's lit with hundreds of candles. Price includes meals.

$$$-$ Haritagiri, Padmaprabha Rd, T04936-203145, www.hotelharitagiri.com.

A modern building in the heart of Kalpetta just off the highway, some a/c rooms, clean and comfortable, restaurant 'reasonable', good value but rather noisy.

Nagarhole National Park

Safari lodges within Nagarhole are uniformly very expensive, though rates generally include jeep safaris. More affordable rooms are available in homestays around Kutta on the western fringe of the park.

$$$$ Kabini River Lodge, at Karapur on reservoir bank, bookings on T080-4055 4055, www.junglelodges.com. 14 rooms in Mysore Maharajas' 18th-century hunting lodge and bungalow, 6 newer cabins overlooking lake, 5 tents, simple but acceptable, good restaurant, bar, exchange, package includes meals, sailing, rides in buffalo-hide coracles on the Kaveri, jeep/minibus at Nagarhole and Murkal complex, park tour with naturalist, very friendly and well run.

$$ Spice Garden, Nellore Estate, Kutta, T(0)99406-87782. Lovely homestay set on a 40-ha (100-acre) coffee and pepper plantation, with simple comfortable cottages and a handful of tent cabins.

Mysore

$$$$-$$$ Lalitha Mahal Palace (ITDC), Narasipur Rd, Siddartha Nagar T0821-252 6100. 54 rooms and suites in the palace built in 1931 for the maharaja's non-vegetarian, foreign guests. Regal setting near Chamundi Hill, old fashioned (some original baths with extraordinary spraying system), for nostalgia stay in the old wing, attractive pool, but avoid the below par restaurant.

$$$$-$$$ Royal Orchid Metropole, 5 JLB Rd, T0821-425 5566, www.royalorchidhotels.com. After languishing in disrepair for years, the Karnataka government has resuscitated the glorious colonial Metropole building. Airy, high-ceilinged rooms, massage and yoga classes plus a small pool and excellent restaurant.

$$$$-$$ Green Hotel, Chittaranjan Palace, 2270 Vinoba Rd, Jayalakshmipuram (near Mysore University), T0821-251 2536, www.greenhotelindia.com. Princess's beautiful palace lovingly converted with strong sustainable tourism ethos: hot water from solar panels, profits to charity and staff recruited from less advantaged groups. The best of the 31 rooms are in the palace but if you stay in the cheaper, newer block you can still loll about in the huge upper lounges: excellent library, chess tables and day beds. Unique, but beyond walking distance from Mysore centre.

Western Plateau

$$$$ Hoysala Village Resort, Belur Rd, 6 km from Hassan, T08172-256764, www.hoysalavillageresorts.in. 33 big cottage rooms with hot water, TV, tea and coffee maker and fan spread out across the landscaped, bird-filled resort. Rustic, with small handicraft shops, good restaurant, very attentive service, good swimming pool.

$$$ The Ashhok Hassan (ITDC), BM Rd, 500 m from bus stand, T08172-268731, www.hassanashok.com. Dramatic renovation creating 37 lovely rooms in immaculate, soundproofed central Hassan hotel. It's all been done on clean lines, with modern art and all mod cons from a/c to Wi-Fi. Charming suites have big rattan armchairs, and the Presidential suite has its own dining room, bar and steam bath (**$$$$**). Excellent service and tidy garden grounds with pool.

RESTAURANTS

Mysore

$ Anu's Bamboo Hut, 367 2nd Main, 3rd Stage, Gokulam, T0821-428 9492. In the midst of the Western yogi ghetto of Gokulam, this friendly little rooftop café serves the kind of light, fresh and healthy food you begin to pine for after a period in India. The vegetarian buffet (daily except Thu, 1300-1500) is packed with salads and bean dishes, and always sells out quickly; Anu also does good smoothies and *lassis* from 1700-1900, and offers vegetarian cooking classes. Call ahead.

$$ Park Lane, 2720 Sri Harsha Rd, T0821-400 3500. Red lights hang from the creeper-covered trellis over this courtyard restaurant: turn them on for service. Superb classical music played every evening 1900-2130, good food, including barbecue nights. Popular, lively and idiosyncratic. Upstairs you'll find good-value **$$** hotel rooms, done out in folk-art-rustic style

$ Mylari, Hotel Mahadeshwara, Nazarbad Main Rd (ask rickshaw driver). The best *dosas* in town served on a banana leaf, mornings until 1100, basic surroundings, may have to queue. Biriyanis also legendary.

$ RRR, Gandhi Sq. Part a/c, tasty non-vegetarian on plantain leaves, good for lunch.

BENGALURU (BANGALORE)

IT capital Bengaluru (Bangalore), the subcontinent's fastest-growing city, is the poster boy of India's economic ascendance. Its buoyant economy has cost the so-called 'garden city' and 'pensioner's paradise' its famously cool climate and sedate pace, while its wealthy retirees are long gone. In their place are streets throttled with gridlocked traffic, a cosmopolitan café culture, a lively music scene and dynamic, liberal-minded people, which combine to make the city a vibrant and forward-thinking metropolis, one whose view of the world is as much attuned to San Francisco as to the red baked earth of the surrounding state of Karnataka.

And there's more to Bengaluru than Wipro, Infosys and call centres: Bengaluru rivals Kancheepuram for silk; it's the site of India's aeronautical defence industry's headquarters; it boasts a mammoth monolithic Nandi Bull temple; has boulevards shaded by rain and flame trees and the great green lungs of Lal Bagh Gardens and Cubbon Park; and holds a number of fine administrative buildings left over from the British. For all its outward-looking globalism, if you walk around the jumbles of rope and silk shops, tailors, temples and mosques in the ramshackle and unruly bazars of Gandhi Nagar, Sivaji Nagar, Chickpet and City Market, you can almost forget the computer chip had ever been invented.

ARRIVING IN BENGALURU

Getting there After tangling with Bengaluru's notoriously clogged traffic, buses from Hassan finally pull in to the central Kempegowda Bus Station, commonly but misleadingly known as 'Majestic'. Cheap and generally nasty hotels and seedy bars cling to the fringes of the bus station; unless you're utterly exhausted and desperate this is not an area in which to linger. Trains from Hassan/Arsikere arrive at one of two terminals: Bangalore City, just across the road from Majestic, or Yesvantpur Junction, 7 km north in the elegant Brahmin suburb of Malleswaram. There are prepaid auto-rickshaw stands at all three arrival points to get you to the main hotel precinct around MG Road and Brigade Road.

Moving on The new Bengaluru International Airport, 35 km north of the city in Devanahalli, has direct flights to London, Frankfurt, the Middle and Far East, Sri Lanka and Nepal, as well as all major Indian cities. For flight information see www.bengaluruairport.com, T080-6678 2251. A metered taxi from the centre will cost around Rs 600; auto-rickshaws are not allowed into the airport. Express airport buses (Rs 200) leave from a range of destinations in the centre including Majestic bus station and MG Road; see www.mybmtc.com.

Getting around Bengaluru is very spread out and you need transport to get around. You also need to allow plenty of time: despite a new Metro and highway flyovers being in place, infrastructure has completely failed to keep pace with the city's population explosion. Traffic is so bad that road travel on weekdays is best avoided, and even weekends can see the streets descend into something approaching gridlock. The Metro, touted as Bengaluru's salvation, is at the 'good start' stage: trains currently run along a short stretch to the east of MG Road between 0600-2200. This will soon extend east via the bus and railway stations to Mysore Road, with a north–south line connecting to Yesvantpur station. City buses run a frequent and inexpensive service throughout the city. Taxis and auto-rickshaws are available for trips around town, and should readily use their meters; they charge 50% extra after 2200. There are prepaid rickshaw booths at each of the stations. If you're planning on covering a lot of sights in a day it can work out cheaper to hire a car and driver.

Tourist information Karnataka State Tourism Development Corporation (KSTDC) ⓘ *head office, No 49, Khanija Bhavan, West Entrance, Race Course Rd, T080-2235 2901, www.karnataka holidays.net, Mon-Sat 1000-1730, closed every 2nd Sat; booking counter* for tours and hotels at Badami House, NR Square, T080-4334 4334, has counters at the airport and City railway station. **Karnataka Tourism House** ⓘ *8 Papanna Lane, St. Mark's Rd, T080-4346 4351,* is a one-stop shop for bookings and info. **India Tourism** ⓘ *KSFC Building, 48 Church St, T080-2558 5417; Mon-Fri 0930-1800, Sat 0900-1300,* is very helpful. For events, pick up the fortnightly *Time Out* magazine (www.timeoutbengaluru.net), and the bimonthly *City Info* (www.explocity.com). An excellent online resource is www.bangalore.burrp.com/events.

BACKGROUND

The 16th-century Magadi chieftain Kempe Gowda built a mud fort and four watchtowers in 1537 and named it Bengalaru (you can see his statue in front of the City Corporation buildings). Muslim King Haidar Ali strengthened those fortifications before his death at the hands of the British, leaving his son Tipu Sultan to pick up where he left off. When the British gained control after 1799 they installed the Wodeyar of Mysore as the ruler and the rajas developed it into a major city. In 1831 the British took over the administration for a period of 50 years, making it a spacious garrison town, planting impressive avenues and creating parks, building comfortable bungalows surrounded by beautiful lawns with tennis courts, as well as churches and museums.

PLACES IN BENGALURU

The 1200 ha of **Cubbon Park** in the Cantonment area was named after the 19th-century British representative in Bangalore. The leafy grounds with bandstand, fountains and statues are also home to the Greco-Colonial High Court, State Library and museums, now overshadowed by the post-Independence granite of Vidhana Soudha, the state's legislature and secretariat buildings across the street.

    Government Museum ⓘ *Kasturba Rd, Cubbon Park, T080-2286 4483, Tue-Sun 1000-1700, Rs 4,* is idiosyncratic and slightly dog eared; opened in 1886, it is one of the oldest in the country. There are 18 galleries: downstairs teems with sculptures, huge-breasted Durga and a 12th-century figure of Ganesh from Halebid sit alongside intricate relief carvings of Rama giving his ring to Hanuman, and there are Buddhas from as far afield as Bihar. An upstairs gallery holds beautiful miniatures in both Mysore and Deccan styles, including a painting of Krishnaraj Wodeyar looking wonderfully surly. There are also Neolithic finds from the Chandravalli excavations, and from the Indus Valley, especially Mohenjo Daro antiquities. In the same complex, the **K Venkatappa Art Gallery** ⓘ *Kasturba Rd, Cubbon Park, T080-2286 4483, Tue-Sun 1000-1700,* shows a small cross-section of work by the late painter (born 1887). His paintings of the southern hill stations give an insight into the Indian fetishisation of all things pastoral, woody and above all cold. There is also the story and blueprints of his truncated design for the Amba Vilas Durbar Hall in Mysore and miniatures by revered painter Abanindranath Tajore (1871-1951), alongside a second portrait of Krishnaraj Wodeyar.

Visveswaraya Industrial and Technological Museum ⓘ *Kasturba Rd, next to the Government Museum, Tue-Sun 1000-1800, Rs 15,* will please engineering enthusiasts, especially the basement, which includes a 1917 steam wagon and India's oldest compact

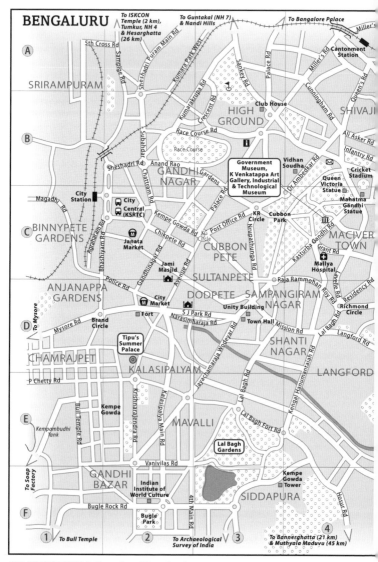

aircraft. Others might be left cold by exhibits on the 'hydrostatic paradox' or 'the invention of the hook and eye and zip fastener technology'. Upstairs is a wing devoted to educating the inhabitants of Bengaluru on genetic engineering. You might find the debate a little one-sided: "agricultural biotechnology is a process … for the benefit of mankind," it states in capital letters. A small corner (next to the placard thanking AstraZeneca, Novo Nordisk Education Foundation, Novozymes and Glaxo-SmithKline), is dubbed 'Concerns', but you can see how cloning and genetically strengthened 'golden' rice might seem more attractive when put in the context of the growling Indian belly.

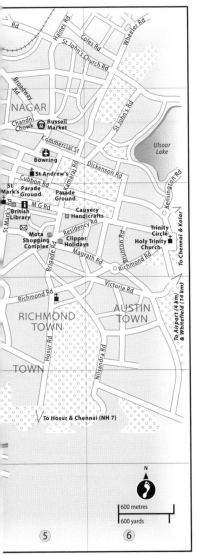

To the southwest lies the summer palace that Tipu Sultan, the perennial thorn in the side of the British, boasted was "the envy of heaven". **Tipu's Summer Palace** ① *City Fort, 0800-1730, foreigners Rs 100, Indians Rs 5, video camera Rs 25*, was begun by his father Haidar Ali and was completed by Tipu in 1789. Based on the Daria Daulat Bagh in Srirangapatnam, the understated two-storey structure is largely made of teak with walls and ceilings painted in brilliant colours with beautiful carvings. A room downstairs is given over to documenting Haidar and Tipu's reigns and struggles against the British.

Lal Bagh Gardens ① *southeast of the Summer Palace, 0600-1900, Rs 10*, were laid out across 97 ha by Haidar Ali in 1760 and are second only to Kolkatta's in size. Tipu added a wealth of plants and trees from many countries (there are over 1800 species of tropical, subtropical and medicinal plants) and the British brought a bandstand. Sadly, the Indian affection for botanical beauty means that the rose gardens are kept behind bars. At dusk, Lal Bagh is popular with businessmen speed-walking off their paunches, and courting couples and newlyweds who sit on the banks of the lotus pond eating ice cream. The rocky knoll around the Kempe Gowda tower has great city views, and is popular at sunset. There are fortnightly Sunday

ON THE ROAD
Health tourism

For decades, Western travel to India was synonymous with emaciated hippies, and backpackers' conversations invariably veered towards the scatological as everyone, at some stage, was sure to catch the dread 'Delhi belly'. It's a sign of the times that, although the British National Health Service failed to award India its whole back-up project in 2004, the country has become a very real alternative to private health care, representing huge cost reductions on surgery.

The centrepiece for this emerging industry is arguably Bengaluru, which has the largest number of systems of medicine approved by the World Health Organization in a single city: cardiac, neurology, cancer care and dentistry are just a few of the areas of specialization, and clients include the NHS and America's largest insurance company. Open-heart surgery will set you back US$4500 in Bengaluru, for example, as opposed to US$18,000 abroad. And afterwards, of course, you can recuperate at an Ayurveda resort. Lately Bengaluru has knitted its medical specialists with its IT cred to pioneer virtual medicine too, whereby cardiac experts in the city hold teleconferences with outposts up and down the subcontinent to treat emergencies, examine and monitor patients via phone, text and video, a method specialists at Narayana Hrudayalaya confidently predict will one day become the norm.

evening performances of Kannada folk theatre, song and dance; go on for supper at **MTR** (see Restaurants, page 256) for a pukka Bengaluru evening. The **Glass House**, with echoes of London's Crystal Palace and Kew Gardens, holds flower shows in January and August to mark Republic and Independence days.

Further south, the hefty **Nandi Bull at Bull Temple** ① *Bull Temple Rd, Basavanagudi, 0600-1300, 1600-2100*, was carved at the behest of Kempe Gowda, making it one of the city's oldest temples. The monolithic Nandi was believed to be growing unstoppably until a trident was slammed into his forehead: he now towers nearly 5 m high and is 6 m in length. His huge proportions, draped imperiously in jasmine garlands, are made of grey granite polished with a mixture of groundnut oil and charcoal. Under his hooves you can make out the *veena* or south Indian sitar on which he's resting. Behind him is a yonilingam. Just outside the temple are two bodhi trees, with serpent statues draped with sacred strands in offering for children. To your right as you exit the temple lies Bugle Park, a pretty little patch of wood whose trees are packed with fruit bats. It also holds one of Kempe Gowda's four 16th-century watchtowers. You can walk past the old fort under the subway to reach the atmospheric City Market, and from there to the busy market area of the Old Town around Avenue Road and Chikpet.

For those interested in ancient Indian astrological practices, the **Palm Leaf Library** ① *33 5th Main Rd, Chamarajpet*, is supposed to be the repository for everyone's special leaf, which gives accurate details of character, past, present and future. Locating each leaf is not guaranteed.

Sri Gavi Gangadhareshwara Temple is most remarkable for its two quirks of architecture. First, the 'open window' to the left of the temple, which only once a year (on **Makara Sankrati Day**, 14/15 January) allows a shaft of light to shine between the horns of the stone Nandi bull in the courtyard and to then fall on the Siva lingam in the inner sanctum. The second quirk can only be seen by bending double to crouch around the back of the cave shrine. The Dravida-style **Venkataramanasvami Temple** is where the Wodeyar Maharaja chose to worship first, when his dynasty's rule was reinstated at the end of the 18th century, before entering the palace.

The grand, Tudor-style **Bangalore Palace** ⓘ *north of Cubbon Park, T080-2336 0818, 1000-1800, foreigners Rs 200, Indians Rs 100, camera Rs 500, video Rs 1000; frequent buses from Majestic/Sivaji Nagar*, built by Chamaraja Wodeyar in 1887, was incongruously inspired by Windsor Castle. The entry price buys you a tour of the Mysore mahahrajas' collection of art and family portraits.

The sprawling modern **International Society for Krishna Conscious temple complex (ISKCON)** ⓘ *Hare Krishna Hill, 1R Block, Chord Rd, Rajaji Nagar, northwest of the centre, 0700-1300, 1615-2030*, holds five shrines, a multimedia cinema showing films on the Hare Krishna movement, lofty *gopurams* and the world's tallest *kalash shikara*. Around 9000 visitors make the pilgrimage every day; *bhajans* (religious songs) are sung daily.

AROUND BENGALURU

Nandidurg, Tipu's fortified summer retreat in the Nandi Hills, lies on top of a granite hil with sheer cliffs on three sides 10 km from Chikballapur, to the north of Bengaluru. Literally 'the fort of Nandi', the place, today a minor hill resort with great views from the 60-m-high 'Tipu's drop', was named after Siva's bull. The ninth-century **Bhoganandisvara Temple** at the foot of the hill is a good example of the Nolamba style; its walls are quite plain but the stone windows feature carvings of Nataraja and Durga. The 16th century brought typical Vijayanagar period extensions such as the *gopuram* at the entrance. To get there, take a bus from the Central Bus Stand (ask for the Nandi Hill bus, not Nandidurga); they leave at 0730, 0830, 0930, returning at 1400, 1630, 1830.

Nrityagram ⓘ *30 km north of Bengaluru, T080-2846 6313, Tue-Sat 1000-1400*, is a dance village where young dancers learn all disciplines of traditional Indian dance. It was founded by the late Odissi dancer Protima Gauri. Guided tours include lunch, dance demonstrations and a short lecture.

BENGALURU (BANGALORE) LISTINGS

WHERE TO STAY

$$$$ Oberoi, 39 MG Rd, T080-2558 5858, www.oberoihotels.com. 160 superb rooms and suites with private sit-outs, all of which have views across the lush tropical gardens. Decent-sized swimming pool. Good restaurants, bar, spa and fitness centre, beauty salon.

$$$$ Taj West End, 23 Race Course Rd, near railway, T080-6660 5660, www.taj hotels.com. Charming 1887 colonial property set in beautiful gardens; much more than a business hotel. 117 immaculately appointed suites and rooms with balconies and verandas, Wi-Fi, flatscreen TV. There's also a splendidly restored Heritage Wing, dating from 1907. **Blue Ginger**, one of Bengaluru's most romantic garden restaurants, serves authentic Vietnamese food in low-lit jungly surroundings.

$$$$-$$$ St Mark's Hotel, 4/1 St Mark's Rd, T080-4001 9000, www.stmarkshotel. com. Nice carpeted rooms in very quiet and capable business hotel. All rooms have Wi-Fi and bath. Good views, questionable decorative taste. Price includes breakfast.

$$$$-$$$ Villa Pottipati, 142 8th Cross, 4th Main Rd, Mallesaram, T080-2336 0777, www.neemranahotels.com. 8 rooms in historic townhouse furnished with rosewood 4-posters and sepia Indian portrait photography. Set in garden in the charming quiet tree-lined avenues of Bengaluru's Brahminical suburbs. A/c and internet facilities, small plunge pool. Atmospheric, but a bit lacklustre. Thin mattresses.

$$ Sri Lakshmi Comforts, 117 MG Rd, next to LIC, T080-2555 9388, www.slcomforts.com. Good lower-range choice right amongst the MG Rd action, with spartan but clean rooms, friendly staff and a good *thali* restaurant.

$$-$ Vellara, 126 Brigade Rd, T080-2536 9116. A grim exterior conceals one of the MG Rd area's best deals. 36 spacious and well-kept rooms, which get better the higher up you go. TV and phone in each room, and the value and location are excellent. Recommended.

RESTAURANTS

$$$ Ebony Restaurant, Ivory Tower, Hotel Ivory Tower, Barton Centre, MG Rd, T080-4178 3344. Open 1230-1500 and 1930-2300. Parsee dishes like mutton *dhansak* and curry *chawal*, along with Muglai, Tandoori and French food, but come for the views from this penthouse terrace restaurant, which are the best in Bengaluru.

$$$ Karavalli, at the Taj Gateway, 166 Residency Rd, T080-6660 4519. Excellent upscale take on Karnataka coastal food.

$ Halli Mane, 12 Sampige Rd, Malleswaram. Fun and buzzing vegetarian canteen decked out like a village house:

order at the counter, present your ticket at the relevant counter and elbow yourself a bit of table space. A good place to try Karnataka specials like *ragi roti*.

$ MTR (**Mavalli Tiffin Rooms**), 11 Lalbagh Rd, T080-2222 0022. Tiffin 0630-1100 and 1530-1930, lunch 1230-1400 and 2000-2100. Closed Mon lunch. The quintessential Bengaluru restaurant: a classic Kannadiga Brahmin vegetarian oozing 1920s atmosphere, full of Bengaluru elders, at the edge of Lalbagh gardens. A 14-course lunch lasts 2 hrs, but you'll be lucky to get a table.

PRACTICALITIES

258 Ins and outs
258   Best time to visit South India
258   Getting to South India
260   Transport in South India
266   Where to stay in South India
268   Food and drink in South India
270   Festivals in South India
273   Responsible travel

274 Essentials A-Z

283 Index

288 Credits

INS AND OUTS

→ BEST TIME TO VISIT SOUTH INDIA

By far the most comfortable time to visit South India is from October to March, when the weather is dry and relatively cool. April and May are intensely hot, especially on the Deccan Plateau and the Tamil Nadu plains – South India's hill stations fill to bursting during this time – with humidity building up as the monsoon approaches. The southwest monsoon hits Kerala in early June, sweeping northward to reach Mumbai about 10 days later; the heaviest rain comes in July and can see large parts of the west coast knee-deep in water for hours at a time. A second monsoon travels up the east coast during September and October. If you're travelling during the monsoon you need to be prepared for extended periods of torrential rain and disruption to travel. The post-monsoon period comes with cool air and clear skies – this is the best time for mountain views – while winter temperatures can drop close to zero in the high points of the Western Ghats. Autumn and winter are also the time of some of India's great festivals, including the wild **Ganesh Charturthi** in Mumbai, **Dussehra** and **Diwali**.

→ GETTING TO SOUTH INDIA

AIR

South India is accessible by air from virtually every continent. By far the most common arrival point is Mumbai, though excellent connectivity through the Gulf and Southeast Asia makes it just as easy to fly directly into Chennai, Bengaluru, Hyderabad, Kochi or Thiruvananthapuram. Several carriers permit 'open-jaw' travel, arriving in and departing from different cities. In 2013 the cheapest return flights to Mumbai from London started from around £500, but leapt to £800+ as you approached the high seasons of Christmas, New Year and Easter.

Once you're on the ground India's comprehensive internal flight network can get you to destinations throughout the south.

From Europe Despite the increases to Air Passenger Duty, Britain remains the cheapest place in Europe for flights to India. **British Airways, Virgin Atlantic, Jet Airways** and **Air India** fly direct from London to Mumbai, while BA also flies direct to Chennai, Bengaluru and Hyderabad. **Air India** and **Jet Airways** also serve several airports in mainland Europe, while major European flag carriers including **KLM** and **Lufthansa** fly to Mumbai from their respective hub airports. In most cases the cheapest flights are with Middle Eastern or Central Asian airlines, transiting via airports in the Gulf. Several airlines from the Middle East (eg **Emirates, Etihad, Gulf Air, Kuwait Airways, Qatar Airways** and **Oman Air**) offer good discounts to Indian regional capitals from London via their hub cities. This adds a couple of hours to the journey time, but makes it possible to fly to less obvious gateway cities such as Kochi and Thiruvananthapuram, avoiding the more fraught route via Mumbai (which involves long immigration queues and shuttling from the international to domestic terminal). Consolidators in the UK can quote some competitive fares, such as: www.skyscanner.net, www.ebookers.com; **North South Travel** ① *T01245-608291, www.northsouthtravel.co.uk (profits to charity).*

From North America From the east coast, several airlines including Air India, Jet Airways, Continental and Delta fly direct from New York to Mumbai. American flies from Chicago. Discounted tickets on British Airways, KLM, Lufthansa, Gulf Air and Kuwait Airways are sold through agents although they will invariably fly via their country's capital cities. From the west coast, Air India flies from Los Angeles to Mumbai, and Jet Airways from San Francisco to Mumbai via Shanghai. Alternatively, fly via Hong Kong, Singapore or Bangkok using one of those countries' national carriers. Air Canada operates between Vancouver and Delhi, with internal connections to airports in the South. Air Brokers International ⓘ www.airbrokers.com, is competitive and reputable. STA ⓘ www.statravel.co.uk, has offices in many US cities, Toronto and Ontario. Student fares are also available from Travel Cuts ⓘ www.travelcuts.com, in Canada.

From Australasia Qantas, Singapore Airlines, Thai Airways, Malaysian Airlines, Cathay Pacific and Air India are the principal airlines connecting the continents, although none have direct flights to the south. Singapore Airlines offer the most flexibility, with subsidiary Silk Air flying to airports in Tamil Nadu and Kerala. Low-cost carriers including Air Asia (via Kuala Lumpur), Scoot and Tiger Airways (Singapore) offer a similar choice of arrival airports at substantial savings, though long layovers and possible missed connections make this a slightly more risky venture than flying with the mainstream airlines. STA and Flight Centre offer discounted tickets from their branches in major cities in Australia and New Zealand. Abercrombie & Kent ⓘ www.abercrombiekent.co.uk, Adventure World ⓘ www.adventure world.net.au, Peregrine ⓘ www.peregrineadventures.com, and Travel Corporation of India ⓘ www.tcindia.com, organize tours.

Airport information The formalities on arrival in India have been increasingly streamlined during the last few years and the facilities at the major international airports greatly improved. However, arrival can still be a slow process. Disembarkation cards, with an attached customs declaration, are handed out to passengers during the inward flight. The immigration form should be handed in at the immigration counter on arrival. The customs slip will be returned, for handing over to the customs on leaving the baggage collection hall. You may well find that there are delays of over an hour at immigration in processing passengers who need help with filling in forms. When departing, note that you'll need to have a printout of your itinerary to get into the airport, and the security guards will only let you into the terminal within three hours of your flight. Many airports require your to scan your bags before checking in, and in rare cases you may also be asked to identify your checked luggage after going through immigration and security checks.

    Departure charges Several airports, including Bengaluru and Hyderabad, have begun charging a Passenger Service Fee or User Development Fee to each departing passenger. This is normally included in international tickets, but some domestic airlines have been reluctant to incorporate the charge. Keep some spare cash in rupees in case you need to pay the fee on arriving at the terminal.

AIR

India has a comprehensive network linking the major cities of the different states. Deregulation of the airline industry has had a transformative effect on travel within India, with a host of low-budget private carriers with a host of low-cost private carriers jockeying to provide the lowest prices or highest frequency on popular routes. On any given day, booking a few days in advance, you can expect to fly from Mumbai to Goa, Bengaluru, Chennai or Kochi for around US$100 one way including taxes, while booking a month in advance can reduce the price to US$60-70.

Competition from the efficiently run private sector has, in general, improved the quality of services provided by the nationalized airlines. It also seems to herald the end of the two-tier pricing structure, meaning that ticket prices are now usually the same for foreign and Indian travellers. The airport authorities too have made efforts to improve handling on the ground.

Although flying is comparatively expensive, for covering vast distances or awkward links on a route it is an option worth considering, though delays and re-routing can be irritating. For short distances (eg Thiruvananthapurm–Kochi), and on some routes where you can sleep during an overnight journey (eg Aurangabad–Hyderabad) it makes more sense to travel by train.

The best way to get an idea of the current routes, carriers and fares is to use a third-party booking website such as www.cheapairticketsindia.com (toll-free numbers: UK T0800-101 0928, USA T1-888 825 8680), www.cleartrip.com, www.makemytrip.co.in, or www.yatra.com. Booking with these is a different matter: some refuse foreign credit cards outright, while others have to be persuaded to give your card special clearance. Tickets booked on these sites are typically issued as an email ticket or an SMS text message – the simplest option if you have an Indian mobile phone, though it must be converted to a paper ticket at the relevant carrier's airport offices before you will be allowed into the terminal. Makemytrip.com and Travelocity.com both accept international credit cards.

RAIL

Trains can still be the cheapest and most comfortable means of travelling long distances saving you hotel expenses on overnight journeys. It gives access to booking station Retiring Rooms, which can be useful from time to time. Above all, you have an ideal opportunity to meet local travellers and catch a glimpse of life on the ground.

High-speed trains There are several air-conditioned 'high-speed' Shatabdi (or 'Century') Express for day travel, and Rajdhani Express ('Capital City') for overnight journeys. These cover large sections of the network but due to high demand you need to book them well in advance (up to 90 days). Meals and drinks are usually included.

Classes A/c First Class, available only on main routes, is the choice of the Indian upper crust, with two- or four-berth carpeted sleeper compartments with washbasin. As with all a/c sleeper accommodation, bedding is included, and the windows are tinted to the point of being almost impossible to see through. A/c Sleeper, two and three-tier configurations (known as 2AC and 3AC), are clean and comfortable and popular with middle class families; these are the safest carriages for women travelling alone. **A/c Executive Class**, with wide reclining seats, are available on many Shatabdi trains at double the price of the ordinary **a/c Chair Car** which are equally comfortable. **First Class (non-a/c)** is gradually being phased out, and is now restricted to a handful of routes through Tamil Nadu and Kerala, but the run-down old carriages still provide a very enjoyable combination of privacy and openable windows. **Second Class (non-a/c)** two and three-tier (commonly called **Sleeper**), provides exceptionally cheap and atmospheric travel, with basic padded vinyl seats and open windows that allow the sights and sounds of India (not to mention dust, insects and flecks of spittle expelled by passengers up front) to drift into the carriage. On long journeys Sleeper can be crowded and uncomfortable, and toilet facilities can be unpleasant; it is nearly always better to use the Indian-style squat loos rather than the Western-style ones as they are better maintained. At the bottom rung is **Unreserved Second Class**, with hard wooden benches. You can travel long distances for a trivial amount of money, but unreserved carriages are often ridiculously crowded, and getting off at your station may involve a battle of will and strength against the hordes trying to shove their way on.

Indrail passes These allow travel across the network without having to pay extra reservation fees and sleeper charges but you have to spend a high proportion of your time on the train to make it worthwhile. However, the advantages of pre-arranged reservations and automatic access to 'Tourist Quotas' can tip the balance in favour of the pass for some travellers.

Tourists (foreigners and Indians resident abroad) may buy these passes from the tourist sections of principal railway booking offices and pay in foreign currency, major credit cards, traveller's cheques or rupees with encashment certificates. Fares range from US$57 to US$1060 for adults or half that for children. Rail-cum-air tickets are also to be made available.

Indrail passes can also conveniently be bought abroad from special agents. For people contemplating a single long journey soon after arriving in India, the Half- or One-day Pass with a confirmed reservation is worth the peace of mind; two- or four-day passes are also sold.

The UK agent is SDEL ① *103 Wembley Park Dr, Wembley, Middlesex HA9 8HG, UK, T020-8903 3411, www.indiarail.co.uk*. They make all necessary reservations and offer excellent advice. They can also book Air India and Jet Airways internal flights.

Cost A/c first class costs about double the rate for two-tier shown below, and non a/c second class about half. Children (aged five to 12) travel at half the adult fare. The young (12-30 years) and senior citizens (65 years and over) are allowed a 30% discount on journeys over 500 km (just show your passport).

Period	US$ A/c 2-tier	Period	US$ A/c 2-tier
½ day	26	21 days	198
1 day	43	30 days	248
7 days	135	60 days	400
15 days	185	90 days	530

Fares for individual journeys are based on distance covered and reflect both the class and the type of train. Higher rates apply on the Mail and Express trains and the air-conditioned Shatabdi and Rajdhani Expresses.

Internet services Much information is available online via www.railtourismindia.com, www.indianrail.gov.in, www.erail.in and www.trainenquiry.com, where you can check timetables (which change frequently), numbers, seat availability and even the running status of your train. Internet e-tickets can be bought and printed on www.irctc.in though it's a fiendishly frustrating system to use, and paying with a foreign credit card is fraught with difficulty. If you plan to do a lot of train travel on popular routes (e.g. Hospet–Goa or Goa–Mumbai) it might be worth the effort to get your credit card recognised by the booking system. This process changes often, so your best option is to consult the very active India transport forums at www.indiamike.com. An alternative is to seek a local agent who can sell e-tickets, which can cost as little as Rs 10 (plus Rs 20 reservation fee, some agents charge up to Rs 150 a ticket, however), and can save hours of hassle; simply present the printout to the ticket collector. However, it is tricky if you then want to cancel an e-ticket which an agent has bought for you on their account.

Tickets and reservations It is possible to reserve tickets for virtually any train on the network from one of the 1000 computerized reservation centres across India. It is always best to book as far in advance as possible (usually up to 60 days). To reserve a seat on a particular train, note down the train's name, number and departure time and fill in a reservation form while you line up at the ticket window; you can use one form for up to four passengers. At busy stations the wait can take an hour or more. You can save a lot of time and effort by asking a travel agent to get your tickets for a fee of Rs 50-100. If the class you want is full, ask if tickets are available under any of Indian Rail's special quotas. **Foreign Tourist Quota (FTQ)** reserves a small number of tickets on popular routes for overseas travellers; you need your passport and either an exchange certificate or ATM receipt to book tickets under FTQ. The other useful special quota is **Tatkal**, which releases a last-minute pool of tickets at 1000 on the day before the train departs. If the quota system can't help you, consider buying a 'wait list' ticket, as seats often become available close to the train's departure time; phone the station on the day of departure to check your ticket's status. If you don't have a reservation for a particular train but carry an Indrail Pass, you may get one by arriving three hours early. Be wary of touts at the station offering tickets, hotels or exchange.

Timetables Regional timetables are available cheaply from station bookstalls; the monthly *Indian Bradshaw* is sold in principal stations. The handy *Trains at a Glance* (Rs 40) lists popular trains likely to be used by most foreign travellers and is available at stalls at Indian railway stations and in the UK from SDEL (see page 261).

ROAD
Road travel is sometimes the only choice for reaching many of the places of outstanding interest, particularly national parks or isolated tourist sites. For the uninitiated, travel by road can also be a worrying experience because of the apparent absence of conventional traffic regulations. Vehicles drive on the left – in theory. Routes around the major cities

are usually crowded with lorry traffic, especially at night, and the main roads are often poor and slow. There are a few motorway-style expressways, but most main roads are single track. Some district roads are quiet, and although they are not fast they can be a good way of seeing the country and village life if you have the time.

Bus Buses now reach virtually every part of India, offering a cheap, if often uncomfortable, means of visiting places off the rail network. Very few villages are now more than 2-3 km from a bus stop. Services are run by the State Corporation from the State Bus Stand (and private companies which often have offices nearby). The latter allow advance reservations, including booking printable e-tickets online (check www.redbus.in and www.viaworld.in) and, although tickets prices are a little higher, they have fewer stops and are a bit more comfortable.

Bus categories Though comfortable for sightseeing trips, apart from the very best 'sleeper coaches' even **air-conditioned luxury coaches** can be very uncomfortable for really long journeys. Often the air conditioning is very cold so wrap up. Journeys over 10 hours can be extremely tiring so it is better to go by train if there is a choice. If you must take a sleeper bus (a contradiction in terms), choose a lower berth near the front of the bus. The upper berths tend to be really uncomfortable on bumpy roads. **Express buses** run over long distances (frequently overnight), these are often called 'video coaches' and can be an appalling experience unless you appreciate loud film music blasting through the night. Ear plugs and eye masks may ease the pain. They rarely average more than 45 kph. **Local buses** are often very crowded, quite bumpy, slow and usually poorly maintained. However, over short distances, they can be a very cheap, friendly and easy way of getting about. Even where signboards are not in English someone will usually give you directions. Many larger towns have **minibus** services which charge a little ·more than the buses and pick up and drop passengers on request. Again very crowded, and with restricted headroom, they are the fastest way of getting about many of the larger towns.

Bus travel tips Some towns have different bus stations for different destinations. Booking on major long-distance routes is now computerized. Book in advance where possible and avoid the back of the bus where it can be very bumpy. If your destination is only served by a local bus you may do better to take the Express bus and 'persuade' the driver, with a tip in advance, to stop where you want to get off. You will have to pay the full fare to the first stop beyond your destination but you will get there faster and more comfortably. When an unreserved bus pulls into a bus station, there is usually an unholy scramble for seats, whilst those arriving have to struggle to get off! In many areas there is an unwritten 'rule of reservation' using handkerchiefs or bags thrust through the windows to reserve seats. Some visitors may feel a more justified right to a seat having fought their way through the crowd, but it is generally best to do as local people do and be prepared with a handkerchief. As soon as it touches the seat, it is yours! Leave it on your seat when getting off to use the toilet at bus stations.

Car A car provides a chance to travel off the beaten track, and gives unrivalled opportunities for seeing something of India's great variety of villages and small towns. Until recently, the most widely used hire car was the romantic but notoriously unreliable Hindustan Ambassador. You can still find them for hire in parts of Tamil Nadu and

Kerala, but they're gradually giving way to more efficient (and boring) Tata and Toyota models with mod cons such as optional air conditioning – and seat belts. A handful of international agencies offer self-drive car hire (Avis, Sixt), but India's majestically anarchic traffic culture is not for the faint-hearted, and emphatically not a place for those who value such quaint concepts as lane discipline, or indeed driving on your assigned side of the road. It's much more common, and comfortable, to hire not just the car but someone to drive it for you.

Car hire If you fancy the idea of being Lady Penelope and gadding about with your own chauffeur, dream no more. Hiring a car and driver is the most comfortable and efficient way to cover short to medium distances, and although prices have increased sharply in recent years car travel in India is still a bargain by Western standards. Even if you're travelling on a modest budget a day's car hire can help take the sting out of an arduous journey, allowing you to go sightseeing along the way without looking for somewhere to stash your bags.

Local drivers often know their way around an area much better than drivers from other states, so where possible it is a good idea to get a local driver who speaks the state language, in addition to being able to communicate with you. The best way to guarantee a driver who speaks good English is to book in advance with a professional travel agency, either in India or in your home country. Recommended operators with English speaking drivers include **Milesworth Travel** ① *Tamil Nadu, www.milesworth.com,* **Skyway** ① *Karnataka, www.skywaytour.com,* and **Intersight** ① *Kerala, www.intersighttours.com.* You can, if you choose, arrange car hire informally by asking around at taxi stands, but don't expect your driver to speak anything more than rudimentary English.

On pre-arranged overnight trips the fee you pay will normally include fuel and inter-state taxes – check before you pay – and a wage for the driver. Drivers are responsible for their expenses, including meals (and the pervasive servant-master culture in India means that most will choose to sit separately from you at meal times). Some tourist hotels provide rooms for drivers, but they often choose to sleep in the car overnight to save money. In some areas drivers also seek to increase their earnings by taking you to hotels and shops where they earn a handsome commission; these are generally hugely overpriced and poor alternatives to the hotels recommended in this book, so don't be afraid to say no and insist on your choice of accommodation. If you feel inclined, a tip at the end of the tour of Rs 100 per day is perfectly acceptable.

	Tata Indica non-a/c	Tata Indigo non-a/c	Hyundai Accent a/c	Toyota Innova
8 hrs/80 km	Rs 1200	Rs 1600	Rs 2200	Rs 2500
Extra km	Rs 8	Rs 10	Rs 15	Rs 15
Extra hour	Rs 80	Rs 100	Rs 200	Rs 180
Out of town				
Per km	Rs 8	Rs 10	Rs 15	Rs 15
Night halt	Rs 200	Rs 200	Rs 300	Rs 250

Taxi Taxi travel in India is a great bargain, and in most cities in the south you can take a taxi from the airport to the centre for under US$10. Yellow-top taxis in cities and large towns are metered, although tariffs change frequently. These changes are shown on a fare conversion chart which should be read in conjunction with the meter reading. Increased night time rates apply in most cities, and there might be a small charge for luggage. Insist on the taxi meter being flagged in your presence. If the driver refuses, the official advice is to contact the police. When a taxi doesn't have a meter, you will need to fix the fare before starting the journey. Ask at your hotel desk for a guide price. As a foreigner, it is rare to get a taxi in the big cities to use the meter – if they are eager to, watch out as sometimes the meter is rigged and they have a fake rate card. Also, watch out for the David Blaine-style note shuffle: you pay with a Rs 500 note, but they have a Rs 100 note in their hand. This happens frequently at the prepaid booth outside New Delhi train station too, no matter how small the transaction.

Most airports and many major stations have booths where you can book a **prepaid taxi**. For slightly more than the metered fare these allow you to sidestep overcharging and give you the security of knowing that your driver will take you to your destination by the most direct route. You might be able to join up with other travellers at the booth to share a taxi to your hotel or a central point. It's OK to give the driver a small tip at the end of the journey.

At night, always have a clear idea of where you want to go and insist on being taken there. Taxi drivers may try to convince you that the hotel you have chosen 'closed three years ago' or is 'completely full'. Say that you have a reservation.

Rickshaw Auto-rickshaws (autos) are almost universally available in towns across South India and are the cheapest and most convenient way of getting about. It is best to walk a short distance away from a hotel gate before picking up an auto to avoid paying an inflated rate. In addition to using them for short journeys it is often possible to hire them by the hour, or for a half or full day's sightseeing. In some areas younger drivers who speak some English and know their local area well may want to show you around. However, rickshaw drivers are often paid a commission by hotels, restaurants and gift shops so advice is not always impartial. Drivers generally refuse to use a meter, often quote a ridiculous price (Chennai's 'rickshaw mafia' are particularly notorious for overcharging) or may sometimes stop short of your destination. If you have real problems it can help to note down the vehicle licence number and threaten to go to the police. Beware of some rickshaw drivers who show the fare chart for taxis.

Cycle-rickshaws and **horse-drawn tongas** are more common in the more rustic setting of a small town or the outskirts of a large one. You will need to fix a price by bargaining. The animal attached to a tonga usually looks too undernourished to have the strength to pull the driver, let alone passengers.

India has an enormous range of accommodation, and you can stay safely and very cheaply by Western standards right across the country.

The mainstay of the budget traveller is the ubiquitous Indian 'business hotel': walking distance to train and bus stations, anonymous but generally decent value, with ensuite rooms of hugely variable cleanliness and a TV showing 110 channels of cricket and Bollywood MTV. At the top end, alongside international chains like ITC Sheraton (ostentatious) and Radisson Blu (dependable), India boasts several home-grown hotel chains, best of which are the exceptional heritage and palace hotels operated by the Taj group. Meanwhile, Kerala and Tamil Nadu offer abundant opportunities to stay in fine style in converted mansions and farmhouses – a great way to help preserve architectural heritage while keeping your money in the local economy. And while the coastal holiday belts of Goa and Kerala have their share of big and bland resorts, you'll also find a huge variety of individual lodgings, from porous coconut-fibre beach shacks that don't even come with a lock to luxurious restored forts overlooking the Arabian Sea and minimalist Zen retreats hidden in paddy fields.

In the high season (October to April, peaking at Christmas/New Year and again at Easter) bookings can be extremely heavy in popular destinations. It is generally possible to book in advance by phone, fax or email, sometimes on payment of a deposit, but double check your reservation a day or two beforehand and always try to arrive as early as possible in the day to iron out problems.

HOTELS

Price categories The category codes used in this book are based on prices of double rooms excluding taxes. They are **not** star ratings and individual facilities vary considerably. Modest hotels may not have their own restaurant but will often offer 'room service', bringing in food from outside. In temple towns, restaurants may only serve vegetarian food. Expect to pay more in Mumbai and, to a lesser extent, Chennai for all categories. Prices away from large cities tend to be lower for comparable hotels.

Off-season rates Large reductions are made by hotels in all categories out-of-season in many resorts. Always ask if any is available. You may also request the 10-15% agent's commission to be deducted from your bill if you book direct. Clarify whether the agreed figure includes all taxes.

Taxes In general most hotel rooms rated at Rs 3000 or above are subject to a tax of 10%. Many states levy an additional luxury tax of 10-25%, and some hotels add a service charge of 10% on top of this. Taxes are not necessarily payable on meals, so it is worth settling your meals bill separately. Most hotels in the **$$** category and above accept payment by credit card. Check your final bill carefully. Visitors have complained of incorrect bills, even in the most expensive hotels. The problem particularly afflicts groups, when last-minute extras appear mysteriously on some guests' bills. Check the evening before departure, and keep all receipts.

PRICE CODES

WHERE TO STAY

$$$$ over US$150   **$$$** US$66-150
$$ US$30-65   **$** under US$30

Price for a double room in high season, excluding taxes.

RESTAURANTS

$$$ over US$12   **$$** US$6-12   **$** under US$6

Price for a two-course meal for one person, excluding drinks and service charge.

Hotel facilities You have to be prepared for difficulties which are uncommon in the West. It is best to inspect the room and check that all equipment (air conditioning, TV, water heater, flush) works before checking in at a modest hotel. Many hotels try to wring too many years' service out of their linen, and it's quite common to find sheets that are stained, frayed or riddled with holes. Don't expect any but the most expensive or tourist-savvy hotels to fit a top sheet to the bed.

In some states **power cuts** are common, or hot water may be restricted to certain times of day. The largest hotels have their own generators but it is best to carry a good torch.

In some regions **water supply** is rationed periodically. Keep a bucket filled to use for flushing the toilet during water cuts. Occasionally, tap water may be discoloured due to rusty tanks. During the cold weather and in hill stations, hot water will be available at certain times of the day, sometimes in buckets, but is usually very restricted in quantity. Electric water heaters may provide enough for a shower but not enough to fill a bath tub. For details on drinking water, see opposite.

Hotels close to temples can be very **noisy**, especially during festivals. Music blares from loudspeakers late at night and from very early in the morning, often making sleep impossible. Mosques call the faithful to prayers at dawn. Some find ear plugs helpful.

Some hotels offer 24-hour checkout, meaning you can keep the room a full 24 hours from the time you arrive – a great option if you arrive in the afternoon and want to spend the morning sightseeing.

HOMESTAYS

At the upmarket end, increasing numbers of travellers are keen to stay in private homes and guesthouses, opting not to book large hotel chains that keep you at arm's length from a culture. Instead, travellers get home-cooked meals in heritage houses and learn about a country through conversation with often fascinating hosts. Kerala in particular has embraced the homestay model – though the term is increasingly abused as a marketing term by small hotels – while Chennai has a number of smart family-run B&Bs. Tourist offices have lists of families with more modest homestays. Companies specializing in homestays include **Home & Hospitality** ① *www.homeandhospitality.co.uk*, **MAHout** ① *www.mahoutuk.com*, and **Sundale Vacations** ① *www.sundale.com*.

FOOD

You find just as much variety in dishes crossing India as you would on an equivalent journey across Europe. Combinations of spices give each region its distinctive flavour.

The South has given rise to a particularly wide variety of cuisine. Most ubiquitous are the humble snacks that appear on the menu in South Indian cafés the length and breadth of India: *masala dosa*, a crispy rice pancake folded over and stuffed with a lightly spiced potato filling; *uttapam*, a cross between a pancake and a pizza, topped with tomato and onion or slices of banana; and *idli*, soft steamed rice cakes served with a spicy stew called *sambar* and coconut chutney. Every town in the south has a slew of places serving these staples, and for less than US$1 you can fuel yourself up for a full morning's sightseeing.

Vegetarian food is still prevalent throughout the Hindu-dominated states of Maharashtra, Tamil Nadu, Kerala and Karnataka. Along the Kerala coast, with its largely Christian and Muslim population, you'll find excellent seafood and fish dishes, which might be served grilled or stewed in a potent coconut-laden curry with tapioca. Goa, meanwhile, is the birthplace of the vindaloo – a more subtle, sweet-sour ancestor to the highly flammable offerings found in your local curry house – and also does a nice line in Portuguese pastries. And if you find yourself in Hyderabad, don't miss the opportunity to try India's most famous biryani, a succulent mound of rice and spices piled high with chunks of lamb or goat.

Throughout Indis the best value food comes in the shape of the traditional *thali*, a complete meal served on a large stainless-steel plate, or on a banana leaf in traditional Brahmin restaurants. Several preparations, placed in small bowls, surround the central serving of wholewheat chapati and rice. A typical vegetarian *thali* will include dhal (lentils), two or three curries (which can be quite hot) and crisp poppadums. A variety of pickles are offered – mango and lime are two of the most popular. These can be exceptionally hot, and are designed to be taken in minute quantities alongside the main dishes. Plain *dahi* (yoghurt), or *raita*, usually acts as a bland 'cooler', and there's usually a bowl of sweet *kheer* (rice pudding) to finish off.

If you're unused to spicy food, go slow. Food is often spicier when you eat with families or at local places, and certain cuisines (notably those of Andhra Pradesh and the Chettinad region of Tamil Nadu) are notorious for going heavy on the chilli. Most restaurants are used to toning things down for foreign palates, so if you're worried about being overpowered, feel free to ask for the food to be made less spicy.

Food hygiene has improved immensely in recent years. However, you still need to take extra care, as flies abound and refrigeration in the hot weather may be inadequate and intermittent because of power cuts. It is safest to eat only freshly prepared food by ordering from the menu (especially meat and fish dishes). Be suspicious of salads and cut fruit, which may have been lying around for hours or washed in unpurified tap water – though salads served in top-end hotel restaurants and places primarily catering to foreigners (eg in Goa and Puducherry) can offer a blissful break from heavily spiced curries.

Choosing a good restaurant can be tricky if you're new to India. Many local eateries sport a grimy look that can be off-putting, yet serve brilliant and safe food, while swish four-star hotel restaurants that attract large numbers of tourists can dish up buffet food that leaves you crawling to the bathroom at 0200. A large crowd of locals is always a good sign that the food is freshly cooked and good. Even fly-blown *dhabas* on the roadside can be safe, as long as you stick to freshly cooked meals and avoid timebombs like deep-fried samosas left in the sun for hours.

Many city restaurants and backpacker eateries offer a choice of so-called European options such as toasted sandwiches, stuffed pancakes, apple pies, fruit crumbles and cheesecakes. Italian favourites (pizzas, pastas) can be very different from what you are used to. Ice creams, on the other hand, can be exceptionally good; there are excellent Indian ones as well as some international brands.

India has many delicious tropical fruits. Some are seasonal (eg mangoes, pineapples and lychees), while others (eg bananas, grapes and oranges) are available throughout the year. It is safe to eat the ones you can wash and peel.

Don't leave India without trying its superb range of indigenous sweets. Srikhand is a popular dessert in Maharashtra, a thick yoghurt laden with sugar, while a piece or two of milk-based peda or Mysore pak make a perfect sweet postscript to a cheap dinner.

DRINK

Drinking water used to be regarded as one of India's biggest hazards. It is still true that water from the tap or a well should never be considered safe to drink since public water supplies are often polluted. Bottled water is now widely available although not all bottled water is mineral water; most are simply purified water from an urban supply. Buy from a shop or stall, check the seal carefully and avoid street hawkers; when disposing bottles puncture the neck which prevents misuse but allows recycling.

There is growing concern over the mountains of plastic bottles that are collecting and the waste of resources needed to produce them, so travellers are being encouraged to carry their own bottles and take a portable water filter. It is important to use pure water for cleaning teeth.

Tea and **coffee** are safe and widely available. Both are normally served sweet, and with milk. If you wish, say 'no sugar' (*chini nahin*), 'no milk' (*dudh nahin*) when ordering. Alternatively, ask for a pot of tea and milk and sugar to be brought separately. Freshly brewed coffee is a common drink in South India, but in the North, ordinary city restaurants will usually serve the instant variety. Even in aspiring smart cafés, espresso or cappuccino may not turn out quite as you'd expect in the West.

Bottled **soft drinks** such as Coke, Pepsi, Teem, Limca and Thums Up are universally available but always check the seal when you buy from a street stall. There are also several brands of fruit juice sold in cartons, including mango, pineapple and apple – Indian brands are very sweet. Don't add ice cubes as the water source may be contaminated. Take care with fresh fruit juices or *lassis* as ice is often added.

Indians rarely drink **alcohol** with a meal. In the past wines and spirits were generally either imported and extremely expensive, or local and of poor quality. Now, the best Indian whisky, rum and brandy (IMFL or 'Indian Made Foreign Liquor') are widely accepted, as are good Champagnoise and other wines from Maharashtra. If you hanker after a bottle of imported wine, you will only find it in the top restaurants or specialist liquor stores for at least Rs 1000.

For the urban elite, refreshing Indian beers are popular when eating out and so are widely available. 'Pubs' have sprung up in the major cities. Elsewhere, seedy, all-male drinking dens in the larger cities are best avoided for women travellers, but can make quite an experience otherwise – you will sometimes be locked into cubicles for clandestine drinking. If that sounds unsavoury then head for the better hotel bars instead; prices aren't that steep. In rural India, local rice, palm, cashew or date juice *toddy* and *arak* is deceptively potent.

Most states have alcohol-free dry days or enforce degrees of Prohibition. Some upmarket restaurants may serve beer even if it's not listed, so it's worth asking. In some states there are government approved wine shops where you buy your alcohol through a metal grille. For information on liquor permits, see page 282.

→ FESTIVALS IN SOUTH INDIA

India has a wealth of festivals with many celebrated nationwide, while others are specific to a particular state or community or even a particular temple. Many fall on different dates each year depending on the Hindu lunar calendar; there's an amazingly thorough calendar of upcoming major and minor festivals at www.drikpanchang.com.

THE HINDU CALENDAR

Hindus follow two distinct eras: The *Vikrama Samvat* which began in 57 BC and the *Salivahan Saka* which dates from AD 78 and has been the official Indian calendar since 1957. The *Saka* new year starts on 22 March and has the same length as the Gregorian calendar. The 29½-day lunar month with its 'dark' and 'bright' halves based on the new and full moons, are named after 12 constellations, and total a 354-day year. The calendar cleverly has an extra month (*adhik maas*) every 2½ to three years, to bring it in line with the solar year of 365 days coinciding with the Gregorian calendar of the West.

Some major national and regional festivals are listed below. A few count as national holidays: **26 January**: Republic Day; **15 August**: Independence Day; **2 October**: Mahatma Gandhi's Birthday; **25 December**: Christmas Day.

Jan New Year's Day (1 Jan) is accepted officially when following the Gregorian calendar but there are regional variations which fall on different dates, often coinciding with spring/harvest time in Mar and Apr. **Makar Sankranti** (14 Jan), marks the end of winter and is celebrated with kite flying. In the south, particularly Tamil Nadu, this date marks the 4-day festival of **Pongal**, when houses are decorated with colourful *kolam* designs and cows are worshipped to promote a good harvest.
Feb **Vasant Panchami**, the spring festival when people wear bright yellow clothes to mark the advent of the season with singing, dancing and feasting.
Feb-Mar **Maha Sivaratri** marks the night when Siva danced his celestial dance of destruction (*Tandava*), which is celebrated with feasting and fairs at

Siva temples, but preceded by a night of devotional readings and hymn singing.
Mar **Holi**, the festival of colours, marks the climax of spring. The previous night bonfires are lit symbolizing the end of winter (and conquering of evil). People have fun throwing coloured powder and water at each other and in the evening some gamble with friends. If you don't mind getting covered in colours, you can risk going out but celebrations can sometimes get very rowdy (and unpleasant). Some worship Krishna who defeated the demon Putana.
Apr/May Kerala's *pooram* season reaches full swing, with elephant parades, fireworks and cacophonous drumming in honour of the goddess Kali. **Buddha Jayanti**, the 1st full moon night in Apr/May marks the birth of the Buddha.

Jul/Aug Raksha (or Rakhi) Bandhan symbolizes the bond between brother and sister, celebrated at full moon. A sister says special prayers for her brother and ties coloured threads around his wrist to remind him of the special bond. He in turn gives a gift and promises to protect and care for her. Sometimes *rakshas* are exchanged as a mark of friendship. **Narial Purnima** on the same full moon. Hindus make offerings of *narial* (coconuts) to the Vedic god Varuna (Lord of the waters) by throwing them into the sea. **Independence Day** (15 Aug), is a national secular holiday marked by special events.

Aug/Sep Ganesh Chaturthi was established just over 100 years ago by the Indian nationalist leader Lokmanya Tilak. The elephant-headed God of good omen is shown special reverence. On the last of the 5-day festival after harvest, clay images of Ganesh are taken in procession with dancers and musicians, and are immersed in the sea, river or pond. Kerala celebrates the 10-day harvest festival of **Onam** with processions, snake boat races and sumptuous feasts. **Janmashtami**, the birth of Krishna is celebrated at midnight at Krishna temples.

Sep/Oct Dasara has many local variations. Celebrations for the 9 nights (*navaratri*) are marked with **Ramlila**, various episodes of the Ramayana story are enacted with particular reference to the battle between the forces of good and evil. In some parts of India it celebrates *Rama*'s victory over the Demon king *Ravana* of Lanka with the help of loyal *Hanuman* (Monkey). On the 10th day (**Dasara** or **Dussehra**) huge effigies of Ravana made of bamboo and paper are burnt in public open spaces. Mysore has South India's most spectacular Dussehra, with the final day marked by a parade led by caparisoned elephants.

Oct/Nov Gandhi Jayanti (2 Oct), Mahatma Gandhi's birthday, is remembered with prayer meetings and devotional singing.

Diwali/Deepavali (*Sanskrit ideepa* lamp), the festival of lights. Some Hindus celebrate Krishna's victory over the demon *Narakasura*, some Rama's return after his 14 years' exile in the forest when citizens lit his way with oil lamps. The festival falls on the dark *chaturdasi* (14th) night (the one preceding the new moon), when rows of lamps or candles are lit in remembrance, and *rangolis* are painted on the floor as a sign of welcome. Fireworks have become an integral part of the celebration which are often set off days before Diwali. Equally, Lakshmi, the Goddess of Wealth (as well as Ganesh) is worshipped by merchants and the business community who open the new financial year's account on the day. Most people wear new clothes; some play games of chance.

Guru Nanak Jayanti commemorates the birth of Guru Nanak. **Akhand Path** (unbroken reading of the holy book) takes place and the book itself (*Guru Granth Sahib*) is taken out in procession.

Dec Christmas Day (25 Dec) sees Indian Christians celebrate the birth of Christ in much the same way as in the West; many churches hold services/mass at midnight, particularly in Goa and the Christian belt of central Kerala. There is an air of festivity in city markets which are specially decorated and illuminated. Over **New Year's Eve** (31 Dec) hotel prices peak and large supplements are added for meals and entertainment in the upper category hotels. Some churches mark the night with a Midnight Mass.

MUSLIM HOLY DAYS

These are fixed according to the lunar calendar. According to the Gregorian calendar, they tend to fall 11 days earlier each year, dependent on the sighting of the new moon.

Ramadan, known in India as 'Ramzan', is the start of the month of fasting when all Muslims (except young children, the very elderly, the sick, pregnant women and travellers) must abstain from food and drink, from sunrise to sunset.

Id ul Fitr is the 3-day festival that marks the end of Ramzan.

Id-ul-Zuha/Bakr-Id is when Muslims commemorate Ibrahim's sacrifice of his son according to God's commandment; the main time of pilgrimage to Mecca (the Hajj). It is marked by the sacrifice of a goat, feasting and alms giving.

Muharram is when the killing of the Prophet's grandson, Hussain, is commemorated by Shi'a Muslims. Decorated *tazias* (replicas of the martyr's tomb) are carried in procession by devout wailing followers who beat their chests to express their grief. Lucknow is famous for its grand *tazias*. Shi'as fast for the 10 days.

As well as respecting local cultural sensitivities, travellers can take a number of simple steps to reduce, or even improve, their impact on the local environment. Environmental concern is relatively new in India. Don't be afraid to pressurize businesses by asking about their policies.

Litter Many travellers think that there is little point in disposing of rubbish properly when the tossing of water bottles, plastic cups and other non-biodegradable items out of train windows is already so widespread. Don't follow an example you feel to be wrong. You can immediately reduce your impact by refusing plastic bags and other excess packaging when shopping – use a small backpack or cloth bag instead – and if you do collect a few, keep them with you to store other rubbish until you get to a litter bin.

Plastic mineral water bottles, an inevitable corollary to poor water hygiene standards, are a major contributor to India's litter mountain. However, many hotels, including nearly all of the upmarket ones, most restaurants and bus and train stations, provide drinking water purified using a combination of ceramic and carbon filters, chlorine and UV irradiation. Ask for '*filter paani*'; if the water tastes like a swimming pool it is probably quite safe to drink, though it's best to introduce your body gradually to the new water. If purifying water yourself, bringing it to a boil at sea level will make it safe, but at altitude you have to boil it for longer to ensure that all the microbes are killed. Various sterilizing methods can be used that contain chlorine or iodine and there are a number of mechanical or chemical water filters available on the market.

Bucket baths or showers The biggest issue relating to responsible and sustainable tourism is water – particularly relevant in arid areas such as the Deccan plateau where a poor monsoon can result in severe drought. The traditional Indian 'bucket bath', in which you wet, soap then rinse off using a small hand-held plastic jug dipped into a large bucket, uses on average around 15 litres of water, as compared to 30-45 for a shower. These are commonly offered except in four- and five-star hotels.

Support responsible tourism Spending your money carefully can have a positive impact. Sleeping, eating and shopping at small, locally owned businesses directly supports communities, while specific community tourism concerns, such as those operated by **Be The Local** ① *Mumbai, www.bethelocaltoursandtravels.com*, **The Blue Yonder** ① *north Kerala, www.theblueyonder.com*, and the **Ex-Vayana Bark Collectors Eco Development Commitee** ① *Periyar Tiger Reserve, www.periyartigerreserve.com*, provide an economic motivation for people to stay in remote communities, protect natural areas and revive traditional cultures, rather than exploit the environment or move to the cities for work.

Transport Choose walking, cycling or public transport over fuel-guzzling cars and motorbikes and travel by train rather than plane wherever possible.

ESSENTIALS A-Z

Accident and emergency

Contact the relevant emergency service (police T100, fire T101, ambulance T102) and your embassy. Make sure you obtain police/medical reports required for insurance claims.

Customs and duty free
Duty free

Tourists are allowed to bring in all personal effects 'which may reasonably be required', without charge. The official customs allowance includes 200 cigarettes or 50 cigars, 0.95 litres of alcohol, a camera and a pair of binoculars. Valuable personal effects and professional equipment including jewellery, special camera equipment and lenses, laptop computers and sound and video recorders must in theory be declared on a **Tourist Baggage Re-Export Form** (TBRE) in order for them to be taken out of the country, though in practice it's relatively unlikely that your bags will be inspected beyond a cursory X-ray. Nevertheless, it saves considerable frustration if you know the equipment serial numbers in advance and are ready to show them on the equipment. In addition to the forms, details of imported equipment may be entered into your passport. Save time by completing the formalities while waiting for your baggage. It is essential to keep these forms for showing to the customs when leaving India, otherwise considerable delays are very likely at the time of departure.

Prohibited items

The import of live plants, gold coins, gold and silver bullion and silver coins not in current use are either banned or subject to strict regulation. Enquire at consular offices abroad for details.

Drugs

Be aware that the government takes the misuse of drugs very seriously. Anyone charged with the illegal possession of drugs risks facing a fine of Rs 100,000 and a minimum 10 years' imprisonment. Several foreigners have been imprisoned for drugs-related offences in the last decade.

Electricity

India's supply is 220-240 volts AC. Some top hotels have transformers. There may be pronounced variations in the voltage, and power cuts are common. Power back-up by generator or inverter is becoming more widespread, even in humble hotels, though it may not cover a/c. Socket sizes vary so take a universal adaptor; low-quality versions are available locally. Many hotels, even in the higher categories, don't have electric razor sockets. Invest in a stabilizer for a laptop.

Embassies and consulates

For information on visas and immigration, see page 281. For a comprehensive list of embassies (but not all consulates), see http://india.gov.in/overseas/indian_missions.php or http://embassy.goabroad.com. Many embassies around the world are now outsourcing the visa process which might affect how long the process takes.

Health

Local populations in India are exposed to a range of health risks not encountered in the Western world. Many of the diseases cause major problems for the local poor and destitute and, although the risks to travellers is more remote, they cannot be ignored. Obviously 5-star travel is going to carry less risk than backpacking on a budget.

Health care in the region is varied. There are many excellent private and government clinics/hospitals. As with all medical care, first impressions count. It's worth contacting your embassy or consulate on arrival and asking where the recommended clinics are (ie those used by diplomats). You can also ask about locally recommended medical dos and don'ts. If you do get ill, and you have the opportunity, you should also ask your medical insurer whether they are satisfied that the medical centre/hospital you have been referred to is of a suitable standard.

Before you go

Ideally, you should see your GP or travel clinic at least 6 weeks before your departure for general advice on travel risks, malaria and vaccinations. Make sure you have travel insurance, get a dental check (especially if you are going to be away for more than a month), know your own blood group and if you suffer a long-term condition such as diabetes or epilepsy make sure someone knows or that you have a Medic Alert bracelet/necklace with this information on it. Remember that it is risky to buy medicinal tablets abroad because the doses may differ and India has a huge trade in counterfeit drugs.

Vaccinations

If you need vaccinations, see your doctor well in advance of your travel. Most courses must be completed by a minimum of 4 weeks. Travel clinics may provide rapid courses of vaccination, but are likely to be more expensive. The following vaccinations are recommended: typhoid, polio, tetanus, infectious hepatitis and diptheria. For details of malaria prevention, contact your GP or local travel clinic.

The following vaccinations may also be considered: rabies, possibly BCG (since TB is still common in the region) and in some cases meningitis and diphtheria (if you're staying in the country for a long time). Yellow fever is not required in India but you may be asked to show a certificate if you have travelled from Africa or South America. Japanese encephalitis may be required

for rural travel at certain times of the year (mainly rainy seasons). An effective oral cholera vaccine (Dukoral) is now available as 2 doses providing 3 months' protection.

Websites

Blood Care Foundation (UK), www.bloodcare.org.uk A Kent-based charity 'dedicated to the provision of screened blood and resuscitation fluids in countries where these are not readily available'. They will dispatch certified non-infected blood of the right type to your hospital/clinic. The blood is flown in from various centres around the world.

British Travel Health Association (UK), www.btha.org This is the official website of an organization of travel health professionals.

Fit for Travel, www.fitfortravel.scot. nhs.uk This site from Scotland provides a quick A-Z of vaccine and travel health advice requirements for each country.

Foreign and Commonwealth Office (FCO) (UK), www.fco.gov.uk This is a key travel advice site, with useful information on the country, people, climate and lists the UK embassies/consulates. The site also promotes the concept of 'know before you go' and encourages travel insurance and appropriate travel health advice. It has links to Department of Health travel advice site.

The Health Protection Agency, www.hpa.org.uk Up-to-date malaria advice guidelines for travel around the world. It gives specific advice about the right drugs for each location. It also has useful information for those who are pregnant, suffering from epilepsy or planning to travel with children.

Medic Alert (UK), www.medicalalert.com This is the website of the foundation that produces bracelets and necklaces for those with existing medical problems. Once you have ordered your bracelet/ necklace you write your key medical details on paper inside it, so that if you collapse, a medic can identify you as having epilepsy or a nut allergy, etc.

Travel Screening Services (UK), www.travelscreening.co.uk A private clinic dedicated to integrated travel health. The clinic gives vaccine, travel health advice, email and SMS text vaccine reminders and screens returned travellers for tropical diseases.

World Health Organisation, www.who.int The WHO site has links to the *WHO Blue Book* on travel advice. This lists the diseases in different regions of the world. It describes vaccination schedules and makes clear which countries have yellow fever vaccination certificate requirements and malarial risk.

Books

International Travel and Health, World Health Organization Geneva, ISBN 92-4-15802-6-7.

Lankester, T, *The Travellers Good Health Guide*, ISBN 0-85969-827-0.

Warrell, D and Anderson, A (eds), *Expedition Medicine (The Royal Geographic Society)*, ISBN 1-86197-040-4.

Young Pelton, R, Aral, C and Dulles, W, *The World's Most Dangerous Places*, ISBN 1-566952-140-9.

Language

Hindi, spoken as a mother tongue by over 400 million people, is India's official language, but in the South it is only widely spoken in Mumbai, Maharashtra and Goa. The regional languages you'll come across in South India are mostly from the Dravidian family, with Telugu spoken by 8.2% of Indians (mainly in Andhra Pradesh), Tamil (Tamil Nadu, 7%), Kannada (Karnataka, 4.2%) and Malayalam (Kerala, 3.5%). Of the Indo-Aryan languages, Marathi (Maharashtra, 8%) and Urdu (Hindi's almost-identical twin, spoken by Muslims throughout the country) are the most common, with Konkani spoken only in Goa and coastal Maharashtra.

Owing to India's linguistic diversity, English is also enshrined in the Constitution for a wide range of official purposes, notably communication between Hindi and non-Hindi speaking states. It is widely spoken in towns and cities and even in quite remote villages it is usually not difficult to find someone who speaks at least a little English. Outside of major tourist sites, other European languages are almost completely unknown. The accent in which English is spoken is often affected strongly by the mother tongue of the speaker and there have been changes in common grammar which sometimes make it sound unusual. Many of these changes have become standard Indian English usage, as valid as any other varieties of English used around the world. It is possible to study a number of Indian languages at language centres.

Money → *UK £1 = Rs 100, €1 = Rs 84.5, US$1 = Rs 63.3 (Sep 2013)*

Indian currency is the Indian Rupee (Re/Rs). It is **not** possible to purchase these before you arrive. If you want cash on arrival it is best to get it at the airport bank, although see if an ATM is available as airport rates are not very generous. Rupee notes are printed in denominations of Rs 1000, 500, 100, 50, 20, 10. The rupee is divided into 100 paise. Coins are minted in denominations of Rs 10, 5, Rs 2, Rs 1 and (the increasingly uncommon) 50 paise.

Note Carry money, mostly as traveller's cheques or currency card, in a money belt worn under clothing. Have a small amount in an easily accessible place.

Currency cards

If you don't want to carry lots of cash, prepaid currency cards allow you to preload money from your bank account, fixed at the day's exchange rate. They look like a credit or debit card and are issued by specialist money changing companies, such as Travelex and Caxton FX. You can top up and check your balance by phone, online and sometimes by text.

Traveller's cheques (TCs)

TCs issued by reputable companies (eg **Thomas Cook**, **American Express**) are widely accepted. They can be easily exchanged at small local travel agents and tourist internet cafés but are rarely used directly for payment. Try to avoid changing at banks, where the process can be time consuming; opt for hotels and agents instead, take large denomination cheques and change enough to last for some days.

Credit cards

Major credit cards are increasingly accepted in the main centres, though in smaller cities and towns it is still rare to be able to pay by credit card. Payment by credit card can sometimes be more expensive than payment by cash, whilst some credit card companies charge a premium on cash withdrawals. **Visa** and **MasterCard** have an ever-growing number of ATMs in major cities and several banks offer withdrawal facilities for Cirrus and Maestro cardholders. It is however easy to obtain a cash advance against a credit card. Railway reservation centres in major cities take payment for train tickets by Visa card which can be very quick as the queue is short, although they cannot be used for Tourist Quota tickets.

ATMs

By far the most convenient method of accessing money, ATMs are all over India, usually attended by security guards, with most banks offering some services to holders of overseas cards. Banks whose ATMs will issue cash against Cirrus and Maestro cards, as well as Visa and MasterCard, include **Bank of Baroda**, **Citibank**, **HDFC**, **HSBC**, **ICICI**, **IDBI**, **Punjab National Bank**, **State Bank of India** (**SBI**), **Standard Chartered** and **UTI**. A withdrawal fee is usually charged by the issuing bank on top of the conversion charges applied by your own bank. Fraud prevention measures quite often result in travellers having their cards blocked by the bank when unexpected overseas transactions occur; advise your bank of your travel plans before leaving.

Changing money

The **State Bank of India** and several others in major towns are authorized to deal in foreign exchange. Some give cash against Visa/MasterCard (eg **ANZ**). American Express cardholders can use their cards to get either cash or TCs in Mumbai. The larger cities have licensed money changers with offices usually in the commercial sector. Changing money through unauthorized dealers is illegal. Premiums on the currency black market are very small and highly risky. Large hotels change money 24 hrs a day for guests, but banks often give a substantially better rate of exchange. It is best to exchange money on arrival at the airport bank or the Thomas Cook counter. Many international flights arrive during the night and it is generally far easier and less time consuming to change money at the airport than in the city. You should be given a foreign currency encashment certificate when you change money through a bank or authorized dealer; ask for one if it is not automatically given. It allows you to change Indian rupees back to your own currency on departure. It also enables you to use rupees to pay hotel bills or buy air tickets for which payment in foreign exchange may be required. The certificates are only valid for 3 months.

Cost of living

The cost of living in India remains well below that in the West. The average wage per capita is about Rs 68,700 per year (US$1200). Manual, unskilled labourers (women are often paid less than men), farmers and others in rural areas earn considerably less. However, thanks to booming global demand for workers who can provide cheaper IT and technology support functions and many Western firms transferring office functions or call centres to India, salaries in certain sectors have sky rocketed. An IT specialist can earn an average Rs 500,000 per year and upwards – a rate that is rising by around 15% a year.

Cost of travelling

Most food, accommodation and public transport, especially rail and bus, is exceptionally cheap, although the price of basic food items such as rice, lentils, tomatoes and onions have skyrocketed. There is a widening range of moderately priced but clean hotels and restaurants outside the big cities, making it possible to get a great deal for your money. Budget travellers sharing a room, taking public transport, avoiding souvenir stalls, and eating nothing but rice and dhal can get away with a budget of Rs 400-600 (about about US$7-11 or £6-7) a day. This sum leaps up if you drink alcohol (still cheap by European standards at about US$2, £1 or Rs 80 for a pint), smoke foreign-brand cigarettes or want to have your own wheels (you can expect to spend between Rs 150 and 300 to hire a scooter per day). Those planning to stay in fairly comfortable hotels and use taxis sightseeing should budget at US$50-80 (£30-50) a day. Then again you could always check into the **Falaknuma Palace** for Christmas and notch up an impressive US$600 (£350) bill on your B&B alone. India can be a great place to pick and choose, save a little on basic accommodation and then treat yourself to the type of meal you could only dream of affording back home. Also, be prepared to spend a fair amount more in Mumbai, where not only is the cost of living significantly higher but where it's worth coughing up extra for a half-decent room: penny-pinch in places like Hampi where, you'll be spending precious little time indoors anyway. A newspaper costs Rs 5

and breakfast for 2 with coffee can come to as little as Rs 100 in a basic 'hotel', but if you intend to eat banana pancakes or pasta in a backpacker restaurant, you can expect to pay more like Rs 100-150 a plate.

Opening hours

Banks are open Mon-Fri 1030-1430, Sat 1030-1230. Top hotels sometimes have a 24-hr money changing service. **Post offices** open Mon-Fri 1000-1700, often shutting for lunch, and Sat mornings. **Government offices** open Mon-Fri 0930-1700, Sat 0930-1300 (some open on alternate Sat only). **Shops** open Mon-Sat 0930-1800. Bazars keep longer hours.

Safety
Personal security

In general the threats to personal security for travellers in India are remarkably small. However, incidents of petty theft and violence directed specifically at tourists have been on the increase so care is necessary in some places, and basic common sense needs to be used with respect to looking after valuables. Follow the same precautions you would when at home. There have been much-reported incidents of severe sexual assault in Delhi, Kolkata and some more rural areas in 2013. Avoid wandering alone outdoors late at night in these places. During daylight hours be careful in remote places, especially when alone. If you are under threat, scream loudly. Be cautious before accepting food or drink from casual acquaintances, as it may be drugged – though note that Indians on a long train journey will invariably try to share their snacks with you, and balance caution with the opportunity to interact.

The left-wing Maoist extremist Naxalites are active in east central India. They have a long history of conflict with state and national authorities, including attacks on police and government officials. The Naxalites have not specifically targeted

Westerners, but have attacked symbolic targets including Western companies. As a general rule, travellers are advised to be vigilant in the lead up to and on days of national significance, such as Republic Day (26 Jan) and Independence Day (15 Aug) as militants have in the past used such occasions to mount attacks.

Following a major explosion on the Delhi to Lahore (Pakistan) train in Feb 2007 and the Mumbai attacks in Nov 2008, increased security has been implemented on many trains and stations. Similar measures at airports may cause delays for passengers so factor this into your timing. Also check your airline's website for up-to-date information on luggage restrictions.

That said, in the great majority of places visited by tourists, violent crime and personal attacks are extremely rare.

Travel advice

It is better to seek advice from your consulate than from travel agencies. Before you travel you can contact: **British Foreign & Commonwealth Office Travel Advice Unit**, T0845-850 2829, www.fco.gov.uk. **US State Department's Bureau of Consular Affairs**, Overseas Citizens Services, Room 4800, Department of State, Washington, DC 20520-4818, USA, T202-647 1488, www.travel.state.gov. **Australian Department of Foreign Affairs Canberra**, Australia, T02-6261 3305, www.smartraveller.gov.au. Canadian official advice is on www.voyage.gc.ca.

Theft

Theft is not uncommon. It is best to keep TCs, passports and valuables with you at all times. Don't regard hotel rooms as being automatically safe; even hotel safes don't guarantee secure storage. Avoid leaving valuables near open windows even when you are in the room. Use your own padlock in a budget hotel when you go out. Pickpockets and other thieves operate in the big cities. Crowded areas are particularly high risk. Take special care of your belongings when getting on or off public transport.

If you have items stolen, they should be reported to the police as soon as possible. Keep a separate record of vital documents, including passport details and numbers of TCs. Larger hotels will be able to assist in contacting and dealing with the police. Dealings with the police can be very difficult and in the worst regions, such as Bihar, even dangerous. The paperwork involved in reporting losses can be time consuming and irritating and your own documentation (eg passport and visas) may be demanded.

In some states the police occasionally demand bribes, though you should not assume that if procedures move slowly you are automatically being expected to offer a bribe. The traffic police are tightening up on traffic offences in some places. They have the right to make on-the-spot fines for speeding and illegal parking. If you face a fine, insist on a receipt. If you have to go to a police station, try to take someone with you.

If you face really serious problems (eg in connection with a driving accident), contact your consular office as quickly as possible. You should ensure you always have your international driving licence and motorbike or car documentation with you.

Confidence tricksters are particularly common where people are on the move, notably around railway stations or places where budget tourists gather. A common plea is some sudden and desperate calamity; sometimes a letter will be produced in English to back up the claim. The demands are likely to increase sharply if sympathy is shown.

Telephone

The international code for India is +91. International Direct Dialling is widely available in privately run call booths, usually labelled on yellow boards with the letters

'PCO-STD-ISD'. You dial the call yourself, and the time and cost are displayed on a computer screen. Cheap rate (2100-0600) means long queues may form outside booths. Telephone calls from hotels are usually more expensive (check price before calling), though some will allow local calls free of charge. Internet phone booths, usually associated with cybercafés, are the cheapest way of calling overseas.

A double ring repeated regularly means it is ringing; equal tones with equal pauses means engaged (similar to the UK). If calling a mobile, rather than ringing, you might hear music while you wait for an answer.

One disadvantage of the tremendous pace of the telecommunications revolution is the fact that millions of telephone numbers go out of date every year. Current telephone directories themselves are often out of date and some of the numbers given in this book will have been changed even as we go to press. Our best advice is if the number in the text does not work, add a '2'. **Directory enquiries**, T197, can be helpful but works only for the local area code.

Mobile phones are for sale everywhere, as are local SIM cards that allow you to make calls within India and overseas at much lower rates than using a 'roaming' service from your normal provider at home – sometimes for as little as Rs 0.5 per min. Arguably the best service is provided by the government carrier **BSNL/MTNL** but security provisions make connecting to the service virtually impossible for foreigners. Private companies such as **Airtel, Vodafone, Reliance** and **Tata Indicom** are easier to sign up with, but the deals they offer can be befuddling and are frequently changed. To connect you'll need to complete a form, have a local address or receipt showing the address of your hotel, and present photocopies of your passport and visa plus 2 passport photos to an authorized reseller – most phone dealers will be able to help, and can also sell top-up. **Univercell**, www.

univercell.in, and **The Mobile Store**, www. themobilestore.in, are 2 widespread and efficient chains selling phones and sim cards.

India is divided into a number of 'calling circles' or regions, and if you travel outside the region where your connection is based, you will pay higher 'roaming' charges for making and receiving calls, and any problems that may occur – with 'unverified' documents, for example – can be much harder to resolve.

Time

India doesn't change its clocks, so from the last Sun in Oct to the last Sun in Mar the time is GMT +5½ hrs, and the rest of the year it's +4½ hrs (USA, EST +10½ and +9½ hrs; Australia, EST -5½ and -4½ hrs).

Tipping

A tip of Rs 10 to a bellboy carrying luggage in a modest hotel (Rs 20 in a higher category) would be appropriate. In upmarket restaurants, a 10% tip is acceptable when service is not already included, while in places serving very cheap meals, round off the bill with small change. Indians don't normally tip taxi drivers but a small extra is welcomed. Porters at airports and railway stations often have a fixed rate displayed but will usually press for more. Ask fellow passengers what a fair rate is.

Tourist information

There are **Government of India** tourist offices in the state capitals, as well as state tourist offices (sometimes **Tourism Development Corporations**) in some towns and places of tourist interest. They produce their own tourist literature, either free or sold at a nominal price, and some also have lists of city hotels and paying guest options. The quality of material is improving though maps are often poor. Many offer tours of the city, neighbouring sights and overnight and regional packages. Some run modest hotels and midway motels with restaurants and may also arrange car hire and guides. The staff in the regional and local offices are usually helpful.

Visas and immigration

For embassies and consulates, see page 274. Virtually all foreign nationals, including children, require a visa to enter India. Nationals of Bhutan and Nepal only require a suitable means of identification. The rules regarding visas change frequently and arrangements for application and collection also vary from town to town so it is essential to check details and costs with the relevant embassy or consulate. These remain closed on Indian national holidays. Now many consulates and embassies are outsourcing the visa process, it's best to find out in advance how long it will take. For example, in London where you used to be able to get a visa in person in a morning if you were prepared to

queue, it now takes 3-5 working days and involves 2 trips to the office.

At other offices, it can be much easier to apply in advance by post, to avoid queues and frustratingly low visa quotas. Postal applications take 10-15 working days to process.

Visitors from countries with no Indian representation may apply to the resident British representative, or enquire at the **Air India** office. An application on the prescribed form should be accompanied by 2 passport photographs and your passport which should be valid 6 months beyond the period of your visit. Note that visas are valid from the date granted, not from the date of entry.

Tourist visa Normally valid for 3-6 months from date of issue, though some nationalities may be granted visas for up to 5 years. Multiple entries permitted, and it is worth requesting this on the application form if you wish to visit neighbouring countries.

Liquor permits

Periodically some Indian states have tried to enforce prohibition. When applying for your visa you can ask for an All India Liquor Permit. Foreigners can also get the permit from any Government of India Tourist Office in Delhi or the state capitals. Instant permits are issued by some hotels.

Weights and measures

Metric is in universal use in the cities. In remote areas local measures are sometimes used. One lakh is 100,000 and 1 crore is 10 million.

INDEX

A

Abbé Faria 103
Abbi Falls 247
Abul Hasan 74
accidents 274
accommodation 266
  price codes 267
Agastya 157
Agonda, Goa 97
Aihole 89
airport information 259
air travel 258, 260
Ajanta 55
Alappuzha 211
alcohol 269
Alfassa, Mirra 156
Ali, Haidar 141
Alleppey 211
Amber Vilas, Mysore 239
Anaimudi 218
Andhra Pradesh State
  Museum, Hyderabad 70
Anjuna, Goa 117
Arambol, Goa 119
Arossim, Goa 113
Ashtur 81
Asvem, Goa 122
Athangudi 175
ATMs 277
Aurangabad 51
Aurangabad Caves 53
Auroville 159
auto-rickshaws 265
Avudayarkoil 175
Ayurvedic medicine 221

B

Backwaters 210
Badami 86
Baga 115
Bahubali 244
Bakr-Id 272
Bandipur National Park 233

Bandora, Goa 126
Bangalore
  See Bengaluru 250
Barid Shahi tombs 82
Basavanagudi 254
Belur 244
Benaulim, Goa 113
Bengaluru 250
  history 251
  tourist information 251
Betalbatim, Goa 113
Bhagamandala 247
Bhagwan Mahaveer
  Sanctuary, Goa 129
Bhusawal 55
Bibi ka Maqbara 53
Bidar 79
Bijapur 83
black dhotis 190
Blue Mountain Railway 232
Bodinayakkanur 220
Bogmalo, Goa 113
Bolghatty Island 207
Bombay
  see Mumbai 35
Bondla Wildlife Sanctuary,
Goa 128
bus travel 263

C

Cabo de Rama, Goa 97
Candolim 115
Cape Rama, Goa 97
Car Festival 245
car hire 264
car travel 263
cave painting 59
caves
  Ajanta 55
  Aurangabad 53
  Elephanta 46
  Ellora 60
  Kanheri 48
cave sanctuaries 53
Champakulam 211

Chamundi Hill 238, 239
Chandor, Goa 111
Chapora Fort, Goa 118
Chaukhandi of Hazrat
  Khalil-Ullah 82
Chellarkovil 191
Chennai 137
  Central Chennai 143
  George Town 141
  history 139
  Marina 143
  Mylapore 147
  South Chennai 147
  St George 141
Cheruthuruthy 225
Chettinad 174
Chidambaram 164
Chinnar Wildlife Sanctuary
  222
Chowara 196
Christmas 271
climate 258
Cochin 203
coffee 269
Colomb, Goa 98
Colva, Goa 112
consulates 274
Coonoor 231
Coorg 246
Cortalim, Goa 113
Cotigao Wildlife Sanctuary,
  Goa 99
credit cards 277
cuisine 268
currency 276
currency cards 276
customs, local 273
customs regulations 274

D

dabbawallahs 45
Danushkodi 182
Darasuram 169
Dasara 238, 271

Daulatabad Fort 54
Day, Francis 139
Deogiri Fort 54
departure tax 259
Devakottai 175
Dhanuskodi 183
Diwali (Divali) 271
Dodabetta 230
Dravida 150
drinks 269
driving 263
Droog 232
drugs 274
Dudhsagar Falls, Goa 129
Dutch, The 206
duty free 274

E

East India Company 140
Edathna 212
Egmore, Chennai 146
electricity 274
Elephanta Caves 46
elephants 233
Elk Falls 232
Ellora 60
embassies 274
emergencies 274
Eravikulam 222
Ernakulam 203
Esch, Vincent 68
Ettumanoor 212
exchange rates 276

F

Farmagudi, Goa 125
Fatorpa, Goa 97
festivals 270
flamingos 172
food 268
Fort Aguada 116
Fort Kochi 203
French, The 157

G

Galgibaga 98
Gandhamadana Parvatam 183
Gandhi Museum, Madurai 181
Gandhi, Rajiv 153
Ganesh 166
Gangaikondacholapuram 167
Gateway of India, Mumbai 37
Gingee 161
Goa 96
Golconda 72
Gommateshwara 243
Goregaon 48
Gulbarga 82
Guru Nanak Jayanti 271
Guruvayur 224

H

Halebid 245
Hampi 90
    Krishnapura 93
    Royal Enclosure 93
Hanamakonda 76
Harmal, Goa 119
Hassan 243
health 274
health tourism 254
Hindu calendar 270
Holi 270
holidays 270
Hollant Beach, Goa 113
homestays 267
Hope diamond 73
Hospet 94
hotels 266
    price codes 267
Hunsur 236
Husain Sagar Lake 70
Hyderabad 65
    Char Minar 67
    New City 68
    Old City 67
    transport 65

I

Id ul Fitr 272
Id-ul-Zuha 272
Ikshvakus 77
immigration 281
Independence Day 271
Indrail passes 261
innoculations 275
Irwin, Henry 142, 238

J

Jambukesvara 174
Jang, Salar 74
Janmashtami 271

K

Kailasanatha Temple, Ellora 61
Kakkabe 247
Kalady 207
Kalpathy 226
Kambam Valley 186
Kanadukathan 175
Kanheri caves 48
Kanyakumari 197
Karaikkudi 175
Karapur 236
Kavale, Goa 126
Keerana Rayar 183
Keri, Goa 122
Khandepar, Goa 125
Kindlebaga Beach, Goa 98
Kochi 203
Kodagu 246
Kodaikkanal (Kodai) 186
Koh-i-noor diamond 73
Kollam 214
Kolukkumalai 220
Kotagiri 232
Kottar 198
Kottayam 212
Kovalam 195
Kumarakom 212, 213
Kumbakonam 167

L

Lakhnavaram Game Sanctuary 76
language 276
laws 273
liquor permits 282
litter 273
Luz Church, Chennai 148

M

Madgaon, Goa 111
Madikeri 246
Madras
  See Chennai 137
Madurai 176
Mahabalipuram 149
Mahakuta 87
Mahalaxmi Temple 104
Mahasivaratri 270
Mahavir 63
Majorda, Goa 113
Mamallapuram 149, 150
Mandrem, Goa 123
Mangaladevi Temple 191
Mapusa, Goa 116
Mararikulam 211
Mardol, Goa 126
Margao, Goa 110, 111
Matrimandir 160
Mattupetty Lake 220
medicines 274
Meenakshi 178
Meenakshi Temple, Madurai 178
Meenmutty Falls 235
Menino Jesus 113
Mercara 246
Mettupalayam 232
mobile phones 280
Mobor, Goa 114
Moira, Goa 116
Molem, Goa 129
Molem National Park, Goa 129
money 276
Morji, Goa 122

Morjim, Goa 122
Mudumalai Wildlife Sanctuary 233
Muharram 272
Mukurti Peak 231
Mumbai 35
  CST 40
  Fort 38
  Gateway of Indian and Colaba 37
  history 36
  Malabar Hill 42
  Marine Drive 42
  tourist information 36
  transport 35
  'VT' 40
Munnar 218
Muslim holy days 272
Muthanga Wildlife Sanctuary 236
Mysore 237

N

Nagarhole (Rajiv Gandhi) 236
Nagarjunakonda 76
Nallamalais Hills 77
nalukettu 206
Nandidurg 255
Narasimhavarman I 150
Narial Purnima 271
national holidays 270
Navaratri 271
Nayakas 178
Nayaka, Thirumalai 180
Nehru Zoological Park 71
New Year's Day 270
Nilgiri Ghat Road 232
Nisargadhama 247
Nrityagram 255

O

Old Goa 101
Ooty 229
opening hours 278
Osmania University 71

P

Palakkad 225
Palampet 76
Palghat 225
Palolem, Goa 98
Panaji, Goa 101
Pan Chakki 53
Pandikuzhi 191
Panjim, Goa 101
  Fontainhas 104
  history 101
  San Thome 104
  waterfront 103
Partagali, Goa 99
Patnem Beach, Goa 98
Pattadakal 88
Periyar National Park 188
Pernem, Goa 119
Point Calimere Wildlife and Bird Sanctuary 172
Ponda, Goa 124
Pondicherry 156
  See also Puducherry
Poovar Island 196
Priol, Goa 125
prohibitions 274
property 108
Puducherry 156
Pudukkottai 175
Punnathur Kotta Elephant Yard 224

Q

Querim, Goa 122
Queula, Goa 126
Quilon 214
Qutb Shahi tombs 73

R

Rabia Daurani 53
Rajamalai National Park 222
Rajaraja I 171
Rajaraja II 169
Rajbag Beach, Goa 98
Rajendra, King 167

Rajiv Gandhi National Park 236
Raksha Bandhan 271
Ramachandran 143
Ramadan 272
Ramanuja 153, 174
Ramesvaram 182, 183
Ramlila 271
Ramoji Film City 71
Ranganathittu Bird Sanctuary 241
Ravana 182
Raya, Krishna Deva 165
Raymond, Michel 71
responsible tourism 273
restaurants 268
    price codes 267
rickshaws 265
River Nila 223
River Pykara 231
Rock Fort, Tiruchirapalli 173

S
Sabarimala 190
safety 278
Salcete Coast, Goa 110
Salcete, interior 124
Saluvankuppam 153
Sandalwood Oil Factory 239
Sangam literature 179
Santra Beach, Goa 113
Sarangapani 168
Savoi, Goa 127
Secunderabad 65
Setupatis 182
Shilod 55
Shitab Khan 75
Shravanabelgola 243
Sinquerim 115
Siolim, Goa 118
Sirumalai Hills 187
Sita 182
Sittannavasal 176
Sivaratri 270
Sivasamudrum Falls 242
soft drinks 269
Somnathpur 241

Spice Hills, Goa 127
Sravanabelagola 243
Sri Aurobindo Ashram, Puducherry 157
Sri Krishna Pattabhi Jois 240
Sri Mahalingeshwara Temple, Mysore 240
Sri Padmanabhaswamy Temple 193
Sriperumbudur 153
Srirangam 173
Srirangapatnam 240
St Andrew's Church 147
St Catherine Falls 232
St Francis Xavier 106
Suchindram 198
Sultan, Tipu 141
Sulthan Bathery 236
Sundareswarar (Siva) 178
swastika town plan 75

T
Tambdi Surla, Goa 130
Tambraparni Teertha 100
Tanjore 169
taxis 265
tea 269
telephone 279
Terekhol, Goa 122
Thandiandamole 247
Thanjavur (Tanjore) 169
Tharangampadi 166
theft 279
Thekkadi National Park 188
Thirukokarnam 175
Thiruvaiyaru 172
Thiruvananthapuram 193
    See also Trivandrum
Thrissur 223
time 280
tipping 280
Tipu's Summer Palace, Bangalore 253
Tiracol Fort, Goa 122
Tiracol, Goa 122
Tiruchirappalli 172
    See also Trichy

Tirukkalukundram 153
Tiruvanaikkaval 174
Tiruvannamalai 161
Top Station 220
tourist information 280
train travel 260
Tranquebar 166
transport 258
    air 258, 260
    bus 263
    car 263
    rail 260
    rickshaw 265
    taxi 265
traveller's cheques 277
travel tips, bus 263
treks, Kerala 222
Trichur 223
Trichy 172
Triplicane, Chennai 143
Trivandrum 193
    See also Thiruvananthapuram
Tughluq, Muhammad bin 54
Tungabhadra Dam 94
turtles, Goa 99

U
Udhagamandalam
    See also Ooty 229
Utorda, Goa 113

V
vaccinations 275
Vagator, Goa 118
Vaigai Lake 186
Valia Palli, Kottayam 212
Vandiyur Mariammam Teppakulam 180
Varkala 191
Varushanad Hills 186
Vasant Panchami 270
Vasco da Gama 206
Velinga, Goa 125
Velsao, Goa 113
Verna, Goa 113

Vijayapuri 77
visas 281
Vishnu 174
Vizhinjam 196
Vypeen Island 207
Vythiri 235

W
Warangal 75
water, drinking 269
Wayanad 235
Western Ghats 235

Y
yoga 120, 240

CREDITS

Footprint credits
Editor: Nicola Gibbs and Felicity Laughton
Production and layout: Emma Bryers
Maps: Kevin Feeney
Cover and colour section: Pepi Bluck

Publisher: Patrick Dawson
Managing Editor: Felicity Laughton
Advertising: Elizabeth Taylor
Sales and marketing: Kirsty Holmes

Photography credits
Front cover: f9photos/Shutterstock.com
Back cover: Mazzzur/Shutterstock.com;
v.s.anandhakrishna/Shutterstock.com
Inside front flap: AJP/Shutterstock.com; Pikoso.
kz/Shutterstock.com; Ewamewa2/Dreamstime.
com; Rajesh Narayanan/Shutterstock.com
Colour pages: title page: Mohamed Abdul Rasheed/
Dreamstime.com. p2: Lola Tsvetaeva/Shutterstock.com;
reddees/Shutterstock.com. p3: Zzvet/Shutterstock.com.
p4: Ailisa/Shutterstock.com. p6: reddees/Shutterstock.com.
p7: Dmitri Mikitenko/Shutterstock.com. p8: filmlandscape/
Shutterstock.com. p9: Mukul Banerjee/Shutterstock.com;
JeremyRichards/Shutterstock.com. p10: vicspacewalker/
Shutterstock.com; Dirk Ott/Shutterstock.com; Radiokafka/
Shutterstock.com. p11: Eduard Derule/Shutterstock.
com; Jigmenamdol/Dreamstime.com. p12: SNEHIT/
Shutterstock.com. p13: Mazzzur/Shutterstock.com. p14:
Anatoli Styf/Shutterstock.com. p16: jaume/Shutterstock.
com. p17: Polina Ryazantseva/Dreamstime.com;
Jayakumar/Shutterstock.com; Hemis.fr/SuperStock. p18:
Nagel Photography/Shutterstock.com; Jaume Juncadella/
Dreamstime.com. p19: PhotoBarmaley/Shutterstock.com;
saiko3p/Shutterstock.com. p20: f9photos/Shutterstock.
com. p22: Zzvet/Shutterstock.com. p23: Nickolay Stanev/
Shutterstock.com. p24: Daniel J. Rao/Shutterstock.com.
p25: ostill/Shutterstock.com; AJP/Shutterstock.com;
Andrey Armyagov/Shutterstock.com. p26: Dscmax/
Dreamstime.com; Nickolay Stanev/Shutterstock.com;
Jayanand Govindaraj/Dreamstime.com. p27: jorisvo/
Shutterstock.com; Johan_R/Shutterstock.com; Brandon
Bourdages/Shutterstock.com. p28: Noppasin/Shutterstock.
com. p29: Igor Plotnikov/Shutterstock.com. p30: AJP/
Shutterstock.com. p32: Pikoso.kz/Shutterstock.com.

Publishing information
Footprint DREAM TRIP South India
1st edition
© Footprint Handbooks Ltd
September 2013

ISBN: 978 1 907263 82 8
CIP DATA: A catalogue record for this book
is available from the British Library

® Footprint Handbooks and the Footprint
mark are a registered trademark of
Footprint Handbooks Ltd

Published by Footprint
6 Riverside Court
Lower Bristol Road
Bath BA2 3DZ, UK
T +44 (0)1225 469141
F +44 (0)1225 469461
footprinttravelguides.com

Printed in Spain by GraphyCems

Every effort has been made to ensure that
the facts in this guidebook are accurate.
However, travellers should still obtain
advice from consulates, airlines etc about
travel and visa requirements before
travelling. The authors and publishers
cannot accept responsibility for any loss,
injury or inconvenience however caused.

Distributed in the USA by Globe Pequot
Press, Guilford, Connecticut